Yakuza

The Japanese characters for the Yamaguchi-gumi, Japan's largest crime syndicate, are depicted on the front cover. The symbols on pages 11, 41, 125, 187, and 283 are adapted from the gang insignia for, respectively, the Inagawa-kai, the Sumiyoshi-rengo, the Yamaguchi-gumi, the Toa Yuai Jigyo Kumiai, and the Nippon Kokusui-kai.

YAKUZA

The Explosive Account of Japan's Criminal Underworld

David E. Kaplan and Alec Dubro

▲▼▼
Addison-Wesley Publishing Company, Inc.

Reading, Massachusetts   Menlo Park, California
Don Mills, Ontario   Wokingham, England   Amsterdam
Sydney   Singapore   Tokyo   Madrid   Bogotá
Santiago   San Juan

The excerpt on p. 17 is reprinted with permission from *The East,* October 1981, Tokyo, vol. xvii, nos. 9 & 10, pp. 47–48.

The excerpt on p. 20 is reprinted with permission from an article entitled "Delinquent Groups and Organized Crime," in the *Sociological Review Monograph,* no. 10, 1966, published by Routledge & Kegan Paul PLC, London.

Library of Congress Cataloging-in-Publication Data

Kaplan, David E., 1955–
  Yakuza: the explosive account of Japan's criminal underworld.

  Bibliography: p.
  Includes index.
  1. Yakuza—Japan—History. 2. Yakuza—History.
3. Organized crime—Japan—History. 4. Crime and
criminals—Japan—History. 5. Gangs—Japan—History.
I. Dubro, Alec. II. Title.
HV6453.J33Y355 1986   364.1'06'052   85-28664
ISBN 0-201-11151-9

Cover design by Richard Adelson
Text design by Douglass G. A. Scott
Set in 11-point Times Roman by Camden Type 'n Graphics, Camden, ME

ABDCEFGHIJ–DO–89876
First printing, April 1986

Contents

Acknowledgments

This book is a collaborative effort, the result of more than four years of work. During this time, the authors were aided by some fifty researchers and reporters spread across five continents. We have, in addition, drawn on the work of countless others from academia, the media, law enforcement, and the underworld. Many of our sources cannot be named due to concern over job security and, in some cases, personal safety. We regret if others' contributions pass unnoticed here; this book would have been an impossible task without the assistance of our many friends and colleagues, and our heartfelt thanks go to all who helped in any way.

We owe a tremendous debt to the staff and associates of the Center for Investigative Reporting. Our gratitude goes out to Laura Lent, Dan Noyes, and David Weir for their long and steady encouragement; to Mark Schapiro for saving the project when it nearly died an unnatural death; to Liza Pike for her negotiating skill, James Curtiss for his administrative talents, and to Judy Coburn, Diana Hembree, Howard Kohn, and the rest of the CIR family who contributed in so many ways to this work.

We owe two of our colleagues in Japan an equally important debt. John Roberts and Glenn Davis, two veteran Tokyo correspondents, contributed enormously at virtually every step of this project – from commenting on our initial proposal to arranging interviews, performing research, and critiquing our huge manuscript. Their expertise and experience helped produce the vast store of information that forms the heart of this book. In addition, their friendship, and that of their families, greatly warmed what was an otherwise freezing Tokyo winter.

Our colleagues at Nippon Hoso Kyokai (NHK), Japan's public broadcasting system, also are deserving of great thanks. Their careful arrangements secured interviews with leading yakuza, allowing American journalists an unprecedented look at the Japanese underworld. Despite countless cultural blunders on our part, NHK producers patiently and skillfully guided us along a sometimes treacherous path. Thanks to Sadaharu Inoue, who helped from the beginning, and to Hajime Suzuki, Atsushi Karube, and Yasuo Onuki.

Our translators and interpreters performed admirably both at home and abroad. Thanks to Reiko Makeuchi for courage far beyond the call of our meager payments; Professor Yuzuru Katagiri, Ike Matsuzaki, and K. T. for offering invaluable help in understanding not only a difficult language but a complex culture as well; and James Chun, Jon Joseph, and Taka Yamada for filling in at critical moments.

A special thanks goes to those around the globe who helped us with research and interviews: Mike Kepp in Brazil, Ramon Tulfo in the Philippines, Stan Correy in Australia, Kay Landmann in West Germany, Toshimitsu Shigemura in South Korea, and others in Thailand, Hong Kong, and elsewhere who must remain unnamed. Our researchers at the Center for Investigative Reporting also deserve enormous credit for digging up and compiling key sources of information: Susan Moran bore the brunt of this work. The efforts of Frances Dinkelspiel, Jennifer McNulty, Brenda Sunoo, and the rest of the center's talented interns are also greatly appreciated.

In Tokyo, a hearty thanks goes to the estimable Bernard Krisher for his unique contributions to our project. Jean Sather, now with Asahi News Service, also contributed mightily with research and newsclips. We extend thanks as well to the staffs of the Foreign Press Center (especially Shigeyoshi Araki) and the Foreign Correspondents Club of Japan. In the Japanese law enforcement community we warmly thank Hiroto Yamazaki for his help and hospitality, and Kanehiro Hoshino for his patience and wisdom. Hajime Takano and Takao Toshikawa were generous with needed advice and research assistance, and Goro Fujita and Kenji Ino provided invaluable insights into the strange patterns of the underworld.

In the San Francisco Bay Area we thank Professors Harumi Befu and Chalmers Johnson for making available their considerable expertise in Japanese culture and politics. Barbara Faison and Loren Kelly of the Japanese Consulate's Information Service also helped a great deal, as did our colleagues Lowell Bergman, Brad Bunin, and Bonnie Burt. Thanks to Inspector John McKenna of the San Francisco Police Department, Tony Crittenden of the California Department of Justice, Mike Sterrett, and others unnamed.

Special thanks go to Bill Sweet, Mike Fleming, and the staff of the U.S. Customs Service in Honolulu. Also in that city, we owe a good bit of Japanese *giri* to Professor Joe Tobin of the University of Hawaii, who painstakingly went over our manuscript and made invaluable comments. And thanks to our colleague and friend Jim Dooley of the *Honolulu Advertiser;* Bernie Ching and Ron Higa, formerly of the Honolulu Police Department; Hilton Lui of the FBI; Don Carstensen of the Honolulu Public Prosecutor's Office; and Steve Lane.

In Los Angeles we thank George Min, John Vach, and Jimmy Sakoda of the LAPD; also Dwight Chuman, Shigeharu Higashi, and Kurashima-san. In New York, thanks to ABC's Peter Lance for helping start it all; also to Marnie Inskip and Charles Kades, and to our law enforcement sources in the region. In Washington, D.C., we thank Pharis Harvey for his help and expertise on Korean affairs; John Mintz of the *Washington Post;* Don Goldberg of Jack Anderson's office; and Manuel Gonzalez and John Leonard from the President's Commission on Organized Crime.

Thanks also to Karl Schoenberger, now with the *Hartford Courant,* Frank Joseph Shulman and Tamiko Cooke of the University of Maryland, Fred Pernell of the National Records Center, Thomas Burkman of Old Dominion College, and Professor Howard Schonberger of the University of Maine.

We are greatly indebted to Howard Bray and the Fund for Investigative Journalism, who generously supported this project from the very beginning. Our gratitude also goes to the PEN Writers Fund for their important contribution, and to our colleagues in the National Writers Union for their friendship and efforts to improve the plight of American authors.

At Addison-Wesley we thank our friend and first editor, Robin Manna, for her patience and commitment to a long-overdue manuscript. We thank, equally, our talented second editor, Theresa Burns, for picking up an enormously complicated project and throwing her enthusiasm and editorial skills into the fray, and helping two exhausted authors clear the final hurdles.

Alec Dubro extends a personal note of thanks to Ruth Dubro, Leon and Shirley Becker, Ben and Toni Coplan, Lee Hamilton, Steve Krinsky, Julie and David Marino, Jim Tobias, and, of course, Vivian Becker for her support over the years. David E. Kaplan gives thanks to Pam Eichner for sharing the trials of life in San Francisco and the Far East, to Phil Cook and Rocky Kistner, to the Kaplan and Eichner families, and to his parents, who made it all possible.

About the Authors

DAVID E. KAPLAN, a staff writer at the Center for Investigative Reporting in San Francisco, is editor of the book *Nuclear California* and the recipient of several journalism awards, including the 1984 Thomas M. Storke International Journalism Award. His articles have appeared in major newspapers and magazines, and he has worked as a consultant to NHK (Japan's public broadcasting network), the Australia Broadcasting Corporation, ABC News, CBS News, and television stations on the West Coast.

ALEC DUBRO, a New York–based journalist, began his career as a rock music critic for *Rolling Stone* magazine in 1968 and has since written about such diverse subjects as drug enforcement agencies, anti-submarine warfare, and surveillance technology. He has worked as a private investigator, editor, television news writer, and consultant to the President's Commission on Organized Crime. He is Vice President for Organizing of the National Writers Union.

THE CENTER FOR INVESTIGATIVE REPORTING, founded in 1977, is the only independent, nonprofit organization in the country established as an institution to do investigative reporting. From their offices in San Francisco and Washington, D.C., the CIR staff writes for leading newspapers and magazines and works closely with television news programs in the U.S. and abroad, including "60 Minutes" and "ABC World News Tonight." Center stories have helped spark Congressional hearings and legislation, U.N. resolutions, public interest lawsuits, and changes in the activities of multinational corporations, government agencies, and organized crime figures. Its stories have won numerous awards, including the National Magazine Award and the National Press Club Award. For more information contact CIR at 54 Mint Street, 4th floor, San Francisco, CA 94103.

Yakuza

Prologue
Enter the Yakuza

If you want the *yakuza* stuff taken seriously, the man from Justice said, start by getting rid of those stories about tattoos and missing fingers. That was the message from Washington, D.C., to Michael Sterrett in Hawaii.

It was the spring of 1976 and Sterrett, the sharp young federal prosecutor, was making headlines in Honolulu. For three years he had journeyed to Hawaii to initiate a remarkable set of prosecutions. Working out of any available desk in Honolulu's old federal building, Sterrett obtained a series of convictions that set back organized crime in the islands for years. Now he was pushing hard to open the federal government's first Organized Crime Strike Force office in the fiftieth state, but some of his organized crime reports were generating considerable skepticism.

It had been difficult enough just to gain permission for the flights to Hawaii. Unlike trips to other states, travel to the islands required approval from the number-two man at the Department of Justice, the assistant attorney general. And it didn't help that Sterrett's home office at the San Francisco regional headquarters wasn't always taken seriously, or that Hawaii was hardly a priority for Washington policymakers. The state's criminal gangs – an array of Asians, whites, blacks, and Pacific Islanders – received little attention from a federal agency preoccupied with the traditional American mob. No one in Washington had ever built a career on chasing crime around the mid-Pacific.

But Sterrett was getting results. Capitalizing on a rare moment of cooperation between local and federal lawmen, he had prosecuted and put away "Nappy" Pulawa, the Hawaiian gambling kingpin whose connections included top Las Vegas mobsters. And Sterrett had successfully gone after Pulawa's successor, Earl K. H. Kim, and the members of his gambling syndicate.

It was during his work on those cases, as he pored over police reports, that Sterrett first began to notice the presence of Japanese nationals. Federal officials in Honolulu already were concerned over the growing ties between mainland and Hawaiian crime syndicates. Now a third leg of an underworld triangle began to emerge, one that had been apparent to local police since the late 1960s.

The tattoos and missing fingers comprised the most striking, immediate features of these new criminals. They were not ordinary tattoos, but magnificent, full-color designs of samurai warriors, flowers, and dragons that stretched across the body from neck to calf. And the mutilated fingers – these were the ceremoniously severed tops of the smallest digit, lopped off at the joint and presented to the gang leader as a mark of atonement.

Sterrett's memos to Washington, filled with such bizarre descriptions, accurately depicted the classic traits of Japanese organized crime syndicates. After 250 years of crime in the Far East, the yakuza had finally arrived in the West.

At first, Sterrett was puzzled by the appearance of the yakuza. What were they doing in Honolulu, and who did they know? One fact was clear, however – the islands hosted the right elements in which organized crime could flourish: machine party politics coupled with a tough labor movement; a hedonistic culture with widespread acceptance of prostitution, gambling, and drugs; and a massive tourist industry that each year gathered millions of visitors from around the world and turned them loose on Honolulu streets.

Perhaps most important was Hawaii's geographic position in the mid-Pacific, a convenient stopping-off point for international trade and travelers from throughout the Orient and North America. It was here that the much-heralded era of the Pacific Basin could be seen firsthand. Trade among the Pacific Rim nations was booming, threatening to overtake the North Atlantic as the world's major market area. The rapidly expanding economies of East Asia, the steady growth of Japan and California, and the emergence of China left little doubt about the region's potential.

Hawaii itself comprised an ethnic mirror of the entire basin. Once populated solely by Polynesians, the islands were now one-third white and one-quarter ethnic Japanese. An assortment of other Asians and Pacific Islanders made up much of the rest. Asian investment capital streamed into the islands from Hong Kong, Japan, and Singapore; investors bought up hotels, banks, real estate, and, in the eyes of the locals, anything that could be purchased.

If this were the dawn of the Pacific Era, reasoned Sterrett, it would follow that the rapid development of legitimate business might be paralleled by an equally burgeoning underworld economy. The American Mafia, after all, had gone international years before with their investments in Europe and the Caribbean, and through their ties to the Italian Mafia, the Corsican mobs, and heroin refiners from Bangkok to Marseilles. It seemed logical, then, that the linking of the Pacific Rim economies would bring new criminal groups into the picture. Reports were already coming into Honolulu about counterfeiters from Taiwan, drug dealers from Hong Kong and Thailand, and suspect investors from Las Vegas, Tokyo, and Seoul. Another set of Asian crime syndicates – the Chinese Triads – was also beginning to cause trouble for authorities in both Europe and America.

The potential for organized crime to expand in the Pacific was enormous. Already in the region there existed the power of what Sterrett liked to call shadow governments – underworld states that collect their own taxes and enforce their own laws. Sterrett could see future glimpses of a vast criminal empire that reached across national boundaries, accountable to no one but the underworld, in which drugs and guns and huge amounts of money moved across the Pacific. The possibilities were endless; who could estimate the impact of a U.S.-Japan crime syndicate on the $85 billion worth of goods shipped between the two countries each year? What might be the effect of a "yakuza connection" on both sides of the Pacific?

The scenario, though intriguing, seemed a bit too far off and alarmist for a young prosecutor already having trouble getting his memos read. So at first Sterrett hedged, refusing to exaggerate the possible importance of a few Japanese crooks lurking around Hawaii. But in time he changed his mind. "It took a lot of learning to understand what was involved," he recalled. "Slowly, though, it began to dawn on us that we were dealing with a completely different kind of organized crime problem."

Detailed information in English about the yakuza was at best scarce. There were translation problems, and, strangely, the Japanese police appeared reluctant to cooperate. Much to the amazement of the U.S. lawmen, requests for information were answered slowly and incompletely. Japanese authorities refused to provide their American counterparts with a list of known yakuza members. Apparently, there were some formidable legal – and cultural – obstacles at hand. What little intelligence did become available, however, raised eyebrows around the old federal building.

Sterrett leafed through a handful of reports on the yakuza from Japan's National Police Agency and scanned the sketchy profiles then developed by police in Honolulu. The figures cited were striking: 110,000 gangsters lived and worked in Japan, neatly organized into 2500 "families" and federations. In the United States, with twice Japan's population, the Justice Department estimated that there were only 20,000 organized crime members. It seemed a remarkable statistic for Japan, a country famous for its low crime rates. Yet even the figure of 110,000 gangsters, according to Japanese police, was down from a peak of 180,000 only fifteen years earlier. The huge yakuza syndicates, furthermore, seemed well financed and highly organized – the criminal counterpart to the country's efficient, finely tuned corporations.

Sterrett found that, like the American mob, the yakuza service the covert vices: prostitution, pornography, drugs, gambling. He learned that the Japanese gangs share other similarities with their American equivalents: large chunks of the construction and entertainment industries lie under their control, including movie studios, nightclubs, and professional sports. Half the Japanese mob's sizable income comes from drug dealing, say police, particularly in amphetamines – what the Japanese call "awakening drugs." The yakuza portfolio also includes loan sharking, trucking, and an array of strong-arm, smuggling, and extortion rackets. According to the National Police Agency, the yakuza control some 26,000 legitimate businesses and countless illegal ones; their impact is felt from small street-side businesses to the country's largest corporations. And, for a price, they break strikes and help silence dissenters. The gangs are politically powerful as well, extending their influence through shadowy figures to the highest levels of Japanese government.

That, however, is where the similarities with the American mob end. The yakuza are accepted into Japanese society in a way that confounded Sterrett and the few other U.S. officials who bothered to investigate them. Yakuza groups, for example, maintain offices that prominently display the gang emblem on their front doors, much as if they were the local loan company (which, in fact, they often are). This is equivalent to a New Jersey crime family opening an office in Newark emblazoned with the sign, MAFIA HEADQUARTERS, LOCAL 12. Yakuza members are also in the practice of sporting on their suits lapel pins that identify their gang, displaying them with the same pride as Rotarians and fraternity brothers. Several of the largest gangs publish their own newspapers or magazines, complete with feature articles, legal advice, and even poetry written by gang members. After a recent gang war, the feuding leaders went so far as to call a press conference, announcing that the fighting had ended and apologizing to the public for any inconvenience they had caused.

Clearly, there was a very different tradition of organized crime at work here, one that Western cops had never encountered before. Some of the material Sterrett came across seemed pretty farfetched. The yakuza appeared to be living anachronisms, samurai in business suits. They cast themselves as the moral descendants of Japan's noble warriors, the last upholders of the nation's traditional values. The Japanese public, furthermore, seemed to accept this. The gangsters had somehow developed an enduring image as patriots and Robin Hoods. They seemed not so much a Mafia as a loyal opposition, the honorable members of Japan's criminal class.

Out of all his research, though, what struck Sterrett most were the reports of ritual finger-cuttings – the very items he was told to keep out of his memos to Washington. They symbolized to him in one act the radically different nature of the Japanese gangsters. "Here were individuals so devoted they were willing to endure amputating their own fingertips for the boss. The motivation, the loyalty of these people were things we'd just never seen before."

Impressed with their organization, their size, and reports of their increasing activity in Hawaii, Sterrett began building a file. He soon learned that his vision of a trans-Pacific criminal cartel might not be so far off the mark. Yakuza members had been seen by Honolulu police mixing with both local and mainland organized crime figures. They had become involved on the islands in prostitution, pornography, extortion, and gunrunning. Apparently, they were venturing to the mainland as well – to San Francisco, Los Angeles, and Las Vegas. Other reports showed that, since the early 1970s, the Japanese mob had gone international, expanding into South Korea, Southeast Asia, and a host of other regions around the Pacific Rim. By the early spring of 1976, Sterrett was finally convinced that the yakuza did in fact pose a problem meriting federal attention.

The watershed event for Sterrett, though, occurred in May of that year, when Wataru "Jackson" Inada was found murdered in his Honolulu apartment. Inada, a small, tough ex-boxer, got caught up in Hawaiian rackets and drug dealing upon his arrival from Tokyo in 1972. He bore on his back the ornate tattoos of a yakuza, which he acquired as a soldier in the 6000-member Sumiyoshi federation, one of Japan's largest syndicates. Police believe Jackson's murder was a result of an ambitious, though ill-fated, heroin deal involving West Coast Mafiosi.

The Inada case was what Mike Sterrett calls the beginning of the institutionalization of the yakuza in the United States. Within two short years, Jackson Inada had made connections to high-ranking members of the mainland Mafia. He had allied himself with the leading figures of Hawaiian organized crime, while maintaining his relationship to the yakuza in Japan. And he had made American law enforcement take a hard, second look at the potential impact of the tattooed men. Sterrett's Strike Force office was opened a year later, in 1977.

It had been a frustrating fight for recognition, Sterrett recalled. "You have to remember," he said, "that it had been only ten or eleven years since the Mafia's existence was officially even acknowledged by the FBI and Justice. They didn't want to hear about non-Mafia activity; their priority was La Cosa Nostra. Now imagine: there I was, someone who took over twenty trips from, of all places, San Francisco, to Honolulu, warning the Justice Department about yet another organized crime group whose members amputated their own fingers. . . ."

Sterrett's work, however – including his exotic memos – began to get closer attention from Washington, and in 1979 he was given charge of the San Francisco regional office. Before leaving, he would see his hunches about the yakuza start to come true.

By 1979, the Japanese gangs had become big news in Hawaii, with extensive press and television coverage of their involvement in drugs, gambling, and prostitution. But it took a second smuggling case, after Inada, to really set off the alarm. In May 1979, a trio of yakuza "mules," or couriers, were arrested at Honolulu International Airport.

Each man held one pound of white Asian heroin stuffed into his carton of Dunhills. A passport check revealed a total of sixteen trips to Bangkok, Thailand – the probable source of the heroin – and twelve subsequent journeys to Hawaii, Guam, and San Francisco. A search of their homes in Tokyo by Japanese authorities turned up a strange set of instructions carefully spelling out the duties of the smugglers: "You should obey whatever you are told to do by your group leader," the document read. "You have no choice, you cannot refuse or complain of the leader's instruction. The above instructions are given at the request of the financier in order to protect ourselves and to accomplish our work."

U.S. officials were alarmed. According to a classified report by the Drug Enforcement Administration, the arrests "clearly demonstrate" that the yakuza are "furiously engaged in heroin smuggling. . . ." The DEA's fears were echoed by federal investigators at a 1981 congressional hearing, who warned: "It's only a matter of time before the yakuza groups become seriously involved in the smuggling of heroin into the United States." Authorities had become justifiably concerned that, given the yakuza's excellent organization and reserves of cash and men, they could develop into the most efficient importers of heroin into the West Coast.

American lawmen, meanwhile, began finding extensive yakuza investment in Hawaii and California. Hidden by the vast movement of capital between Japan and the United States, the yakuza's illicit profits were being laundered through American real estate, hotels, and what the Japanese call *mizu shobai* – literally, "water business" – bars, restaurants, and nightclubs. Using souvenir shops as fronts, the yakuza muscled into the lucrative Japanese tourist trade in Los Angeles and San Francisco. They developed as well a multimillion-dollar racket in the smuggling of hard-core pornography and handguns to Japan. There were also charges of white slavery rings in which fraudulent talent scouts recruited young female entertainers in the United States and, once in Japan, forced them to work as prostitutes and sex show performers.

By 1981, the yakuza began earning their share of attention from the American public as well as the police. A parade of stories on the coming of Japan's Mafia marched out of the media. In *Newsweek,* the *Los Angeles Times,* Jack Anderson's column, and on local and national television, the groups were profiled, their activities exposed. Most of the coverage, while at times sensational, was accurate, quoting police about the extent of yakuza heroin dealing and dwelling on the huge size of the gangs and their strange customs.

Predictably enough, a handful of reports began to surface, laced with what might charitably be called latent racism. One news headline, summoning fears of another era, spoke of Japanese criminals "invading" the West Coast. Another publication went further, depicting on its cover a monstrous gangster looming out of Japan, enshadowing Hawaii and threatening Los Angeles. It was the yakuza as yellow peril, an easy jump for people needing scapegoats for U.S. foreign trade problems.

Particularly shocking was the strong reaction of listeners to a popular radio talk show on the yakuza held in politically liberal San Francisco. A series of callers took the opportunity to denounce the Japanese as the cause of our economic malaise, with one enterprising woman suggesting a full trade boycott until "these people" stop sending their criminals here. The media prize, though, goes to the September 1983 issue of the porno magazine *Chic*. While most readers seldom get past the month's glossy photos, few would have missed the bold headlines in that issue's nine-page feature on the yakuza: "First came the Japanese televisions, stereos and radios that flooded the American marketplace. Next was the invasion of Japanese-made autos that helped cripple our economy. Now an even greater threat to America has arrived – the Yakuza, Japan's version of the Mafia."

The yakuza do indeed pose a threat to the United States, but it hardly merits archaic racist stereotypes bound up in the frustrations of an economic trade war. The problems, of course, are more complex, involving what Mike Sterrett called the institutionalization of the yakuza. It is the prospect that, like other organized crime groups, once entrenched in American society, the yakuza will be extremely difficult to dislodge. They will have found a home abroad.

There is another, equally compelling reason for the West to be wary of the yakuza, a reason more profound, yet at first perhaps less alarming: organized crime in Japan is extraordinarily politicized. The modern history of the yakuza is intertwined with that of Japan's extreme right wing, a bizarre group of emperor-worshiping activists who were the most virulent force behind that country's rise to domestic fascism and military expansion. Although currently less powerful than in the prewar period, the ultranationalist right still makes waves in Japan. So closely associated with the yakuza are these extremist bands that at times the groups are indistinguishable. There is no near analogy in American society. In some respects it is as if the Ku Klux Klan and the Mafia formed an enduring, politically potent alliance.

Over the years, this often violent coalition of rightists and gangsters has served as a paramilitary force for Japan's ruling Liberal Democratic Party, the LDP, which has exercised a virtually unbroken hold over the nation's postwar politics. It is a history that rivals the worst traditions of corruption in America. So rooted in Japanese culture are these practices that at times they defy the very meaning of corruption as used in the West. More important, the political workings of the yakuza have over the years influenced critical events in Japan, at one point with the active complicity of U.S. intelligence agencies. Today, their activities continue to bear heavily on the future of America's chief Pacific ally and largest overseas trading partner, influencing key issues that include, foremost, the rearming of Japan.

When Michael Sterrett first investigated Honolulu's Japanese gangsters, he could not have realized how true his intuition would prove: the yakuza are not simply another organized criminal gang. But then, they have always been something more.

Part I
Early History

Chapter 1
The Honorable
Outlaws

One might call Goro Fujita the Bard of the Yakuza and he would not object. His business card, ornate even by Japanese standards, introduces the man by asking for forgiveness, explaining in humble terms that he drinks too much but is devoted to his work. He is a short, round fellow whose bushy hair hangs around a face that might belong either to a comedian or a thug, depending on his mood. He is, in fact, a former gangster, a veteran of the Tosei-kai, the largely ethnic Korean gang known for its ruthless control of nightclubs in Tokyo's famous Ginza district. But Goro Fujita no longer patrols the night streets for the "Ginza Police," as they once were called. He is now something of a celebrity among the yakuza, as novelist, historian, and storyteller of Japan's underworld.

Fujita is the proud author of some thirty novels about the yakuza, romantic works that dwell on a particularly Japanese brand of virility, bravery, and fatalism, of noble values that can be traced back to the samurai warriors of feudal Japan. They are books with names like *Big Gambler, Cemetery of Chivalry, Poetry of the Outlaw,* and *I Don't Need My Grave*. He is master of the swordfight scene, interpreter of arcane custom, and archivist of criminal history. He beams while presenting, alongside his many novels, three encyclopedic tomes that comprise the core of his lifework: the first, a massive genealogical dictionary of the complex kinships among the yakuza; the others, two volumes of the *One Hundred Year History* of right-wing politics and organized crime in Japan, a history, says the author, dating back over 300 years.

At his comfortable home on the outskirts of Tokyo, Fujita carries on a rare seminar for special guests on the history of the yakuza. He lovingly pulls out old photos of early bosses, pressed between the pages of a dozen hardbound volumes stored on his fine wooden shelves. His office library bulges with a unique Japanese literary collection – books on swords, guns, martial arts, general history, regional history, war, and the right wing.

Fujita is a man who spins a good yarn, tells long-winded jokes, and can hold even the demanding attention of a yakuza boss. He writes fiction because he doesn't like to use real names. "Too many demands would be placed upon me," he explains. Fujita's characters nonetheless manage to convey his profound feelings for the yakuza world, sentiments that have found a welcome audience among the Japanese reading public. His work belongs to a genre of Japanese literature that has long extolled the image of the romantic gangster. The yakuza, in fact, form a central theme of popular culture in Japan, with heroes and anti-heroes enshrined in countless movies, books, ballads, and short stories.

For Fujita and his colleagues, the history of organized crime in Japan is an honorable one, filled with tales of yakuza Robin Hoods coming to the aid of the common people. The heroes of these stories are society's victims who made good, losers who finally won, men who lived the life of the outlaw with dignity. These tales stand at the heart of the yakuza's self-image, and – much to the chagrin of Japanese police – of public perception as well. The police challenge the accuracy of these portrayals, as do most scholars of Japanese history; but the feeling persists among the Japanese that organized crime in their country bears a noble past. To understand this romantic image of the gangster, one must go back nearly four centuries to the country's Middle Ages, the source of countless modern legends that in Japan take the place of the frontier West in American culture – where the sword replaces the six-shooter and the cowboy is a samurai.

Samurai Bandits and Chivalrous Commoners

To the commoners of feudal Japan they were known as *kabuki-mono,* the crazy ones, and as early as 1612 they began attracting the attention of local officials. Like rebels of a more recent era, they wore outlandish costumes and strange haircuts; their behavior was often equally bizarre. At their sides hung remarkably long swords that nearly trailed along the ground as the outlaws swaggered through the streets of old Japan. Terrorizing the defenseless townspeople almost at will, these outlaws were not above using them to practice *tsuji-giri,* a hideous rite in which a samurai would waylay a passerby to test a new blade.

The kabuki-mono comprised the legendary crime gangs of medieval Japan, eccentric samurai warriors known also as the *hatamoto-yakko,* or, loosely, the servants of the shogun. They made heavy use of slang and

14 | *Early History*

adopted outrageous names, such as Taisho Jingi-gumi, or the All-Gods Gang. They displayed an unusual loyalty among themselves, swearing to protect one another under any circumstance, even against their own parents.

It was the Tokugawa era, the time of the shogunate. Centuries of civil war had come to a historic end when Ieyasu Tokugawa unified the island country in 1604, thereby becoming the first great shogun. But Japan was not yet stable. Peace in the nation meant that as many as 500,000 samurai were suddenly unemployed, workers whose best skills lay largely in soldiering and the martial arts. Eventually, most samurai joined the growing merchant class, as large villages like Osaka and castle towns like Tokyo and Nagoya were transformed into bustling urban centers. Others found jobs in the expanding civil bureaucracy, or as scholars and philosophers. But not all were success stories. The kabuki-mono – nearly all of them samurai of good standing – found themselves caught within a rigid medieval society about to enter a 200-year period of self-imposed isolation, with few opportunities beyond those offered by street fighting, robbery, and terror.

Such a life was not a new one for the *ronin,* or masterless samurai. In earlier times, many had turned to banditry when their lords were defeated in battle, looting the towns and countryside as they meandered across Japan. Traditionally, these renegade warriors were taken into the armies of the feudal lords then warring over Japan, but now, in the relative peace of Tokugawa society, these new groups of outlaw samurai began to take on a life of their own. (The gangs of roving bandits from this era would later be brought to life in the Japanese movie *Seven Samurai,* which in turn inspired the American Western *The Magnificent Seven.*)

While these criminal servants of the shogun – the hatamoto-yakko – might appear to be the true forebears of the Japanese underworld, today's yakuza identify not with them but with their historic enemies, the *machi-yakko,* or servants of the town. These were bands of young townsmen who, as fear and resentment grew, formed to fend off the increasing attacks by hatamoto-yakko. While sporting at times the same odd habits as their opponents, their leaders were often of different stock – clerks, shopkeepers, innkeepers, artisans. Others were laborers rounded up by local construction bosses, including a good many homeless wanderers and stray samurai. Like the gangs of today, the machi-yakko were adept at gambling, and developed a close relationship with their leaders that may well have been a precedent for the tightly organized yakuza.

The townspeople naturally cheered on the machi-yakko, elated to watch fellow commoners stand up to the murderous samurai. Indeed, among the citizens of Edo, as Tokyo was then called, the town servants quickly became folk heroes. It is understandable, then, that the yakuza – who see themselves as honorable outlaws – have chosen to look upon the machi-yakko as their spiritual ancestors. But a direct connection is difficult to make. Kanehiro Hoshino, a criminologist with Japan's Police Science Research Institute, points out that both yakko groups disappeared by the late seventeenth century after repeated crackdowns by an alarmed shogunate. Tokyo's All-Gods Gang, for example, met its fate in 1686 when officials rounded up 300 of its members and executed the ringleaders. Although occasionally the gangs no doubt performed honorable acts, they seem largely to have been what one scholar called "disorderly rogues."

Like most Robin Hoods throughout history, the machi-yakko owe their reputation not to deed but to legend, in this case the numerous eighteenth-century plays in which they are invariably portrayed as heroes and champions of the weak. So popular were these dramas that the Japanese theater itself owes much of its early development to the depiction of these marauding bands of eccentrics. They were further heralded in assorted folk tales and songs that remain among the most popular of Japan's past. In these stories and plays they are billed as the *otokodate*, or chivalrous commoners. There is the tale, for example, of Ude no Kisaburo, or One-armed Kisaburo, immortalized in a Kabuki play. Kisaburo, a skilled swordsman who protects the townspeople, is excommunicated by his fencing teacher after having an affair with a woman. Seeking his teacher's forgiveness, he severs his right arm in an act of remorse, and then goes on to battle the thugs of Tokyo.

The most celebrated tale of the machi-yakko is that of Chobei Banzuiin. Born into a ronin family in southern Japan, Chobei journeyed to Tokyo around 1640, where he joined his brother, who was the chief priest of a Buddhist temple. Chobei became a labor broker, recruiting workers to build the roads surrounding Tokyo and to repair the stone walls around the shogun's palace. Using a ploy that would become a yakuza mainstay, Chobei opened a gambling den. The betting served not only to attract workers, but enabled him to retrieve a portion of the salaries he paid them.

According to the stories and kabuki plays about his life, Chobei became the leader of Tokyo's machi-yakko. The tales are filled with his great deeds – a town girl rescued from assault; the marriage of two lovers previously unable to wed because of their different social class. Whenever thanked by those he helped, he would answer: "We have made it our principle to live with a chivalrous spirit. When put to the sword, we'll lose our lives. That's our fate. I just ask you to pray for the repose of my soul when my turn comes." As his words predicted, he was put to the sword, slain by his archenemy Jurozaemon Mizuno, the leader of Tokyo's hata-moto-yakko. Although the circumstances leading to Chobei's death are uncertain, one kabuki play offers the following finish:

> One day, Mizuno invites Chobei through his messenger to come to his residence and have a drink together in token of reconciliation. Chobei and his many followers immediately determine that the invitation is a trap. Not listening to his followers, who ask him not to go, Chobei goes to Mizuno's house alone.
>
> Mizuno receives Chobei respectfully at his home, and before long, a banquet begins. At the banquet, one of Mizuno's followers spills sake from a large cup on Chobei's kimono under pretense of a slip of his hand. As planned, another of Mizuno's followers takes Chobei to a bathroom, suggesting he have a quick bath and change his kimono. When Chobei becomes defenseless in the bathroom, four or five samurai, all Mizuno's followers, attack him. But being proud of his physical strength, he defeats them without any difficulty. Holding a spear in his hand, Mizuno himself then appears in the bathroom. Looking into the eyes of Mizuno, Chobei says calmly, "Certainly, I offer my life to you. I'm ready to throw away my life, otherwise I'd never have accepted your invitation and come here alone; I'd have listened to my followers who worried about my life. Whether one lives to be a hundred or dies as a baby depends on his fate. You are a person of sufficient status to take my life because you are a noted hatamoto. . . . . I offer my life to you with good grace. I knew I would be killed if I came here; but, if it was rumored that Chobei, who had built up a reputation as a machi-yakko, held his life so dearly, it would be an everlasting disgrace upon my name. You shall have my life for nothing. I have iron nerves, so lance me to the heart without the slightest reluctance!"
>
> Though tough, Mizuno shrinks from these words and hesitates to spear him. His followers urge him [on]. Finally, he makes up his mind and stabs Chobei through the heart with his long spike. The curtain falls with Mizuno's line: "He was too great to be killed."

Another play climaxes with the gallant Chobei being sliced to death "like a carp on a chopping block." Whatever the hero's final fate, his story has made quite an impression on today's yakuza, who claim him as one of their own.

The Yakuza Emerge

The legends and traditions of the machi-yakko were inherited by a later generation of "chivalrous commoners." Among them were Japan's old firemen – gutsy, quick-tempered fellows who usually did construction work but also served as the community's volunteer fire department. Other common heroes included police detectives, leaders of labor gangs, sumo wrestlers, and the members of Japan's eighteenth-century crime syndicates.

These early yakuza would not appear until a hundred years after the death of Chobei Banzuiin, in a society still bound by the feudal laws of the shogun. They were the enterprising members of a medieval underworld who today are widely seen as the true ancestors of the modern yakuza: the *bakuto,* or traditional gamblers, and the *tekiya,* or street peddlers. So distinctive were the habits of the two groups that Japanese police today still classify most yakuza members as either bakuto or tekiya (although a third group, the *gurentai,* or hoodlums, was added after World War II). The ranks of both groups were largely filled from the same quarters – the poor, the landless, and the delinquents and misfits found in any large society. Each group, however, stuck closely to its unique area of control, to such an extent that they could operate within the same small territory without conflict: the bakuto along the busy highways and towns of old Japan, the tekiya amid the nation's growing markets and fairs.

It is to these rustic bands of itinerant traders and roadside gamblers that Goro Fujita traces back yakuza genealogy in his *One Hundred Year History*. Through his oral histories with yakuza elders, his research at Japan's modern libraries, and even his field trips to the tombstones of ancient yakuza, Fujita claims to be able to link today's godfathers to a criminal lineage extending back to the mid-1700s. The genealogical charts within Fujita's books, however, only embellish the preoccupation with history among the varied yakuza clans. Alongside the pictures of great godfathers that adorn the walls of gang headquarters today are family trees that link the group, however precariously, to these noble outlaws of old. What is unusual is that such ancestral connections are invariably made not by blood, but through adoption.

Like the Italian Mafia, the yakuza began organizing in families, with a godfather at the top and new members adopted into the clan as older brothers, younger brothers, and children. The yakuza, however, added to that structure the unique Japanese relationship known as *oyabun-kobun,* or, literally, father-role/child-role. The *oyabun* provides advice, protection, and help, and in return receives the unswerving loyalty and service of his *kobun* whenever needed.

In the feudal society of eighteenth-century Japan, the oyabun-kobun system often provided the basis for relations between teacher and apprentice, between lord and vassal, and, in the nascent underworld, between boss and follower. It was a mirror of the traditional Japanese family in which the father held great and final authority, including the power to choose marriage partners and occupations for his children.

Within the early yakuza gangs the oyabun-kobun relationship created remarkable strength and cohesion, leading at times to a fanatic devotion to the boss. Today, despite encroaching modernization, it continues to foster a loyalty, obedience, and trust among the yakuza unknown within American crime groups except between the closest of blood relatives. Sociologist Hiroaki Iwai, an authority on delinquent groups in Japan, wrote of the devotion traditionally required to the oyabun: ". . . new kobun will be expected to act as *teppodama* ('bullets') in fights with other gangs, standing in the front line, facing the guns and swords of the other side, risking his life. . . . On occasion he will take the blame and go to prison for a crime committed by his oyabun."

Like other organized crime groups, the early yakuza developed an elaborate ceremony to initiate new recruits into the organization. Within the Triad societies of the Chinese underworld, the rites involved the killing of a young rooster, the reciting of thirty-six oaths before an altar, and the pricking of the recruit's middle finger by a silver needle. The cutting of a new member's skin, done to symbolize blood relations, was also heavily practiced by the Sicilian Mafia until the 1930s. The old Mafia initiations had religious overtones as well. As paper was burned representing the immolation of a saint, the recruit swore an oath pledging his honor, loyalty, and blood to the Mafia.

Within the yakuza, bakuto and tekiya began using a formal exchange of *sake* cups to symbolize the blood connection. These rites, however, have represented not only entry into the gang, but also entry into the oyabun-kobun relationship as well. The ceremony also holds religious significance, typically being performed before a shrine devoted to Shinto, the indigenous religion of Japan. The amount of sake in the cups depends upon one's status. If the participants are not father and child, but brother and brother – as in treaties between gang bosses – equal amounts are poured into each cup. If the relationship is one of elder brother and younger brother, the elder brother's cup is filled six-tenths and the younger brother's cup four-tenths. Various other combinations exist, each coming with its own carefully prescribed set of duties within the "family."

Such initiations continue today, although usually in abbreviated form. One ceremony between oyabun and kobun, held in its full formality, was described by sociologist Iwai:

> . . . an auspicious day is chosen, and all members of the organization will attend, with torimochinin or azukarinin ("guarantors") present as intermediaries. Rice, whole fish, and piles of salt are placed in the Shinto shrine alcove, in front of which the oyabun and kobun sit facing each other. The torimochinin arrange the fish ceremonially and fill the drinking-cups with sake, adding fish-scales and salt. . . . They then turn solemnly to the kobun and warn him of his future duties: "Having drunk from the oyabun's cup and he from yours, you now owe loyalty to the ikka [family] and devotion to your oyabun. Even should your wife and children starve, even at the cost of your life, your duty is now to the ikka and oyabun," or "From now on you have no other occupation until the day you die. The oyabun is your only parent; follow him through fire and flood."

The oyabun-kobun system reached its peak around the turn of the twentieth century, influencing the structure of political parties, social movements, the military, business and industry, and the underworld. Today it remains a concept with which most Japanese are intimately familiar, and while it continues to carry certain responsibilities, the relationship is generally treated far less seriously than in the past. An oyabun, for example, is now often a senior at work with whom one is especially close – the equivalent, perhaps, of a mentor in the West. It is almost exclusively within the yakuza that the oyabun-kobun system remains unchanged from its past, existing in a world where kobun will kill others or even kill themselves for the sake of the oyabun. An old adage still popular among gang members goes: "If the boss says that a passing crow is white, you must agree." It is this relationship that stands at the heart of the present, and future, of the Japanese underworld.

Tekiya: The Peddlers

There are various theories offered about the origin of the tekiya. Goro Fujita believes they began as nomads, peddling their goods at castle towns and trading centers. Other ideas center around the word *yashi*, an earlier name used for the peddlers. Because yashi connotes banditry, they may have begun as ronin outlaws combing the countryside. The most widely accepted theory, though, revolves around the fact that the yashi's patron god was Shinno, a Chinese god of agriculture believed to have discovered medicine to help the sick and poor. This account holds that the yashi were groups of medicine peddlers, something akin to the traveling snake-oil salesmen of America's Wild West (the word *shi* can mean medicine and *ya* a merchant or peddler). Over time the name became a catch-all for peddlers of various kinds.

Whatever their origins, by the mid-1700s the tekiya had banded together for mutual interest and protection from the perils of Tokugawa Japan. The gangs were able to establish control over the portable booths in market fairs held at temples and shrines. They were men with a well-deserved reputation for shoddy goods and deceptive salesmanship, a tradition that survives today among the nation's estimated 24,000 tekiya members. The early peddlers developed a proven repertoire of cheating techniques: they would lie about the quality and origin of a product; act drunk and make a show of selling items cheaply so customers believe they don't know what they're doing; or delude the customer with such enterprising tricks as selling miniature trees (*bonsai*) without roots.

The tekiya were organized according to feudal status, with members falling into one of generally five ranks: the boss or oyabun, the underboss, officers, enlisted men, and apprentices. The gang became a sophisticated operation in certain respects. The oyabun's home served as both gang headquarters and training center for new members, who began by living in the boss's home and learning the business. They would later join the enlisted men who were required to peddle the boss's goods through the countryside. Only after they returned with good results were they admitted as full-status members. All members, however, were bound by a strict organization, a domineering oyabun, and, among most groups, the following "Three Commandments of Tekiya":

Do not touch the wife of another member (a rule established because wives were left alone for long periods while their husbands went peddling).

Do not reveal the secrets of the organization to the police.

Keep strict loyalty to the oyabun-kobun relationship.

The boss controlled not only his kobun, but the allocation of stalls and even the availability of certain goods. He would collect rents and protection money, and pocket the difference between them and the rental payment required by the shrine or temple. It was a kind of extortion that would continue to the present day: tekiya bosses demanding payment from street peddlers for the privilege of opening their stalls. Those who refused would find their goods stolen, their customers driven away, and risk being physically assaulted by gang members anxious to maintain their monopoly over the region. Disagreements between tekiya bosses over territory inevitably led to frequent fights. Nevertheless, a good deal of cooperation existed among the gangs, for as the peddlers trekked from fair to fair they inevitably fell under the care of other bosses who, upon payment, would see to it that the vendors were assigned a favorable place to open their stalls.

Unlike the gamblers, the tekiya operation was by and large legal work. Indeed, feudal authorities greatly increased the power of tekiya bosses by granting official recognition of their status between the years 1735 and 1740. In order to reduce the widespread fraud among tekiya vendors and to prevent future turf wars, the government appointed a number of oyabun as "supervisors" and allowed them the dignity of "a surname and two swords," symbols of near-samurai status. With such legitimacy, and with the rapid growth of towns over the next century, the gangs began to expand. Some started organizing additional fairs of their own, becoming, in a sense, the "carnival people" of Japan. They put on festivals resembling circuses with colorful sideshows, and numerous tekiya stands selling food, gifts, housewares, and whatever might attract a buyer. Despite their newfound legitimacy, however, the gangs continued to nurture some thoroughly criminal traits. They would take into their vast network wanted criminals and other fugitives; their protection rackets expanded along with their territory; and their frequent brawls with other gangs often turned tekiya meeting places into armed camps.

Although the early tekiya were made up largely of the same types of misfits as their gambling cousins, the bakuto, they also attracted the members of Japan's ancestral class of outcasts. These were the *burakumin,* or "people of the hamlet," who comprised a separate caste somewhat similar to the untouchables of India. The burakumin were an arbitrary class, comprising largely those who worked with dead animals, such as leather workers, or in "unclean" occupations such as undertaking. Discrimination directed against the burakumin was cruel and relentless. They were popularly referred to as *eta* (heavily polluted) or *hinin* (nonhuman). Just as the samurai were able to abuse the commoners, so were the commoners allowed to torment the burakumin.

In his book *Peasants, Rebels, and Outcasts,* historian Mikiso Hane describes the conditions under which the burakumin lived:

They were restricted in where they could live, quality of housing, mobility in and out of their hamlets, clothing, hairdo and even footwear. . . . In some areas they were required to wear special identification marks, such as a yellow collar. They were banned from the shrines and temples of non-eta communities, and inter-marriage with other classes was strictly forbidden.

In relation to the underworld, the system seemed to feed on itself. Under the Tokugawa regime, those who violated laws or customs could be relegated to the status of eta or hinin; some tekiya members, therefore, already were branded as nonhuman. At the same time, many born into burakumin families joined the tekiya gangs, which provided a path out of abject poverty and disgrace. Peddling offered the burakumin one of the few opportunities to leave their birthplace, where they would forever be known as outcasts. It was a significant pool of potential outlaws; by the end of the Tokugawa era in 1867, the burakumin numbered about 400,000 of Japan's 33 million people.

Legal discrimination against the burakumin was officially ended in 1871 by a government decree. However, the abuse and victimization of these people remains to this day, and continues to drive substantial numbers of burakumin into the hands of the yakuza.

Bakuto: The Gamblers

While Japan's outcasts helped swell the ranks of the tekiya, the bakuto also had little trouble finding members. The first gambling gangs were in fact recruited by government officials and local bosses who, under the Tokugawa administration, were responsible for a variety of irrigation and construction projects. These efforts required the payment of substantial sums to the workers, money that their employers schemed to get back in much the same way as Chobei Banzuiin a century earlier: by hiring a motley crew of outlaws, laborers, and farmers to gamble with the workers.

The hired gamblers gradually began attracting misfit merchants and artisans, as well as Japanese of higher status, such as samurai and sumo wrestlers. As they organized into disciplined bands, these early gamblers found their niche along the nation's great trunk roads, where their colorful lives formed the basis for countless tales of old Japan. Their contribution, though, would be far greater than enriching Japanese folklore: the bakuto became what Tokyo criminologist Hoshino calls "the kernel of organized crime groups" in Japan. They would give that country's underworld not only its central tradition of gambling, but also its custom of finger-cutting and the first use of the word "yakuza."

The highways of feudal Japan proved a benign environment for the gamblers. As a deterrent to misbehavior in the provinces, the Tokugawa government decreed that all lords visit Tokyo once a year, and that their families reside in the city permanently. The main highways thus became the political lifelines of the country, carrying frequent processions of nobles and servants, as well as an almost constant stream of couriers. Spaced at convenient intervals along the road were stopping places where the traveler might find a night's rest and some entertainment, including the chance to wager a coin or two. Japan's most famous route, the Tokaido Highway, was built in 1603, joining Kyoto – the ancient capital and home of the emperor – with Tokyo, seat of the shogun and real power of the Tokugawa government. In all, there were fifty-three of these way stations along the highway; most of these, by the mid-nineteenth century, played host to a local bakuto gang.

It was along the Tokaido and other highways that the gamblers first began using the word "yakuza". According to the most widely held belief, the term derives from the worst possible score in the card game *hanafuda* (flower cards). Three cards are dealt per player in the game, and the last digit of their total counts as the number of the hand; therefore, with a hand of 20 – the worst score – one's total is zero. Among the losing combinations: a sequence of 8-9-3, or in Japanese, ya-ku-sa.

The losing combination of ya-ku-sa came to be used widely among the early gambling gangs to denote something useless. It was later applied to the gamblers themselves, to mean they were useless to society, born to lose. For years the word was limited to the bakuto gangs – there are still purists today among the Japanese underworld who insist that the only true yakuza are the traditional gamblers. As the twentieth century progressed, however, the word gradually received wide use by the general public as a name for bakuto, tekiya, and a host of other organized crime groups in Japan.

Like the tekiya, the early bakuto groups developed a set of rules that included strict adherence to secrecy, obedience to the oyabun-kobun system, and a ranking order determining one's status and role within the group. It was a feudal organization with almost total control resting with the oyabun. Promotions were likely to be based on members' performances during gang fights; gambling skills and loyalty to the oyabun also figured greatly. For the lowly kobun, promotion through the ranks could be an arduous task. He would generally be assigned such jobs as polishing dice, cleaning the house of the oyabun, running errands, and baby-sitting.

The gamblers dealt severely with those who broke the gang's rules. Cowardice, disobedience, and revealing gang secrets were treated not only as acts of betrayal but also as affronts to the reputation and honor of the gang. Certain offenses were particularly taboo, including rape and petty theft. Short of death, the heaviest punishment was expulsion. After banishing the transgressor, the oyabun notified other bakuto gangs that the gambler was no longer welcome in his group; by general agreement, the outcast could not then join a rival band. It is a tradition that survives today. In the event of expulsion, the gang sends a volley of open-faced postcards via regular mail to the various underworld families. The cards comprise a formal notice of expulsion, and ask that the gangs reject any association with the former member.

For serious violations not meriting death or expulsion, the bakuto introduced the custom of *yubitsume,* in which the top joint of the little finger is ceremoniously severed. The practice of finger-cutting was not confined to the bakuto. Others in the lower rungs of Tokugawa society later employed it, including the prostitutes of Tokyo's famous Yoshiwara district, who saw it as a mark of devotion to their special lovers. The yakuza, however, used the ritual amputations more practically. Finger-cutting reportedly began as a means of weakening the hand, which meant that the gambler's all-important sword could not be as firmly grasped. Such an act, whether forced or voluntary, succeeded in making the errant kobun more dependent on the protection of his boss.

When amputated in apology, the severed phalanx is wrapped in fine cloth and solemnly handed to the oyabun. The oyabun generally accepts, for great merit has traditionally been accorded this act. Further infractions, however, could mean another amputation at the second joint of the same digit, or at the top joint of another finger. Often yubitsume occurs just prior to expulsion, as a lasting punishment inflicted by the gang.

The practice of finger-slicing spread to the tekiya and other crime groups, and, according to Japanese authorities, has actually increased since feudal times. A 1971 survey by government researchers found that 42 percent of modern bakuto members had severed finger joints, and that 10 percent had performed the act at least twice.

The other great trademark of the yakuza, the tattoo, also won widespread acceptance among the bakuto during Japan's feudal period. The yakuza's tattoo originally was a mark of punishment, used by authorities to ostracize the outlaws from society; criminals generally would be tattooed with one black ring around an arm for each offense.

There is, however, a nobler tradition of tattooing in Japan. Its remarkable designs, considered by many to be the world's finest, date back hundreds of years. As early as the third century, a Chinese account of the

Japanese noted: "Men both great and small tattoo their faces and work designs upon their bodies." Over the years the patterns grew more complex, blending a striking array of famous gods, folk heroes, animals, and flowers into one fluid portrait. By the late seventeenth century, intricate, full-body designs became popular with the gamblers and with laborers who worked with much of their bodies exposed: porters, stable hands, carpenters, masons. Occasionally, the *geisha* (Japan's professional female entertainers) would indulge, as did the prostitutes of Tokyo and Osaka, who would tattoo the name of a favored client on their arm or inner thigh. The Tokugawa government, which tried periodically to prohibit tattooing, was unable to curb its popularity.

The traditional tattooing process is an agonizing one. Using a tool carved from bone or wood, and tipped with a cluster of tiny needles, the artist punches into the skin with a succession of painful jabs. The thrusting action of the tattooer is particularly stinging to such sensitive parts as the chest and buttocks. The operation, furthermore, is a prolonged one. A complete back tattoo, stretching from the collar of the neck down to the tailbone, can take 100 hours.

Such extensive tattooing, then, became a test of strength, and the gamblers eagerly adopted the practice to show the world their courage, toughness, and masculinity. It served, at the same time, another, more humble purpose – as a self-inflicted wound that would permanently distinguish the outcasts from the rest of the world. The tattoo marks the yakuza as misfits, forever unable or unwilling to adapt themselves to Japanese society.

As with ritual finger-cutting, the tattooing spread from the bakuto to the tekiya and other Japanese gangs, and the practice became increasingly confined to the underworld. So closely associated with the yakuza is the custom today that saunas and public baths, wanting to protect their clientele from gangsters, hang signs reading "No tattoos allowed." Today an estimated 73 percent of the yakuza bear some tattooing, although many employ modern electric needles, which are faster and less painful. Still, it is a mark of great respect within the underworld to have endured the torture of the traditional method.

The bakuto's contributions to criminal history extend to traditions other than tattoos and finger-cutting. Certain early gangster bands were granted a measure of official sanction and became adept at working with authorities, though less formally than the tekiya. Some oyabun were even deputized. Such agreements with the police often allowed the gangs to consolidate and expand their power. Other gangs, however, viewed cooperation with the police as contrary to the gambler's code of conduct, and often attacked the errant bakuto. Nevertheless, these early moves by authorities to recognize, work with, and even co-opt the underworld broke important ground. Similar agreements later formed the basis for political corruption that reaches the highest levels of Japanese government.

Despite official cooperation by some groups, and occasional bloody disputes over territory by others, the early bakuto generally helped one another. Indeed, at times they resembled an underworld mutual aid society. Of particular note was the bakuto's system of "travelers," a custom by which itinerant gamblers would visit the boss of each region on their route, stay for several days, and receive a small amount of money for expenses. The traveler was treated with the great courtesy reserved for an invited guest: according to bakuto etiquette, although host and visitor were strangers, they were in the same profession.

The travelers were among the most colorful figures of the Tokugawa era; even today their outfits are easily recognized by most Japanese through the countless plays and movies about their lives. They wore hats of sedge that almost covered their faces; caped overcoats that flapped in the wind as they walked; straw sandals and gaiters; a strapped pair of bundles slung over their shoulders; and a single sword at their side, unlike the two blades worn by samurai.

Ritual and custom pervaded the life of the bakuto, and the travelers were no exception. Upon arrival at the house of the oyabun, the traveler introduced himself, using archaic Japanese, to the kobun answering the door. "I was born in so-and-so place. I am so-and-so of the so-and-so group. I am a humble man, and as we have now made acquaintance, I would like you to support me from today onwards." The traveler then presented a hand towel to the kobun as a gift and, according to etiquette, it would be returned with a small amount of money and the phrase, "Your courtesy is enough appreciation." In exchange for his meals, the traveler would do menial tasks in the oyabun's house, such as cleaning or drawing bath water from the well. The boss, for his part, would treat him as his guest. In the event the traveler was a wanted man – which was often the case – the oyabun would take responsibility for sheltering him.

The Gambler as Hero

The bakuto in general, and the travelers in particular, became the basis for the leading characters in the *matabi-mono* (stories of wandering gamblers), a genre of Japanese literature that has enjoyed great popularity since the turn of this century. Among the authors was Shin Hasegawa, a pulp novelist whose widely read works beginning around 1912 turned the yakuza into popular heroes. His stories depicted the gamblers as faithful and humane people, men whose loneliness and sorrow few outsiders could understand. Like Goro Fujita's novels of seventy years later, Hasegawa's stories portrayed men of questionable backgrounds who fought as hard as they gambled, yet maintained a philosophy of supporting the underdog and never troubling the common folk. Above all, they remained loyal to those who helped them. A virtuous traveler would be willing to sacrifice his life for the oyabun who for one day had opened the gang's home to him.

The aggressive yet compassionate outlaw, useless to society but willing to stand up for the common man – these are the essential components of the yakuza legend. It is a tradition inherited not only from the machi-yakko but from the samurai as well, and it spread through the feudal underworld.

The yakuza were especially keen on the values embodied in *bushido,* the much-heralded code of the samurai. Like the warriors, they would prove their manliness by the stoic endurance of pain, hunger, or imprisonment. Violent death for the yakuza, as for the samurai, was a poetic, tragic, and honorable fate. But the value system developed by the early yakuza endured because it went far beyond a mere reflection of the samurai's code. At its heart rested the concepts of *giri* and *ninjo,* two terms not easily translated into English. The ideas behind giri and ninjo had a formidable impact on the samurai, and continue to exert a powerful influence on Japanese society at large.

Giri loosely means obligation or a strong sense of duty, and is tied up with complex Japanese values involving loyalty, gratitude, and moral debt. In a sense, giri is the social cloth that binds much of Japan together; its observance figures centrally in such matters as the *oyabun-kobun* system. Still, such explanations fall far short of conveying the intricacies implied by the word. Ruth Benedict, in her classic 1946 account of Japanese culture, *The Chrysanthemum and the Sword,* cited the country's old saying that "Giri is hardest to bear." Wrote Benedict, "There is no possible English equivalent and of all the strange categories of moral obligations which anthropologists find in the cultures of the world, it is one of the most curious. It is specifically Japanese." The obligations encompassed by giri range from "gratitude for an old kindness to the duty of revenge."

Ninjo is roughly equivalent to "human feeling" or "emotion." Among its many interpretations is generosity or sympathy toward the weak and disadvantaged, and empathy toward others. It is typically used in conjunction with giri, and the tension created by these two forces – obligation versus compassion – forms a central theme in Japanese literature. By adopting giri-ninjo, the yakuza greatly enhanced their standing in society, showing that, like the best samurai, they could combine compassion and kindness with their martial skills.

Among those who follow the yakuza there is a spirited debate about whether these old values still exist. The oyabun of Japan's great syndicates, cast in their Confucian roles as teachers and preservers of tradition, are outspoken on the yakuza's position. According to Kakuji Inagawa of the Inagawa family, perhaps the most powerful oyabun in Japan today, "The yakuza are trying to pursue the road of chivalry and patriotism. That's our biggest difference with the American Mafia, it's our sense of giri and ninjo. The yakuza try to take care of all society if possible, even if it takes one million yen to help a single person." Adds a ranking boss from the rival Sumiyoshi syndicate: "In the winter we give the sunny half of the street to the common people because we survive on their work. In the summer we yakuza walk on the sunny side, to give them the cool, shaded half. If you look at our actions, you can see our strong commitment to giri-ninjo."

Nowhere do the old values shine brighter than in the tale of Shimizu no Jirocho (Jirocho of Shimizu). This is the story, taught to millions of Japanese children, about the man who is undoubtedly the country's most famous gangster.

Jirocho was the third son of a sailor, born, according to legend, on New Year's Day of 1820 in the thriving seaport of Shimizu. His hometown lay along the great Tokaido Highway, on a stretch between Tokyo and what was then a quiet fishing village called Yokohama. Because of a local superstition that New Year's babies grew up to be either great geniuses or hopeless villains, his father took no chances and gave the boy up for adoption by a wealthy relative. As a young boy, Jirocho was a terror, but eventually he settled down to become a model rice merchant in his adoptive father's business.

Soon his father died, however, and at sixteen Jirocho inherited the business. There he stayed until age twenty, when one day he encountered a wandering monk standing in his doorway. The monk warned him he would die before his twenty-sixth birthday, a prediction Jirocho took to heart. Jirocho, by then bored with his job, considered joining up with the bands of gamblers that flourished in Shimizu and up and down the Tokaido. After a drunken brawl with local hoodlums, he finally left his wife and business, and took to the road for three years as a "traveler." During that time he made a name for himself as an exceptional fighter, mediator, and leader of men.

Upon returning to Shimizu, he set about organizing his own gang, and soon attracted gamblers and would-be gamblers from miles around: there were street toughs, construction workers, ronin; Jirocho put together the classic bakuto gang. According to one account, at his peak he commanded an army of 600 gamblers, and held sway over the heartland of the Tokaido, stretching along eight coastal stations from the Fuji River near Tokyo to the Oi River toward Kyoto. Jirocho's men, in fact, became the law of the land along their stretch of the Tokaido, for the Tokugawa police were often undisciplined and notoriously corrupt. Under Jirocho's able leadership, his men would fight heroic battles against dishonorable gamblers and thieves, and guard the common people against the brutal ways of the samurai and their lords.

Jirocho's heyday spanned the turbulent years of the mid-nineteenth century in Japan. The Tokugawa shogunate was in decline, weakened by assaults from every side: there were powerful nobles and merchants who wanted change and recognition; foreign navies who demanded that the country open its doors to the West; repeated uprisings by an oppressed peasantry; and a growing hostility from the imperial court in Kyoto, whose own power over Japan was fast increasing.

A mighty movement was gaining strength to install the emperor as actual head of state. (His role heretofore had been largely symbolic.) Among its supporters were those who hoped to keep the nation closed to foreigners, for the shogun had bowed to Commodore Perry's demands in 1854 and was gradually opening Japan's ports to the West. Spouting the slogan "Revere the emperor, expel the barbarians," these traditionalists would inadvertently hasten the end of over 200 years of isolation, for the emperor would swing Japan's doors open far wider than the shogun ever did.

This was to be the final chapter of the Tokugawa era, the end of Japan's long immersion in feudalism. It was in these confused final days of near civil war that Jirocho, like many yakuza, finally chose sides, lending his support to help enshrine the emperor as the divine ruler of the Japanese islands. Other yakuza joined ranks with the embattled forces of the shogun. The motivation for both groups was not ideological: gamblers that they were, the bakuto were merely playing the odds, hoping to win political advantage from the victors.

Jirocho's gamble was a wise one, for all his past crimes were pardoned, and he became a powerful man in his community. The bakuto boss promoted improvements in farming, fishing, and the development of the city of Shimizu. In keeping with the new surge toward modernization, Jirocho started one of Japan's first English schools. To the likely amazement of his old colleagues, he even established a penitentiary. His followers, meanwhile, continued to keep order and run the gambling games in the region.

Jirocho died in 1893 at the age of seventy-three. Thousands today still visit his grave each year, where he lies buried with his followers in a local temple. It is said that at the foot of Mount Fuji there stands still another monument to the old outlaw, a Shinto shrine dedicated to Jirocho, built by farmers who work the land he once reclaimed.

That, more or less, is how Japan's most famous yakuza has been depicted in countless ballads and tales over the years. But not everyone agrees with the legend. Among the dissenters is the *Asahi Shimbun,* Japan's most prestigious newspaper, which ran a story in January 1975 entitled " 'Robin Hood' of Shimizu Was Nothing but a Thug." According to old administrative documents discovered in a town next to Shimizu, says the story, Jirocho, far from inspiring worship among the people, "was in truth nothing but a gangster who oppressed the farmers." The documents reveal that Jirocho, who was entrusted to rule over the area by the government, remained a gang boss at heart, controlling Shimizu through violence and intimidation. Like most of the world's great outlaws, Jirocho is best remembered through legend, not history.

The Yakuza Modernize
The forces of historical change swirling around Jirocho's life had climaxed in 1867 when, bowing to the inevitable, the fifteenth and final shogun of the Tokugawa family resigned and was replaced by the young Emperor Meiji. It was the dawn of the Meiji Restoration, in which all the pent-up commercial and intellectual power of Japan would be released and the Japanese would perform their first economic miracle, breaking the last bonds of feudalism and swiftly transforming their country into an industrial power.

By the turn of the century, Japan had evolved into a complex, rapidly modernizing society populated by some 45 million people. Between 1890 and 1914, the country's total industrial production had doubled, while its share of factories more than tripled. Politically, too, the country was fast changing. The Japanese witnessed the birth and maturation of their first parliament and political parties, and the growth of a powerful, autonomous military that would invade China, annex Korea, and in 1905 defeat the Russians in war.

As the country modernized, the yakuza expanded their activities in step with the growing economy. The gangs gained a foothold in organizing casual laborers for construction jobs in the big cities, and in recruiting stevedores for the booming business on the docks. Also, with the introduction of the metal wheel, the underworld influenced control of the new carts, called rickshaws, which by the turn of the century numbered 50,000 in Tokyo alone.

Gambling remained the center of life for the bakuto gangs, although better police control forced them to take their games farther underground into urban hideaways and private homes. Many bosses started legitimate businesses to act as fronts for the gangs' rackets, and began an enduring custom of making payoffs to local police. The tekiya also maintained their traditional livelihood, the street stalls. The peddlers were able to expand their territory more easily, for unlike the gamblers, their work was not on the surface illegal. Determined police efforts, however, were making it clear to both groups that the all-out, open brawls and territorial wars of the past would be far less tolerated in the new state.

The bakuto and tekiya gangs also continued to play politics, and gradually some gangs developed close ties to important officials. These gangs wanted some measure of government sanction, or at least some freedom from government harassment, and saw cooperation as the key. On the other side, the government continued to find uses for the organized gangs, as it had since before Jirocho's day.

At first, the use of this muscle was somewhat haphazard, as it had been with Jirocho's men, and ideology had little to do with the association between politician and hit man. It remained as pure opportunism on both sides. There was always a strongly conservative cast to the relationship, but late in the nineteenth century that conservatism began to veer to the right. Japan now began its climb to militarism abroad and its descent into repression at home, for just as the nation began experimenting with democracy, so was an ominous new force being born – the ultranationalists.

Patriotic Gangsters

Modern ultranationalism, the force behind Japan's rightward swing, harks back to the 1880s. It was first defined in Kyushu, the southernmost of the four major islands, and at the time a poor fishing and coal mining region. Kyushu was home to a large community of disgruntled ex-samurai, many of whom had taken part in rebellions against the new social order. The discontent of these soldiers was exploited by patriots and politicians critical of the new regime's corruption and disregard of tradition. Particularly affected was the city of Fukuoka, in the corner of the island closest to the Asian mainland. The city developed into a breeding ground for antigovernment thought, and within a few years became the center of a new militarism and patriotism in Japan.

Out of Fukuoka emerged a leader who would forever change the course of both organized crime and politics in Japan, joining those two forces together in a way that would endure to the present day. He was Mitsuru Toyama, born the third son to a family of obscure samurai rank. Information on his early years is difficult to verify. It is said that Toyama spent his childhood in poverty, peddling sweet potatoes on the streets of Fukuoka, and developed into a tough, streetwise teenager who idolized the samurai tradition.

By the time Toyama reached his twenties, his activities turned political. He took part in one of the final samurai uprisings, earning a three-year jail sentence from the Meiji government. Upon his release, the young patriot enlisted in his first nationalist group, the Kyoshisha (Pride and Patriotism Society), and for the first time began to gather a following. Toyama took to the streets and set about organizing the listless toughs of Fukuoka. His men became both a disciplined work force and a tough fighting force used to keep labor unrest at a minimum in the region's coal mines.

Like others before him, Toyama gained a reputation as a local Robin Hood, handing out money to his followers on the streets of Fukuoka without bothering to count it. He became known as "Emperor of the Slums," and earned the respect of local politicians, who knew and feared his frequent use of violence.

Toyama's rise to national power came with his founding of the Genyosha, or Dark Ocean Society, in 1881. Genyosha, a federation of nationalist societies already in operation, was to be the forerunner of Japan's modern secret societies and patriotic groups. The articles of its charter were vague: revere the emperor, love and respect the nation, and defend the people's rights. The ambitious Toyama, however, knew exactly what the organization was about – tapping directly into the powerful sentiment among the ex-samurai for expansion abroad and authoritarian rule at home. Even the name Dark Ocean suggested expansion, symbolizing to Toyama and his followers the narrow passage of water separating Japan from Korea and China.

It was Toyama who foresaw and formed, almost singlehandedly, a new patriotic social order that would be used as a paramilitary force in Japanese politics. Through a campaign of terror, blackmail, and assassination, the Dark Ocean Society's work would prove highly effective, exerting particular influence over members of the officer corps and the government bureaucracy, and playing an instrumental role in sweeping Japan into East Asia and, ultimately, into war with the United States.

Genyosha members worked as bodyguards for government officials, as strong-arm persuaders for local political bosses, and in legitimate jobs as skilled laborers – plumbers, carpenters, masons – in unions affiliated with the society and its successors. These new yakuza considered themselves at the opposite end of the underworld spectrum from the bakuto and tekiya, as high-class gangsters imbued with the righteousness of Toyama's superpatriotic politics.

The society's agents were sent far and wide to China, Korea, and Manchuria as spies. They operated schools where an entire generation of ultranationalists were trained. Through studies in the martial arts, foreign language, and spying techniques, Genyosha graduates formed the basis of a sophisticated intelligence network created by the Japanese prior to World War II.

In Japan, Toyama deployed his men with equal skill. They were used to foment or subdue public unrest, intimidate both political candidates and voters, suppress dissident laborers, and punish anyone of whom their bosses disapproved. The Dark Ocean Society and its ilk were especially useful to mining and manufacturing companies, who employed them not only as strikebreakers, but as hired political muscle who helped promote or shatter the careers of would-be politicians.

Toyama and his Dark Ocean followers possessed their own agenda, however. Using money gained from their growing rackets, Toyama launched a campaign of terror and assassination aimed at achieving a new social order in Japan. Genyosha activists hurled a bomb into the carriage of Foreign Minister Shigenobu Okuma, who lost a leg to the explosion; stabbed the liberal politician Taisuke Itagaki; and murdered Toshimichi Okubo, perhaps the Meiji era's most brilliant statesman.

The year 1892 saw a new phenomenon in Japan: a national election. Toyama and company greeted it with the first large-scale cooperation between rightists and the underworld. The society, already making deals with conservatives inside the Meiji government, launched a violent campaign in support of conservative incumbents.

Fearing that his forces might not be adequate, Toyama called on the leader of a gang in nearby Kumamoto, who sent 300 of his men to Fukuoka as reinforcements. This combined force was joined by the local police, who had been mobilized by none other than the minister of home affairs to assist the gangsters in harassing antigovernment opponents. The result was the bloodiest election in Japanese history, with scores dead and hundreds wounded. Genyosha, for its part, stated openly in its official account that the purpose of the Fukuoka campaign was to uproot all democratic and liberal organizations in the region.

Genyosha's next mission was more ambitious. Toyama, acting on a secret request from the minister of war, was to "start a fire" in Korea, creating a pretext for Japanese troops to move in. In 1895, a squad of Genyosha agents, trained as assassin-spies in the martial arts of the *ninja,* infiltrated the Korean Imperial Palace and murdered the queen. This act, in part, did indeed precipitate Japan's invasion of that country. The Japanese would not leave for fifty years.

From then on, ultranationalism became a more or less permanent fixture on the political landscape. The Dark Ocean Society provided the model for hundreds of secret societies reaching into every corner of Japan and, eventually, through much of East Asia as well. They sported such colorful names as the Blood Pledge Corps, the Loyalist Sincerity Group, the Farmers' Death-Defying Corps, and the Association for Heavenly Action. Some groups were supported by wealthy patrons; others financed their work through an array of crimes that today still form the daily bread of yakuza gangs: gambling, prostitution, protection rackets, strikebreaking, blackmail, and control of labor recruiting, entertainment, and street peddling. The secret societies attracted the bosses of local tekiya and bakuto groups, and began a process that a hundred years later would continue to blur the distinction between gangsters and rightists in the minds of Japanese.

Initially, the more traditional yakuza groups had no real ideology and seemed to stand at some distance from the Genyosha and its successors. But the similarities among them were very strong. All shared a mystical world view that worshiped power, resented foreigners and foreign ideas (especially liberalism and socialism), revered a romanticized past, observed Shinto as the core of their belief systems, and deified the emperor as a living Shinto god. Equally important was structure: the groups traditionally organized along rigid oyabun-kobun lines and used similar ceremonies to tighten those ties. Many of the ultranationalist groups, then as now, were often nothing more than gangs of violent thugs whose "patriotic" purpose tended to be as much financial as political.

Ultimately, these social patterns produced virtually identical politics among most rightists and gangsters. Local gang bosses – whether they controlled dockworkers, street stalls, or village politics – realized that the entire basis of their authority was threatened by left-wing attacks on traditional society. With the emergence of a noticeable left and labor movement at the turn of the century, this understandable fear among the oyabun made them easy converts to the new ultranationalism.

Among the groups that the yakuza found appealing was a successor of Genyosha called Kokuryu-kai, or the Amur River Society, founded in 1901 by Toyama's right-hand man, Ryohei Uchida. The name of this secretive group hinted at its purpose: the expansion of Japanese power to the Amur River, the boundary between Manchuria and Russia. The group would become far better known by a different title, however: the characters for the word Kokuryu-kai could also be read as the Black Dragon Society, a name that caught the fancy of Western journalists.

The ultimate objective of the Black Dragons was no less than the domination and control of all Asia. To the more fanatic visionaries, the society was destined for the calling of Hakko-ichi-u – the Eight Corners of the World Under One Roof. The roof, of course, was that of the Emperor of Japan, descended from the Sun God in an unbroken line. The Black Dragon Society became the natural successor to Toyama's Dark Ocean, taking over its followers, its policies, and its goals. Under the patronage and guidance of Toyama, it would push Japan into a victorious war with Russia, commit political assassinations, and do for China what the Dark Ocean activists had done for Korea – help create the conditions for a Japanese invasion. For some thirty years the organization flourished, exhorting the Japanese to wage a holy war against capitalism, bolshevism, democracy, and the West. Through it all, Toyama and Uchida would reign as the Marx and Lenin of the Japanese ultranationalist movement.

The 1920s, the so-called period of Taisho democracy, represented the peak of Japan's prewar liberalism. Despite a political climate plagued by assassination, police repression, and an increasingly renegade military, the country continued to prosper. Universal suffrage was introduced, labor unions grew, and, spurred on by further economic growth, the middle class greatly expanded. But ominously in the background stood Toyama, who had continued to increase in stature. The patriot was courted by leading politicians, and even received money from the imperial family.

Toyama's next underworld achievement – the first national federation of gangsters – occurred in 1919, with the formation of the Dai Nippon Kokusui-kai (Great Japan National Essence Society). This organization of more than 60,000 gangsters, laborers, and ultranationalists was the brainchild of Toyama and Takejiro Tokunami, then minister of home affairs. The new federation fit neatly into the mold set nearly forty years earlier by Toyama's Dark Ocean Society. Its platform spoke vaguely of honoring the emperor, the "spirit of chivalry," and ancient Japanese values. Practically, however, the Kokusui-kai served as a massive strikebreaking force, and introduced an unprecedented level of violence into the ultranationalist movement. Headed by Tokunami himself, with Toyama as chief adviser, the organization functioned quite similarly to its Fascist contemporaries in Italy – Mussolini's Black Shirts. The Kokusui-kai operated with the strong support of the Home Ministry, the police, and certain high-ranking military officials. Its members were deployed not only against strikers but against any target deemed subversive by Toyama and friends. Among the group's many actions was an attack on the 28,000 men who had walked out in the great 1920 Yawata Iron Works strike. The Kokusui-kai gangs worked side by side with police, military gendarmes, firemen, veterans, and muscle men of other ultranationalist groups to break the strike.

Tokunami's Kokusui-kai evolved into the paramilitary arm of the Seiyu-kai, one of the two dominant political parties of the day. Seeing the example set, by the end of the decade Seiyu-kai's principal opposition, the Minseito party, had organized its own gangster force: the Yamato Minro-kai, filled with yakuza also drawn largely from construction gangs. So integrated into their respective political parties did these gangs become that more than a few bosses ran successfully for national office. Their presence in the Diet, Japan's parliament, was but another sign that all did not bode well for Japan's future.

By the 1930s, rightist groups had proliferated tremendously. The country was destabilized as moderate politicians fell victim to assassination or withdrew completely from public life. From 1930 until the end of the war, Japanese police would officially record a total of twenty-nine rightist "incidents." Among them were attempted coups d'état by military officers and ultranationalists, and repeated attacks on leading politicians and industrialists – including the assassinations of two prime ministers and two finance ministers.

Toyama's star continued to rise through the tumultuous 1930s as the practice of democracy nearly vanished in Japan. The aging leader, now possessing great prestige and wealth, arranged cabinets as well as assassinations. He was invited to dinners at the imperial palace and at ultranationalist societies. He addressed key patriotic gatherings, at which he would invariably be asked to lead the three cheers for the emperor. Symbolic of Toyama's new power was his introduction to the Japanese of their new prime minister, Prince Konoe, before a crowd of 18,000 in 1937. With many of Toyama's allies now in power, the country slid deeper into a decade of repression known to many Japanese as *Kuroi Tanima,* the Dark Valley. As the Nazis seized control in Germany and the Fascists rose to power in Italy, so did a ruthless militarism erupt in Japan. Every sector of society was organized for political regimentation and indoctrination. The era was at hand of the Greater East Asia Co-Prosperity Sphere, in which Japanese might would sweep over the Western colonies of the Orient. To the aging Toyama and his fellow ultranationalists, their dream was coming true.

The varied yakuza and strong-arm gangs continued to contribute men and muscle to the patriotic cause. Yakuza groups cooperated with the militarists by going to occupied Manchuria or China to participate in "land development" programs. For Japan's gangs, the exploitation of resource-rich Manchuria meant open season on the Chinese. It was, as one scholar put it, "the heyday of the yakuza, a return to the good old days of feudalism." Among the vocations attractive to the gangs was assisting the government's Opium Monopoly Bureau in its dual job of making money and weakening public resistance by fostering drug addiction. It was a page taken from British colonial handbooks of a century earlier, and the Japanese employed it skillfully. The military estimated its revenue from Japan's narcotization policy in China at $300 million a year.* When not spent on graft and corruption, the money went into the industrial development of the occupied lands.

Outside their political pursuits, the more traditional yakuza gangs were busy expanding their financial base at home. Military expansion brought more money into Japan, and the yakuza were well situated to grab a large share of the booty. Like Tokunami's labor bosses and their construction gangs, the yakuza organized the laborers along Japan's waterfronts. In the port city of Kobe, for instance, yakuza gangs gathered up groups of otherwise unemployable men and sold their labor cheaply to longshore firms in need of docile, unskilled workers. So lucrative was this racket that various oyabun fought over contracts and territories. The Kobe group that emerged victorious was the Yamaguchi-gumi, under the able leadership of Kazuo Taoka. Over the next quarter century, he would transform his waterfront gang into the largest yakuza syndicate in Japan, reaching a peak of more than 13,000 members in 36 of Japan's 47 prefectures. (A prefecture is roughly equivalent to a U.S. state.) The infamous Yamaguchi syndicate would become a household word in Japan, and Taoka the undisputed godfather of Japanese crime.

---

*All yen-to-dollar conversions are given in rates current at the time.

While Taoka organized the docks and laid ground for the future of the yakuza, a remarkably similar process was then occurring in the United States. The Lucky Luciano mob had taken over much of the Manhattan and Brooklyn waterfronts, acting through "Tough" Tony Anastasia and Joe "Socks" Lanza, and work on the docks functioned in an almost oyabun-kobun fashion. So tightly did the mob control the waterfront that during the war, the Office of Naval Intelligence felt it prudent to make a deal with Luciano, then in a New York prison, to make sure the docks remained free of saboteurs.

In other respects, though, the American mob had outstripped its Japanese counterparts. Despite the widespread integration of gangsters into the ultranationalist movement, city or neighborhood gangs were still the rule in Japan. American gangs, meanwhile, flush with the huge cash reserves generated by liquor sales during Prohibition, were growing into a sophisticated national syndicate. Equally important, U.S. gangsters were learning how to invest their newfound capital and manage it according to modern corporate practice. These historic changes came about when Luciano joined forces with the gangsters under Meyer Lansky and Benjamin "Bugsy" Siegel and, for the first time, organized crime moved beyond strictly ethnic groupings. These New York gangsters combined with Cleveland's Mayfield Road Gang, Detroit's Purple Gang, the Chicago mob, and others to apportion large sections of the country for specific rackets, such as gambling, drugs, and labor racketeering. By the 1930s, the mob was so strong a force that it had influence in presidential elections.

The bombing of Pearl Harbor, however, changed life radically for both the U.S. and Japanese Mafias. With the advent of war with the West, the Japanese government's love affair with the far right and the yakuza came to an abrupt end. The wartime government, having moved as far to the right as big business and the army wished, no longer needed the rightists or gangsters as an independent force. Upper-echelon rightists either worked for the government or were imprisoned. Likewise, yakuza either put on a uniform or saw the war from the inside of a cell. Among those spending time in prison was the waterfront boss Kazuo Taoka, who passed his time reading books about Toyama and the Dark Ocean Society.

Mitsuru Toyama finally died in 1944 at the age of 89, but not before seeing his beloved Japan conquer much of Asia and the Pacific. His influence would live on through innumerable gangster-rightist organizations, and two generations later his portrait adorns the walls of nearly all rightist offices and of many yakuza ones as well. Unfortunately, this grand old man of the Japanese right did not see the final result of his long years of militancy, as the war thrust Japan to both the height and depth of its political power, all within four years. By August 1945, the Americans had dropped the atom bomb and the Soviets invaded Manchuria, and within a few days the Japanese had finally had enough.

Part II
The Kodama Years

Chapter 2
Occupied Japan

The ranking military officers of the U.S. occupation often gave press conferences, but this one was a bit out of the ordinary. It was not held in the General Headquarters building, and it was unusually combative in tone. The date was September 19, 1947, and the place was Tokyo.

The principal speaker told the press that he had just finished addressing a meeting of Japanese public procurators – the equivalent of district attorneys – and he was now taking his case to the people. The speaker was Colonel Charles L. Kades, a former New York attorney, the assistant chief of Government Section and one of the most influential men in the occupation hierarchy. Colonel Kades told the journalists that he had warned the procurators of a web of criminal gangs and influential gangsters throughout Japan that formed "a massive underground network extending from the smallest rural village to the highest echelons of the national government."

The statement may have been a revelation to the American journalists present, but it was hardly a surprise to the Japanese. This was a part of their culture that most citizens, and all journalists, knew at least by reputation.

Kades, a genial yet forceful New Dealer who had been the principal architect of the new Japanese constitution, concluded to the press, "This clannish and clandestine combination of bosses, hoodlums, and racketeers is the greatest threat to American democratic aims in Japan." At the time, Kades was only dimly aware that this same combination had been a threat to democratic aims of the Japanese people for the past fifty years.

The American press found the story titillating. The Hearst papers began grinding out breathless crime stories that sounded very close to wartime propaganda. There was an "invisible government" in Japan. The gangs were a threat to the occupation forces. They would bring back militarism and ultranationalism. In other words, more yellow peril. Exaggerated and alarmist as these articles were, they were also naively prescient. The mobs would indeed help steer Japan backward and to the right, but not by attacking the occupation directly. On the contrary, like other Japanese, gangsters knew who was in charge and wanted to form alliances with the people in power. In fact, Kades himself was approached by a gang leader and asked if he needed anyone beaten up.

Occupation officials decided to look into the threat. Investigations, some of which had been begun prior to Kades's announcement, yielded piles of evidence attesting to the power of the gangs. Occupation offices poured forth a stream of press releases and fact packets. In November 1947, the *Christian Science Monitor* devoted a full page to the issue in which reporter Gordon Walker considered the prospects for a concerted campaign against organized crime in Japan. "If these and other measures are [not] effective in breaking down the labyrinth of undercover controls and influences now operating behind the scenes," wrote Walker, ". . . many occupation authorities frankly admit the long-term prospects for a truly free Japan are endangered."

The reaction of the Japanese officials was a loud, dull thud. The procurators made a few cases – if the occupation police led them by the hand. But the political hierarchy tied the hands of the procurators and ignored the issue publicly. Prime Minister Katayama simply denied the existence of underground organizations, much as J. Edgar Hoover was then denying that any Mafia functioned in the United States. By the beginning of 1948, the gangs began to disappear from the newspapers. The campaign against the underworld diminished in intensity, and soon it was dead.

Paradoxically, while the occupation's Government Section was fulminating about the yakuza, and the press was drawing some trenchant conclusions about the peril posed by the gangs, other forces in the occupation were aiding the yakuza. For one thing, American policies in Japan – particularly in regard to food rationing – helped perpetuate the black market, which brought many gangs wealth and power. Also, the complete disarming of the civil police allowed the gangs to run free. But most disturbing is the fact that some occupation officials actively aided the gangs, encouraged them, and even paid their leaders.

Japan in Ruins
Officially, the U.S. occupation of Japan began on September 2, 1945, with the signing of the surrender aboard the U.S.S. *Missouri* in Tokyo Bay. On September 8, General Douglas MacArthur flew from Okinawa

and arrived at Atsugi Air Base, which had been rebuilt for his coming in four days. He drove solemnly through the charred streets of Tokyo to the American Embassy. There, he raised the American flag and directed the Eighth Army to occupy and administer the defeated nation.

The widespread devastation wreaked on Japan was staggering. Virtually every major city except historic Kyoto had been severely damaged by high explosives, firebombs, or nuclear weapons. The military of Japan was in disarray, its soldiers disgraced and hungry. Over four million remained in East Asia, outside of Japan. The civilian population was suffering, uncertain, stunned. Never before had an enemy conquered the home islands. In the city of Tokyo, one million out of 1,650,000 buildings had been demolished, mostly by the 1945 fire raids. Nationwide, one-quarter of the wealth, one-third of the manufacturing machinery, four-fifths of the shipping, one-fifth of the vehicles were destroyed.

But there was a great deal left. American industrialist Edwin Pauley, in surveying the damage for the occupation, found that, "In spite of extensive destruction, especially in the closing phases of the war, Japan retains more industrial capacity than she needs or has ever used for her civilian economy." This was a fact not lost on either the Americans or the neighboring Soviets. While the Western European allies scrambled to regain their lost Asian colonies, America had plans for Japan itself.

It was clear from the beginning that the running of Japan was going to be an American show. In theory, the supreme power over the defeated Axis combatant lay in the Allied Council for Japan, a group consisting of the foreign ministers of the U.S., the U.S.S.R., China, and three Commonwealth countries (Britain, Australia, and New Zealand). It was supplemented by a thirteen-member Far Eastern Commission. Neither organization accomplished much more than the maintenance of offices in Tokyo. The real seat of government was the office of the Supreme Commander for the Allied Powers (SCAP), General Douglas MacArthur, who assumed the post on August 15, 1945.

MacArthur's mission was simple in concept: remake Japan. Justin Williams, writing in *Japan's Political Revolution under MacArthur*, neatly summarized the work awaiting SCAP:

[The] . . . quick demobilization of Japan's military forces, total destruction of her war equipment, complete closure of her war factories, arraignment of Gen. Tojo Hideki and other wartime leaders, arrest and trial of hundreds of war criminals, institution of a far-reaching purge in all walks of Japanese life, abolition of secret societies and the though-control police, removal of all re-

strictions on civil liberties, release of Japanese political prisoners, the outlawing of a state-supported Shinto religion, the large-scale shake-up of the Japanese school system, free discussion of the Emperor system, cleanup of the Japanese press, breakup of the large industrial and banking combinations, sale of large landholdings to Japanese peasants, legalization of labor unions and encouragement of collective bargaining, enfranchisement of women, liberalization of the election law, adoption of a democratic constitution and a general election of members to the lower house of the Diet (Parliament).

If Japan were to be reoriented, the tools used by MacArthur were orders, called SCAPINS, which dropped from his office at the Dai Ichi Building as if bearing revealed truths. To interpret these truths to the Japanese, some 6000 civilians, including a host of Japanese-American translators, supplemented the U.S. military, which numbered 200,000 in early 1946.

SCAP was an American bureaucracy, and had the usual political divisions and cliques that the Japanese learned to exploit for their own ends. Above it all, MacArthur reigned serenely, a latter-day American shogun. Just below him, General Courtney Whitney headed Government Section. A successful Manila lawyer, Whitney felt that implementing the Post-Surrender Directive, the comprehensive plan for the occupation, meant inhibiting Japan's warmaking desires and capabilities. This, in turn, meant strengthening the Japanese left – unions, liberals, socialists, and Communists. Whitney was opposed by General Charles A. Willoughby, head of intelligence, or G-2. Willoughby feared the Japanese left, Chinese and Soviet Communists, and American liberals. He used G-2 to give aid, comfort, money, and position to precisely those Japanese whom Whitney and Kades sought to remove from public life – the ultranationalist right.

Whitney and Willoughby were, in a sense, merely actors in a larger drama. Through much of the war, the New Dealers in the Roosevelt administration were lobbying for elimination of the emperor and a general suppression of Japanese nationalism when the war ended. On the other side were American conservative business interests, who feared a leftist Japan and lobbied to keep the socioeconomic structure more or less intact.

SCAP was generally effective in running the defeated and destitute Japan. It was, by and large, a humane and generous way to treat a vanquished enemy. It is much more doubtful whether the occupation achieved its other aim – cleaning up Japanese politics. Japanese institutions, including corrupt ones, proved far more hardy than anyone had expected. Some undesirable elements, such as the yakuza, seemed not only to survive, but to flourish, even in the dismal wreckage of the bombed-out cities.

The first year of the occupation was a very grim one for most Japanese. Ten yen was a typical day's salary for a working Japanese, enough to buy a dozen sardines or one small orange. The Americans saw no need to provide more than a bare minimum of food while shortages plagued their wartime allies. With the demobilization of Japan's huge army, and industry at a standstill, there were plenty of people eager to deal in black market rice and other goods. There was money to be made this way. It gave rise to a host of nouveaux riches, called the New Yen class.

Another new class arose in the occupation years. This comprised the newly liberated Asian minorities living in Japan, the so-called *sangokujin*. Literally "people of three countries," the sangokujin were Chinese, Taiwanese, and Koreans who had been brought into Japan to replace the many workers who had been drafted into the army. Working in what were often conditions of virtual slavery, the sangokujin served as forced labor in factories and various unskilled jobs. An estimated 2.6 million Koreans and 50,000 Chinese entered wartime Japan, and eventually some 2 million were repatriated. The others stayed behind to try their luck under the American administration.

After the surrender, the rage of the minorities – a rage built up from years of prejudice and exploitation – exploded into vicious attacks on Japanese citizens. Those sangokujin who remained in Japan, still excluded as they were from the economic mainstream, built up a flourishing business controlling many of the nation's major black markets. Initially, they had a leg up on the native Japanese black marketeers. The occupiers distrusted the Japanese and favored other nationals; the sangokujin became aides and informers to U.S. officials. At the same time, SCAP literally disarmed the civil police, as swords were replaced with nightsticks. In addition, SCAP purged the upper echelons of the police force. Some had been members of the feared *Tokko,* or "Thought Police," while others had connections to the ultranationalist right. Lacking effective leadership, the Japanese police became too confused or timorous to act against the sangokujin.

Into this breach strode the yakuza. It is difficult to say whether the yakuza were at the time more outraged by the sangokujin attacks on Japanese, or by the usurpation of lucrative black market space by the "foreigners." In either case, yakuza groups openly clashed with the sangokujin, often under the eyes of the beleaguered police.

In Kobe, a group of some 300 sangokujin invaded a police station and held hostages as a show of force. According to Yamaguchi-gumi boss Kazuo Taoka, the mayor of Kobe approached the yakuza leader for help. Taoka and his allies ambushed the sangokujin at the police station, stampeding them with swords, guns, and grenades. The yakuza's reward was twofold: the hated sangokujin were undercut, and the police owed the yakuza a long-term debt of giri.

In Tokyo, the sangokujin were strong enough to parade in front of the emperor's palace. They had also managed to take over the rackets along the Ginza, where they clashed with furious yakuza gangs. Another pitched battle took place in the summer of 1946 in a section of Tokyo known as Shimbashi. In the bombed-out area near the train station, a black market had been established, with a group of Taiwanese taking control of the street stalls.

Goro Fujita tells the tale of how tekiya gangsters fought back with a machine gun salvaged from a crippled fighter plane. The peddlers crept to the top of a nearby elementary school, mounted the gun, and began firing volleys at the sangokujin, forcing them to scatter, leaving behind their new businesses in the Shimbashi market. Fujita and other champions of the yakuza would consider the fight over Shimbashi, like the Kobe police station fracas, a major battle of a great patriotic stand. Among many older Japanese today, the battles are fondly remembered, with the yakuza cast as embattled heroes saving a prostrate Japan from evil foreigners. It was, once again, the yakuza as champion of the common people. These stories would be retold until, like a tattered newsclip, they were blurred and indistinct.

Although American military police were aware of the "Korean problem" and the armed clashes, they did not really understand the nature of the conflicts. Public Service Department Police Investigator Harry Shupak changed all that when he arrived in Shimbashi in late July 1946.

Shupak found that Giichi Matsuda, boss of the gang battling the sangokujin, had been shot by one of his own men, apparently in an abortive coup attempt. Matsuda's wife, Yoshiko, then took over the day-to-day operation of the Kanto Matsuzakaya Matsuda-gumi, as the gang was formally known. On August 26, she was called before the Metropolitan Police Board for questioning and provided Shupak and his PSD associates with their first explanation of the way things work in Tokyo. She freely and proudly described the workings of what the Americans began to call the Oyabun-Kobun System.

According to Mrs. Matsuda, Giichi had organized the gang in 1945 when it became evident that the outdoor market business was, in her words, "very booming." The gang established itself after driving out the other thugs. As stalls rapidly increased in number, Matsuda installed his kobun in the marketplace and, in cooperation with the ward office and the police, formed all the stalls into the open-air stall market, or black market.

Matsuda, in the time-honored tekiya fashion, ordered his lieutenants to charge the stall operators for their license, and to bill them monthly for lease, cleaning, and electricity. The Matsuda-gumi also kept the competition away – until the sangokujin decided to make a stand. Giichi Matsuda had gotten his feet wet in the coming yakuza wave, and was already riding the crest when he was assassinated. The tekiya business was very booming, indeed.

Black Market Underworld

Although the occupation police could not see it easily, a new type of oyabun-kobun group was forming, one that would be a model for most of the yakuza groups soon to follow. This was the gurentai, a far more ruthless form of yakuza than the traditional gamblers and peddlers. The occupation had, by sweeping away the top layer of control in government and business, left a power vacuum. The results were described in Gordon Walker's 1947 *Christian Science Monitor* story: ". . . into this vacuum has sprung a degenerate 'boss' system reminiscent of the Capone gangster days. Largest and strongest of these organized gangs are the so-called Gurentai, or armed hooligan mobs, which have sprung up like mushrooms all over Japan. Drawing upon demobilized young men without jobs, repatriates without incomes, and capitalizing upon the lowered moral standards resulting from military defeat, the gangs operate through the use of threat, extortion, and violence."

One of the most visible gurentai had been the subject of a Counter Intelligence Corps (CIC) investigation as early as February 1946: Akira Ando. Although Ando was convicted by a military court of possessing black market items, he continued to receive money, work, and friendship from many high-ranking occupation officials. Apparently, many Americans needed him, as the Japanese government had once needed him. In 1941, for instance, the Tokyo Metropolitan Police named him "Guardian of Korean Laborers and Protector of Korean Juveniles." This seemingly benevolent title was an acknowledgment that Ando controlled Korean labor – a valuable commodity in labor-short wartime Japan. With this work force, Ando's outfit, the Dai-An Construction Company, built infrastructure and moved factories for the government after the air raids began.

When Japan surrendered, Ando was commissioned by the Americans for construction work. In 1945 he spruced up Atsugi Air Base in preparation for MacArthur's landing. That same year, Ando received additional contracts and, while millions of Japanese barely survived on less than a thousand calories a day, he made a tidy multimillion-dollar profit.

Ando was something of a prototype of the modern yakuza leader. Born in 1901, he was forty-four years old at the war's end. He headed the Ando-gumi, a cross between a gurentai gang and a construction company, and was on close terms with the black market oyabun in the major cities. Equally important, he was on more than speaking terms with Prince Takamatsu, the emperor's brother, as well as with wartime politicians of national stature.

Favors did not, of course, run just to Ando; he had to reciprocate. Japanese politicians who wanted to ensure the position of the emperor system used Ando to help in lobbying the American brass. Ando ran a string of eighteen clubs – expensive whorehouses, actually. The most famous was the Dai-An, which was closed by SCAP and reopened under another name, the Wakatombo. At his Ginza clubs, Ando's frequent guests included a handful of the highest-ranking officials of the Eighth Army. It is doubtful that Ando alone swung MacArthur to a pro-emperor position, but his work didn't hurt. Ando's motivation, one that would be heard ad nauseam, was simple. "I shall fight communism as long as I live," he explained. "I stand for democracy and the preservation of the imperial system."

Although Ando's blend of hustle and graft played very well as an occupation tactic, Ando himself disappeared into obscurity in the mid-1950s. He may have been the most successful gang boss of the occupation, but he certainly wasn't the most famous. That honor probably went to Kinosuke Ozu, the tekiya boss of Tokyo. Ozu was actually oyabun of just one section of Tokyo, Shinjuku, but like Al Capone, who officially ran only the West Side of Chicago, Ozu's power and fame went much further. In fact, in October 1947, *Saturday Evening Post* reporter Darrell Berrigan profiled Ozu in a story entitled "Tokyo's Own Al Capone."

Ozu was a garden-variety thug until the end of the war. He then capitalized on the death of Giichi Matsuda, taking over most of the Shinjuku section in which the Shimbashi market stood. Ozu amassed considerable money and power, but like so many gangsters, he wanted respectability as well. His base remained in the tekiya groups, where he controlled hundreds – even thousands – of street peddlers; he also established control over the various bakuto and gurentai gangs operating in Shinjuku. With this base, he forced his way onto the Tokyo Chamber of Commerce, which he proceeded to terrorize for his own uses.

Ozu cowed the Chamber of Commerce, but he failed to do the same to the people of Shinjuku. He ran for the Diet seat from that district in 1947, and lost. His opponent was Sanzo Nozaka, the popular Communist leader. Ozu promised during the election to donate most of his millions to the poor, but somehow his brand of socialism was less appealing than Nozaka's. Ozu, however, did get 12,000 votes.

Most of the time, the links between the mob and politicians were too strong and too obvious for anyone to ignore entirely. Yet as late as 1950, some occupation personnel were still marveling over these links. That year, the Office of the Political Advisor (POLAD), the State Department's provisional office under SCAP, cabled Washington concerning gang activities in the Tokyo area. The telegram stated that a well-organized band of gangsters, headed by Masajiro Tsuruoka and Kakuji Inagawa and supported by unidentified high-level rightist politicians, had been operating on a large scale throughout the Tokyo-Yokohama-Shizuoka area since the end of the war. Exactly why Tsuruoka and Inagawa could claim this patronage is clear later in the cable. Apparently, the gang had collected some 50,000 yen for building construction, repair of streets and roads, and other work. With rebuilding of cities moving ahead rapidly, gangs with this sort of muscle could make a lot of yen. And this was just one gang.

This was not a case of simple extortion. Construction companies themselves were traditionally so similar to gangs as to be often indistinguishable. Both groups employed the same word, *gumi* (meaning gang or association), to describe their organizations. The construction companies, furthermore, often exerted political influence in their own right. In the northern island of Hokkaido, for instance, a gumi boss and public works builder, Chiizake Usaburo, gave money to the Liberal Party, ordered his newspaper to support the Communists, and ran himself as an independent, all in one Diet election. Usaburo's influence would be felt no matter who won, and he would most likely continue to draw lucrative public works contracts.

There were, of course, times when politicians didn't want to get into bed with the gangs, and many times when businesses didn't want to make payoffs. Often, such refusals brought fires in the night, or brutal attacks. So entrenched and widespread were these practices that when SCAP ordered that "All the people of Japan must be urged to stop paying tribute to bosses and gangsters," it was a futile demand. SCAP, furthermore, was hardly taking steps to remedy the situation. Indeed, between 1945 and

1950, the occupation failed miserably to protect the Japanese people from the gangs. Even the Eighth Army did not stop the sangokujin, and in all, little was ultimately done about the power of the gurentai. Furthermore, American GIs fed the black markets with an endless supply of goods. Nevertheless, for a brief period, SCAP did make an effort to combat the gangs.

In September 1947, SCAP's Controls Coordinating Committee established the Oyabun-Kobun Subcommittee, composed of representatives from fourteen major and minor SCAP staff sections. Although established primarily to look into criminal activity, the subcommittee found itself exploring the structure on Japanese society. Oyabun-kobun was, as pointed out, a structure that included many legitimate relationships, such as owner-manager, editor-reporter, and others. SCAP was surprised. The subcommittee issued a full report on the oyabun-kobun within two weeks, perhaps a peacetime bureaucratic record. Some of the findings were startling.

According to the report, of the 14-million-person labor force in Japan, 3 million were part of the oyabun-kobun system. Two-thirds of these were construction gangs, and the rest mainly casual labor. However, it was discovered that a 20,000-man work force was kept confined in the Hokkaido coal mines under terms that hovered between indentured servitude and slavery. A Tokyo newspaper concluded that workers were held in virtual slavery and would be freed when their contracts ran out. The subcommittee also found that the oyabun were engaged in anti-union activity, controlling the black market rice and using it as an economic weapon to force new kobun to join and remain outside of any labor union.

A related report by the Public Safety Division repeated the analysis of the three major oyabun-kobun groups – bakuto, tekiya, and gurentai. They observed that "political pressure often prevented effective action on the part of the police." In summation, the analysis concluded that the oyabun-kobun system "extends into politics, controls the price of everyday commodities, controls the flow of goods through regular channels, and performs local government functions in the issuance of licenses and the collection of taxes. In addition to these functions the Gurentai terrorize a large portion of the population of the large cities who are engaged in the restaurant business and other public amusement enterprises."

The subcommittee found that the gurentai groups had grown more than anyone had anticipated. The report of the Public Safety Division calculated that the centers of gurentai strength were Tokyo, with 7400 kobun in the employ of 181 oyabun, and Kobe, with 6400 kobun working beneath 82 oyabun. Living was good for the gurentai, said the report, with shakedowns of small and medium-sized businesses bringing in a large and constant income. "The average take seems to be about 5000 to 10,000 yen for each establishment," noted the PSD report, enough to make rich men out of those living on the criminal fringe.

The tekiya did not slip by uncounted. Said the PSD, the tekiya "grew to amazing proportions, controlling 88 percent of the 45,000 stalls in Tokyo and having partial interest in the remaining 12 percent." Known as the Street-Stall Tradesmen's Cooperative Union (Roten Dogyo Kumiai), it comprised at the time 200 bosses, 4000 followers, and 22,557 lesser followers under the leadership of Kinosuke Ozu, "a ruffian of the lowest type."

The reports were reasonably accurate and presented a picture of crime out of control. In spite of Kades's efforts to publicize the problem, though, there seemed to be a roadblock along the way. When the reports were taken to the Dai Ichi building for MacArthur's perusal, they never got past his aides. Frequent weekly and monthly reports also died in the antechambers.

It soon became clear that the United States high command had no real desire to root out organized crime, despite the efforts of men like Kades and a number of Government Section officials. It wasn't just the Japanese police who were constrained; the problem simply wasn't a priority for American MPs. Although the alarm sounded that the yakuza were working hand-in-glove with remnants of ultrarightist groups – groups that were illegal under the occupation – MacArthur apparently didn't want to be bothered. Inertia and a desire to look good were two reasons to avoid the yakuza problem, but there were far more disturbing reasons.

Basically, elements in the occupation were finding it expedient to go easy on the right side of the Japanese political spectrum. Among the components of the right were the yakuza gangs, many of which were tied to conservative politicians ranging from right-centrists to closet ultranationalists. The gangs were almost always thoroughgoing anticommunists, and this, for some SCAP officials, was good enough. The fact that they made life miserable for a sizable section of the Japanese public was merely an unfortunate side effect.

But why? The extreme right had just plunged the Pacific Basin into its most destructive war ever, and the Americans were determined to make Japan pay in one way or another for that war. How policy changed, and how the right and its yakuza allies found the climate improving over the course of the occupation, is a story that begins not in Tokyo but in Washington.

SCAP Changes Course

Long before the occupation began, a critical diplomatic struggle broke out in State Department circles over the administration of Japan and the rest of East Asia after the war was won. Basically, there were two distinct factions: the so-called China Crowd, left of center and disciples of *Amerasia* magazine; and the Japan Crowd, centering around associates of the former American ambassador to Japan, Joseph Clark Grew.

Simply put, the China Crowd wanted China, and a China under Mao at that, as the centerpiece of American foreign policy in East Asia. Mao's opponent, Chiang Kai-shek, had through the years generated great antipathy and distrust among American liberals because of his corruption and indifferent war effort against the Japanese. With Mao's China as a U.S. ally, reasoned these strategists, Japan's future was that of a neutral country. Japan would be reduced to a nonmilitary power, shorn of its emperor, and purged of its bellicose right wing. The nation, if it behaved itself, would be allowed to become the Switzerland of East Asia.

The Japan Crowd, on the other hand, wanted Japan's military power to be reduced and realigned, not eliminated. They wanted the economic structure to be left largely as it was before the war. Japan would be the keystone of America's Asian interests, and Japan would provide a line of defense against the Soviet Union, clearly a rival for the riches of northeast Asia. Japan could also partially counter the threat posed by a Communist China, if it came to that.

The appointment of MacArthur as administrator of Japan initially delighted the Japan Crowd. MacArthur – Republican, anticommunist, scourge of the Bonus Marchers – was an ideal conservative. But they were quickly disappointed for two reasons. One, MacArthur had suffered military defeats and personal humiliations at the hands of a right-wing Japan. Two, MacArthur and his staff simply disliked the Japan Crowd's old-boy network and generally disregarded their advice.

As a result, MacArthur approved, although he did not initiate, reforms for Japan that might in another context be easily considered anticapitalist. Some of his noneconomic measures were not overly controversial, at least to Americans, although they were often misunderstood by the Japanese: human rights, female emancipation, freedom of the press, elimination of secret police. But the simultaneous enactment of labor rights, land reforms, and the attempted breakup of Japan's huge financial combines – the *zaibatsu* – sent American conservatives into a frothing rage.

In the first months of MacArthur's tenure, pressure was kept on the right. Some zaibatsu were forced to divest. The Kempei Tai, the internal military police, were disbanded, as were the Thought Police. Meanwhile the Japanese left was actively encouraged. All political prisoners – including the Communists – were released, and exiles returned home. Labor was encouraged by the New Dealers in SCAP to flex its muscle. Within a year, Japanese organized labor grew from nothing to 5 million members, ten times its prewar high.

Then there were the purges. SCAP's Basic Initial Post-Surrender Directive, the 1945 mandate for carrying out the occupation, ordered the incarceration of high-ranking wartime political and military leaders. In addition, read the order, "Persons who have been active exponents of militarism and militant nationalism will be removed and excluded from public office and from any other position of public or substantial private responsibility." Eventually, over 200,000 persons were purged.

The purges had not a vestige of democratic process to them, convicting men on unsupported word and denying the accused a fair trial. But the punishment, for the most part, was neither harsh nor lengthy. By 1947, SCAP began to indicate that enough social reorganization was enough. A return to normalcy, minus the military expansionism, was called for: it was time for Japan to take its rightful place as the linchpin of U.S. strategy in the Far East.

The Cold War was beginning. Chiang Kai-shek was losing ground and the Russians were seizing territory in Eastern Europe. Suddenly, anything that served to strengthen the American position vis-à-vis world communism was deemed good and proper. By 1948, the New Dealers in Government Section, men such as Kades and T. A. Bisson, had resigned or been sent home. The China Crowd was discredited, shortly to be blamed for the "loss" of China.

Japanese of all political persuasions were somewhat bewildered by this apparently arbitrary change. Later, the term *gyakkosu*, or reverse course, was coined to explain America's political about-face. Some historians have doubted that such a reversal took place, citing that the United States never intended to allow a social revolution in the first place. But internationally, the change was noted; the Soviets believed that Japan was about to be used as a springboard for an attack on the USSR, according to a 1947 CIA report. And, from the perspective of Japanese liberals and leftists, a change most certainly happened, no matter what SCAP stated. SCAP, it appeared, had suddenly acquired a fear of the left.

The fear wasn't SCAP's alone. The conservative government of Japan, headed by Shigeru Yoshida, an aristocratic anticommunist, also wanted the left dealt with, and quickly. In April 1949, SCAP responded with the so-called Red Purge. Leftist unions and groups were forced to register under the Organizational Control Ordinance.

The real object of the Red Purge, from SCAP's point of view, was primarily the Japanese Communist Party (JCP), which was seen by the Americans as not merely a civil disrupter, but an instrument of the Soviets and others. The JCP's membership had grown from 8000 in 1946 to 100,000 in 1949, and the party controlled to varying degrees an estimated half of organized labor. Despite its growth, though, politically the JCP never won more than 10 percent of the electoral vote in any Diet election. Yet so alarmed were SCAP officials, there was consideration of banning the party altogether. Although this never occurred, measures were enforced against it, and, much as in the United States, the legal position of its members grew increasingly precarious.

Even though the JCP was the prime target, a wholesale purge took place against anyone found annoying or dangerous by the increasingly dominant conservatives. Labor unions were undermined with growing regularity, their leaders harassed and assaulted, and membership declined; 20,000 civil servants and schoolteachers were dismissed; newspaper and radio offices were the subject of police raids; universities were urged to rid themselves of leftist professors. There were other changes as well. The breakup of the huge financial combines like Mitsui and Mitsubishi was discontinued; the emperor, it was decided, would not be tried as a war criminal; SCAP officials began to make plans for "housebreaking the unions"; and the original policy for complete demilitarization of Japan was abandoned as unrealistic.

Why was SCAP so willing to acquiesce to the Japanese rightists, the very group responsible for the war that had cost the United States so dearly? Foremost, it was a strategic move: use the rightists to help secure Japan while fighting communism on the Asian mainland. It was imperative that Japan's demobilized army of nearly 6 million – the largest in Asia – not pose the slightest risk to American aims. But partly, it was the reluctance of the U.S. military to socially reform Japan. SCAP became far more interested in reducing the economic burden on the United States, and saw stability rather than reform of the nation as the key. Equally important, wealthy American businessmen, many of whom filled SCAP's higher ranks, were anxious to stake out shares in Japan's future. The country's defeat provided a historic opportunity to influence or control one of the world's great industrial systems.

Given these American motives, and the self-preserving instincts of the Japanese conservatives, it is not surprising that no tactic in support of these motives was rejected as too brutal or unfair. The problem was how to form a phalanx of loyal troops who could counter the threat, both real and perceived, from the left. This force, which would continue to function in some form up to the present, was a loose, familiar assemblage of rightists and yakuza.

Gangsters and Dirty Tricks

A strikingly similar set of events was then unfolding half a world away in Western Europe. The CIA was paying Corsican gangsters in France, particularly in the city of Marseilles, to disrupt Communist strikes in 1947 and 1950, and to attempt to break the back of the French Communist Party. As was the case in Japan, much of France then lay in ruins. Unemployment was high, wages low, and amid shortages of every kind, the black markets had become a way of life.

Alarmed by electoral gains of the French Communists and by Soviet expansion into Eastern Europe, U.S. officials quickly began implementing their own plans for the continent, and began a secret war against the left. Only months before the 1947 strike in France, the Truman administration had established the CIA and introduced the multibillion-dollar European Recovery Plan, popularly known as the Marshall Plan.

The small, sophisticated Corsican gangs were, like the yakuza, accustomed to doing battle with leftists and labor unions. The French Fascists had used them to battle Communist demonstrators in the 1930s, and during the war, the Gestapo had found them useful for spying on the Communist underground. But it was the CIA's alliance with the Corsican mob that proved the most significant, according to journalist Alfred McCoy in his seminal book, *The Politics of Heroin in Southeast Asia*. As the CIA funneled cash and arms to the French underworld, wrote McCoy, the Corsicans were put "in a powerful enough position to establish Marseilles as the postwar heroin capital of the Western world and to cement a long-term partnership with Mafia drug distributors." Within a year of the CIA's 1950 operation, the Corsican mob opened Marseilles' first heroin labs and began shipments that over the next twenty years would dump thousands of pounds of heroin onto American streets – a pipeline of drugs that would later be called the French Connection.

While that story has been told before, few understand that Americans were hiring mobsters in Japan as well, in a secret war against the left that began as early as 1946. At its helm stood Major General Charles Willoughby, MacArthur's intelligence chief – both during the Pacific campaigns and under SCAP, where he headed G-2 (intelligence). Willoughby and his trusted aides in G-2 served both to directly repress the left, as did G-2's Counter Intelligence Corps, and indirectly, by aiding and financing rightist thugs or yakuza to do the job. To help run his covert operations, the general followed another pattern similar to that which U.S. officials were then secretly employing in Europe: recruiting for intelligence use key members of the enemy who probably should have been tried as war criminals. Willoughby succeeded in freeing from the purge in Japan certain well-placed officers from the Imperial Army and Navy. Many of these held extreme right-wing views, and their attitudes toward communism would be put to good use. As U.S. agents made life easier for Nazis like Klaus Barbie ("The Butcher of Lyon") and General Rienhard Gehlen (the Wehrmacht's intelligence chief in Russia), so did Willoughby recruit such men as Lt. General Seizo Arisue, former chief of military intelligence for the General Staff. Arisue and other officers were incorporated into G-2's "Historical Section" and into a number of secret agencies. In addition to supplying U.S. officials with intelligence gleaned from years of work on Korea, China, and the Soviet Union, Willoughby's new recruits made a second career spying on and disrupting the left in Japan for G-2.

Major General Charles Andre Willoughby seems to have been naturally inclined toward the role of guardian of the extreme right. Born Adolf Weidenbach in Germany, Willoughby was called by one fellow officer "our own Junker general." His mentor, General MacArthur, referred to him as "my loveable Fascist."

Willoughby had functioned under MacArthur in Manila, and there became close to the Falangist Spaniards who supported Franco. After the war, Willoughby served as advisor and intermediary for Franco in Spain, and devoted himself to extreme right-wing causes in the United States, such as Billy James Hargis's Christian Crusade.

Willoughby was forever discovering Communist spy plots, some of which, particularly those revolving around the Soviet liaison offices, did exist. But his paranoia and sense of drama tended to blur his perceptions. According to one former colleague, Kenneth Colton of Government Section, Willoughby circulated memos on blue paper – called Willoughby Chits by staffers – that were sometimes "far-fetched." One SCAP veteran asserted that Willoughby was "horribly involved with the right wing."

The full scope of spying and disruption under Willoughby's command is difficult to assess, let along prove, and the answer may have died with Willoughby in October of 1972. American researchers have been stymied in their attempts to locate and review Willoughby's own G-2 files, which seem to have disappeared.

Perhaps Willoughby was somewhat embarrassed by G-2's frequent ineptitude. One former military intelligence officer who worked under the general recalled, "We were supporting every right-wing jerk who came along. It was so chaotic in the postwar years that American agents were stumbling over each other. Five different guys were running one Japanese, and the Japanese were collecting money from each of them. Most of them [the Japanese rightists] had their own agendas anyway. It was hard to say who was running who."

Nonetheless, there emerged a series of highly suspicious incidents that discredited the left, particularly the JCP, which critics in Japan have long blamed on "dirty tricks." The most famous of these incidents is the Matsukawa case. In August 1949, saboteurs derailed a Japan National Railways train in the town of Matsukawa, killing three people and injuring many more. The case came to be known as the greatest cause célèbre in the history of lawsuits in Japan. In a highly politicized atmosphere, twenty workers – all but one either Communists or trade union leaders – were charged and convicted of the crime. Their case assumed the proportions of the Rosenberg, Oppenheimer, and Hiss cases in the United States, with support committees, demonstrations, and enormous press coverage. The convictions were overturned by the Japanese Supreme Court in 1963, but legal proceedings dragged on for another seven years until, in 1970, the accused were paid damages by the Japanese government for possibly having been the victims of a frame-up by the prosecution.

It has never been proven exactly who did sabotage the Matsukawa train; fingers have been pointed at both U.S. and Soviet intelligence agents, as well as the JCP. All had conceivable motives for creating such an incident. One persistent theory, introduced by defense lawyers in the case, maintains that the saboteurs – all men – were members of an obscure traveling band, the Japan Girls' Opera Troupe (Nihon Shojo Kageki Dan). Typical of the yakuza's tekiya-style operations, the troupe had mysteriously appeared for an unscheduled one-night stand in Matsukawa the day before the incident.

Matsukawa, though, was but one of a whole string of mysterious incidents befalling the JCP and the labor movement. It was a time of great unrest in the railroad industry, with widespread layoffs aimed at leftist organizers as part of GHQ's purge. One month before the Matsukawa line careened off its tracks, the Shimoyama incident occurred, in which the president of the National Railways fell in front of a train. It was widely believed to be murder, and blame was laid upon the JCP. Another case was the Mitaka incident, an earlier train crash blamed as well on JCP sabotage; also the Shiratori incident, involving the murder of a policeman, again blamed on the JCP.

It is possible, of course, that the JCP was involved in one or more of these incidents. The Communists were engaged in an often violent battle for control of the labor movement, and their leaders talked loosely about the inevitability of armed struggle in the country. But the leadership, which previously had shown a talent for manipulation and public demonstrations, would have had to be wholly mindless to engage in mass murder. The JCP was never more than a relatively small political minority in Japan, even at the height of its popularity, which, by coincidence, was concurrent with these incidents. On the other hand, if the events were indeed part of a G-2 campaign to discredit the nation's Communists, it couldn't have been more successful. The bad publicity and court trials turned public opinion against the JCP.

There is one case in which Japanese rightists and American intelligence were caught red-handed. This was the Kaji affair, which began in late 1951. A leftist writer named Wataru Kaji was kidnapped by G-2 and handed over to the newly ensconced CIA. Up until this point Willoughby had assiduously refused to allow the CIA or its predecessor, the OSS, to operate freely in any of his domain. Intelligence in Japan was an Army affair. But Kaji was held incommunicado for more than a year by the CIA, and was allegedly subjected to torture. He was apparently suspected of working as a Soviet spy, although the U.S. Embassy claimed he was a double agent. When the affair came to light, the Japanese were outraged because Kaji's detention lasted past April 1952, when Japanese sovereignty was restored. The press also discovered the existence of a Japanese espionage group that aided the Americans in the kidnapping.

This group was one of several operating under Willoughby and G-2, and was named for its principal officer, ex-Colonel Takushiro Hattori, a former aide to General Tojo. His group, the Hattori Kikan (Hattori Agency), was made up of a dozen colonels and 300 lower ranks. Another group, the Cannon Agency, named for American Colonel J. Y. Cannon, was also accused of involvement in the Kaji affair, although here the hard evidence was lacking. Perhaps the least-known was the Katoh Agency, whose name was an acronym of five Japanese rightist officers. One of these was General Arisue, who had formerly been assigned to G-2's Historical Section. Katoh was so shadowy that Government Section assigned Major Jack Napier to conduct an investigation into Katoh's purpose. Napier, in turn, handed it over to the Japanese attorney general, who pursued the matter. One report, dated December 23, 1948, connected Arisue with Major General Willoughby. A later report noted that Arisue worked inside G-2 and that the "contents of [his] business are supposed to be related to information on the Soviet situations and the 'Red' activities within Japan."

Katoh, Cannon, and the other agencies operated under the unofficial mandate of protecting Japan from internal and external communism. But while Willoughby's officers were undoubtedly helpful to G-2's plans, for certain uses they were not always practical. Dirty tricks were one thing, but countering street demonstrations and strikes took another breed. For really unpleasant work, men without commission had to be discreetly called upon. In 1947, for instance, Chinese in Yokohama were abusing the Japanese population. For reasons not apparent, SCAP officials did not take action against the sangokujin. However, one member of the Cannon Agency, a Korean Navy commander, took care of the disturbance. He appealed for help to a Korean-Japanese named Hisayuki Machii, who was then in the process of forming one of the major gangs of the yakuza, the Tosei-kai. In spite of the Chinese being fellow sangokujin, Machii told his followers to gather rifles and machine guns and end the problem. Apparently, a show of force was all that was necessary.

Machii had sufficient strength, and solid connections through Cannon Agency and elsewhere, to be useful to G-2. The aging oyabun currently presents himself as a legitimate businessman, although, according to Japanese police, he still maintains close ties to his old fellows. Mr. Machii does not grant interviews, but his American business partner, former California assemblyman Kenneth Ross, told the authors that his partner was no gangster, that his occupation activities were limited to "strong-arm" tactics used to "break up Communist demonstrations, kind of like union busting. It was illegal in the pure sense, but it was done under the quasi-jurisdiction of our occupation forces."

Among the groups that exercised "quasi-jurisdiction" was the Counter Intelligence Corps of G-2. "You had to be lily white to get into CIC and turn coal black to stay in," recalls Harry Brunette, who served as a special agent with CIC during the occupation. "That CIC badge was your authority to do anything. If they told you to break in and steal some documents, you did it. We'd trade with the devil if we had to." Brunette remembers the specially commissioned agents affiliated with the Cannon Agency and similar outfits. "They were almost always linguists, Japanese-Americans, and they were directly responsive to CIC headquarters. They'd only come into our field office to get paid and drop off sealed reports for Tokyo."

At times CIC's special agents intervened directly in disturbances. Chicago *Sun* correspondent Mark Gayn, reporting in Japan from December 1945 to May 1948, described their work as part of a "campaign of union busting." In his remarkable account of the occupation years, *Japan Diary,* Gayn makes note of the hypocrisy of SCAP's labor policy. As early as October 1946, wrote Gayn, "[while] the Labor Division was talking in pious phrases to Japanese union leaders, Counterintelligence agents were breaking up labor demonstrations." Indeed, Japan's famously cooperative company unions are due more to the antilabor activities of some SCAP officials than to the docile nature of Japanese workers.

There existed a growing force of other thugs and gangsters that certain occupation officials could count on in their campaign against the left. These were the new ultranationalist gangs. In the same tradition of earlier yakuza-rightist gangs, they were organized along the traditional oyabun-kobun lines, and engaged freely in the black markets, racketeering, and extortion. But most conspicuous of their activities were strikebreaking and murderous attacks on trade union and leftist leaders. The new gangs were characterized by an ideology that was simultaneously anticommunist, anti-Korean, and anti-American.

Despite the official condemnation by SCAP, during much of the occupation the gangs freely launched attacks on leftists and labor unions. The fact that the Americans in 1946 originally banned all ultranationalist groups and purged their leaders appears to have been a minor inconvenience for the extreme right. The agency responsible for enforcing the ban on such groups was none other than G-2, which was not only unenthusiastic about the whole program, but was accused of actually using the gangs in its own campaigns to spy on and disrupt the left.

By 1947, the purge against the right seems to have been thoroughly undercut. Mark Gayn, writing in May of 1948, summed up the sorry state of affairs. "The purge, as of this date, has become a sham," he wrote. "War criminals sit in the Diet, the Cabinet and the imperial court, draw new 'democratic' legislation and administer the purges to fit their political ends. War criminals are 'revising' the textbooks, running the press, dominating the radio and moving picture industries. Thought Control agents, purged and purged again, keep reappearing in positions of responsibility – often with American encouragement."

By 1949, policy crept even with reality as SCAP launched its full-scale depurge. It was to be one of the last formidable acts of the reverse course: by the start of the Korean War, SCAP released 10,000 people from purge restrictions, and over the next year and a half freed a total of some 200,000.

The official lifting of the purges added even more recruits to the rightist gangs, which by the end of the occupation numbered as many as 750 separate groups. The new gangs of rightists sported evocative names reminiscent of those organizations founded by Mitsuru Toyama and fellow ultranationalists in the 1920s and 1930s. There was, for example, the New and Powerful Masses Party, begun in June 1946 in Tokyo by a gambling boss. In response to the growing labor movement, the enterprising "party" leader expanded the gang's interests to violent anti-union and anticommunist activity. In 1946, a truckload of its members, militantly adorned with white headbands and shoulder sashes, arrived at the headquarters of the National Railway Workers Union to persuade them to cancel their threatened strike. Within the year, the gang would be involved in a more highly publicized incident. Two members paid a visit to Katsumi Kikunami, a JCP Diet member and chairman of the Congress of Industrial Unions, and exhorted him to use his influence to call off a planned general strike. To emphasize their point, they slashed Kikunami's forehead with a dagger.

In the face of such blatant acts of violence, SCAP officials had little choice but to take action. In 1947, the Masses Party had the distinction of being the first postwar rightist group to be specifically ordered to disband. During the occupation years, however, the gang's members would be arrested for gambling, extortion, assault, robbery, murder, fraud, and other crimes.

Another such group was the aptly named Japan Goblin Party (Nihon Tengu To), whose aims seemed to weigh heavily on the gangster side despite its avowed political beliefs. The group was founded in 1945, with its headquarters located in Tokyo's Ginza district; among its most prominent members were local political bosses and gamblers. Its known political acts included plastering public places with anticommunist posters. When this sort of activity proved to be not very lucrative, the Goblins moved on to more remunerative work, such as robbing a post office, stealing stores of occupation cigarettes, and various acts of extortion, robbery, and fraud, until that party, too, was finally banned.

Although the rightists' political acts were no doubt appreciated by certain U.S. officials, no one in SCAP, not even Willoughby, really wanted to soil his hands dealing with the country's gangs of rightists and crooks. If hired muscle for intimidation or worse was needed, SCAP could usually count on the many rightists on G-2's payroll to arrange something. But while the staffs of Willoughby's clandestine agencies played a major role, they were not always effective. What G-2 needed was a central go-between, someone who had power in his own right, and who would not succumb to anti-American sentiments; someone brutal, but not too treacherous. It turned out that SCAP had just the man.

G-2, the CIA, and Mr. Kodama

From 1946 until late 1948, Yoshio Kodama languished in Tokyo's Sugamo Prison, the holding tank for many of the accused war criminals awaiting trial or sentencing by the International Military Tribunal for the

Far East. Kodama was Class A, a designation reserved for cabinet officers, military men, and ultranationalists. On December 23, 1948, the
Class A criminals separated into two groups: seven of those convicted by
the Tribunal, including former prime minister Tojo and four military men,
dropped from the gallows. Hours later, sixteen others, including Kodama,
stepped out into the cold night air.

It had not been Kodama's first incarceration, but it was undoubtedly
the most profitable. In his three years behind bars, Kodama wrote two
books, *I Was Defeated,* a turgid political analysis of his life on the right,
and *Sugamo Diary,* an amusing and perceptive report of life in prison.
More important, Kodama made or solidified friendships with other
Japanese rightists who would someday run the country. When Kodama
left Sugamo at age thirty-seven, he was just starting a new phase of his old
work. Through his ties to the right, the underworld, and American intelligence, Kodama would become one of the most powerful men in postwar
Japan – and the mastermind behind the yakuza's rise to political power.

He began life in 1911, the fifth son of a Nihonmatsu City gentleman
who was down on his luck. In 1920, at age eight, Yoshio was placed with
distant relatives in Korea, where he suffered through isolation and child
labor in a variety of exceedingly unpleasant industrial jobs. In his teens,
young Kodama, sensitive to the exploitation of the worker, turned first to
socialism and then to ultranationalism as a solution to personal and social
problems. As a theorist, he was less than convincing, but he turned out to
be extremely adept at organizing, profiteering, and violence.

Beginning in the late 1920s, Kodama enlisted in a series of ultranationalist groups, apprenticing himself to the infamous Mitsuru Toyama of
the Dark Ocean Society. In 1929, he joined Kenkoku-kai (Association of
the Founding of the Nation), begun by Dr. Shinkichi Uesugi and Bin
Akao, one of Japan's best known, most virulent rightists. Kenkoku-kai
had a reputation as the most radical of the rightist groups. Upon joining,
Kodama tried to hand the emperor a written appeal urging increased patriotism. Kodama was seized by the police at a motorcade before he could
serve Hirohito with the papers, and Yoshio drew six months in jail. Three
years later Kodama founded the Dokuritsu Seinen Sha (Independence
Youth Society). This group collaborated with Tenko-kai (Society for
Heavenly Action) in 1934 in an abortive attempt to assassinate cabinet
members, including Prime Minister Admiral Saito. Kodama was caught
but sentenced to only 3½ years in prison.

Kodama was released from Fuchu Penitentiary in 1937. He had
served a total of six years in various prisons and jails. "During my six
years of imprisonment," he wrote in *I Was Defeated,* "the rightist move-

ment had been completely castrated while the reform ideals that had risen all over the country since the Manchurian incident [1931] had been completely canalized into the field of foreign policies."

Not one to miss an opportunity, Kodama used his rightist connections to move into the world of "foreign policies." According to the book *Uyoku Jiten* (Right-Wing Dictionary), after becoming a staff officer at Army headquarters, Kodama entered the Foreign Ministry's information bureau. He later joined the expeditionary force to China and the East Indies, and was also attached to the Navy, Air Force, and Ministry of the Interior as a nonregular.

Kodama's talents were recognized by his superiors, and from 1939 through late 1941 the young rightist toured East Asia, spying for the government. His frequent trips between China and Japan caught the attention of U.S. Army intelligence agents, who credited him with setting up a network of Manchurian spies and collaborators that stretched across China. On December 8, the day after the Japanese attack on Pearl Harbor and much of Southeast Asia, the thirty-year-old Kodama set up shop in Shanghai. He started an operation called Kodama Kikan (Kodama Agency) with an exclusive contract from the Navy Air Force to supply strategic materiel needed for the war effort.

Kodama operated as a sort of Imperial Japanese version of *Catch-22*'s Milo Minderbinder, buying tungsten here, guns there, reselling them, and peddling vast stores of radium, cobalt, nickel, and copper. He obtained the materials in China and Manchuria, forcing the Chinese at gunpoint to sell at pitifully low prices. It was an incredibly lucrative effort, one that might easily be termed looting. Kodama, however, saw it differently. His enterprises, unlike other so-called development firms in the conquered territories, grew out of an ill-suppressed idealism. His agency, said Kodama, was "an organization with no thought of profit and since it was simply composed of a group of self-sacrificing youths, I was only able to continue my work through the sincere efforts of the men cooperating with me." Such "sincere" efforts apparently pay off; at the end of the war, Kodama Kikan had become a financial giant with a working capital of $175 million in industrial diamonds and platinum, as well as banknotes.

With so many "self-sacrificing youths" working for him, Kodama found time to continue his intelligence work. He ran operations for Section Eight of the General Staff office in Shanghai, which handled intelligence. In addition, he financed the Shanghai office of the Kempei Tai – the Japanese secret police. Still, the demands of his industrial kingdom must have left increasingly little time for spy missions. By the early 1940s, according to U.S. intelligence reports, the Kodama Kikan controlled iron, salt, and molybdenum mines, and operated farms, fisheries, and secret munitions plants through much of central China. And, although it might not have been his usual line of work, he at times acted as a go-between in major heroin-for-minerals deals.

The end of the war saw Kodama, by then a thirty-four-year-old rear admiral, back in Japan as an advisor to the prime minister, Prince Higashikuni. Kodama did use his influence to help implement the surrender with a minimum of violence, but the Americans were not impressed. In the first days of 1946, he was rounded up with other high-ranking Japanese and sent to Sugamo Prison to await trial. During his three-year imprisonment, he was interrogated at great length concerning his operations in China. In a key report of May 1947, at least one G-2 official summarized Kodama's exploits and argued strongly for his continued internment. Concluded the report:

> *In summary, Kodama appears to be a man doubly dangerous. His long and fanatic involvement in ultranationalist activities, violence included, and his skill in appealing to youth make him a man who, if released from internment, would surely be a grave security risk. In addition, there is the outstanding probability . . . that, as a result of his hearty co-operation with the war effort, he has a large fortune to back up whatever activities he might see fit to undertake . . . [and] could very easily become a big-time operator in Japan's re-constructional period. . . . Kodama's past performance indicates that he is the sort of man G-2 considers more dangerous than either the superannuated ideologists or the professional men who aided Japan's war-time effort for reasons of patriotism or survival of their professional interests. . . .*

Like many veteran ultranationalists, however, Kodama was never tried, nor even formally charged. According to SCAP's Chief of Legal Section, Alva C. Carpenter, the "suspected" Class A war criminal was released because the International Tribunal had found other civilians not guilty, and Legal Section – expecting acquittal for Kodama – declined to bring charges. But the historical record is not that simple.

It appears that Kodama's release may have involved a deal he had struck with G-2 officials, then increasingly obsessed with communism, to share both his wealth and his considerable intelligence on China and the Japanese left. If not in prison, it was shortly after his release that Kodama's work began with U.S. intelligence.

At the time of his release from Sugamo, Kodama had already begun the machinations that would soon create a powerful rightist bloc inside and outside the government. In fact, prior to his arrest, Kodama entrusted a good part of his fortune – he was the second-richest man among the 644 suspected war criminals – to another influential rightist, Karoku Tsuji. Occupation officer Harry Emerson Wildes, in a 1946 internal report on Tsuji, called him the "mystery man of Japanese politics" because of his ability to make lavish campaign donations without any visible means of income. Only later would it be revealed how Tsuji used Kodama's booty to finance the founding of the Liberal Party. That money firmly established the close relationship that would exist between Kodama and the ruling conservatives in Japan for the next thirty-five years. In 1955, the Liberal Party merged with the Democratic Party to form the Liberal-Democratic Party, or LDP, which has run Japan ever since. From that point on, over the next two decades, Kodama was perhaps the most powerful single individual within the LDP.

Karoku Tsuji was a powerful figure in his own right. He was a major financier of the dominant party before the war, and had a say in the opposing party as well. In 1946 Tsuji was sixty-nine years old, but still enjoyed being called Japan's Al Capone (as opposed to Kinosuke Ozu, who was merely Tokyo's Al Capone). Before the war, Tsuji, along with Black Dragon godfather Mitsuru Toyama, ran many of the bands of political thugs in Tokyo that effectively controlled voting through the usual strongarm intimidation. Tsuji and Toyama stood at the center of what Harry Wildes called "Japan's Tammany Hall . . . one of the most corrupt political machines in Japanese history." By 1946, according to Wildes, Tsuji had garnered even more power, ruling over the black markets, crime gangs, and political life of greater Tokyo.

Upon release from Sugamo, Kodama found two bases of power that would serve him well – the yakuza and American intelligence. Kodama quickly showed that he had the support of the yakuza legions whenever he needed it. In 1949, for instance, he led the Meiraki-gumi against labor unions at the Hokutan Coal Mine. These unions had been the most effective and militant of the miners' unions, and all the governing forces, Japanese and American, wanted them brought into line. When a frontal assault on the union proved insufficient because of the miners' willingness to do battle, Kodama's men tried to foment internal strife, also with limited success.

By 1950, it appears that Kodama had solidified his position as a principal go-between for G-2 and the various yakuza bands. One aging gangster, the retired boss of Tokyo's Takinogawa gang, summed up Kodama's work in a 1984 interview: "None of us gang bosses had much connection with GHQ. Kodama was the one who did that." Kodama was able to swing that much weight because he knew the essential element of power – money. Not only did he have a lot of it, but he knew how to move it around as well.

Kodama also retained an interest in another major component of political power, intelligence. However, his first known venture in concert with G-2 did not turn out to be particularly auspicious for either party. Kodama was involved in an operation to send a spy ship, sailing under merchant marine cover, to Shanghai to gather intelligence on the new Communist regime. Kodama was of particular interest to G-2 because of his extensive China background. However, when the *Choshu Maru* docked at the port city in January 1951, it was promptly seized by the suspicious Chinese.

In 1949, the Central Intelligence Agency had begun to take over Japanese intelligence operations over General Willoughby's objections. Kodama's next venture was with the agency and, despite his earlier failure, he was assigned another maritime black-bag job. This time he was given $150,000 up front to smuggle a cargo of tungsten out of China. An official, later with the CIA, who was involved in the deal said that the ship never arrived. Kodama, he said, kept the money and told the U.S. Embassy that the ship had sunk.

One might think that these fiascoes would be enough to make the Americans drop Kodama altogether. Far from it. This was the beginning of a long-standing relationship between Kodama and the CIA. Kodama's approach wasn't original – rightists around the world have been using it for generations – but it was effective: cry red and the Americans will usually pony up. In fact, it was highly effective. The use of organized crime and ultranationalists by the occupation kept the Japanese left on the defensive and off balance, just as the CIA's use of the Corsican mob did against the French Communists. But such policies create unwanted side effects. In France, the CIA's use of the underworld enabled the Corsican gangs to establish the French Connection for massive heroin shipments to the United States. And in Japan, the aftereffects were at least as profound.

The money, the favored treatment, and the privileged relationships accorded to rightists and their gangster allies by U.S. officials created a corrupt power structure that would last for decades. The yakuza now resumed their role in Japanese politics – providing money and muscle – in a stronger position than ever. They continued to act as company goons and strikebreakers. Their strength enabled them to grab increasingly larger segments of the economy, drawing money from the Japanese people far in excess of any services they provided. And the country's rightist politicians benefited from having a private yakuza army at their disposal.

Colonel Kades was prescient in his 1947 press conference when he claimed, "This clannish and clandestine combination of bosses, hoodlums and racketeers is the greatest threat to American democratic aims in Japan." The colonel also might have noted that this was the greatest threat to Japanese democratic aims, and would continue to be for years to come. It is an unfortunate fact that American misuse of power helped undermine Japanese democratic goals. It is not an exaggeration to say that the occupation gave the yakuza its biggest lease on life. The best for the yakuza was yet to come.

Chapter 3
Nexus on the Right

As the occupation drew to a close, many Japanese, especially those on the political right, were fearful of a leftist move toward power. One of those worried was Tokutaro Kimura, the powerful minister of justice under Prime Minister Yoshida.

As 1952 began, Kimura was nervously anticipating the April signing of the peace treaty with the United States. He called together a group of influential rightists to discuss the future. In his book *The Great History of the Right Wing*, rightist historian Bokusui Arahara recreated that scene in a Tokyo meeting room. Kimura spoke in ominous tones to his assembled colleagues:

> "It is clear as day that Communists will rise in revolt all over Japan and a bloody revolution will begin. I already have information that a standing government of the Communist Party would be formed in Nagano Prefecture.
>
> "There is information that the police are infiltrated by the reds, and there are many Communist Party members among high-ranking officers of the Reserve Corps [the forerunner of the Self-Defense Forces, or army]. Furthermore, there are many who are not regular members of the Communist Party but have pledged loyalty to the Party. If so, we cannot depend on the police, and there is a strong possibility that the Reserve Force will become our foe.
>
> "Can't you call together men with common beliefs to fight desperately against the Communist Party, to preserve the national policy?"

Kimura's plea was quickly answered by his henchman Nobuo Tsuji:

"Justice Minister, there is nobody who would risk their lives but gamblers, racketeers, and hoodlums. If the Communists should arise in revolt, those who talk about theories are not useful when it actually comes to a fight. There are none but those fellows, who risk their lives for their bosses. However, we may have difficulty in recruiting them since their bosses were hunted and the groups dispersed by the Occupation policy."

Tsuji estimated to the Minister that if money were available, he could possibly organize a special attack unit of criminals, and that of the number of bakuto, tekiya, and gurentai – whose population he generously estimated at several million – he thought that 200,000 could be considered reliable, dedicated anti-Communist fighters. Replied Kimura: " 'Oh, two hundred thousand courageous persons can be called! Thank God! It's providential. If they can be gathered, the nation can be saved!' "

Kimura then shook hands with his three closest cronies and said through his tears of joy, " 'I beg you to work for the country. I will never let you worry about money.' "

The Minister of Drawn Swords
The meeting may not have taken place precisely as Bokusui Arahara depicted it, for Arahara, a former yakuza and a Christian pastor, was a right-wing partisan as well as a writer. But less biased historical sources confirm that such an event did indeed occur, and preparations were made to launch a 200,000-man force. It was to be called Aikoku Hankyo Battotai, or the Patriotic Anti-Communist Drawn Sword Regiment. The Japanese Youth Guidance Association, Nihon Seishonen Zendo Kyo-kai, would be used as a front group, and Kimura planned that ultimately the Japanese government would take the whole project under its wing.

Kimura was unusual not because he sought to reinstitute the rightist/ gangster nexus from inside the Japanese government, but because he sought to do so during the American occupation, and in such a crude prewar fashion. Kimura's success, though, was due in part to the same SCAP policy that let Kodama and other prewar ultranationalists back out on the streets and into the elective offices and the corporate boardrooms. Much as Tokunami had done thirty years earlier, by the end of the occupation Kimura would sweep across the nation, organizing postwar Japan's first national alliance of gangsters and rightists. It was a remarkable feat: the nation's highest-ranking law enforcement official attempting to form the splintered yakuza bands into a single cohesive underworld force.

Kimura rose to prominence as a lawyer. He hung out his shingle in 1911, and after functioning as a private attorney, became chairman of the Japan Lawyers' Association. During the war, he assumed the directorship of one of the many ultranationalist groups, the Dai Nippon Butoku-kai (the Great Japan Military Virtue Society), as well as a local post in the Imperial Rule Assistance Youth Association.

At the war's end, Kimura entered the Yoshida government, first as procurator general, then as attorney general (later retitled minister of justice) from May 1946 until a year later, when his past caught up with him. The rightist attorney was pronounced a Class D war criminal and purged from public life. He didn't suffer too badly, as he resumed his private practice and served on the boards of two Tokyo industrial firms.

By the summer of 1948 Kimura was itching for return to power, and his former boss, Prime Minister Yoshida, tried to pull some strings. A SCAP Government Section investigation was less than complimentary: "The entire record of Mr. Kimura's association with SCAP has been one of opposition, of recalcitrance, and of defiance by delay and misfeasance. . . . He is undesirable for any position of power and influence over the people of Japan." MacArthur himself wrote to Yoshida saying that he could do nothing "regardless of the fine reputation for personal integrity which you tell me Mr. Kimura enjoys."

Less than a year later, in May 1949, Yoshida was again asking for Kimura to be granted reinstatement, claiming that Japan's recovery was "seriously impeded by a lack of talent." Kimura, claimed Yoshida, was not a rightist, but had been merely head of the fencing division of Butoku-kai, a position offered to him "because of his preeminence as a citizen and his hobbies of fencing and sword collection which of course have nothing to do with militarism and aggression." This time it worked, for SCAP's reverse course had begun and thousands of rightists were being depurged. On October 13, 1950, Kimura was reinstated and became once again justice minister.

From there it was a short hop to the Drawn Sword Regiment, a name chosen no doubt by the fencing buff. For a justice minister, Kimura showed less interest in justice than in cozying up to powerful gangsters. According to Arahara, Kimura met with tekiya leader Eiji Sekiguchi and helped create the nationwide Street Peddlers Union, which was loyal to the justice minister. Kimura also engineered the release of "Tokyo's Al Capone," Kinosuke Ozu, who then joined with the Drawn Swordsmen. Kimura went straight to the top as well, securing the loyalty of perhaps the most influential of occupation-era bosses, Kanbei Umezu, who at the time was in prison. From there, Japan's highest lawman urged a consortium of

Tokyo oyabun to create a new association, the Nippon Kokusui-kai, and received their support in the fight against communism.

Kimura had underworld support, but he failed at the other end. His main stumbling block was Prime Minister Yoshida, who knew better than Kimura that the Americans – while suddenly tolerant of the old ultranationalists – were not prepared to let the reverse course run back to 1937. Somewhat dismayed at his minister's zeal, Yoshida squelched the Drawn Sword Regiment. Complicating matters for Kimura, major funding failed to appear, and what money was raised somehow didn't make it to the various rightists and yakuza. Kimura, it seemed, had his faults. In fact, among the legal profession he was called the "Sweetfish of Tamagawa," because he promised colleagues this delicacy and then neglected to make good. He was also known as "Venerable Ready Consent, Man of Non-Performance," a phrase that flows better in Japanese.

Although stymied in his plan to create a private army, Kimura did not retire in defeat. In 1954, Yoshida appointed him to head the National Defense Agency, overseeing the new Self-Defense Forces and sniffing out Communists in the nascent army and throughout Japan: he would, in fact, become known as "Japan's Joe McCarthy." Kimura, who lived until past ninety, was also an unreconstructed militarist. In 1953, he put together a coalition of thirty-seven rightist organizations under the name Hoyu-kai, and used it as a pro-military lobbying group. He was later elected to the upper house of the Diet, where he pushed for a number of perennial planks in the rightist platform: a sovereign emperor, elimination of the Mac-Arthur constitution, revising the textbooks, and strengthening the army.

Kimura was by no means the most important postwar rightist; he was merely one fish in a whole school of ex-officers, old ultranationalists, new rightists, yakuza bosses, and others. His career in public service, though, was a clear indication of just how lenient the occupation and the new independent Japan would be with the personnel and the ideas that had steered the nation to disaster. The failure of his Drawn Sword Regiment was merely a tactical defeat, and others picked up the banner.

The 1950s were a time of rapid and bewildering changes for the Japanese. The country began to regain its industrial base, and the social system moved rapidly into the realm of the Western industrial democracies, although Japan would never become Westernized per se. Nonetheless, great changes swept through Japanese society: women began to work outside the home in greater numbers; labor continued to organize; elections were regularly held; and the old order lost much of its control over individual citizens. At the same time, though, the zaibatsu, Japan's massive financial combines, regained much of their hold on the national economy, and the conservatives continued to run the government.

The San Francisco Peace Treaty came into force in April 1952, and marked the formal end to the occupation, although many Japanese regarded it as just that – a formality. There was, for one thing, the rather suspect nature of the treaty: the three major Asian powers – China, India, and Russia – were nonsignatories, and a number of smaller Asian countries also refused to ratify. The treaty provided only a partial end to the occupation, since American military bases on the home islands and complete American control over Okinawa were mandated, and the basic instrument of government, the American-written constitution, remained in effect. Moreover, there is little argument over the fact that Japanese foreign policy, particularly regarding China and Russia, was closely bound up with American aims.

But if Japan had a semicolonial status, it was hardly an exploited nation. Freed from the burden of equipping and maintaining a large standing army – indeed, enjoined from it under the terms of the constitution – the nation could devote most of its energies to improving the material lot of its citizens. This, as the world already knows, Japan did, emerging from the ruins in 1945 to become the world's third largest economy by 1968.

Politically, Japan's governments have been nominally middle-of-the-road conservative since the surrender. In spite of pressures from the left, the conservatives strengthened their hand in the 1950s. In 1955, the Liberal Party, begun with funds from Yoshio Kodama's hoard of plundered wealth, merged with the Democratic Party, and under the leadership of Nobusuke Kishi, together they formed the Jiyu-Minshuto, or Liberal-Democratic Party, the LDP. The Socialist Party often mounted well-organized challenges to conservative rule, but except for the brief period from April 1947 to February 1948, it never participated in any government, much less controlled one. The Japanese Communist Party was held in check by the deep-seated conservatism of the rural Japanese, and by legal, economic, and physical force directed by the LDP and the far right.

In spite of relative political stability – relative certainly to many other Asian nations and to the previous two decades in Japan – there was a good deal of public disorder from both the right and the left in the 1950s. Issues such as the contamination of a Japanese fishing vessel in the mid-Pacific by American nuclear tests in 1954 touched off a lengthy round of leftist protests. The right, on the other hand, found it more convenient to agitate against the Soviet Union, and there was a good deal to complain about:

continued internment of Japanese prisoners of war; seizure of the Kurile Islands to the north; harassment of the Japanese fishing fleet.

The left in the 1950s maintained control of large sectors of the labor movement, such as the Nikkyoso, or Japan Teachers' Union, and the Sohyo, or General Council of Trade Unions. The right, on the other hand, could muster far less support than even the Communist Party, but the country's arch-conservatives found that grassroots support wasn't the only way to power. There were, as there had been before the war, the old-line political bosses in the countryside, and better yet, the gangsters in the cities.

When Tokutaro Kimura's friend Nobuo Tsuji claimed that there were millions of hoodlums in Japan, he was exaggerating, but not by much. In 1952, there were still millions of people plugged into the black markets and oyabun-kobun rackets that grew up in the war's aftermath. As conditions improved, most of these men drifted off into less precarious pursuits; those who stayed became the core of the new emerging yakuza empire.

From their strongholds in Osaka/Kobe in the west, and Tokyo/Yokohama in the east, gangsters began to consolidate their forces. Out of the thousands of gangs, some began to dominate. In the Kanto region, around Tokyo, names like Kinsei-kai, Tosei-kai, and Sumiyoshi-kai began to sound familiar to newspaper readers. In the Kansai region around Osaka and the nearby port of Kobe, the Yamaguchi-gumi and the Honda-kai began to overshadow their competitors.

As Japan recovered from defeat and destruction, the gangs were forced to move from control of necessities to control of luxuries. The yakuza were no longer needed in the black market, for credit and abundant foodstuffs were again available. But the yakuza found that even before prosperity fully arrived, there was big money to be made in non-essentials – drugs, prostitution, and entertainment.

During the war, Japan, like other countries, discovered that weary soldiers could be kept going on amphetamines, and produced large stocks of the drug. The most famous military users of amphetamines were *kamikaze* pilots (who would at least not suffer through the excruciating comedown that amphetamines produce). In any case, stocks of speed were appropriated from military stores and sold during the occupation, finding a market among the dispirited people of defeated Japan. Although Japanese morale improved as time went on, the demand for amphetamines persisted, fluctuating with supplies and periodic crackdowns by police. It is a market that the yakuza have come to monopolize, and one that has proven to be extremely lucrative.

Prostitution, too, became yakuza business. Traditionally, many forms of prostitution were respectable in Japan, and were certainly not the domain of crude gangsters. But the war's end changed all that. Out of the economic desperation many women were sold by their families to yakuza, who used them as prostitutes in the cities – often for American customers. Public solicitation and management of prostitutes was finally outlawed in 1958, after which time nearly all organized vice fell into the hands of the yakuza and their associates.

Gambling, on the other hand, was in part taken out of the hands of the bakuto, at least as exclusive operators of the games. Most of the popular forms of public gambling were legalized: horse racing, bicycle racing, and later, speedboat racing. The government found them a convenient source of needed revenue. The enterprising bakuto then were suddenly reduced to scalping tickets, touting at races, and running illegal bookie shops. Those bakuto with any vision soon expanded into vice, drugs, or businesses such as bars and restaurants.

As the Japanese gained both money and leisure time, entertainment again became popular, and the yakuza moved to control much of this growing field. Professional sports, from ancient sumo to the more recent import of baseball, came under yakuza influence. Theater, cabarets, and the burgeoning movie industry were all, to some degree, forced to yield control to the gangs.

Government reaction to the growing power of the yakuza was mixed. At the police level, there was a strong response to gang power, and crackdowns and arrests were frequent. But high officials, particularly those in the right wing of the LDP, were less concerned with the day-to-day rackets of the yakuza, and often more interested in making alliances with them. Throughout the 1950s, the right and the new, powerful gangster organizations once again began to assume each other's coloration. By 1959, the national newspaper *Yomiuri* could headline an article "Hoodlum Gangs Become Rightist Organizations." Some gangs, said the paper, had changed into rightists in order to avoid the police crackdown then in progress. The largest of the three new "political parties" was the Kokusuikai, the same group that had been founded by Kimura's associates. According to the article, "The setup of the three organizations is patterned after the Liberal-Democratic Party. . . . These organizations are anticommunist and fervently support the emperor system."

Perhaps the comparison with the LDP was tongue-in-cheek, perhaps not. In any case, it was often very apt. Although this confluence of rightist and gangster was appalling to most Japanese, there were others, including some of the most powerful men in the country, who prospered because of their ties to the gangster/rightist organizations. The gangs played an essential role in the creation of several immense fortunes, and helped others in shaping political careers that reached, in some cases, to the very top.

The Kuromaku Come of Age

Since the late nineteenth century, the *kuromaku* has been a pivotal figure in Japanese politics. Literally "black curtain," the word originated in classic Kabuki theater, in which an unseen wirepuller controls the stage by manipulating a black curtain. Today it connotes a powerful godfather or fixer who operates behind the scenes. Although most political arenas have their kuromaku, the term most often applies to those men on the right – usually the extreme right – who serve as a bridge between the yakuza-rightist underworld and the legitimate world of business and mainstream politics. Most famous of the early kuromaku was Mitsuru Toyama, doyen of the extreme right and head of the Dark Ocean Society.

In postwar Japan, a number of men rose to fill the position of kuromaku, and perhaps the best known of these was a trio of Class A war criminals, all former residents of Sugamo Prison: Yoshio Kodama, Ryoichi Sasakawa, and Nobusuke Kishi. Prewar ultranationalists all, these men lost no time in bringing the right wing up to date and using it to influence business and the ruling Liberal-Democratic Party.

Kodama, as noted earlier, had spent the war largely in China, procuring strategic materials for the Imperial Navy, dealing in looted goods, occasionally brokering heroin, and operating an intelligence net. His activities landed him in Sugamo, but SCAP's G-2 section found him a valuable contact after the war, and Kodama's links to American intelligence, as well as his renewed involvement in Japan's extreme right, began as soon as he was released from prison at the end of 1948.

Kodama brought with him skill at organizing, a fair ability for political theorizing, and immense personal charisma, all of which stood him in good stead with the emerging postwar right. He was only thirty-four at the war's end, and Kodama hit the ground running upon his release. As the eminent historian Ivan Morris wrote in 1960: "Kodama is considered to be extremely influential as an undercover man in conservative and financial circles. At the same time he maintained links with former military men and rightists. . . ." Among Kodama's many associates in the "New Japan" were yakuza boss Karoku Tsuji, Prime Minister Ichiro Hatoyama, political wheeler-dealer Ichiro Kono, and ultranationalist Bin Akao. (The last named was linked to the dramatic 1960 stabbing assassination of Socialist Party leader Inejiro Asanuma, and as late as that year Akao was calling himself the "Hitler of Japan.")

Kodama had been introduced to party politics by Ichiro Kono before the end of the war, and both men immediately afterward began planning new paths to power. During the occupation, Kodama contributed a healthy slice of his vast fortune to the Liberal Party, and by 1954 he had helped engineer the election of Hatoyama to prime minister. He owned outright a real estate firm and several nationally distributed sports (gambling) newspapers; he was suspected of possessing interests in a film company, a baseball team, and a shipping line. In addition, Kodama reportedly owned part of the Ginza nightclub empire that was controlled by his strikebreaking pal, Korean gang boss Hisayuki Machii.

He also returned to his wartime sidelines of intelligence-mongering and running black-bag jobs. By 1958, six years or so after he had left the direct employ of G-2, Kodama was placed on the CIA payroll, with many lucrative spinoffs coming his way. And, from his talents as a strikebreaker, nurtured by General Willoughby's organization, Kodama went into private practice. He hired himself out to industrialists to protect them against undue labor problems – a job that kept him in close contact with underworld bosses.

Kodama worked well with most of the various groups and individuals he cultivated – politicians, businessmen, yakuza, rightists, and spies. During the 1950s and 1960s, he strengthened his ties to the traditional right, and forged new links to the growing gangster conglomerates. Kodama organized, theorized, and moved huge sums of money around. He paid politicians and they paid him – if not with money, then in giri, or favors and obligations. But he was certainly not the only kuromaku following such a path. One of Kodama's former cellmates accumulated enough money and power to also alter Japan's postwar history.

Ryoichi Sasakawa used a slightly different road to power than did Kodama, and placed a greater emphasis on money over loyalty to ideals. But both men would inhabit essentially the same circles, and both came from the very same roots. Not merely an ultranationalist before the war, Sasakawa was an open admirer of Mussolini, and ordered his private militia to don black shirts in imitation of the Italian Fascists. Among his followers was an ardent young rightist named Yoshio Kodama.

Sasakawa was tossed into Sugamo in 1945 for three years where, for a time, he shared a cell with Kodama. It was there he learned an important lesson that he could continue to build upon: cultivate the Americans. But the Americans in SCAP were not all enamored of Sasakawa. The final prison report on the Fascist leader admonished: "In summary, Sasakawa appears to be a man potentially dangerous to Japan's political future. . . . He has been squarely behind Japanese military policies of aggression and anti-foreignism for more than twenty years. He is a man of wealth and not too scrupulous about its use. He chafes for continued power. He is not above wearing any new cloak that opportunism may offer."

The report was not well heeded, for Sasakawa took precisely that course. He moved steadily toward a less aggressive form of foreign intervention, making friends around the world with right-wing despots and ministers. He would also find that once the liberals from SCAP departed, the Americans weren't such bad fellows after all. He began making trips to the United States, spreading largesse among influential Americans for both personal and political advantage.

Sasakawa began his postwar life of opportunism while still in Sugamo, where he devised a plan to make it big in the gambling business. Upon leaving the prison in December 1948, he approached various local governments in Japan. Would they consider splitting the take with him from motorboat races? They were only too glad to have the income. Over the next thirty-five years, Sasakawa built an enormous gambling empire, the Japan Motorboat Racing Association, which sets up the race course, operates the stands and the boats, pays the drivers, pays the parimutuel windows, and cleans up – in every sense. By 1980, Sasakawa's company grossed a remarkable $7.4 billion – larger than the gross national product of many countries. At the same time, Sasakawa won over the various bakuto gangs. He bragged publicly that he was a drinking companion of Japan's leading godfather, Yamaguchi-gumi head Kazuo Taoka. In the kuromaku tradition, Sasakawa also reportedly served as a mediator between feuding yakuza gangs. And, like his cohort Kodama, he employed squads of financial racketeers to push along his controversial investments.

Sasakawa also resumed his right-wing activities, taking care to adapt his schemes to changing conditions. For instance, his prewar group, the Kokusui Taishuto, or Patriotic People's Mass Party, was transmogrified into the postwar Zenkoku Kinrosha Domei, or All-Japan White Collar Workers' League. Sasakawa also found it expedient to ally himself with non-Japanese rightists. He counted himself among the founders of the Asian Peoples' Anti-Communist League, and its stepchild, the World Anti-Communist League (WACL), along with such early supporters as Syngman Rhee and Chiang Kai-shek. In 1963, Sasakawa became an advisor to Reverend Sun Myung Moon's Japanese branch of the Unification Church, known in Japan as *Genri Undo*. Moon and Sasakawa brought a number of Japanese rightist groups together in a WACL subsidiary known as Kokusai Shokyo Rengo, the International Federation for

Victory over Communism, and Sasakawa assumed the roles of both patron and president. He continued to advise and fund rightist groups until, by the late 1970s, he could claim to have the allegiance of some eight million Japanese.

This huge number, however, included the entire memberships of groups that were simply traditionalist rather than politically right, organizations ranging from karate federations to sword dancing groups. As he was funding these groups, Sasakawa was also marching off to regions not even rightists could easily comprehend, promoting the "science" of Waterology, a collection of crackpot ecological notions. He also bought up huge blocks of television air time to exhort youngsters to honor their parents and keep the earth clean. He embarked on a thirty-year career of shameless self-aggrandizement, running hundreds of print and television ads bearing his smiling visage and reminding Japan of his beneficence. "Formerly I had Yoshio Kodama and many other roughnecks around me," he once said. "I was their leader. So, some may call me a rightist. But I am not a rightist, I am a humanitarian." But as late as 1974, *Time* magazine would quote him as repeatedly boasting, "I am the world's wealthiest Fascist."

The names of Kodama and Sasakawa would become synonymous in Japan with the dark side of the nation's politics. Both men would exert enormous influence over the LDP and have a say in the naming of cabinet ministers, even the prime minister himself – much as Kodama did with the third Sugamo power, Nobusuke Kishi.

In some ways, Kishi's story is the most remarkable of the three. He began his political career as a follower of the influential Fascist Ikki Kita in the early 1930s, and by the end of the decade had moved into a position of power within the government. Kishi's real base of power was Manchukuo, the Japanese puppet state in conquered Manchuria. From 1936 to 1939, Kishi was officially the second-highest-ranking civilian in Manchukuo, although some referred to him as the ruler of the province. There, he maintained office with the help of those rightists and gangsters who came to help with the "development" of Manchukuo. After leaving the province, Kishi went on to hold the offices of minister of trade and industry, and vice munitions minister in Tojo's wartime cabinet.

Kishi was held as a Class A war criminal by the Americans, but left Sugamo along with Kodama and the others who were mysteriously released on December 23, 1948. Kishi then staged one of the world's greatest political comebacks. He was depurged in 1952 and immediately entered politics. By allying himself with key rightists within the government, and through a series of shrewd maneuvers, Kishi soon moved to center stage. He became secretary-general of the LDP in 1955, and pushed on to become deputy prime minister under Yoshida's successor, Tanzan Ishibashi. But when Ishibashi was forced to resign after only three months for health reasons, Kishi went all the way. Backed by Kodama's money and influence, he staged an unstoppable run for prime minister. When Kishi assumed office in March 1957, he took the nation's highest post only five years after depurge, and nine years after release from war criminal status. This mutual assistance among the Sugamo graduates would mark Japanese electoral politics for years to come.

Kishi managed to help return to center stage a whole galaxy of prewar rightists and yakuza allies. Among them were two symphonious, and notorious, names – Ichiro Kono and Bamboku Ohno. Kono was a part of many major LDP decisions, including those to name Prime Minister Kishi and his successor, Eisaku Sato. Kono himself was minister of agriculture and was an elected member of the Diet. He was also a sworn brother to Yoshio Kodama.

Perhaps even more critical to the rightist alliance was Bamboku Ohno, an old-line rightist who controlled an important faction in the LDP. Backed by Kishi and Kodama, Ohno assumed the secretary-general post in the party, where he remained until his death in 1965.

In 1963, Ohno revealed his connections by publicly addressing a gathering of Kobe yakuza. The occasion was a reception for Katsuichi Hirata, godfather of the Yamaguchi-gumi subgroup, the Honda-kai. Over 2500 people crowded into the plush Shin-Seiki Club to hear Hirata take the oath of office. Ohno arrived to speak to the crowd; he was accompanied by six husky bodyguards wearing black suits and sunglasses. In a rousing speech, the LDP's secretary-general told the assembled that *ninkyo,* or chivalry, was part of Japan's best traditions, and that this very tradition was being kept alive by the Honda-kai gang. Said Ohno, "Politicians and those who go the way of chivalry [yakuza] follow different occupations. But they have one thing in common and that is their devotion to the principles of giri and ninjo." He concluded, "I offer my speech of congratulations by praying that you would further exert yourself in the ways of chivalry in order to make the society and our country better." He led the crowd in three *banzai* – cheers for the emperor – and received a thunderous ovation. The guests then moved on to a reception where they were entertained by a host of geisha.

Ohno and Kono were merely the most visible members of the right to be helped by the Kishi regime. Many of those in Kishi's Manchuria crowd, for instance, received offices under his stewardship. For three years, from 1957 until 1960, Kishi strengthened the position of the far right in the LDP, and fostered antipathy to the constitution. He kept an eye toward the future as well: the youngest member of the Kishi cabinet was Yasuhiro Nakasone, a member of the Kono faction and a protégé of Kodama, with whom he shared a secretary-adviser. Twenty-two years later, in 1982, the hawkish Nakasone finally became Japan's prime minister with the help, not surprisingly, of Kodama.

But despite Kishi's seemingly firm hold on the right and on the prime ministry, he would, during his term, encounter furious opposition from an unexpected quarter – the student left.

The Ampo Struggle

In 1960, there erupted a prolonged period of demonstrations and conflict in Japan that would strain the LDP hold on the country, threaten briefly the relationship between the United States and Japan, and prove that the old alliance between rightist and gangster was more valuable than ever to those in power.

The Americans had been attempting to renegotiate the U.S.-Japan Security Pact, the mutual defense treaty between the two nations. Although it stipulated that America would continue to maintain bases in Japan, as it had under the terms of the peace treaty, the security pact put little actual burden on Japan. America was required to come to the aid of Japan if the latter were attacked, but Japan had no responsibility to help the Americans if that country were under attack elsewhere in the world. The Kishi government was anxious to see that the pact be swiftly concluded and ratified, but the treaty contained a number of provisions that many Japanese, particularly anyone even slightly left of center, thoroughly disliked.

The pact allowed American forces in Japan to be equipped with nuclear weapons – a matter of grave concern to the Japanese after Nagasaki and Hiroshima. It also allowed the United States to take action within Japan if the Japanese government requested aid to quell any internal disturbances, something the left believed was aimed at them. Basically, American interests were an outgrowth of later occupation goals – protecting their flank against Soviet and Chinese communism, and keeping Japan in the American orbit. American aims, though, did not necessarily sit well with the Japanese.

In the spring of 1960, an international incident polarized Japanese and American interests. On May 1, the Soviet Union shot down an American CIA reconnaissance plane, the U-2, over Russian territory. Although this particular overflight originated in Pakistan, another major U-2 base was at Atsugi, Japan. Japanese who were opposed to the stationing of the

U.S. military on Japanese soil saw the U-2s as a magnet for Soviet bombers.

But even before the U-2 incident, grassroots opposition to the security pact had been brewing in Japan. By March 1959, in fact, a wide-ranging progressive coalition was formed – the People's Council for Preventing Revision of the Security Treaty, the *Ampo Joyaku Kaitei Soshi Kokumin Kaigi,* generally called simply *Ampo.* This coalition contained every left-of-center group and then some. There were labor, education, women's, and Marxist groups, ranging from the Japan Anarchists League to the Executive Committee of the Japan Group Singing Association. But when it came time to take the case to the streets of Tokyo, Ampo drew its troops primarily from the city's huge student population, from the leftist movement known as Zengakuren.

Quickly, the right responded, and it was immediately evident that the old alliance was working. According to a contemporary newspaper account, "In an attempt to cope with rallies staged by leftist forces against the security pact, rightist bodies organized a number of public meetings favoring the pact. Among them were a rally sponsored by the Patriotic Party at the Hibya Public Hall on July 25, 1959, and another held by the Matsuba-kai [The Pine Needle Association, a major yakuza gang] at the same site on September 25."

The appearance of the yakuza group was the first indication that the right might not be content merely to sway public opinion. By themselves, rightists and yakuza would get nowhere with the public who, for the most part, supported the leftist position. But the momentum produced by the Ampo forces frightened the more conservative elements in the business and political communities. Kishi, in particular, had a lot of personal ambition staked on the passage of the treaty, and did not want to let the despised left do anything to endanger its ratification.

On May 19, 1960, amid a series of massive public demonstrations by the Ampo people, the LDP took the extraordinary step of physically barring the Socialists from the Diet chambers and ramrodding the treaty through to ratification. All that remained was the formal signing in June. This was to coincide with a state visit from President Eisenhower. The demonstrations, however, did not subside and the government was forced to take the Ampo factions seriously. Not that the treaty should be reconsidered, but that the demonstrators ought to be silenced, or at least contained.

By the May 19 ratification, events had grown noisy, with frequent fighting between demonstrators and police or, often, rightist thugs. But there had been a certain restraint on both sides and no loss of life on either.

The Kishi people, though, were not at all confident that their police and rightist supporters could contain the Ampo demonstrators at a critical time. With Ike's visit imminent, the LDP's top leadership then took a historic step backwards – it turned to the underworld in the hopes of fashioning a criminal reserve army comprised of the yakuza and the far right.

The initial conduit between the LDP and the mob was Yoshio Kodama, who pledged his support and assured the politicians that this could indeed be accomplished. The LDP then sent its emissary, the head of the party's "Welcome Ike" committee, Tomisaburo Hashimoto, to a meeting of gangster bigwigs. Hashimoto contacted a number of influential yakuza: Kakuji Inagawa, head of the huge Kinsei-kai; Yoshimitsu Sekigami, oyabun of the Tokyo-based Sumiyoshi-kai; and "Tokyo's Al Capone," Kinosuke Ozu, still leader of the massive tekiya association. All agreed to help. To make sure the organization was tight, Kodama remained the linchpin of the operation. To him, it must have been the call of the wild: the government of Japan was once again, as in prewar days, summoning a patriotic underworld army. It was as if the Black Dragon Society itself were reborn.

In a sense, the government had no choice. Eisenhower was expected to arrive on June 21 and to drive from Tokyo airport accompanied by the emperor in an open limousine. The idea of an attack on the car was horrifying to the LDP politicos planning the motorcade. In the face of the anticipated demonstration, authorities planned to mobilize 18,000 police – enough to line the route with cops stationed every two yards. There were up to 15,000 Tokyo police available, and there were plans to requisition police from cities hundreds of miles away, but the LDP decided to rely on irregulars as well.

Three rightist coalitions were called upon for troops. One, the New Japan Council, organized in 1958 by Kishi himself and headed by Tokutaro Kimura, was to be a source of nonviolent types, people who would mass themselves in support of Ike. For heavier action, the government could draw on the All-Japan Council of Patriotic Organizations, composed of rightists and gangsters. In the distant reserve were some 300,000 members of the Japan Veterans League, a group that included some of the ultranationalist wartime leaders.

The final plans for June 21 were described by veteran Tokyo journalist Koji Nakamura, writing in the *Far Eastern Economic Review:*

"Kodama persuaded yakuza leaders of organized gamblers, gangsters, extortionists, street vendors and members of underground syndicates to organize an 'effective counter-force' to ensure Eisenhower's safety. The final plan called for the deployment of 18,000 yakuza, 10,000 street vendors [tekiya], 10,000 veterans and members of rightist religious organizations. They were supported by government-supplied helicopters, Cessna aircraft, trucks, cars, food, command posts, and first-aid squads, in addition to some 800 million yen [about $2,300,000] in 'operational funds.' "

It was a remarkable feat of organization, and from the point of view of the Japanese government, concluded none too soon. Eleven days before Eisenhower's scheduled arrival, the Japanese got a taste of what the President's visit might be like. U.S. Ambassador Douglas MacArthur II (nephew to the general) met Eisenhower's press secretary, James Hagerty, at the Tokyo airport, and on the return drive their limousine was cut off, surrounded by angry demonstrators. MacArthur and Hagerty had to be rescued by military helicopter.

Five days later, MacArthur cabled State Department headquarters and conveyed the Japanese plans to protect Ike, although his notion of these plans was at some divergence with reality. In addition to police, wrote MacArthur, waiting along the route would be welcoming groups of Boy and Girl Scouts, as well as adults friendly to the President. These, he said, "will be in sufficiently great numbers to overwhelm any unfriendly demonstration and will ensure that [the] president receives [a] proper welcome." But in case the scouts failed to deter the Ampo demonstrators, MacArthur wrote, ". . . 30,000 young men of various athletic organizations and strongly opposed to zengakuren [the students] are being issued arm bands for identification and will, if required, assist police."

The "athletes" never got the call, because at the very same time as MacArthur was cabling Washington with the good news, the demonstrations reached a new peak. The left did not back down in the face of the rightist threats, but pushed on against the treaty. Finally, on the evening of June 15, the demonstrations outside the Diet building reached another peak and this time events went too far. Gangsters and rightists battling the students seriously injured a number of protestors and killed a young co-ed from Tokyo University.

It was enough. The Japanese government withdrew the invitation to Eisenhower, fearing more deaths and even greater embarrassment. The confrontation between left and right over the visit would probably have been more disastrous than the shame of cancellation. But the drama was not yet over.

Three days later, 300,000 leftists moved through the streets of Tokyo shouting "Ampo hantai" (Down with the treaty) and "Kishi taose" (Overthrow Kishi). But at midnight on the 18th of June, the treaty was automatically afforded final ratification, and on the 21st, the emperor's seal was fixed upon the security pact. It is very unlikely that the United States would have removed its bases had the treaty been rejected, but with the ratification, both the LDP and Washington were satisfied.

Someone still had to pay for the massive anguish and disruption the country had suffered through, and on June 23, Kishi announced that he would resign as prime minister, an act that indeed defused the Ampo demonstrations. Three weeks later he turned the government over to another conservative, Hayato Ikeda. The Ampo forces at the time believed that they had effected an important change, but the LDP was returned to office by a wide margin at the next election, and the security pact remained in effect.

Kishi had not been personally popular as prime minister, and never recovered his position of public power, but he continued to work behind the scenes. By giving the coalition of rightists and yakuza the official imprimatur of the government, Kishi reinstated a tradition dating back to the dark days of ultranationalism. His actions, furthermore, legitimized the postwar ties between the government and the underworld and ushered in a twenty-year period of gangster-rightist cooperation.

Perhaps the most enduring institution on the right stemming from the Ampo period is the Zen Nippon Aikokusha Dantai Kaigi, the All-Japan Council of Patriotic Organizations. By the early 1960s, Zen Ai Kaigi, as it was invariably known, had quickly grown into the leading Japan-wide federation of rightist groups, with a total membership of over 150,000. It was from the outset a true coalition, with 440 groups ultimately participating. In the subsequent years, Zen Ai Kaigi provided both political theory and political muscle to the right, and many of its ventures were under the direction of Kodama and his close allies.

Kodama did not create Zen Ai Kaigi by himself. He was only one of a network of influential rightists behind the organization, all aided by a number of yakuza leaders as well. The oyabun of Nippon Kokusui-kai, Matsuba-kai, Gijin-to, and others were "advisers" to the group. And on the board of directors were names out of the past: Tatsuo Amano, who led an abortive coup in 1933; Kozaburo Tachibana, who was involved in the prewar assassination of a prime minister; and Tadashi Onuma, the murderer of Finance Minister Junosuke Inouye. Ryoichi Sasakawa, with his growing financial clout, sat on the Board, as did former G-2 sidekick Giichi Miura.

Although Zen Ai Kaigi adhered to general rightist principles, it did not have a clear program. It did, however, launch actions that went beyond mere advocacy. Early in its existence, for instance, Zen Ai Kaigi received a request from a steel fabricating firm in Chiba, a prefecture near Tokyo, to help the company with its labor problems. Specifically it was asked to break up a strike. So well did Zen Ai Kaigi tackle the task that the union was broken up and 680 people were hospitalized. These were obviously not theoreticians at work.

In fact, so prevalent were yakuza among Zen Ai Kaigi's membership that some observers called it Yakuza Kaigi. It was fitting, then, that the organization chose its leadership with an eye to holding the yakuza within the coalition. The organization's second chairman and longtime boss was a Buddhist priest named Keizo Takei, a man who had been a yakuza in his youth, and a spy and saboteur in the 1930s.

Factions within the huge coalition were common. In April 1961, yakuza groups within Zen Ai Kaigi – Matsuba-kai, Nippon Kokusui-kai, Nippon Yoshihito-to – withdrew from the alliance and formed an all-yakuza rightist coalition, the Nippon Jiyu Shugi Renmei. That same year, a more activist group loyal to Yoshio Kodama formed within the Zen Ai Kaigi. This was the Seinen Shiso Kenkyu-kai, known as Seishi-kai, the Youth Ideology Study Association. Despite its innocent-sounding name, Seishi-kai was far more criminally inclined than the parent group. Its chairman and actual organizer was one Tomeo Sagoya, the former head of the Fatherland Protection Corps, who was implicated in the 1930 assassination of Prime Minister Osachi Hamaguchi and imprisoned in 1955 for extortion. Seishi-kai had its subgroups as well; one of these was headed by a former boss of Tokyo's huge Sumiyoshi syndicate, and another by the Korean crime boss, Hisayuki Machii.

Kodama assumed greater control over Seishi-kai in the 1960s until, at the end of the decade, amid intense factional infighting, he withdrew the organization from Zen Ai Kaigi. Shortly thereafter, 120 Seishi-kai stalwarts headed for the mountains of Niigata Prefecture, north of Tokyo. There they established a military training camp and learned the basics of street fighting, physical fitness, and bomb throwing. Kodama maintained a watchful eye on his troops, and at the end of the training, he sent them off with an inspirational message: "I hope that each of you will kill one hundred enemies for one, instead of one for one."

Just how many enemies, if any, Seishi-kai killed is unknown, but Kodama's efforts were not in vain. Instead of being used on the front lines against Communist revolution, Seishi-kai members fought against unfavorable publicity in Japan. In early 1971, a journalist named Hisatomo

Takemori was in the process of publishing a book on Kodama and friends, entitled *Black Money*. When Seishi-kai chairman Masayoshi Takahashi heard of this blasphemous act, he leaned rather heavily on the publisher, preventing the printing and distribution of the work. He was subsequently charged with threatening the publisher, but the message came through – no books about Kodama unless the boss agrees.

The legacy of Ampo, then, was a power base that could not actually seize the reins of government, but was a constant, simmering force. Men like Kodama could use it either for their own personal ends – such as silencing an unfriendly book publisher – or for larger political aims – breaking a strike, collecting funds for candidates, intimidating leftists. The real winners were Kodama and those aligned with him.

Rise of the Gangster Shoguns

The war's aftermath continued to produce changes in yakuza methods and structure. For one thing, the yakuza became individually and collectively more violent. The older bakuto gangs were often appalled at the lack of ceremony in the newer mobs, the so-called gurentai, but there was usually little anyone could do. Swords were on their way out and guns were coming in. Ordinary citizens now could be the targets of yakuza as robberies and street shakedowns increased. The yakuza did not necessarily walk in the shadows while the commoners walked in the sun, as they traditionally claimed to do.

The yakuza also began to look different. Under the steady influence of the Americans, both during and after the occupation, the yakuza began to assume some of the characteristics of their American gangster counterparts. Yakuza who swore to uphold traditional values were as entranced with American styles as any Japanese, but as often was the case, Japanese perceptions of Americans were somewhat skewed. Since yakuza didn't know any real American gangsters, they turned to the movies instead. They seemed to focus in on gangster parodies, and the result was that the characters of *Guys and Dolls* rather than *White Heat* or *The Petrified Forest* were their models. The kobun took to dressing in dark suits, dark shirts, and white ties. Sunglasses were *de rigueur,* and in the 1960s, yakuza affected crewcuts and kept them for a longer time perhaps than anyone else in the world. To match their outfits, they affected a leer and a swagger that set them apart from the ordinary citizens. Yakuza leaders also acquired a taste for an imported luxury that may seem ironic today – foreign (principally American) cars. Even today, yakuza leaders are among the few customers for large American sedans in Japan.

The structure of the gangs started changing as well. Out of the chaos of the occupation, some syndicates began to enlarge and dominate their regions through war or alliance. Where prewar gangs tended to remain small – an oyabun and up to fifty kobun – postwar gangs began to swell up to hundreds, sometimes thousands, of members overseen by dozens of sub-oyabun. The postwar tekiya gangs had already formed into the massive Roten Dogyo Kumiai under Tokyo boss Ozu, but by the time of the peace treaty, the new gangs began to make moves to consolidate the underworld. Observed the newspaper *Mainichi* in 1964, "As Japan's economy grows, the big companies expand their markets and absorb smaller enterprises under their control and become mammoth in size. So does the same process take place in the world of violence."

In addition to centralization of power, the gangs added numbers. The Tokyo metropolitan police estimated that in 1958 there were 70,000 yakuza in the whole of Japan; five years later the number had swelled to 184,000, possibly the largest organized crime syndicates in history, more men than in Japan's entire army that year. The actual number was probably less than the number of people engaged in criminal activity under the occupation, but these were not mere black-market swindlers. Most were committed criminals aligned in some 5200 gangs, preying upon an economy growing at breakneck speed.

Some analysts, such as noted yakuza expert Kenji Ino, a Tokyo-based journalist, believe that the high membership was due in part to large numbers of shop owners and operators of entertainment businesses who joined as associates. This period saw the entertainment districts more crowded than ever, and club and restaurant owners were anxious to avoid trouble with the gangs, so they enlisted. By the time the 1964 Tokyo Olympics rolled around, though, the police had finally begun a systematic crackdown on the gangs, ending the postwar period of official tolerance.

During the twenty years following the war, there was one gang that prospered mightily under the new regime of violence and acquisition – the Yamaguchi-gumi. Beginning life as an ordinary Kobe waterfront mob, the Yamaguchi-gumi grew rapidly during the occupation. Like many of the others, it was patterned on the structure of the ancient bakuto gangs, but used the violent tactics of the newer gurentai. Within five years of the end of American rule, the gang came to control most of the area around the nearby metropolis of Osaka, and by the end of the decade had begun to expand nationally. The story of the postwar Yamaguchi mob begins before the war and is very much the story of its longtime boss, Kazuo Taoka.

Born in a small village on the southern island of Shikoku in 1913, Taoka was orphaned at a young age and sent to work at a Kobe shipyard. There, at age fourteen, he began to associate with members of a small gang headed by Noboru Yamaguchi, a gang that took its name from its titular head. For nine years, Taoka was basically an apprentice member and ran errands, waited on the boss, and worked himself up to regular gang tasks. He earned a reputation for ferocity in fights, gouging opponents' eyes out with his fingers. Taoka's comrades soon nicknamed him *Kuma*, "The Bear." In 1936, he became a blood member of the group and the same year found himself looking at an eight-year prison sentence for slashing to death a rival gang member.

Kazuo Taoka spent half the war in prison, and when he walked out in 1943 he was welcomed back to a gang decimated by police crackdowns and the military draft. Shortly after the war, in October 1946, Taoka, thirty-three, assumed the mantle of oyabun when Noboru Yamaguchi died of illness. The young boss had only twenty-five devoted kobun, but he had developed a remarkable talent for organization. Those resources, combined with his legendary ruthlessness, would propel him to greatness in the underworld.

The Bear learned that enterprise was as valuable as brutality, and he quickly discovered new ways to prosper. On the Kobe docks, he founded the Yamaguchi-gumi Construction Company and began work on local projects with his obedient work force. At the same time, he moved to grab a greater share of the local gambling and extortion rackets. In the late 1940s, he formed an alliance with the largest local bakuto gang, the Honda-kai, but Taoka was too ambitious to remain locked in a relationship of parity. The ensuing gang war showed the superiority of Taoka's killers over traditional gamblers, and Taoka took over Honda-kai's rackets, incorporating the weaker gang into his own. A Korean mob, the Meiyu-kai, was next, and Taoka took over their Osaka territory. Then the Miyamoto-gumi fell to Taoka's men. He operated like a smart guerrilla leader, concentrating his forces and attacking savagely when the time was right.

Taoka also expanded the role of the traditional Osaka underworld and vastly increased his income. He launched into show business, forming a talent agency that pushed Osaka-area performers. Taoka put together a package of performers called Home Run Hit Parade and sent them on the road around Japan. The heart of his operation, however, remained in the Kobe docks. He continued to broker day laborers, and even took a financial interest in a number of cargo firms. By the mid-1960s, the

Yamaguchi syndicate controlled an estimated 80 percent of all cargo load-
ing on the Kobe docks. At the same time, Taoka had a piece of some
fourteen firms in the area – mostly cargo transport companies – that
grossed him nearly $17 million in 1965 alone.

By 1964, Taoka controlled 343 different gangs under the Yamaguchi
umbrella, and at the end of the decade could boast 10,000 kobun. His
success was noted by political figures on the right. Taoka's front company, the Association of Harbor Stevedoring Promotion, received financial backing from Tokyo rightist Seigen Tanaka and political support from
Kodama ally Ichiro Kono, then minister of transportation. Taoka was
viewed as a controller of labor, one who could keep leftist unions off the
docks. By the late 1950s, Taoka was a political power to be reckoned with
and was feared and courted widely.

In the area around Tokyo, no one gang came to dominate as the
Yamaguchi-gumi had done in Osaka. But even in this competitive situation, a very few gangs rose to the top, either through muscle, influence, or
both. One of the premier gangs was that of Kakuji Inagawa, a Yokohama
bakuto with talents that in many ways equaled those of Kazuo Taoka.

During the occupation, ethnic Koreans and Chinese became particularly powerful in the port city of Yokohama, outside Tokyo. Not only did
they control that city's black market, but they expanded their operations
down the coast to the hot springs resort of Atami. Dismayed at the influence
of these "foreigners," Inagawa decided to help his mentor, Yokohama
oyabun Masajiro Tsuruoka, whose territory included Atami. Inagawa organized a small gang to fight the Chinese and Koreans alongside Tsuruoka's men. Inagawa's gangsters displayed a legendary ruthlessness in
chasing the non-Japanese from the area, and within several years Inagawa
had built his own gang to equal that of Tsuruoka. Together, their activities
expanded through the region, including among other places Shimizu, historic fighting ground of that most famous of all yakuza, Jirocho of Shimizu.

By 1950, both Inagawa and Tsuruoka had come to the attention of
the occupation authorities. The American consul general in Yokohama
cabled Washington with this observation: "The activities of this gang
ranged from blackmail and intimidation, in connection with the collection
of 'protection' money, to control and direction of bands of thieves which
were regularly placed aboard foreign merchant ships calling at Yokohama
and Shimizu in the guise of cleaning crews."

Inagawa weathered the displeasure of the American authorities. By
the early 1960s, Inagawa and his gang, the Kakusei-kai, had spread from
their initial territory in Yokohama and Atami to Tokyo and even to parts
of the northern island of Hokkaido. By 1964, more than 2700 yakuza

stood under his command. The gang's major source of money came from gambling enterprises. Despite the widespread legalization of betting on races, cards and casino gambling were still forbidden, and bakuto such as Inagawa could make a sizable fortune running such games. According to the Tokyo Metropolitan Police, Inagawa took in $175,000 from one high-stakes card game in 1965, a fee just for running the game.

By 1963, Inagawa was feeling the heat of too much police attention and changed the name of his gang to Kinsei-kai. The new name would go along with his new status – he applied for the registration of Kinsei-kai as a political party. Political solidarity for the gangs was usually problematic. Although Inagawa's syndicate, like others, shared a gut-level ideology of anticommunism and a rightist outlook, alliances were hard to come by. The day-to-day enemy most gangs dealt with was certainly not the remote threat of a Communist takeover of Japan, but that of other gangs, a factor that made yakuza unity a pleasant fiction. At least one person, though, had the vision and the power to deal with the factionalization in the underworld. He would forge alliances and speed the modernization of the yakuza, ensuring that the political and financial development of Japan's underworld kept pace with the nation's rapidly expanding economy. That person was Yoshio Kodama.

Kodama saw that the gangster coalition he put together during the Ampo crisis could perhaps be reconstituted as a permanent entity. It would also provide Kodama with a valuable source of power. Certainly Kodama would strengthen his own hand with the LDP by showing an ability to control both the far right and the warring gangster clans. That control would soon alarm much of the Japanese government.

In December 1963, an unusual leaflet was sent out to all national LDP legislators. It warned Diet members:

> While the Liberal-Democratic Party is occupied incessantly in factional feuds, the leftist influences in Japan are accumulating their energy for revolution. . . . You should realize that what is contaminating Japan the most today is the factional policies of the Liberal-Democratic Party and its intra-party feuds. . . . Before the public's goodwill toward the party changes into a feeling of hatred, all of you should cease intra-party feuds.

Several members of one LDP faction were identified by name in the leaflet, but that was not the most startling thing about it. Such alarmist statements from the right were common enough, and would ordinarily be ignored. But the signers of the statement were a combination of seven yakuza groups, some of the most powerful in Japan. Japanese Diet members were stunned. That gangsters were involved in politics was no surprise, but that a giant federation had formed and was pointedly suggesting national policy was a new and generally unwelcome development.

These seven participating gangs were the components of a coalition formed in December 1963 at the Tsuruya Hotel in Inagawa's resort town of Atami, under the guidance of Kodama. After the meeting commenced with the singing of the national anthem and three hearty banzai, Kodama got to the crux of the matter:

> When we have scuffles, before we shed our blood, let us solve them by discussion. Let us only use our physical strength when we are in danger of a leftist revolution in Japan or when some natural calamity visits us. I hope with this as a starting point, each group would try to maintain friendly relations with the others, and thus try to improve the character of your organizations.

It was true that there were "scuffles" among the gangs, although murderous vendettas would better describe them, and perhaps Kodama genuinely deplored the violence. But he was motivated more by a political vision than anything else. The ideology behind the new alliance grew out of the prewar rightist concept of a Toa Doyu-kai, or Asian Federation, to be used "as a breakwater against communism in time of national crisis," as one commentator put it. The fact that Japan in 1963 was not by any stretch of the imagination facing that sort of national crisis did nothing to deter Kodama.

Rather than a pan-Asian federation, Kodama now envisioned an all-Japan gangster coalition. But in February 1963, when Kodama was holding preliminary talks on the subject, Kazuo Taoka abruptly withdrew his Osaka gang from any proposed federation. From all-Asia, Kodama eventually wound up with an all-Tokyo coalition – the Kanto-kai, named after the Kanto Plain encompassing Tokyo. Nonetheless, it was a formidable organization, comprised of 13,000 gangsters from seven major gangs and headed by Kakuji Inagawa. If Kodama could now pull the gangs together as a functional unit, he would have one of Japan's strongest organizations at his disposal.

Kodama was aided in his task by a group of rightist theorists who bombarded Kanto-kai with messianic dogma. One popular theory was the Showa 45 Crisis theory, which stated that in 1970 (Showa 45, or the forty-fifth year of Emperor Hirohito's reign) Japan would face a leftist revolution. The right, the gangsters were told, had to present a united front. But for most of the members, rightist thought was uncomplicated and direct. Perhaps Kakuji Inagawa said it most eloquently: "We gamblers cannot walk in broad daylight. But if we unite and become a wall to stop communism, we can be of service to the nation. If anything happens, we would like to stake our lives for the good of the country."

Not all participants found these political aims worthy or even necessary. Yoshimitsu Sekigami, president of the Sumiyoshi-kai, said: "We are in the Kanto-kai with the idea that it is an association for amity. I do not believe that Japanese politics is in such a poor state that gamblers must interfere with it."

For some of the gangs, though, political action and posturing were long a part of their repertoire, and Kanto-kai represented no more than a formalization of that tactic. Uichiro Fujita, boss of the 2400-member Matsuba-kai, for instance, publicly fulminated against the "subversive" nature of the Japan Teachers' Union – a favorite target of the right – and demanded that the government fund a school for military arts. The Matsuba-kai also threatened the leadership of the communications workers for daring to engage in a strike. And, Fujita took his members to a mass rally of 3000 gangsters and rightists protesting the Tokyo visit of Soviet Deputy Premier Anastas Mikoyan. Matsuba-kai was of course criminally active as well; members averaged one arrest for every day of the year, the second highest rate of any Tokyo-area gang. This record led police to conclude that Fujita's political involvement was largely a smoke screen for his far more lucrative criminal activities.

Kodama's attitude toward the overtly criminal activities of the gangs was ambivalent. On the one hand, he saw fit to attack the growing problem of street crime, the *gyangu,* or teenage wolf packs. ("Gyangu" can mean "stupid," "pigheaded," or simply "gang.") "There are too many petty hoodlums," Kodama said. "It made me angry to see them loitering around and causing trouble to passersby. . . . That is why I tell the oyabun to rectify their own character first and control the petty hoodlums themselves." Clearly, organized rackets did not fall into the same category; these Kodama did not condemn.

Kodama walked a thin line with Kanto-kai, trying to whip the gangs into a unit, but ultimately it was beyond even his organizational abilities. In slightly more than a year the federation began to fall apart under the strain of competing interests. In January 1965, the thirty executive members of the seven bodies voted to dissolve Kanto-kai, after only fifteen months. But if the organization failed, Kodama did not go down with it.

During the mid-1960s, everything seemed to turn Kodama's way. Not only top LDP figures, but business and professional and even academic people paid him honors with their presence. His house in Tokyo's Setagaya district was the scene of constant meetings and audiences before the great Kodama *sensei* (teacher). Kodama sometimes received prominent foreign visitors. With a surgeon, he would discuss how to raise money for a research facility, while with a politician he would offer help in campaigning.

To the oyabun who stopped by, Kodama was a towering figure. Said Inagawa: "I am sometimes made to wait for seven hours at his house, but when I listen to his talk, I come to understand the world." Even Taoka, who refused to join Kanto-kai, found Kodama a figure worthy of some respect. "I am positively opposed to the idea of his reigning as the boss of the yakuza," said Taoka, "but if he stays a patriot, I am most willing to become his companion." In fact, Taoka would come to depend on Kodama for more than ideological inspiration.

Kodama's pivotal role as a bridge between the gangs and the echelons of legitimate power was understood by many, but not generally acknowledged. It was, therefore, something of a milestone when, in July 1964, the national *Mainichi* newspaper published an exhaustive fourteen-part series on the underground gangs and their relation to aboveground power. Investigative reporting in Japan does not have the tradition that it enjoys in the United States, and for a major daily to commit itself to a six-month investigation and risk treading on the toes of some dangerous and powerful people was a major accomplishment. Although the paper was attacked for the series, it had its supporters. In its final segment, *Mainichi* quoted Toshio Eguchi, director of the National Police Agency (NPA). Eguchi took to task what he perceived as the hypocrisy of Japanese power:

> *"Although our political and financial circles ever complain about organized violence, they continue to contribute money to the various groups. In order to eradicate violence from our society, we must give the underworld no political consideration. It must be relentlessly smashed from all directions."*

It was a courageous statement, but it had little effect on those rightist politicians and financiers who customarily worked with the yakuza. Police did crack down on the gangs, but otherwise it was business as usual, and Kodama, for the time being, remained untouched.

The structure of the gang world continued to change in the 1960s. Previously, Taoka's Yamaguchi-gumi had confined their predatory activities to the Kansai area around Osaka and Kyoto, generally avoiding Tokyo and its surrounding regions. One of the purposes of Kanto-kai, from the point of view of the participants, if not of Kodama, was to present a united front to any moves Taoka might make into Kanto. There was more than just economic interest at play. Residents of Kansai and Kanto foster a great regional rivalry, like Americans on opposite sides of the Mason-Dixon line. There are cultural and political differences, of course, but they are not usually a serious issue. In a gang war, though, these differences can be expected to exacerbate matters.

Kanto-kai did not have any deterrent effect on Taoka. During the short tenure of the alliance, Taoka's syndicate, Yamaguchi-gumi, began sending people into Yokohama and incurring the wrath of Inagawa. There was, in fact, such friction between Inagawa's men and the arriving Yamaguchi thugs that an armed battle known as the Grand Palace incident took place on the streets of Yokohama.

Kodama viewed the warfare as deplorable, a threat to anticommunist unity, and used his connections to secure a peace. His solution was to facilitate an expedient alliance between Taoka and Machii, Korean boss of Tokyo's Tosei-kai. Machii traveled to Kobe for the ceremony uniting the two gangs, and the ensuing alliance helped break Kanto-kai for good. Again Kodama used his good offices to mediate between Inagawa and his Kanto allies, and Taoka. A truce was called, and Taoka accepted a limitation of no more than ten men in the Yokohama area.

Taoka sought to evade this restriction by an elaborate ploy devised by his friend Seigen Tanaka, rightist and Kodama rival. Together they created the cynically named League for the Stamping Out of Drug Traffic, and promoted it in both Kansai and Kanto. Taoka asserted that he began the organization because of the damage to his men caused by drug use during the occupation. "It was simply agonizing to see them when they were out of the drugs," he claimed. "Their wives had an awful time, and they tried to have their husbands recuperate by imprisoning them in the house, but half of them died and half of them became invalid."

In the Osaka area, Taoka used some of Tanaka's connections and found unusual allies. President Masatoshi Matsushita of Rikkyo University and Masako Hika, head of the Kansai Housewives Association, joined with the gang boss in publicly demonstrating against drug use. Taoka then sent his men to the Tokyo area under the guise of fighting the drug menace. In Yokohama, Yamaguchi men were in the streets in October 1963 attempting to gather signatures for a petition denouncing drugs, an act that infuriated the Inagawa gang.

The police and the public, as well, rightly viewed with some suspicion a notorious crime syndicate vowing to stamp out drug traffic. It was a remarkable display of yakuza nerve, but it worked. The Yamaguchi gang maintained their presence in the Tokyo-Yokohama area and continued to pressure the other gangs, especially Inagawa's Kinsei-kai.

The antidrug campaign took a new turn in November 1963 when Tosei-kai member Haruo Kinoshita shot and seriously wounded Seigen Tanaka, architect of the campaign. Kinoshita had seen that Taoka, by allying himself with the Tosei-kai boss Machii, had forced the Korean gang into an isolated position in Tokyo. Other Kanto gangs were now blaming Tosei-kai for the Yamaguchi move into the capital region, so Kinoshita tried to remedy the situation.

Taoka took the assassination attempt as a personal attack, although Tanaka made a remarkable recovery and left the hospital after only four months. Machii felt himself responsible for the assassin's action, even though the latter had acted on his own. Machii traveled to Kobe to make his amends. With him he brought two items that would prevent a possible gang war: two million yen for Tanaka, and his fingertip for Taoka.

Tensions between Taoka and Inagawa remained high, however, until the Tokyo oyabun was found guilty of operating an illegal gambling casino and sentenced to three years in prison. Taoka took stock of the situation and directed all Yamaguchi members in Fukushima Prison to help make Inagawa's stay as pleasant as possible, reasoning that Inagawa would then be in his debt. When Inagawa was released in January 1969 he found that his gang had been seriously reduced by disorganization, mutiny, and arrest. In fact, three-quarters of his members had been arrested in the previous year. The situation called for strong action: first, through a series of decisive moves, he subdued the unrest among the various gangs in his fiefdom. Of far greater importance to Japan's underworld, Inagawa decided that the Yamaguchi gang was too powerful to fight any longer. Inagawa, faced with both the carrot and the stick, found that alliance with Taoka was both reasonable and possibly beneficial.

To lay the groundwork for the alliance, Inagawa turned to Kodama, who then made the arrangements. On October 24, 1972, the long-range plans came to fruition. That day, ten men wearing crewcuts and dark suits got out of four black American cars in front of Taoka's Kobe house. Because of the heavy police surveillance, no bosses from other gangs were invited to the ceremony.

In Taoka's living room, his two top men, Kenichi Yamamoto and Yoshio Masuda, faced off against Inagawa lieutenants Susumu Ishii and Hsiao Chun-shu. It was a classic rite of *sakazuki*, the choreographed exchange of sake to create a blood brotherhood between two forces. Small altars, called *sambo,* were placed before Yamamoto and Ishii, and the go-between said solemnly:

"The ritual to tie the bond of brotherhood between Kenichi Yamamoto, representing leader Taoka of the Yamaguchi gang, and Susumu Ishii, representing the Inagawa gang will now commence."

Sake was poured into unglazed ceremonial cups and drunk. The two then wrapped the cups in special paper and put them into their kimono. They then clasped each other's hands. The go-between held their clasped hands and announced:

"The sake cup [brotherhood] ritual on even terms is now over."

A quiet reception followed, almost masking the enormity of the occasion. Between them, the two syndicates controlled or had alliances with gangs in virtually all of Japan; only four prefectures were wholly independent of the Yamaguchi-Inagawa combine. A process of conglomeration begun in the early 1950s was reaching its peak, and Yoshio Kodama, the underworld's visionary godfather, was reaping the benefits.

Kodama himself always scoffed at the notion of being boss of the yakuza, but then he also denied that he enjoyed immense power. His goal, as he told the newspaper *Mainichi* in 1964, was simply to retire.

"I would like to wash my hands of the worthless everyday world and enjoy my life fishing, for instance," he said. In fact, Kodama was quite the fisherman. He even included a photo of himself flycasting from a boat midstream, on the flyleaf of his autobiographical *Sugamo Diary*. Given the purpose of the photo, it's unlikely that Kodama's mind at the time was only on trout or carp. For him, the period from 1960 to the middle of the 1970s was one where nearly every cast brought in a fish. He, and the organizations he represented – from the thugs in the streets, to the yakuza, to his minions inside the government – had reached the summit of power. Kodama had an army of rightists and gangsters at his call, millions of dollars in his hands, and a government both corrupt and complicit. The underworld's scowling power broker had become the most powerful man in Japan.

Chapter 4
The Black Mist

As the lights glared in room 4221 of the Dirksen Senate Office Building, the Honorable Frank Church pored over his voluminous notes. Assembled before him stirred a huge, expectant crowd of reporters, spectators, and the investigative staff of his own Subcommittee on Multinational Corporations. It was Wednesday, February 4, 1976, and Frank Church, Democratic senator from Idaho and presidential aspirant, was ready to deliver the fruit of six months' labor.

At 10:01 A.M, Church called the hearing to order:

> *"We will hear today first from Lockheed's accounting firm, Arthur Young and Company, and then from the responsible Lockheed executives themselves, about bribes and questionable political payments made in Europe and Japan.*
>
> *"We will find that the company has used an off-the-books account to buy business intelligence and pay the officials of major European consortia . . . we will see that Exxon and the CIA have not been the only ones making million-dollar political contributions to parties and government ministers in Italy . . . and, most disturbing of all, we will show that Lockheed has for many years employed as its agent a prominent leader of the ultra-right wing militarist faction in Japan and has paid him millions of dollars in fees and commissions over the last few years.*
>
> *"In effect, we have had a foreign policy of the U.S. Government which has vigorously opposed this political line in Japan and a Lockheed foreign policy which has helped to keep it alive through large financial subsidies in support of the company's sales efforts in the country."*

To the witness stand that week in Washington, D.C., Church summoned forth a nervous handful of top officials and accountants representing the Lockheed Aircraft Corporation. The witnesses for the first time publicly testified how during the past twenty years Lockheed had secretly funneled more than $12.6 million into Japan, much of it apparently spent on illegal payoffs to the country's most powerful political figures. This huge sum was expended in an effort to sell more than $1 billion worth of Lockheed aircraft to Japan's number-two airline, All Nippon Airways, and to the defense agency of the Japanese government. Roughly $7 million of the amount, most of it in yen bills packed in cardboard boxes, had been covertly passed to Lockheed's secret sales agent in Japan – the ubiquitous Yoshio Kodama.

Headlines raced across Japan's newspapers about the "Rokkiedo Jiken" (Lockheed Incident), and for the next year the scandal dominated the country's affairs. Lockheed became Japan's Watergate, the nation's biggest scandal in postwar history. The Japanese press recounted in minute detail the testimony of the subcommittee's star witness, Lockheed president Carl Kotchian, who reluctantly detailed the company's long history of secret payments to Kodama. Spurred by Kotchian's admissions, investigators would soon reveal that Lockheed's men had bribed their way into deals with Japan's leading politicians of the day. Before the scandal subsided, the list of bribed officials included Prime Minister Kakuei Tanaka; the secretary-general of the LDP; the ministers of industry and transportation; the chairman of the LDP's Special Committee on Aviation; and the current and former parliamentary vice-ministers of transportation. In addition, said investigators, Lockheed had thrown in a kickback of $50,000 to the president of All Nippon Airways on each airplane sold.

The revelations should not have come as a shock to the Japanese, given the postwar history of collusion between the nation's political and criminal underworlds. But the Japanese public had studiously ignored the warning signs. Although some journalists in Japan knew of the Lockheed payoffs as far back as the early 1960s, the press showed little interest in pursuing such a controversial story. The scandal brought up too much of what the Japanese had come to call *kuroi kiri* ("black mist"), the dark history of dirty tricks, corruption, and organized crime in Japan.

By 1976, however, the political system that Kodama helped create had begun to unravel. The Lockheed revelations struck in an atmosphere already charged by the resignation fourteen months earlier of Prime Minister Kakuei Tanaka. Tanaka had been stung, in November 1974, by a two-part exposé in *Bungei Shunju,* a prestigious and widely read monthly. An unusual team of investigative reporters detailed for the first time the enormous sums of so-called black-money running through Tanaka's political network – more than $250 million channeled through dummy corporations from big business to members of his party faction. The reporters further estimated that some $15 million of this amount was used for payoffs within the LDP to secure the post of prime minister for Tanaka.

These revelations, coming only three months after Nixon's resignation over Watergate, threatened to cause heavy political damage to the prime minister. But Tanaka, nicknamed "The Computerized Bulldozer" for his political and financial skill, seemed undaunted. The prime minister, after all, had only expanded and shrewdly employed an already existing system of political gifts and payoffs.

Tanaka had good reason to believe that, like other postwar scandals, this one would pass quickly. Indeed, for the next week the Japanese press refused to touch the story. That changed, however, with Tanaka's appearance before the Foreign Correspondents' Club of Japan, where he was subjected to questions unusually direct and probing for the Japanese. The prime minister, humiliated and unnerved, stormed out of the club, but with the world's press onto the story, the scandal could no longer be ignored. Now, with a vengeance, the Japanese went after Tanaka's politics, his personal finances, and his evasion of income taxes. Two weeks after the *Bungei Shunju* story first appeared, Tanaka resigned as prime minister.

If the Japanese were getting ideas that even the office of prime minister could be bought and sold, the Lockheed scandal confirmed them. The Lockheed scandal went far beyond Tanaka's "money-power politics" to expose in three dimensions the extent of corruption in Japan. One authority on Japan, political scientist Chalmers Johnson of the University of California at Berkeley, summed up the scandal this way:

> *The details were shocking not so much because the Lockheed Company had smoothed the way for its sales of airplanes in Japan – there was plenty of evidence that Boeing, McDonnell Douglas, and Grumman were engaged in similar operations – but because the case took the Japanese back in time, to periods and people they would have liked to forget, to rightwingers and gangsters. . . . The case was serious since it deeply implicated officials of the transportation ministry, plus one of Japan's leading trading companies and the prime minister himself. Worst of all, it brought up the name Yoshio Kodama.*

The Lockheed Corporation and Mr. Kodama

Kodama's relationship with the Lockheed Corporation dates back to early 1958, when the forty-seven-year-old rightist was expanding his political power over both the rapidly growing yakuza gangs and the increasingly entrenched Liberal-Democratic Party. Kodama's contact was Taro Fukuda, a close friend from his postwar stay at Sugamo Prison. An interpreter by trade, Fukuda was born and educated in the United States, and came to Japan to attend Waseda University. U.S. officials revoked his American citizenship upon learning that he had worked for the Japanese government in occupied Manchuria.

Fukuda translated and published Kodama's rhetorical autobiography, *I Was Defeated,* and later, with Kodama's financial backing, founded a public relations agency. That agency was hired by Lockheed's man in Japan, John Kenneth Hull, to conduct a press campaign in the fast-growing country. Hull had arrived in Tokyo in December 1957, when his company moved into Japan to sell its F-104 Starfighter. Hull also put on Lockheed's payroll an assistant named Yoshiyoshi Oni, who would later become Lockheed's Tokyo office manager. Oni had served as an espionage agent in China during the war and later worked for the U.S. occupation, apparently as one of General Willoughby's recruits in G-2.

Worried that the Starfighter sales campaign was not going well, Hull asked Fukuda to suggest Japanese politicians who might help Lockheed present its case to the government. Instead, Fukuda recommended Kodama, and arranged for the two men to meet. Kodama subsequently agreed to become Lockheed's secret "consultant," with Fukuda as the go-between. This arrangement would last for the next eighteen years.

Kodama went to work and performed admirably for his new American client. By using his political connections, he lobbied successfully for Japan's defense agency to choose Lockheed's Starfighter over the Grumman F-11F. His key contacts in the government centered around three of Japan's most yakuza-tainted politicians: Bamboku Ohno, a leading Diet member and, at the time, the LDP's vice president; the powerful Ichiro Kono, another senior LDP official; and Nobusuke Kishi, who, of course, had risen to become prime minister with Kodama's backing.

Lockheed continued to rely on Kodama's services through the mid-1960s, although the company's demands were relatively light. That was probably just fine with Kodama, who had many other tasks before him. Infighting then plagued Zen Ai Kaigi, his national alliance of gangsters and rightists, until in 1969 the group's most activist members splintered off into the even more radical Seishi-kai, taking Kodama with them. But turning the yakuza into superpatriots was not always very lucrative, so when Lockheed had further plans for Japan, Kodama was glad to be of assistance.

By the end of the decade, Lockheed had renewed Kodama's contract and extended it to include South Korea as well. Soon he was at work again, this time unsuccessfully lobbying for the government purchase of yet another jet fighter. His failure may well have been due to a weakening hold over those controlling the LDP. Both Ohno and Kono had died in the mid-1960s, and Kodama had less influence over Prime Minister Kishi's successors, Eisaku Sato and Kakuei Tanaka. But Kodama was not easily discouraged. To underscore his sincerity to the prime minister, Kodama wrote Sato an open letter in 1968, stating: "If there was the smallest act of corruption among the parties directly or indirectly concerned with the selection of Japan's next fighters, it should be denounced severely as immoral conduct corrupting the politics of this country."

It was at about this point that Lockheed approached Kodama with its most critical task yet: the sale of its new wide-bodied passenger plane, the TriStar L1011. A large sale in Japan was deemed crucial by Lockheed executives, who needed it to help overcome financial problems elsewhere in the company. It was to be the jumbo jet sales war of the 1970s, with Lockheed going up against both Boeing and McDonnell Douglas in Japan.

In January 1969, Lockheed apparently began its first formal contract with Kodama, and from then on the money poured in. Kodama received $138,000 a year for "consultation," and was guaranteed a commission of $4 million for an initial order of three to six TriStars to any major Japanese airline. Kodama was also promised $120,000 each for the sale of the seventh through the fifteenth TriStars, and $60,000 more for each additional plane.

With the Kodama machinery now well oiled, Japan's leading power broker went into action. Lacking close connections to certain key LDP leaders, Kodama began to rely increasingly more on money to make things happen. A major problem was how to get to Tanaka, then chief of the powerful Ministry of International Trade and Industry and a candidate to succeed Sato as prime minister. Not having a close relationship with Tanaka, Kodama turned to a mutual friend, Kenji Osano.

Osano, one of Japan's wealthiest men, was a formidable kuromaku in his own right. He was a close friend and the largest individual backer of Tanaka. Osano was also the largest private shareholder in Japan Air Lines and a major investor in All Nippon Airways (ANA). So successful was Osano that the press, in tribute to his financial skill, had dubbed him with a host of titles: "The Takeover King," "The Business Sphinx," "The Ambulatory Cashbox," and "Monster Osano."

As Tanaka rose in political might after the war, Osano scored business success after success. By the mid-1950s, Osano had parlayed a dilapidated fleet of charcoal-burning buses into a fortune, in good part by supplying U.S. forces during the Korean War. In 1964 he bought his friend Tanaka's faltering construction firm for $6 million, an incredibly good deal for Tanaka.

It was at about the time Osano picked up Tanaka's company that he apparently became close to Yoshio Kodama. The newspaper *Asahi,* citing court records, states that in 1965 Osano provided Kodama with 200 million yen (about $550,000). "Mr. Kodama needed money for political purposes and asked for my help," reportedly testified Osano, "so I gave him a 200 million yen bill. . . ." Kodama, then busily organizing yakuza into rightist groups, no doubt put the money to use quickly.

By the time Kodama approached Osano in 1972 – this time on behalf of Lockheed – the latter had become a billionaire. Kodama's fellow kuromaku had built up a financial empire of real estate, hotels, airplanes, and banks. The $6 million development company he had bought from Tanaka in 1964 was by 1972 producing some $330 million in revenues. Osano's flagship company – Kokusai Kogyo – boasted 38 subsidiaries, all under his personal control. By the early 1970s, Osano's assets included nearly 40 hotels in Japan, Hawaii, and California, as well as ski areas, bowling alleys, taxi and bus companies, and restaurants. Osano's companies traded across the Pacific in everything from golf clubs to automobiles.

As he did in business, Osano made his political investments aggressively. Over the years, the tycoon had gained a reputation for making massive contributions to political candidates of both the LDP and the Socialist Party, contributions that rarely appeared on official lists of campaign spending. In the tradition of the kuromaku, Osano was owed a lot of debts by a lot of people. So when Kodama came knocking with a lucrative proposal regarding U.S. aircraft sales, Osano listened intently.

Of Money Changers and Mobsters

By 1971, the jumbo jet war was in full swing and Lockheed's president, Carl Kotchian, had arrived in Japan to personally take charge of the TriStar sales campaign. Although Kotchian had visited Japan at least once a year since 1961, it was only now that he finally met Kodama. Kotchian had read Kodama's *Sugamo Diary* before their first meeting, and although he knew his salesman bore an unsavory reputation, it hardly mattered to the corporate chieftain. In a 1976 interview with the newspaper *Asahi,* Kotchian admitted, "I was not much concerned about Mr.

Kodama's political ideas or behavior. It was enough to be told that he had an excellent record as an agent. . . ."

Kodama had indeed been confirming his worth during the past year. One of Lockheed's biggest obstacles was the president of All Nippon Airways, Tetsuo Oba, who had already taken an option for the McDonnell Douglas DC-10. Kodama knew that for Lockheed to be successful, Oba would have to go.

First, Kodama turned to Osano and advised his friend to move up as an ANA stockholder from 28th to 10th place, thus guaranteeing inside information on the company's affairs. (This cost Lockheed more than $200,000 in payments to Osano.) Next, Kodama activated one part of a large force of *sokaiya* under his command, financial racketeers who specialize in the extortion of Japanese corporations. The day before the ANA stockholders' meeting that year, Kodama's people leaked embarrassing information about a bogus one-million-dollar loan with which president Oba was connected. Kodama's racketeers then packed the shareholders' meeting, demanding information about the loan.

That was enough to topple Oba, who never showed up at the meeting and resigned the following day. In Oba's place Kodama installed a more pliable candidate, a recently retired vice-minister of transportation.

At one point, when Lockheed seemed in danger of losing the TriStar sale, Kodama pulled into the fray other movers and shakers in Japan. Among those he contacted, according to Kotchian, was Kodama's old friend and sometime rival, Ryoichi Sasakawa. Godfather of Japan's multibillion-dollar boat racing industry, Sasakawa was, like Kodama, no stranger to political and financial intrigue. Kodama had asked his former cellmate to intervene on behalf of Lockheed, for there were protests over landing the TriStar at Osaka's already too noisy Itami Airport. Sasakawa, among his many titles, was chairman of the Aircraft Nuisance Prevention Association, and although no payment was ever revealed, he saw to it that the TriStar would have no trouble meeting the airport's noise control levels.

Kotchian must have been impressed with these feats, for between 1970 and 1972 Kodama's fees jumped more than twentyfold, to more than $2.2 million. Kotchian soon came to call Kodama his "Department of State" in Japan. Although the deal was yet to be clinched, Kotchian could see the wind shifting in Lockheed's favor.

In July of 1972, Kakuei Tanaka became prime minister, and events began to unfold rapidly. At a summit meeting with President Nixon in Hawaii the following September – in a hotel owned by Osano – Tanaka promised that Japan would buy $320 million worth of civil aircraft to help alleviate the U.S. trade deficit. Japanese officials, according to press accounts, stated that Nixon actually suggested that the aircraft come from Lockheed. Upon his return home, the prime minister summoned the president of All Nippon Airlines and there immediately followed reports in Japan and the United States that the company would buy the TriStar.

Lockheed suddenly began to covertly move large sums of money through its Tokyo office to Kodama. Within days of Tanaka's meeting with the ANA president, Kodama was signing receipts for more than $3 million in payoff money. The receipts were ably translated into English by Taro Fukuda, Kodama's old friend and longtime Lockheed connection. In addition, several million flowed to Lockheed's acknowledged sales representative in Japan, the giant Marubeni Trading Company. Marubeni executives signed coded receipts for "100 peanuts" or "120 pieces," each unit signifying one million yen (about $3000). The money, like much of that sent to Kodama, was used to bribe leading government and airline industry officials.

By 1973 the TriStar sale was secure, but Lockheed payoff money continued to flow into Japan. The reason: an even more lucrative deal loomed ahead – the sale of Lockheed's P-3C Orion antisubmarine plane to the Japanese Air Force. The order, for some 100 planes, could have been worth as much as $1 billion. Kodama reportedly stood to take in $9 million, partly as his commission, and partly for use as bribes. The deal was about to go through just when Lockheed officials were summoned before Congress and began telling U.S. senators about their payoff practices overseas.

There were logistic problems for Lockheed in moving so much unattributable cash into Japan. The vast amount of the more than $12.6 million Lockheed sent to Kodama and Marubeni was transferred from Switzerland or Los Angeles through Deak & Company, a New York-based firm of international currency dealers. Kodama may well have known of Deak before his payments from Lockheed, because for years the company had served as a covert channel for moving CIA funds. The firm was founded before World War II by Nicholas Deak, a Hungarian émigré who had belonged to the CIA's wartime predecessor, the OSS (Office of Strategic Services). After the war he built up Deak & Company to fifty-nine offices worldwide, and earned a reputation for discreetly handling the funds of those who wish to avoid the regulations and paperwork of ordinary banks. Ten million dollars of Lockheed money passed through Deak's Hong Kong office between 1968 and 1976, most of it from Switzerland.

Some analysts have speculated that the CIA may have lent a guiding hand to Lockheed's efforts in Japan. Veteran reporter Tad Szulc, writing in *The New Republic* in 1976 on Lockheed's Deak connection, suggested that the millions of dollars funneled to Kodama were not entirely Lockheed's idea. "It appears," wrote Szulc, "that the Nixon and Ford administrations, and specifically [the] CIA, may have used Lockheed as a leading edge in the execution of American policies in Japan, particularly in support of ultraconservative groups." Lockheed officials, in fact, had no knowledge of the ultimate use of their payoff money, and Kodama certainly never let on as to what happened to the cash he received. As one intelligence source told Szulc, "Lockheed . . . would have been a perfect channel for the CIA to move funds secretly to people like Kodama." The involvement of Deak as a conduit would only have made it easier for both Lockheed and the CIA.

Whatever the CIA's role in the Lockheed case, it is clear that almost from the beginning the agency knew of the payoffs and the involvement of Kodama. As early as 1958, a CIA official at the U.S. Embassy had been apprised of the situation, and in turn contacted Washington. The CIA, for the record, has claimed that it has no files of any agency involvement with the Lockheed bribes, and has denied any role in the scandal. Lockheed officials have similarly denied that their company had any dealings with individuals in Japan known to be CIA agents.

The immediate – if unintentional – effect of the Lockheed payoffs, guided by Kodama's well-greased hands, was to bolster the position of America's key ally inside Japan, the LDP. Evidence suggests that much of the Lockheed money was used not only as bribes, but as election funds as well, bankrolling LDP candidates in the 1974 upper-house election campaign. Kodama chose his friends carefully, though, and some of Lockheed's millions may well have ended up in the hands of his pals on the far right and, of course, in the yakuza.

Kodama and Osano soon found other challenges besides Lockheed to keep them busy. By 1973, with the TriStar deal well in hand, they were at work together again; this time, Kodama was helping Osano in his successful takeover of the Kokumin Sogo Bank. It had been a profitable relationship between the two kuromaku, but obviously not one that was meant to go public. Three years later, under the floodlights of the scandal, Osano would testify before the Diet that his relationship with Kodama had never gone beyond "sitting for tea" several times a year.

Osano could say whatever he liked, but for the first time he would have to contend with reporters and prosecutors who displayed an uncharacteristic zeal for investigating powerful figures. And it was not only

Osano they were suddenly after. Each Lockheed payment led to different politicians and power brokers, and to a different stratum of a corrupt society. Lockheed's dealings with Osano, Kodama, and others ultimately brought into public view a broad cross section of the black mist enveloping the nation, where leading politicians met gangsters and questionable financial payments seemed a way of life.

Next to Kodama, perhaps the best example of underworld connections could be seen in the case of his powerful protégé, Dietman Koichi Hamada, a close ally of Tanaka, a rising star in the LDP, and a "former" member of the Inagawa crime family.

The forty-three-year-old Hamada lost an incredible $2 million playing baccarat during a series of Osano-sponsored tours to Las Vegas between 1972 and 1974, losses that were covered by Osano using Lockheed money. Osano's tours had become something of a legend among certain circles in Tokyo and Nevada. One such trip, in April 1974, was a nine-day, all-expense-paid junket of twenty-eight people to Honolulu, San Francisco, and Las Vegas. The guests, to put it charitably, were a rather diverse lot.

Government prosecutors and critics in the Diet later accused Osano and Hamada of including in the tours three top executives of the Inagawa syndicate, as well as a leading racketeer associated with Kodama. Another alleged participant was the notorious Susumu Ishii, the number-two man in the 4300-member Inagawa syndicate. Other mob connections may have been made as well. The FBI later questioned those who kept company with Osano and friends in Las Vegas, including reputed members of the U.S. Mafia.

How did Hamada end up in such good graces with Osano and Japan's ruling party? According to press reports, the wily politician had a police record dating back to 1952, when he was convicted of assault and embezzlement, and served a year in prison. Upon his release, Hamada found that his old gang was among many around Tokyo being absorbed by the rapidly growing Inagawa syndicate. In the mid-1950s, Hamada consulted with Inagawa about succeeding his recently deceased boss. Inagawa advised his ambitious kobun to consider another path, and, when Hamada expressed an interest in politics, Inagawa introduced him to Kodama.

For two to three years Hamada stayed with Kodama, working as secretary and servant, and learning the art of politics, Kodama-style. With Kodama's backing, the enterprising candidate worked his way through a succession of local offices and finally to the national Diet. It was as a prefectural assemblyman that Hamada first met Kenji Osano, and over the next fifteen years the two men speculated together in a series of highly lucrative, and often questionable, real estate deals. Hamada soon came to call Osano *oyaji* (father) and Kodama *sensei* (teacher).

Once made, a relationship with the yakuza is very difficult to end, and Hamada's was no exception. Throughout his career, yakuza, reportedly from the Inagawa-kai, have helped fund-raise and campaign for candidate Hamada. His tactics certainly didn't bother the rest of the LDP, many of whom also employed yakuza as campaign workers. In fact, at the peak of his power in 1980, Hamada held office as the LDP's campaign chief.

Hamada enlisted in Kodama's favored faction in the Diet, the intensely nationalistic Summer Storm Society (Seiran-kai), whose financial backers also included gambling czar Ryoichi Sasakawa and Korean gang boss Hisayuki Machii. Eventually, Hamada served as the group's secretary-general. By the time the Lockheed scandal broke, he had become a leading LDP member, and was appointed vice-minister of the Defense Agency, a prime spot from which to push his views on rapidly re-arming Japan. Along with his newfound political power, Hamada remained close to his old gang. As late as 1978 he would boast, "One of the men whom I respect most is the chief of the Inagawa-kai."

Despite his rather open ties to the yakuza, Hamada seems to have enjoyed popularity with his constituents. It was only his involvement in the Las Vegas gambling trips – and their connection to Lockheed – that finally derailed his political career. In April of 1980, Hamada resigned his seat in the Diet rather than face public exposure of his activities with Osano in Las Vegas. He quickly re-emerged, however, as an independent candidate in his old district, and won back his seat in the Diet. In 1984, after a poor electoral showing by the LDP, he was among nine independent conservatives recruited by a frantic Prime Minister Nakasone to keep control of the Diet's lower house.

The Fall of Kodama

Although Hamada survived the Lockheed scandal, his mentor did not fare as well. After Kotchian's 1976 Senate testimony in Washington, the Japanese press unleashed a merciless crusade against Kodama, atoning for its too many years of silence about the man and his influence. Investigators raided his house – a heretofore unthinkable act – and seized vast quantities of his personal files (those he hadn't burned). Tax officials began probing his labyrinthine financial dealings, searching for evidence of the Lockheed money and possible tax evasion.

The scandal may have taken its physical toll on Kodama as well. Shortly after Kotchian's initial testimony, the sixty-five-year-old Kodama suffered a stroke and was confined to his home. But even Kodama's mansion was no escape now. Demonstrators from both right and left protested outside his house. Leftist radicals even tried storming his gates, but were repulsed by police and still-loyal yakuza. Ultranationalist groups – once Kodama's deepest admirers – sent the bedridden fixer suicide notes, suggesting that he commit *hara-kiri* for having stained Japan's honor. Rumors even floated around that the Yamaguchi-gumi was plotting his assassination.

But the worst was yet to come. Indeed, Kodama himself could not have planned a more dramatic gesture. On the chilly Tuesday morning of March 23, 1976, Mitsuyasu Maeno, a twenty-nine-year-old film actor, arrived with three friends at Chofu Airport on the western outskirts of Tokyo. All were dressed in the style of *kamikaze* pilots. Maeno, a qualified pilot, told flying club officials that he wanted to rent two aircraft to film a sequence on kamikaze flyers.

Maeno had once idolized Kodama. Five years earlier, according to one account, he was part of a select band of ultranationalists gathered in Tokyo's elite Okura Hotel to hear the premiere recital of a proposed new national anthem, "Song of the Race." The anthem, writes Lockheed historian David Boulton, called for "a kamikaze coup d'etat to restore the glories of Imperial Japan." The composer of the song was Yoshio Kodama.

Maeno was then a struggling actor with a large film company in Tokyo. (He had discovered that more money could be made starring in pornographic movies, and by 1976 he could be seen in dozens of seedy theaters lining the back alleys of Japan's entertainment districts.) When he approached airport officials with a camera crew clad in kamikaze outfits, they were convincing enough to obtain the rental of two planes.

Maeno knew the route well. The week before, he had made three flights around Kodama's neighborhood. Before climbing into the cockpit of his Piper Cherokee, he strapped on a headband emblazoned with the Rising Sun, as kamikaze pilots did before their suicide flights during the war. Shouting the kamikaze war cry, *"Tenno heika banzai!"* (Long live the emperor), Maeno flew off, followed by his friends, and proceeded to circle Tokyo in formation for about an hour. Maeno then changed course, telling his cohorts he had some business in Setagaya – a Tokyo suburb and home to Yoshio Kodama.

Maeno approached Kodama's house at low altitude and circled twice, shouting the war cry over his radio. Aiming his aircraft nose first, he dove into Kodama's house, smashing into a veranda and dying instantly – but missing his intended victim, who lay in bed in another part of the house. The attack set the building ablaze, however, and Kodama's yakuza guards worked frantically at dousing the fire. So enraged were

Kodama's bodyguards that later in the day they attacked newsmen outside the house. (Reporters later complained that ten riot police stood by during the assault, warning the newsmen not to "excite the young men.")

Police concluded that Maeno had acted alone, that he was not, as feared, part of a rightist plot. But Kodama's woes were far from over. He survived the kamikaze attack only to face trial in June 1977 for tax evasion and violation of foreign exchange laws. It was Kodama's only appearance in court, and he pleaded not guilty to all charges. From then on he refused to leave his home, claiming ill health. Prosecutors, though, were unimpressed and persistently arrived at his bedside, questioning him on seventy different occasions, according to one account. Worse, in addition to seizing his files, tax officials attached most of his property and assets – including a sizable Asian art collection – to ensure the collection of any back taxes and penalties.

The Lockheed revelations, and the subsequent arrest of Kodama, ended an era in Japan. CIA operative, ultranationalist financier, yakuza godfather, political kingmaker – for a generation, no one could lay a finger on Yoshio Kodama. "Kodama never worried about the police, the tax agency, or the prosecutor's office," said one prominent ex-cabinet minister to a reporter. "He was confident that no one could touch him. . . ." But now, investigating and writing about Kodama's affairs was no longer taboo. Japanese publishers issued some fifty books on the man's life, many of them best-sellers. Scores more were published about the Lockheed scandal and its principal characters, in addition to a host of plays and movies that appeared.

Along with Kodama and his private secretary, fourteen other individuals involved in the scandal were finally indicted, including Kenji Osano. Among the charges: perjury, bribery, and violation of foreign exchange laws. Although at least eight politicians were clearly implicated, prosecutors felt they had enough evidence to indict only three: the prime minister, the LDP's secretary-general, and the parliamentary vice-minister of transportation. Prosecutors in 1981 demanded for Kodama a 3½-year prison term and a fine of about $3 million, but the trial was postponed due to Kodama's worsening health.

The aftermath of the scandal was decidedly mixed. U.S. relations with Japan were not noticeably harmed, despite early fears by American officials. The public, though, has yet to learn the full details of the Lockheed case. U.S. federal courts have prevented full disclosure ever since Secretary of State Henry Kissinger intervened in 1976, arguing that a release of the government's complete records of the case would damage American foreign policy interests. As late as 1983, Lockheed attorneys were in court warning that full disclosure could have a "devastating impact upon the reputations and careers of a number of foreign officials, some of whom hold positions of importance to the foreign relations of this country."

Meanwhile, Lockheed's money changer, Deak & Company, encountered troubles of its own. By early 1985, the firm had filed for bankruptcy, a move caused largely by a run on deposits by customers after the President's Commission on Organized Crime publicly linked the company to money launderers. Deak's troubles ended several months later when the aging spook was murdered in his Manhattan office, apparently by a demented drifter.

The Lockheed revelations did prompt Congress to pass into law the Foreign Corrupt Practices Act of 1977, outlawing overseas bribes by U.S. corporations, but controversy lingers around that event as well. According to political scientist Chalmers Johnson, the well-intentioned law has instead had the effect of "worsening the American balance of payments while enriching several large American law firms . . . [and ensuring] that much future business will probably go to America's competitors instead."

In Japan as well, the impact of the Lockheed scandal has been mixed. All but one of the politicians implicated in the payoffs scored resounding victories in the following general election. They were not as fortunate, however, in the courts. Excluding Kodama, all those indicted were found guilty. The last conviction, in October 1983, fell on former prime minister Tanaka. The Tokyo District Court found that Tanaka had accepted $2.1 million to arrange the purchase of Lockheed's TriStar by All Nippon Airways. He was sentenced to four years in jail and ordered to pay a fine equaling the amount he received as a bribe. The final verdict on the Lockheed defendants, though, has yet to come. Tanaka and the others remain free during their appeals, a process that legal experts believe may take a decade to complete.

Osano seemed largely unaffected by his conviction, and continues investing and making vast sums of money. In 1983 he displayed for the press his latest acquisition – the thirtieth hotel under Osano management. The plush 500-room hostelry sits right across the street from Tokyo Eki, Japan's Grand Central Station. Among the guests at his lavish opening were noted corporate leaders and his old pal, former prime minister Tanaka.

The real comeback story, though, lay with Tanaka himself. As the "shadow shogun" of the LDP, he controlled through his "Tanaka faction" 119 of the 422 LDP seats in the Diet. So powerful did Tanaka remain that he became the party's undisputed kingmaker, ensuring, among other things, the election of Nakasone as prime minister in 1982 and again in 1984. His long years of lavishing huge public works projects on his home district had paid off. Despite opinion polls, front-page newspaper editorials, and widespread calls from both opposition and LDP members suggesting that he resign, Tanaka held onto the Diet seat he had kept for thirty-six years. Just two months after his conviction, in an election that centered around his continued influence over the LDP, the sixty-five-year-old Tanaka won his home district by one of the largest vote margins in Japanese history. The rest of his party did not fare as well; the election nearly cost the LDP its postwar hold over the nation's politics. The press was not kind either, dubbing the new administration the Tanakasone cabinet. But Tanaka was unfazed. Until hobbled by a severe stroke in 1985, the former prime minister reigned as the most powerful man in all Japan.

Kodama could no longer keep up with his old pals, although the aging kuromaku claimed to have had a hand in Nakasone's ascendancy to the LDP throne. Kodama had in fact once said that his last endeavor from the sickbed was to make Nakasone – his old protégé – the prime minister. But under indictment, with his assets frozen and his followers leaving, Kodama's power slipped even further. Many businesses cut off their payments of many years to Kodama's financial racketeers. Lockheed had long ago canceled his once lucrative contract. Scores of politicians and businessmen who once boasted of their friendship with the man claimed to no longer see him. Tax officials and Tokyo police, meanwhile, accused Kodama of tax evasion on 1.36 billion yen (about $6 million) he had received in business deals unconnected to Lockheed.

Kodama spent the next three years hospitalized, his health failing and his empire crumbling. During one bedside interview, Kodama told a prosecutor he had received "divine punishment" for serving a U.S. aircraft company that had killed so many Japanese during the Pacific War. His chief physician later told the press that Kodama's mind had deteriorated to the point of being "deranged." By then, however, the powerful kuromaku was seventy-two years old, and he had made his mark on the world. On the evening of January 17, 1984, Kodama suffered another stroke and silently passed away.

For several day, mourners streamed to Kodama's mansion. The visitors represented a cross section of Kodama's life: leading businessmen, rightists, gangsters, entertainers. Curiously missing, though, were many of his close political allies over the years, politicians he had once funded and even controlled, but who now felt it unwise to publicly honor the man to whom they owed so much. Not so constrained was yakuza godfather Kakuji Inagawa, who repeatedly and rightfully proclaimed, "The world will never see the likes of Yoshio Kodama again."

The Kuromaku Legacy

The "black mists" of Japan did not die with Yoshio Kodama. In the spirit of the late kuromaku, questionable payments and mob connections still stretch far and wide among Japan's elected officials, affecting not only moral standards but public policy as well. Although not as blatant as it once was, the political use of organized crime members in Japanese politics goes well beyond what would now be possible in the United States. Reports of mob ties do create a sensation in Japan, much as they would in the United States, but politicians appear far more able to ignore the allegations and get on with their work. Such smugness is in part the price paid for a one-party rule that has lasted more than thirty years. Another reason lies in the much more public role the yakuza play in Japan, with openly identified members and offices, and a grudging acceptance of the gangs by the society at large. Although political careers are made in the U.S. by prosecuting gangs, little or no political advantage is gained in Japan by publicly fighting the yakuza.

As a result of these conditions, today the yakuza are employed widely in Japanese politics – as fund-raisers, bodyguards, and campaign workers. In return, the gang bosses receive access to many of the nation's leading politicians, and gain through this a host of benefits, not the least of which is legitimacy. A public record exists of these gangland ties to Japan's parliament; it is a remarkable account for a country considered to be the most crime-free in the modern world. Perhaps the most striking is that some of the nation's senior political figures have consciously and publicly demonstrated their support to members of the underworld.

Japanese were stunned when, in 1971, former prime minister Kishi, accompanied by former education minister Umekichi Nakamura and a third politician, guaranteed bail for a Yamaguchi-gumi boss convicted of murder. All three politicians were current LDP members of the Diet; Nakamura was then chairman of the Diet Court Indictment Committee. Such connections apparently did not bother the former prime minister. In December 1963, Kishi had acted as vice-chairman of a committee in charge of arrangements for a yakuza funeral. Later, in 1974, he was among scores of prominent guests invited by Yamaguchi godfather Kazuo Taoka to the lavish wedding of his son. Unable to attend, Kishi made sure the family received a congratulatory telegram, as did Ryoichi Sasakawa and Eitaro Itoyama, Sasakawa's relative and an LDP Diet member.

Although police have grown accustomed to such connections, it still surprises them to learn of ex-prime ministers associating with known gangsters. Kishi is not the only one. During the term of Prime Minister Ohira in the late 1970s, police raiding the home of a Yamaguchi boss made an unexpected discovery: a huge, blown-up photo, proudly displayed, of Mr. Ohira hobnobbing over drinks with the gangster, apparently taken at a party.

These connections have prompted some gang bosses to brag about their influence over the nation's politics. Such statements are not entirely unfounded. Many of Japan's politicians do, of course, scrupulously avoid involvement with the underworld. But association with the yakuza appears quite widespread, and while hardly limited to the LDP, it is in the ruling party that the phenomenon finds its fullest expression. Consider the case of Akira Ohno, minister of labor during the Nakasone government's first term. Ohno, son of the notorious LDP powerhouse Bamboku Ohno, apparently sees mob ties as part of a family tradition.

The younger Ohno has become something of a power in his own right. By 1982, the seasoned fifty-four-year-old politician had been returned to Japan's lower house seven times, and had held such important posts as deputy secretary-general of the ruling party. But the public took a second look upon revelations that from 1980 to 1982 Ohno's office had raised 100 million yen (about $435,000) in campaign funds from a loan-sharking group closely tied to the Yamaguchi-gumi. Ohno again came under fire for a series of visits to mob leaders. Concerning a speech he gave at the wedding of a son of a recently "retired" Yamaguchi boss, the *Mainichi* newspaper cited a secretary to the minister who stated that Ohno's ties to the man were close before the mobster's retirement, and that the man "helped Ohno win elections and promote business." Ohno, however, has firmly denied any yakuza connections.

Other leading lights of the LDP allegedly have made use of characters from the underworld. In 1976, for example, the late Rokusuke Tanaka – then the LDP's chief cabinet secretary – admitted that a "former" gangster actually ran one of his campaign groups. The thirty-four-year-old yakuza strongman had once headed a gang in the conservative Tanaka's home district in Fukuoka, birthplace of Japan's modern yakuza-rightist groups. Although the man had recently served time in prison in connection with a manslaughter case, Tanaka reportedly welcomed him, arguing, "It is the responsibility of a politician to rehabilitate ex-convicts."

Apparently Tanaka's responsibility extended to present gang members as well. In late 1983, two yakuza campaigners for the politician were arrested for violating Japan's Public Offices Election Law. The men belonged to the 330-member Kusano family, which holds sway over Tanaka's district. In the election, Tanaka was returned to the Diet for his eighth consecutive term. His yakuza campaigners didn't seem to bother the LDP hierarchy, which subsequently appointed the sixty-year-old Tanaka as secretary-general of the party.

Sometimes mob contacts are used by Japan's leading politicians for purely personal reasons – to intimidate errant relatives, for example. But the yakuza seem to be most widely employed in political campaigning and fund-raising.

Juichiro Tsukuda, a ruling party elder, sees few problems in working with Japan's crime bosses. Among the man's credentials: former minister of posts and telecommunications, former governor of Niigata Prefecture, and a member of the Diet's upper house since 1968. By 1970, the sixty-seven-year-old Tsukuda had come under fire at least once, for attending the funeral service of a noted gangster. But by 1981, the politician had gone a step farther by offering yakuza members not only condolences but employment as well. Tsukuda had hired Takashi Jo, a fifty-year-old ranking member of the huge Sumiyoshi syndicate. Jo's task was to collect some 250 million yen (about $1 million) worth of unsettled bills and checks Tsukuda issued on behalf of the owner of a Turkish bath as part of a bizarre fund-raising scheme gone awry. Tsukuda told a *Mainichi* reporter he was unaware that his bill collector had a violent record. "Many bills and checks are now held by gangs," said the former minister, "so I hired him." Jo took his job seriously. Police arrested him for punching in the face a Tokyo financial broker trying to cash a 2.1-million-yen check drawn on Tsukuda's name at a bank near the Diet building. Jo was released the same day, thanks to a personal visit by Tsukuda to the police.

Tsukuda does not apparently play favorites among the varied yakuza gangs. Eight months later, he was in the news again for intervening in a police investigation on behalf of another syndicate. This time the yakuza was one of the top eight lieutenants of the Yamaguchi-gumi – Shigemasa Kamoda, the same oyabun whom ex-labor minister Ohno admitted knowing. Tsukuda stopped in on Osaka police officials to advise them that Kamoda – then under suspicion of violating gambling laws – had in fact a good alibi.

Similar tales of political corruption and mob connections appear through much of Japan. Considering the pervasive and open dealings between the yakuza and national politicians, it is not surprising that Japan's "black mist" operates on a smaller level as well. In some communities, the yakuza today exert enormous influence over local politics, much as the Mafia traditionally has in certain American towns and cities.

Recent years have seen city officials and gangsters involved in a long list of bribery, intimidation, and fraud cases, as well as the public sponsoring of "retirement" parties for the community's leading thugs.

The widespread employ of gangsters by political figures in Japan is not without its risks. In Shimizu, three members of an Inagawa gang strangled to death a former city councilman in 1977. The politician's crime: failure to repay millions of yen he had borrowed from the mobsters to win reelection.

The Political Yakuza

Although cases of mob-connected politicians are not unfamiliar to Americans, at times the yakuza go well beyond simply aiding the candidate of choice – they run for office themselves. Ever since Mitsuru Toyama's Dark Ocean Society blurred the distinction between gangster and rightist in the late nineteenth century, the yakuza have been organizing their gangs into political parties.

Even during the occupation, often under the nose of U.S. officials, yakuza bosses were running for office in communities where they wielded power. Tekiya strongman Kinosuke Ozu, "Tokyo's Al Capone," garnered 12,000 votes in a 1947 bid for the Diet. In 1952, the oyabun of the Asano-gumi successfully ran for a seat on the city council of a town on Japan's Inland Sea. The election no doubt boosted the gang's plans for expansion; by 1964 the Asano-gumi had doubled in size (to eighty members) and had become the most powerful gang in Okayama Prefecture, an area inhabited by more than 1 million people.

Traditionally, the yakuza have turned to political organizing as a front for other activities. Recent times are no different. Stung by police crackdowns in the early 1980s, the gangs have sharply increased their sponsorship of rightist groups. In 1981, the National Police Agency reported 90 new such organizations with 2000 members, most of them sponsored by major syndicates like the Yamaguchi-gumi and Inagawa-kai. If groups with indirect ties to the underworld are included, the number jumps to nearly 200, covering fully 37 of Japan's 47 prefectures.

Like the more weathered gangster-rightist groups, many of the newer political gangs enjoy close ties to leading politicians. One group in Gifu Prefecture, according to the newspaper *Asahi,* boasts an LDP Diet member as an "advisor." And in Ehime Prefecture, on the eastern island of Shikoku, "several members of the prefectural assembly reportedly are advisors to a new 'rightist' group." Another group, the Shigemasa Kamoda Association, ran Yamaguchi boss Kamoda for the Diet in 1980. Kamoda, an associate of LDP Dietmen Ohno and Tsukuda, vowed to halt drug abuse across the nation, claiming that he was "a monk following the path of chivalry" laid down by Yamaguchi godfather Kazuo Taoka.

Perhaps the most remarkable is that, occasionally, yakuza candidates are still successful in local elections. At least one of these yakuza councilmen bears a prior conviction for murder: Eiji Sadaoka, oyabun of the Sadaoka-gumi in southern Japan. In a town outside Nagasaki, the forty-one-year-old gangster won a seat on the city council in 1975, checking in with the largest number of votes in that town's election. Several days later, police arrested Sadaoka on a drug trafficking charge, and revealed that their man had a record of five previous convictions, including murder.

Ideology often plays a secondary role in the yakuza's political efforts. The gangs are typically far more interested in maintaining the status quo to continue their assorted underworld pursuits. This attitude is shared by organized crime syndicates worldwide. As Chicago's Al Capone said more than fifty years ago, "I'm a hundred-percent supporter of the American free enterprise system." A survey of yakuza political views by criminologist Kanehiro Hoshino found that more than 50 percent supported the ruling Liberal-Democratic Party. Nevertheless, there is a strong, highly conservative bent to those the yakuza support. Invariably, their candidates are well to the right of center, staunch anticommunists, and highly nationalistic. The involvement of prominent, yakuza-tainted politicians like Koichi Hamada in the ultranationalist Summer Storm Society is no accident.

The effect of the yakuza on public policy is difficult to gauge. Certainly, regulatory reforms in yakuza-dominated industries, such as moneylending and private guard services, have long been delayed, perhaps due to yakuza pressure on their friends in the Diet. But the most crucial area of yakuza political involvement today lies in the debate over Japan's fast-growing military.

The yakuza, to be sure, are but one voice – or set of voices – on the right clamoring for a rapid buildup of Japan's armed forces. Historically, though, the yakuza have been keen and active supporters of a potent military in Japan: in ultranationalistic groups in the 1920s and 1930s, pushing the country into World War II; in "land development" programs to settle occupied Manchuria during the war; and after the war, in paramilitary units designed to help police and the military battle leftist groups. As noted earlier, today's highly politicized yakuza alliances – Zen Ai Kaigi and Seishi-kai, for example – include at the top of their agendas a call for repeal of Article IX of Japan's postwar constitution, an antiwar clause that in effect limits the country to a small, defensive military force.

The cause of rearmament is also taken up by scores of smaller ultranationalist groups and political "parties" across the nation. These rightist gangs, often staffed by yakuza and others on the criminal fringe, are a common sight in Japan's major cities. In a culture that lays great emphasis on harmony, these modern ultranationalists are the nation's most notorious violators of the public peace. Clad in helmets, battle fatigues, and sunglasses, they dart about town in steel-plated trucks sporting military banners and flags adorned with the Rising Sun. Atop the vehicles stand huge loudspeakers blaring martial music in all directions, with breaks in the score to call for strident anti-Soviet measures, repeal of the constitution, a crash military buildup, and restoring the dignity of "the Japanese race." Some groups even call for the nuclear arming of Japan, a thought that should give pause to all in the West. In 1984, police estimated there were about 120,000 of these neo-Fascist characters, split into some 840 groups nationwide. Most are not formal members of the yakuza syndicates, but are frequently used by them for such odd jobs as collecting protection money from recalcitrant nightclub operators.

Although there is surprising sympathy for much of the far right's agenda, the great majority of Japanese look upon the gangs as an oddity, as relics of an era that was long ago and rightfully buried. Of far greater significance than these radical groups is the considerable support that yakuza syndicates lend to mainstream rightist politicians through campaign contributions, manpower, and hired muscle. Of at least equal importance have been the unrepentantly militarist views of rightist kuromaku like Kodama and Sasakawa, who have traditionally wielded great power over conservative members of the Diet.

The steady push toward rearmament by these forces has produced some dramatic results. Prodded by the LDP's right wing – and by pressure from the Reagan administration – Japan's military has undergone a complete transformation. Once the butt of jokes among both Japanese and foreign officers, by 1984 the country's so-called Self-Defense Forces ranked eighth worldwide in military spending, ahead of most NATO nations. Japan's 180,000 ground troops also notched eighth in size, as did the country's submarine fleet. Japan's 52 destroyers and frigates had become the fifth largest such force; only three NATO countries could claim greater naval tonnage. With 470 combat aircraft, Japan ranked fifteenth in air power. And the country's economy – the world's third largest – boasted the seventh largest defense industry. Recent moves in the Diet by high-ranking LDP officials propose vastly increased military spending that would place Japan's defense budget behind only those of the United States, the Soviet Union, and the People's Republic of China.

Talk of Japan's rearmament causes great consternation among neighboring countries that still vividly remember the brutality of Imperial Japan's East Asia Co-Prosperity Sphere. The push to a stronger military has alarmed many Japanese as well, who see it as part of a larger drift back to the old, ultranationalist right. Legislation pending in the Diet, for example, would revise much more in the present constitution than just the antiwar clause. Proposals include giving the emperor a "more than symbolic" role, and restoring state support of certain Shintu religious functions. Both measures hark back to the fanatic days of the prewar era. Other worrisome signs, according to critics, are revisionist changes in Japan's view of World War II. A glorified movie of the life of Hideki Tojo, the militarist who served as Japan's wartime prime minister, recently enjoyed huge popularity throughout the country. And, much to the outrage of China and Korea, Japanese history textbooks were changed to greatly soften descriptions of such wartime atrocities as the 1937 Nanking massacre.

Although fears of a full-scale ultranationalist revival are largely confined to the left in Japan, even political conservatives concede that if such an event should occur, the yakuza would be in the vanguard. Kuromaku like Kodama and Sasakawa have long bragged about the tens of thousands of young Japanese men at their disposal. Kodama spoke of his gangster-rightest groups as part of "an anticommunist popular front." Sasakawa, through his chairmanship of some thirty organizations, has laid claim to "my private army of eight million" ready to strike against leftists for the fatherland.

As long as Japan stays affluent and productive, though, there is little to fear from a resurgence of fascism in the country. The Socialists, the smaller parties, and the liberal wing of the LDP still wield enough power to block any truly outrageous demand from the right. In addition, the public generally views rightist methods with distaste. Occasionally, incidents arise that serve as potent reminders of where the ultranationalist road has taken Japan once before. Most Japanese, for example, were shocked and outraged when, in 1971, the forty-year-old leader of a Fukuoka yakuza gang sent a .22-caliber pistol and 175 bullets to Prime Minister Sato. Included was the following appeal: "You have allowed policemen to be killed, let students storm the Imperial Palace and caused trouble for the Emperor, all because you have remained Prime Minister. Herewith I send you a pistol so you can kill yourself honorably with it."

Today's modern Japanese seem to have little use for such histrionics, and the country's radical right commands for now a relatively small percentage of public favor. Furthermore, most yakuza gangs, despite their public vows of allegiance to the rightist cause, will continue to use the movement primarily as a front for other activities. Indeed, the yakuza's political influence will be felt foremost in terms of money and self-interest. The syndicates will simply be defending their long-held turf: the continued control of gambling, drugs, and other vice crimes, and of their increasingly varied financial rackets. Their primary motivation, like that of organized crime elsewhere, will be profit.

One clear sign of this trend away from ideology is the passing of that great figure in Japanese history: the ultranationalist kuromaku. With Kodama gone and Sasakawa well into his eighties, the stage is shifting for Japan's "black-curtain wirepullers." Certainly there is no replacement for Kodama. The kuromaku mold is much more apt to be filled by men like Osano and Tanaka, postwar businessmen with cunning and connections, but who hardly qualify as ultranationalist godfathers. As Sasakawa, sensing the end of an era, told *Newsweek*'s Bernard Krisher in 1976, "I am one of the last fools in this world."

The passing of Kodama and the others, though, signals much more than the changing nature of Japan's power brokers. Kodama's fall from power, together with the Lockheed scandal and Tanaka's resignation, form a milestone in the development of Japan's still-young democracy. These events have had a cleansing effect, sweeping away for a moment the thickest portions of the black mist enveloping Japan. And if the mist has returned quickly, in the form of yakuza payoffs and political connections, the corruption of the country's politics has had to go deeper underground, for the press and the public have grown increasingly less tolerant of the old ways.

Kodama's passing also marks another, equally important milestone. Japan's rapid economic growth, technological sophistication, and rise to world power have thrust upon the yakuza new problems and opportunities. For even before Yoshio Kodama's last breath, the situation in the streets, among the disciplined bands on which he depended for support – this, too, was rapidly changing.

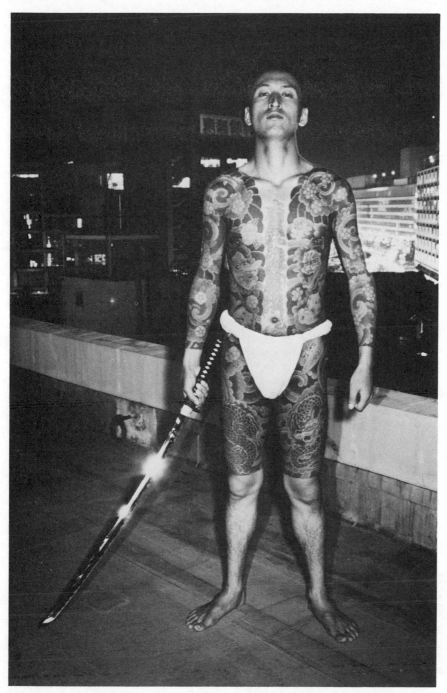

Yakuza in full-body tattoo, posing with samurai sword in the Tokyo night. (Seiji Kurata)

Mitsuru Toyama (seated, with beard), *pioneer of the Japanese ultranationalist movement, with members of his Black Dragon Society, circa 1930. Seated second from right
is student Yoshio Kodama, who would become the single greatest force in the yakuza's
postwar resurrection.*

A young Kodama (left) *in the 1930s as the bodyguard of Wang Ching-wei, chief of the
Nanking (China) puppet government controlled by Japan. Kodama grew fabulously
rich during the war looting the Chinese and supplying the Imperial Navy.*

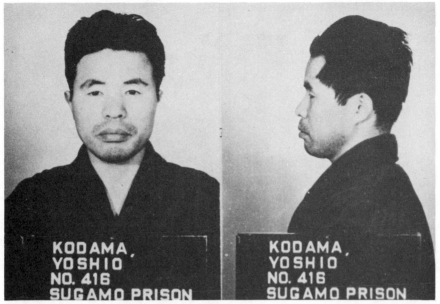

Kodama's mug shot from Sugamo Prison after the war. He was designated a Class A war criminal and spent three years in jail, but was never tried; U.S. intelligence agents needed him elsewhere.

Ryoichi Sasakawu, the self-proclaimed "world's wealthiest fascist" and yakuza associate. Kodama's cellmate at Sugamo Prison, Sasakawa also was designated a Class A war criminal. He became one of Japan's richest men through control of the incredibly lucrative speedboat racing industry.

Sasakawa with Benito Mussolini in 1939. Sasakawa continues to be a great admirer of Mussolini, whom he once called "the perfect fascist and dictator."

Major General Charles Willoughby, commander of U.S. Army Intelligence (G-2) under General MacArthur during the occupation of Japan. Willoughby's men recruited yakuza members to spy on and disrupt the growing left and labor movement. (U.S. Army photograph)

Surveillance photo taken by a U.S. counterintelligence agent during a 1953 May Day parade in Nagoya. The Korean War greatly increased the work of U.S. intelligence agents in Japan, but their reliance on rightists and yakuza often produced mixed results.

Postwar ultranationalism at work: the dramatic 1960 assassination of Socialist Party Secretary-General Inejiro Asanuma by a young right-wing fanatic. The stabbing took place at a public gathering before television cameras, reporters, and a large audience. Asanuma's assassin later committed suicide in his police cell. (Provided by Mainichi Shimbun)

*Kodama with Prime Minister Nobusuke Kishi in 1960. Kishi is looking over galley
proofs of Kodama's memoir,* Sugamo Diary, *before brushing his introduction into the
book. Kodama returned the favor that year by recruiting a 28,000-man army of yakuza
and rightists to protect the planned visit of President Eisenhower.*

A key shot of underworld influence in the early 1960s. From the left: *Yoshio Kodama,
by then one of Japan's leading power brokers; Kakuji Inagawa, godfather of the huge
Tokyo-based Inagawa crime syndicate; Shunji Hasegawa, one of Inagawa's top lieutenants; and Ichiro Kono, secretary-general of the ruling Liberal-Democratic Party.*
(Tokuma Shoten)

A typical tekiya (street stall) setup for a neighborhood festival. Tekiya members have now expanded beyond street stalls into real estate and multimillion-dollar businesses. (Photo by Michio Soejima)

A banquet honoring the installation of a new chief of a major Tokyo gang, circa 1961.
(Photo by Jacqucline Paul)

One of the last times Kodama is seen in public, as he is escorted to his only court appearance in the Lockheed bribery case, January 1984. (Provided by Kyodo News Service)

Part III
The Modern Yakuza

Chapter 5
The Syndicates

He was a man the Sicilians would have called the *capo di tutti capi*. At sixty-five, he reigned as the nation's most powerful gangster, thanks to the help of friends like Yoshio Kodama and to his own extraordinary abilities. He was Kazuo Taoka, third boss of the Yamaguchi-gumi and overlord of 12,000 yakuza throughout the Japanese Islands.

Taoka radiated confidence and power as he rested at his table in the Bel Ami nightclub. The club sat nestled in a crowded entertainment district of Kyoto, Japan's ancient capital and cultural center and long a Yamaguchi stronghold. On stage, a limbo dance being performed was nearing a climax and about fifty guests were applauding. It was early on a Tuesday evening in July of 1978.

A young man in a white shirt arose from his seat and slowly walked toward the table near the stage where Taoka and five bodyguards were sitting. He came no closer than 15 feet, slipped out a .38-caliber pistol, and blasted away at Taoka, leaving a hole in the godfather's neck. As the assassin fled for his own life, Taoka was rushed into a bulletproof Cadillac and sped with police escort to a nearby hospital.

Taoka's assailant, twenty-five-year-old Kiyoshi Narumi, belonged to a gang in the Matsuda syndicate, a bitter Yamaguchi rival also active in western Japan. When a Matsuda boss died in a 1975 turf war with the Yamaguchi-gumi, Narumi and other Matsuda gang members had swallowed the ashes of their murdered oyabun in a pledge of revenge. Taoka, however, survived, as he had other assassination attempts. His assailant was not so lucky; he was found brutally murdered several weeks later on a mountainside near Kobe, headquarters to the Yamaguchi-gumi.

The assassination attempt sparked a gang war right out of Chicago in the 1930s. Gangsters fought gangsters in broad daylight, attacking each other on the streets and raiding each other's offices. At least five more yakuza affiliated with the Matsuda-gumi were murdered in the bloody retaliations that followed.

The shooting swept Taoka out of action for several months, but more important, it signaled the long-term decline of the great godfather and, perhaps, of the immense syndicate he had built. The Yamaguchi-gumi could handle an upstart rival like the Matsuda gangsters, but pressures within the syndicate were changing the face of Japan's biggest crime group. The Yamaguchi-gumi – an alliance of more than 500 gangs – owed much of its strength to Taoka's charismatic leadership, which suddenly seemed highly vulnerable. Taoka had been suffering from an increasingly serious heart ailment for ten years; by the time of his shooting, the godfather found his lieutenants already struggling for his succession.

Another problem facing the syndicate was a growing generation gap between older and younger gang members, with far too few middle-aged mobsters to help fill the void. Yakuza elders, not only in the Yamaguchi-gumi but in gangs throughout Japan, began complaining that their formidable yakuza tradition, unquestioning loyalty to the boss, was no longer blindly accepted by the younger soldiers. Other values, too, were being questioned – of strategy, of leadership – and not just by the under-lings, but by the senior bosses themselves. In the Yamaguchi-gumi alone, as many as twenty-three bosses of affiliated gangs were expelled or disci-plined for opposing syndicate policy. Police theorized that the Ya-maguchi-gumi, which pioneered the modern Japanese crime syndicate, had simply grown too big – and too dependent on Taoka's leadership.

Another new development was the open fighting in the streets. For years the yakuza credo dictated that fights among the gangs would be settled outside the realm of legitimate society; it was part of the image of the noble gangster, never to involve in gang business the common people, the *katagi no shu* (literally, citizens under the sun). But recent gang battles had erupted with little regard for anyone, least of all the general public, and the Japanese were growing tired of the open violence and disregard for custom. So outraged was the public that police launched a much-her-alded eighty-day battle to end the gang war, fielding 1100 officers in what was then the largest mobilization in postwar history. During the first two months of the crackdown, authorities rounded up 2000 gangsters, includ-ing 518 senior members of the Yamaguchi-gumi. Officials went after Taoka's number-two man, Kenichi Yamamoto, nicknamed Yamaken, eventually putting him away for three and a half years of hard labor on charges of firearms possession and intimidation. Prosecutors further pressed a number of old cases against Taoka that included violation of tax laws and blackmail of construction and steamship companies.

Responding to the growing pressures on his huge syndicate, within a year of the shooting Taoka fashioned an uneasy but effective truce with the Yamaguchi-gumi's most bitter enemies. To make sure the public got the message, Taoka did what any modern, self-respecting Japanese godfather would have done: he called a press conference. Under the glare of television lights, some sixty newsmen crowded into Taoka's plush home, sitting cross-legged on tatami mats. For over an hour the reporters listened to Yamaken, flanked by two other gang leaders. (Taoka himself was conspicuously absent.) The boss's right-hand man began by reading from a prepared statement in formal, flowery Japanese. Reporters were able to check his words against copies of the speech distributed earlier as part of a press kit. In the nationally televised address, the Yamaguchi-gumi declared an end to the bloodshed and solemnly apologized to the public and police for the "trouble" caused them. Following the press conference, events finally began to slow down for Japan's largest gang – but not for long.

Yamaguchi-gumi: Death and Succession

Taoka stayed out of public life for much of the following year. He later reemerged for a series of appearances in 1979 to quash rumors that his health was failing, but the yakuza boss looked pale and thin. In the sensational weeklies that chart the movements of Japan's far-flung underworld, Taoka's appearance only increased speculation about who would be his successor, the fourth boss of the Yamaguchi-gumi.

Despite its problems, the Yamaguchi-gumi still stood as Japan's most formidable crime syndicate. As one newspaper remarked, the gang's rhombus-shaped golden pin remained "a persuasive lapel ornament." In much of Japan, the showing of one's pin, combined perhaps with the baring of a tattoo, could get trucks moved, goods discounted, and hallways cleared. Other gangs show off their own badges, of course. Each syndicate wears a different design, proudly displaying its colors on official occasions, much as if they were Rotary brothers. In Japan, where the group, not the individual, defines much of daily life, the pins are an easy mark of identification.

The pins cannot always work their magic, however, particularly when their bearers are faced with police or other gangsters. The emblems were part of the matching outfits worn by Yamaguchi members as the gang made a well-publicized attempt in 1980 to expand its territory to Hokkaido, Japan's northernmost island. Nearly 200 gang members, clad in white blazers and black polo shirts, flew to the capital city of Sapporo for the formal opening of their branch office. They were met at the airport by 800 members of local underworld gangs who had banded together to keep the Yamaguchi-gumi out of their territory. A nervous contingent of some 2000 riot police kept the two groups apart. Officials stopped the Yamaguchi gangsters from opening their office by quarantining the entire delegation in their hotel at a ski resort; a day later, their mission a failure, the gangsters returned to Osaka on a single flight of All Nippon Airways.

Far worse news awaited the Yamaguchi hierarchy than their failure in Hokkaido. One year later, the event long dreaded by the syndicate arrived. Kazuo Taoka's thirty-five-year rule ended with a final heart attack in July 1981. A quiet, private service was held for the immediate family and friends one week later. But a second funeral – an official one – was deemed necessary by the gang. Despite repeated police warnings, after three months of preparation, syndicate leaders arranged to give Taoka an elaborate Buddhist sendoff in the best yakuza tradition. Police responded by raiding gangster homes and offices nationwide, and arresting nearly 900 gang members. Among the contraband seized: 102 guns, 192 swords, and 2 pounds of amphetamines. But the crackdown didn't work: to the Yamaguchi-gumi, the funeral was a matter of honor. On a Sunday in late October, some 1300 yakuza from 200 gangs gathered in Kobe to honor their departed boss. The service took place at a site where a "Taoka Memorial Hall" was to be built, adjacent to the godfather's home in a posh residential area. Three doors down sat the Hyogo Prefecture District Court, located amid the offices of Kobe's most respected lawyers. Surrounding those offices – and the gangsters – stood about 800 helmeted riot police armed with metal shields. Another 500 police checked the arriving visitors at 16 different places, including major airports and train stations.

Flowers arrived from all over the country – from other mob leaders, from prominent businessmen, and from Taoka's old friend Yoshio Kodama, then slowly dying in a Tokyo hospital. For those who came to pay their respects personally, body searches by police were the rule. Among those in attendance was an all-star cast of Japan's entertainment industry: singers, actors, musicians. Said one star, Yoshio Tabata, "From the late fifties to the late seventies, what entertainer in Japan was not helped by Taoka?" Also at the wake appeared Japan's leading man of the cinema, heartthrob Ken Takakura, who, among his numerous roles in yakuza movies, had played Taoka in a film trilogy about the godfather's life.

Taoka had reportedly chosen his ruthless number-two man, Yamaken, as his successor. But shortly after the press conference, Yamaken was thrown into prison and not due out until late 1982. The syndicate, meanwhile, was in such disarray that few could tell who was in charge.

Police thus watched closely to see who would fill the spot of chief mourner at the funeral, a role traditionally assumed by the syndicate's new boss. Much to their surprise, it was the godfather's widow, sixty-two-year-old Fumiko Taoka.

It was, perhaps, a measure of the near panic Yamaguchi leaders felt that, in the heavily macho world of the yakuza, they had openly turned to Fumiko, long a silent power in the organization. Her role was to be a temporary one, bridging the gap until a strong male leader emerged. But in a land where women hold few top jobs and Western-style feminism has made little progress, the appointment was nothing short of remarkable. The place of women in the yakuza has long centered around their roles as prostitutes, hostesses, and housewives for the gangs. Occasionally, though, they amass considerable power in the Japanese underworld. As one gang member explained to a Japanese weekly, "There are women oyabun (bosses), but they don't openly show their faces in the yakuza world. Women don't go about brazenly in a man's world. . . . (Fumiko) will probably be there to act as receiver for others."

For a while, then, the 12,000 men of Japan's largest crime syndicate were led by a woman. Fumiko reportedly occupied her late husband's seat at top-level meetings, and passed judgments on intragang disputes. With Yamaken due out of prison within months, most gang members expected a relatively smooth transition. They were mistaken.

Before he was a free man again, Taoka's heir apparent paid for his long years of heavy drinking. Seven months after his boss's death, Yamaken too succumbed – to cirrhosis of the liver. Suddenly, the entire structure of the Yamaguchi-gumi was thrown into unrelenting confusion. The work of a generation of gangsters – a complex blend of feudalism and corporate management – was now at risk.

During his thirty-five-year rule, Kazuo Taoka had run his syndicate with that famous Japanese knack for using innovative techniques while preserving traditional values. Despite the Yamaguchi-gumi's control of more than 2500 businesses, sophisticated gambling and loan-sharking operations, and heavy investment in the sports and entertainment fields, the organization still functioned along feudal patterns that had existed for 300 years. Day-to-day management of the syndicate – like other yakuza groups – depended on the ancient relationships of oyabun-kobun, with fictive kinships extending from the highest "parent" to the lowest "child." These feudal vestiges certainly didn't hurt the gangs as they adapted to a modern, corporate world. By the time of his death, Taoka's organization was grossing well over $460 million annually, according to police. American executives from General Motors to the Mafia would no doubt give a great deal to manage such fervently dedicated workers as those of the Yamaguchi-gumi.

Above it all, Taoka reigned as an underworld shogun. But as is often the case, the godfather was removed from the daily affairs of the syndicate. That was left to his second-in-command, Yamaken, who had served as a kind of chairman of the board for the Yamaguchi "Corporation." On the fifth day of each month, Yamaken held a meeting with twelve leading bosses who functioned as a board of directors, deciding on syndicate policy and carving up the spoils of underworld Japan.

In all, there were 103 Yamaguchi bosses of various rank from more than 500 separate gangs. The bosses held office according to the parlance of the oyabun-kobun relationship: at the top ruled four *shatei*, or "younger brothers" to Taoka. Also atop the pyramid served the other eight directors, the *wakashira-hosa* (assistant young leaders), one of whom would be appointed a *wakashira* (young leader). Equivalent to the Mafia's *consiglieri*, or counselors, were 6 members of a senior consultative group, the *sanro-kai*. Below this hierarchy lay a series of lesser offices: one *kambu atsukai* (executive), and 83 *wakashu* (young men), who each commanded their own legions of *kobun* (children) or *kumi-in* (enlisted men). Within these individual gangs existed a maze of similar relationships, all based on the oyabun-kobun system. In addition, there were large numbers of apprentices and fringe persons to oversee.

Vast sums of money flowed through this feudal hierarchy. The major affiliated gangs and the syndicate itself each issued an annual financial report. The gangs were required to send monthly amounts to the syndicate headquarters, often in the thousands of dollars. In addition, payments were made as New Year's gifts, for funerals (Taoka's brought in nearly $500,000), for each gangster released from prison, and to help pay for inspection visits by the Yamaguchi brass. By one police estimate, Taoka received annual tribute from his varied gangs totaling more than 500 million yen ($2.1 million).

Those beneath Taoka also fared well. In a revealing 1984 interview with the *Mainichi* newspaper, a Yamaguchi boss let the public know just how well: "A boss of medium rank will make about $130,000 [annually]," he said, "but when you get to the godfather class, you're probably talking more than $400,000. A syndicate head with 1000 men under him can count on bringing in $43,000 a month. . . . Even if you deduct, say, $13,000 for entertainment and office expenses, that still leaves him with $30,000; that's a good $360,000 a year. And he can use it any way he likes."

Those figures were confirmed by a National Police Agency report issued in 1979, which also shed light on the salaries of lower-ranking yakuza. A typical gangster-soldier, said the report, took in around $14,000 a year, about the same as an average salaried worker in Japan. Members who controlled the earnings of women, such as pimps or club managers, fared much better, bringing in more than $45,000 annually. And senior members below the rank of boss could count on twice that amount, or about $90,000. But the big money remained with the men at the top.

"Remember," said the Yamaguchi boss, "a gang leader's income depends on the number of soldiers he has under him. People say the Yamaguchi-gumi controls the Japanese underworld, but we didn't plan it that way. Competition between bosses for a bigger piece of the action has led them to expand their turf, until suddenly the syndicate is everywhere."

To the Japanese on the street, it did indeed seem like the Yamaguchi-gumi was everywhere. In the traditional business of the yakuza world, Taoka's mob commanded the field in western Japan. Its varied gangs controlled day laborers at the ports and in construction jobs; monopolized hundreds of street stall operators; extorted cash from local bars and national corporations; and ran gambling rackets from street-corner numbers operations to high-stakes card games worth millions of dollars a night. They organized political parties and worked as campaign aides for rightist candidates. And they ran nightclubs and cabarets, complete with hostesses, prostitutes, and virtually anything the public wanted but wasn't supposed to have.

Kazuo Taoka's greatest contribution, though, was in forcing open Japan's fast-growing economy to a rapidly modernizing underworld. By the early 1970s, the Yamaguchi-gumi was tied into professional boxing, sumo, and Western-style wrestling. Along with other leading syndicates, it controlled some 100 production companies in the entertainment business. In addition, scores of talent agencies and booking firms were yakuza-controlled. Many performers could not venture onto a stage without the blessing of their yakuza sponsors. Movie companies, too, with their insatiable appetite for yakuza films, fell under the influence of the gangs.

But the Yamaguchi-gumi also led the way into areas beyond entertainment. Despite a formal ban by the big syndicates on the sale of narcotics, Yamaguchi members turned to drug dealing as an easy way of meeting their monthly payments. By the 1970s, police estimated nearly half the yakuza's income was generated by sales of amphetamines, the drug of choice in Japan. Other fields, too, proved especially lucrative.

The gangs moved into moneylending, smuggling, and pornography. Their front companies made bids on huge public works projects, including subways and airport construction. They rigged baseball games, horse races, and public auctions for foreclosed property. The syndicate's aggressive stance and anything-goes policy inspired an entire generation of enterprising mobsters. Yakuza began to move wherever they could find an opportunity. They seized control of hospitals, English schools, amusement halls, and fortune-telling parlors. They bought into real estate, video games, trucking, waste disposal, and security services. They manufactured and distributed counterfeit Japanese stamps and bills, U.S. dollars, Cartier watches, and even brand-name food products.

It took all of Taoka's immense power to bind these varied scams together. The Yamaguchi-gumi was not a monolith; gangs often acted independently of one another, and despite Taoka's unchallenged authority, divisions continually surfaced within the syndicate. Factions developed between militant gangs – anxious for expansion and eager to use violence – and more dovish and neutral groups. Differences existed as well between tekiya and bakuto bosses, and among newer occupations such as financial racketeering and drug dealing. But on important issues – mergers, key promotions, territorial wars – the cabinet was always consulted. And behind every decision stood the authority of the most powerful man in the Japanese underworld. To the yakuza in the street, there seemed to be no problem that godfather Taoka could not solve.

This, then, was the tightly knit structure thrown into confusion by the deaths of Taoka and Yamaken. The once invincible Yamaguchi-gumi suddenly found itself under assault from all sides. Police took the opportunity to launch an "eradication" campaign against the syndicate, arresting many of its top leaders. Squabbling broke out within the organization over how to best manage the conglomerate's vast resources. At the same time, rival gangs, long annoyed by the syndicate's power, began harassing Yamaguchi members, infringing on their territory and picking fights.

To counter these problems, an elite group of eight was selected to run the syndicate's affairs, with guidance and mediation from Taoka's widow, Fumiko. For a time their efforts at collective leadership were successful. Despite all the syndicate's troubles, from Taoka's death in 1981 to 1983 the Yamaguchi-gumi actually grew in size to a peak of 13,346 gangsters. A record 587 gangs comprised the syndicate, stretching into 36 of Japan's 47 prefectures.

Number of Enterprises under Yakuza-influenced Management, 1978—1982

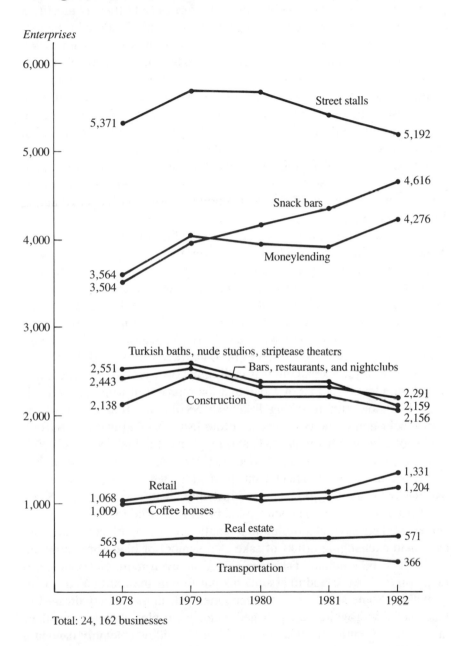

Enterprises

- Street stalls: 5,371 ... 5,192
- Snack bars: 3,564 ... 4,616
- Moneylending: 3,504 ... 4,276
- Turkish baths, nude studios, striptease theaters: 2,551 ... 2,291
- Bars, restaurants, and nightclubs: 2,443 ... 2,159
- Construction: 2,138 ... 2,156
- Retail: 1,068 ... 1,331
- Coffee houses: 1,009 ... 1,204
- Real estate: 563 ... 571
- Transportation: 446 ... 366

1978   1979   1980   1981   1982

Total: 24, 162 businesses

Source: National Police Agency, 1982.

It was clear, though, that the organization would soon have to select a new godfather, and that he would come from the group of eight. Among these eight bosses, men largely in their late forties and fifties, competition already was keen over who would grab the top spot. Feuding broke out. As tempers in the mob reached the breaking point, the contest came down to two veteran mobsters. The first: fifty-eight-year-old Hiroshi Yamamoto, a relative moderate and close associate of Yamaken. Among Yamamoto's qualifications was leading the syndicate in its successful drive into Kyushu, the southernmost island, during the early 1960s. The second candidate: fifty-year-old Masahisa Takenaka, an extremely aggressive but popular leader and longtime friend of the Taoka family. Fumiko reportedly favored Takenaka's militancy over Yamamoto's *interi* (intellectual) yakuza. Among Takenaka's qualifications: eleven convictions for extortion, battery, and other crimes, and pending charges on illegal gambling and tax evasion.

In the end, the selection was made in the finest tradition of gangland democracy, with intense lobbying and several votings by the 104 bosses. Amid charges of bribery and intimidation, a final tally was at last reached: the day had gone to Takenaka, 57 to 19, with numerous abstentions. Playing the role of final kingmaker was Fumiko, who then bestowed the full blessings of the Taoka family on the new leader. But more trouble lay ahead. When Fumiko summoned the defeated Yamamoto to ask his cooperation, the yakuza boss refused to become Takenaka's subordinate.

Within days, Yamamoto was calling his own press conference, and in a short address told all of Japan that the moment of truth had arrived. ". . . I cannot agree to seeing Takenaka become the fourth head of the Yamaguchi-gumi," he announced. "I told [Mrs. Taoka] that I regretfully could not accede to her request. That is my frank and final decision." With that said, on June 19, 1984, at one of Kobe's leading restaurants, Yamamoto and eighteen top lieutenants formed the Ichiwa-kai, taking nearly half the syndicate's 13,000 men and instantly creating one of Japan's top three crime syndicates. The Ichiwa-kai bosses, dressed in dark blue suits, cemented their new relationship in a lengthy ceremony of sakazuki, with each man exchanging drinks of sake as a symbol of blood brotherhood.

Not to be outdone, Takenaka staged an even more elaborate ceremony on Shikoku Island to assume his position as the fourth Yamaguchi godfather. Some 300 fellow mobsters attended, immaculately dressed in black suits with white ties, polished Yamaguchi pins shining from their lapels. At a traditional Japanese inn, Taoka's widow solemnly handed a dagger to the new boss, symbolically marking Takenaka's ascension to the Yamaguchi throne.

For the next six months, tensions remained high between the two syndicates. Slowly, though, the Ichiwa-kai began to lose ground. The parent Yamaguchi syndicate promised amnesty to all those who would rejoin. The syndicate even instituted a new benefit for its members – retirement pay – and awarded the first amount, about $42,000, to a seventy-one-year-old bookie with the gang since 1948. The efforts seemed to work. The Yamaguchi-gumi steadily recaptured much of its lost membership, its ranks swelling to some 10,000, and again became Japan's largest crime organization. The Ichiwa-kai, meanwhile, had been reduced to 2800 men. Worried by the increasing defections, the Ichiwa-kai's Yamamoto took action.

The ambush occurred on January 26, 1985, a Saturday night. At least four Ichiwa-kai hit men arrived in a black car at the Osaka apartment of Takenaka's mistress. As Takenaka and his two highest gang bosses stepped into an elevator, a hail of bullets ripped through their bodies. All would soon die from their wounds. In one attack, the Ichiwa-kai had swept away the top leadership of the Yamaguchi-gumi – but had begun a murderous gang war.

In the midst of more raids and executions, the Yamaguchi-gumi took time to pay respects to Takenaka. In a nationally televised funeral, more than 1000 black-suited gangsters gathered again at Taoka's mansion. Black and white bunting covered the home, and a procession of Mercedes and other foreign luxury cars stretched down the street. The mobsters were in no mood for mourning, however. "We must kill," muttered one to a reporter. "Total slaughter," rumbled another.

By early February, the 83 bosses of the Yamaguchi-gumi had met and unanimously elected sixty-two-year-old Kazuo Nakanishi as their new leader, and then declared open war on the Ichiwa-kai. An immediate bloodbath was averted only by the rapid mobilization of 660 riot police to 184 gangland homes and offices. Over the next month, officials arrested more than 990 mobsters and confiscated some 50 handguns and rifles, among them at least one U.S. Army M-16 automatic. Nonetheless, more than 200 armed attacks between the two syndicates erupted over the next year, leaving 26 gangsters dead. But the biggest surprise was yet to come.

Although the Yamaguchi-gumi held a commanding lead in sheer numbers, the Ichiwa-kai's men had made off with most of the syndicate's arsenal when they seceded. Desperate for firepower, the Yamaguchi hierarchy embarked on an ambitious and ill-fated journey, according to U.S. lawmen.

Events reached a peak in September 1985, when U.S. undercover agents in Honolulu arrested Takenaka's powerful brother, Masashi, and

Hideomi Oda – the syndicate's reputed "financial controller" – for conspiring to buy 3 rocket launchers, 5 machine guns, and 100 handguns from what they thought were Hawaiian organized crime figures. As part of a related deal, claimed U.S. officials, Yamaguchi members sold or conspired to sell 52 pounds of amphetamines and 12 pounds of heroin to the Americans (with a total street value of $56 million). In addition, Takenaka and company were charged with trying to hire one of the undercover agents to assassinate Yamamoto of the Ichiwa-kai, to whom their own members could not get close. It was a remarkable coup for U.S. officials, the payoff from a yearlong multinational investigation involving six federal agencies and local police in Honolulu and Hong Kong. But for the Yamaguchi-gumi the venture was a complete disaster. Instead of gaining a fat arsenal and a foreign assassin, the syndicate had lost a great deal of money, "face," and, pending trial, two of its highest-ranking members to American jails.

Back in Osaka, the episode undoubtedly cost the fingertips of certain Yamaguchi brethren. But tempers slowly cooled down, for the Ichiwa-kai had accomplished its primary task, and the Yamaguchi-gumi was thrown back into a state of utter confusion. In the end, those who had predicted the Yamaguchi-gumi's demise after Taoka's death seemed premature, but not incorrect. By the mid-1980s, it appeared likely that Japan's largest syndicate would never again dominate the yakuza world.

Families, Federations, and the Sumiyoshi-rengo

Although the Ichiwa and Yamaguchi organizations together account for only 13 percent of Japan's underworld, the impact of their gang war has been dramatic. Careful plans for expansion have been disrupted, while other, more stable syndicates vie for a larger piece of the action. The effects, furthermore, have not been limited to Japan. With alliances and enemies extending throughout the nation – and across the Pacific – the underworld map of the region is being recharted. Agreements with Chinese Triad gangs in Southeast Asia, and with the Mafia and other crime groups in the West, are more important than ever to the feuding gangs, who need to ensure a constant flow of handguns and high-profit drugs into Japan.

The splitting of the Yamaguchi-gumi, however, did not change the basic trajectory of organized crime in Japan. Despite police claims of nearly halving the number of yakuza since their peak in the early 1960s, the big syndicates continue to grow. The smaller gangs have borne the brunt of police crackdowns and changing times, succumbing to repeated mass arrests or absorption by the great syndicates. In 1963, the police counted 184,000 yakuza in 5216 groups nationwide. By 1983 the official

Major Yakuza Syndicates I

Syndicate	Sphere of Influence (prefectures)	Affiliated Groups	Membership
Yamaguchi-gumi	29	400	10,400
Sumiyoshi-rengo	20	113	6,723
Motokyokuto Aioh Rengo-kai*	22	105	4,416
Inagawa-kai	12	119	4,347
Ichiwa-kai	30	140	2,800
Matsuba-kai	12	41	2,147
Nippon Kokusui-kai	10	22	943
Dai Nippon Heiwa-kai	13	51	914
Toa Yuai Jigyo Kumiai	NA**	none	796

*Officially disbanded.
**NA = Not Available.
Source: National Police Agency and press reports, 1981–1984.

figure had dropped for the first time below 100,000, to 98,771 yakuza in 2330 groups. At the same time that the yakuza ranks were being cut in half, however, the largest syndicates steadily increased their share of the underworld. Since 1963, Japan's eight largest crime groups have grown from 8 percent to more than 32 percent of all yakuza.

The schisms within Japan's largest syndicate had virtually no effect on this trend. By 1985, the Yamaguchi-gumi, with 10,000 members, was still the largest syndicate in Japan – and among the largest in the world. The splinter Ichiwa-kai, with less than one-third that membership, ranked a respectable fifth among the yakuza. The Osaka gang war, however, did bring to prominence the nation's other major gangs, particularly those based in and around Tokyo. Of growing importance, suddenly, was the number-two syndicate in Japan – the Sumiyoshi-rengo.

The oyabun of the Sumiyoshi syndicate practice a somewhat different form of criminal management than do the Yamaguchi-gumi bosses. Kazuo Taoka had run his syndicate in the traditional way, structured in pyramid fashion, with enormous control vested at the top in a boss of bosses. By contrast, the Sumiyoshi-*rengo*, or "federation," is just that – a federation of crime families. Although both syndicates share many characteristics, they represent the two organizational poles of gang structure in the yakuza world.

Major Yakuza Syndicates II

Syndicate	Headquarters	Year Formed	Syndicate Boss
Yamaguchi-gumi	Kobe/Osaka	1915	Kazuo Nakanishi
Sumiyoshi-rengo	Tokyo	1958	Masao Hori
Motokyokuto Aioh Rengo-kai	Tokyo	1930	Haruo Tanaka
Inagawa-kai	Yokohama	1945	Kakuji Inagawa
Ichiwa-kai	Kobe/Osaka	1984	Hiroshi Yamamoto
Matsuba-kai	Tokyo	1953	Eisuke Sato
Nippon Kokusui-kai	Tokyo	1958	Kyo Koo-soo a.k.a. Seikichi Kimura
Dai Nippon Heiwa-kai	Kobe/Osaka	1965	Katsuyoshi Hirata
Toa Yuai Jigyo Kumiai	Tokyo	1966	Chong Gwon Yong a.k.a. Hisayuki Machii

Source: National Police Agency and press reports, 1981–1984.

The Sumiyoshi-rengo comprises a league of gangs. The pyramid of power in the Yamaguchi-gumi comes to a fine point, headed by a single man. The top of the Sumiyoshi pyramid is broader; while a powerful oyabun reigns over the syndicate, he is only one of several bosses, all considered equal partners. The Yamaguchi-gumi's pyramid resembles that of the traditional Italian Mafia families early in this century, with absolute obedience and close-knit ties throughout much of the organization. The Sumiyoshi-style federation is a more modern development: less money goes to the top as tribute, less authority is vested in the godfather, and, consequently, more autonomy lies with the individual gangs.

This more decentralized structure hasn't hurt the moneymaking ability of Sumiyoshi gangs: officials conservatively estimate that the syndicate brings in more than $276 million per year. Indeed, much as the Yamaguchi-gumi resembles early Mafia families, the makeup of the Sumiyoshi-rengo closely follows that adopted by the American mob when it modernized during the 1930s. It was then, under the leadership of Lucky Luciano and others, that U.S. gangsters first created a national federation of crime families that law enforcement agencies would call La Cosa Nostra, but insiders would simply refer to as the Commission.

Both types of yakuza groups, despite differences in structure, possess the same basic tenets governing gang life. What is more striking is that these unwritten laws have also been shared by American mobs since their formation:

1. Never reveal the secrets of the organization.
2. Never violate the wife or children of another member.
3. No personal involvement with narcotics.
4. Do not withhold money from the gang.
5. Do not fail in obedience to superiors.
6. Do not appeal to the police or the law.

Despite the similarities, though, even the traditional Mafia in America is less intricately structured than comparable yakuza syndicates. There are fewer officers and less control over the varied gangs. Crime families in the United States need this greater autonomy to help ensure the invisibility and mobility on which the American mob depends. The Mafia may be a social institution in the West, but unlike the yakuza, it has little or no public standing and must remain in effect an underground organization. This also bears on why the U.S. Mafia is so much smaller than the yakuza: years of secrecy have kept the mob down to an estimated 2000 to 5000 initiated members in 24 families across America – just half the size of the Yamaguchi alone (although with associates the Mafia may number as high as 50,000).

Traditionally limited to those of southern Italian extraction, the Mafia is only one facet of organized crime in the West. Like the United States itself, American crime syndicates are diverse and multi-ethnic, ranging from drug-dealing motorcycle gangs to small-town bookmakers. The organization of the yakuza, by contrast, is fairly standardized, particularly among the traditional bakuto and tekiya gangs.

Even within the "modern" Sumiyoshi-rengo, for example, one finds yakuza tradition alive and well. Consider the thoughts of Shotaro Hayashi, eighth boss of the syndicate's Doshida gang and one of the Sumiyoshi-rengo's leading powers.

The Doshida family is a Tokyo-based clan of some 200 gangsters. Hayashi, though, is related through kinship ceremonies to six other yakuza bosses; among them, the brothers control about 1000 of the Sumiyoshi's 6700 members. Hayashi's daughter by blood is married to an American, perhaps the reason he is willing to entertain journalists from abroad.

At the residence-office of the gang, the red carpet is rolled out for the foreign guests. The shoes are removed first, of course, and then the visitors are led past a paneled hallway into a room quite large by Japanese standards. Framed photos cover the walls, of old godfathers, of the Doshida family, of Hayashi posed with Masao Hori, the head of Sumiyoshi. Also displayed are fine artworks, and a complex organizational chart that traces the Doshida-gumi back at least several generations of gamblers. The seating is on the floor, cross-legged, at an elegant wood table toward the center of the room.

Hayashi-san appears shortly, wearing traditional Japanese garb. He is beginning to show some of his fifty-five years or so, but still looks like he can handle himself on the back streets of Tokyo. He has a hard face and stern eyes that now peer from behind a pair of thick glasses. There is a hint of kindness there as well, the look of a leader who takes care of his own.

The resident historian, Fujita, is present, and he remarks quietly on the wealth around him. Hayashi is one of the richest men in the Sumiyoshi-rengo, he confides. More than a gang leader, Hayashi is an entrepreneur who owns perhaps 100 buildings on a busy suburban train line out of Tokyo. "There are no stations around which he doesn't own property," assures Fujita.

Introductions are exchanged, and the host suddenly shouts something in guttural Japanese toward the next room. On cue, sixteen immaculate, crew-cut yakuza – his top captains and lieutenants – enter the room in a line against the wall. His men seat themselves on the floor, in martial arts style. They are wearing three-piece suits and looking unamused. Hayashi begins.

"The real yakuza existed until only the start of the Showa era [1925]. The way they're trained now is different. It's questionable whether real yakuza exist today. There was more chivalry in those days. The times have changed.

"I was a gambler since I was eighteen. We are gamblers. But then the government passed this unworkable law making assemblies of gamblers illegal. It forced us to expand to other business. They suddenly put us out of work. But the regulations backfired. The gamblers spread to the tekiya business, and things got mixed up."

It is now clear that this is an audience, not an interview, and that our godfather is holding court. It is an important opportunity for Hayashi, a traditionalist, to explain before the clan what is important within the yakuza world. His men remain seated, motionless, listening attentively to every word.

"My life as a yakuza began with difficulty, when as a young delinquent I joined a gang. The oyabun didn't like me, though. I wanted to be a gambler, but for a long time after joining the family I wasn't allowed to gamble. First I helped with the cooking and cleaning, because the families back then didn't have help or many women. Men did all the housework except clean the toilet – that the women did. The boss had two rooms – one for his wife, the other for his mistresses."

As Goro Fujita and others later explain, his apprenticeship is not very different from what occurs today, although many bosses – including Hayashi – are critical that the training periods have become too short and are sometimes neglected altogether. Still, today's yakuza recruits typically spend from six to twelve months in training, doing menial tasks such as serving guests, answering phones, cooking, cleaning, chauffeuring the boss and his family. The most common complaint is boredom. Perhaps the greatest difference is that the modern yakuza now frequently carries an electronic beeper to help him stay on twenty-four-hour call six days and nights a week. Absence during a time of urgency can cost a fingertip. Hayashi's hands appear unscathed.

"After some months of cleaning duty, I got a position doing *tachiban* [standing guard], but on cold winter days it was difficult. Finally, when new members joined our gang, I was able to do *zoriban* [arranging shoes in order]. These moves were important. For the first time I was not in the house, cleaning. Unless you take these steps, you could not become a card dealer.

"You join this kind of business because you like your boss. What can you do unless you believe your oyabun is the second most powerful man in the world next to the emperor?

"In the old days you had to cut your own skin in a sake glass to join. So this is the world of outlaws. The oyabun can't teach you anything unless you learn yourself. But one must pledge total obedience. To do that you must receive sake from the boss, with a third person as a witness. It is a very important ceremony. . . .

"Yakuza tradition will never cease because we're different from ordinary people. That's why we joined this world. And we share the same idea that if we make one big mistake we die together."

Hayashi's chief complaint, like that of other oyabun, is that the old ways are dying, that the great values of giri-ninjo, of obligation and compassion, have faded. He bares one other complaint as well. He was detained by Customs officials in the United States recently while on a tour organized by a bank. "I was held for two hours, and always followed after that. Tell the Americans that those stories about us operating in the United States are untrue."

The audience is nearly over. Hayashi feels pensive. "The yakuza are a necessary vice for Japanese society. But in the future our biggest task is to become entrepreneurs, to become clean and pay taxes. The age of the tekiya is over; you have to do it aboveboard now. Business will be our main way to survive. As long as you pay taxes you're okay."

The interview ends. The sixteen yakuza – still motionless, still lined up against the wall – finally begin to move. The party shifts upstairs to a long, narrow dining room set for twenty-five. A sumptuous feast has been prepared for the visitors. Amid slices of exotic Pacific fish and drinks of sake, Hayashi encourages his top men to question his guests about the Mafia in America. Few speak up, however. Those that do base their impressions largely on viewings of *The Godfather,* an immensely popular film in Japan, and particularly so among the yakuza of Doshida-gumi.

The offering of a surrogate family is often what attracts recruits to the ranks of the yakuza. The varied gangs serve as a kind of safety valve for the tightly structured Japanese society, in which not having a steady job or an upstanding family can ruin one for life. Indeed, most new recruits are poorly educated, nineteen to twenty years of age, and are living alone when they join, according to data from Tokyo's National Police Science Research Institute. A surprising number come from broken homes: 43 percent have lost one or both parents.

Nearly one-third of the yakuza's recruits come from the infamous *bosozoku,* or hot-rod gangs, the product of a postwar increase in Japanese juvenile delinquency. Like the yakuza, the bosozoku are highly organized within their troublesome groups. Police in 1982 estimated there were 42,510 bosozoku active in 712 gangs, loosely affiliated under five nationwide federations. Sporting swastikas and similar paraphernalia in imitation of Western biker gangs, they bear names like Medusa, Black Emperor, Fascist, and Weatherman, as often as not quite unaware of their symbols' true meaning. A bosozoku specialist with the National Police Agency explained to Tokyo reporter Michael Uehara: "They've created their own world. It's nothing like the world of other kids their age. There are rules and regulations, badges, uniforms of sorts . . . some groups even have membership fees and punishment for members who break rules."

The bosozoku are in fact a mirror of yakuza society, but their members are often no more than adolescents. More than three-quarters are under the age of twenty, nearly 60 percent between sixteen and eighteen years old. Most of them are dropouts from Japan's fiercely competitive school system who soon find themselves frozen out of the country's rigid job market.

Relations between yakuza and bosozoku are not necessarily amicable. Japan's bona fide gangsters tend to look down upon the young hoodlums, secure in the knowledge that they sit atop the criminal hierarchy. Young delinquents are frequently referred to by the term *chimpira,* which appears to be derived from the Japanese word for penis, and is used on the streets as Americans might use the word "prick."

The Medusa and other bosozoku gangs are not the only sources of recruits for the nation's underworld. The ranks of the yakuza also are filled with vast numbers from two groups that have suffered relentless discrimination in today's Japan: the nation's 676,000 ethnic Koreans and its two to three million burakumin – the members of Japan's ancestral untouchable class described earlier. The issue is sensitive enough that police will not officially estimate the numbers of these groups within the yakuza. But unofficially, police believe that in the Yamaguchi-gumi, for example, burakumin comprise some 70 percent of the membership, and Koreans 10 percent.

Similarly, although to a lesser extent, many of the small numbers of resident Chinese are also driven into the yakuza. For these minorities, for the bosozoku, and for the nation's poor, the gangs can easily seem like the only way out of an otherwise miserable life. Like organized crime in America, the yakuza provide a vehicle for upward mobility. Children of successful gangsters are invariably given first-class educations and encouraged to get legitimate jobs. Such are the attractions of adoption into a yakuza family.

The paternalistic structure of the Japanese underworld is not out of character with Japanese society. American anthropologist David Stark, who spent a full year in a remarkable field study of a Japanese gang, writes that ". . . much of what appears so exotic about the gang's organization is actually shared by many of Japan's modern organizations." Stark cites the example of a Japanese bank managed under the principle of *daikazoku,* or "one great family." In a scene reminiscent of yakuza rituals, during the company's annual entrance ceremony, the parents of young recruits symbolically transfer the guardianship of their children to the "family" of the bank. The new workers are given company badges that, like the yakuza's, bear the company logo and list their rank and office within the organization.

There are other similarities. Like Japanese corporations, the yakuza gangs can boast all the trappings of belonging; business cards, used far more widely in Japan than in the United States, are routinely issued to members, embossed with the gang's emblem and clearly identifying the bearer's syndicate, rank, and name. Other symbols are widely used as well, such as flags and lanterns, and even official songs. Anthropologist Stark's host gang, on the Inland Sea, prominently displayed large, round sofa pillows emblazoned with the group's gold emblem, stuffed in the rear window of the boss's Lincoln Continental.

So organized are the yakuza that the larger syndicates even issue their own publications. The Yamaguchi-gumi, for example, publishes the monthly *Yamaguchi-gumi Jiho* and sends it to all gang members. The magazine resembles periodicals published for employees of large corporations and other organizations in Japan, including the prefectural police. In one 1973 issue, a two-page article with photos reported on the meeting of the National Narcotics Banishment and Purification Homeland League, a group composed of uniformed Yamaguchi gangsters from western Japan. Another section, "The Law Classroom," provided four pages of legal advice. There were even two pages of poetry written by gang members, followed by photos and announcements of initiation rites, jailings, prison releases, and funerals. In a later issue, godfather Taoka explained the moral guidelines of the syndicate. "I urge the Yamaguchi-gumi members to do their utmost to avoid being hated by people," he wrote. "Try to have an attitude of gentleness and mildness and always show a smile and act with sincerity."

The gangs use other means as well to ensure cohesiveness. In addition to various rituals, heavy slang – difficult for many Japanese to understand – has been practiced widely for generations; today the words vary even from gang to gang. Certain customs, such as tattooing and finger-cutting, also play a major role, marking the yakuza for life. To demonstrate that infractions of policy are not to be taken lightly, many gangs prominently display the severed fingers, preserved in spirits, at the group's headquarters.

The sense of belonging to the group – so important in Japan – does not come easily in the yakuza world. Indeed, the commitment to the gang is perhaps greater than that demanded by any other group in Japan. Many would-be yakuza fail the requirements of gang life and quit or are expelled. There is a 10 percent annual turnover, but those who survive the first few years adapt as successfully as any Japanese in a society where lifetime employment is an institution.

Inagawa-kai: A Talk with the Godfather

The magazines, badges, and other trappings of gang life in Japan mean very little without the presence of a great boss to hold the group together. If the strength of the yakuza derives in large part from their role as surrogate family, then it is the surrogate father who guides the clan on its way.

With Kazuo Taoka – the godfather of godfathers – gone from the Yamaguchi-gumi, and no one from the syndicate able to fill his shoes, the attention of Japan's seasoned yakuza watchers shifted to the leaders of the other syndicates. Few could match Taoka's experience and seniority in the crime world. Worse, there was no longer a Yoshio Kodama who could mediate among the syndicates and plan great alliances. Although the huge size and aggressive style of the Sumiyoshi-rengo brought the federation considerable attention, it was not to that syndicate that both police and yakuza looked. It was instead to the Sumiyoshi-rengo's long-time Tokyo rival, the enterprising Inagawa-kai, and its remarkable godfather, Kakuji Inagawa.

It was a measure of Inagawa's greatly increased stature that, at the funeral of Taoka, he had served as head of the Taoka funeral committee, a unique position for a godfather of another syndicate. But Kakuji Inagawa had good reason to be there. In a land where age and seniority are not to be treated lightly, the sixty-six-year-old boss carried with him the heart of the yakuza tradition. It was Inagawa who had helped organize Kodama's yakuza army to guard the streets for Ike's 1960 visit; who had served as head of the 13,000-strong Kanto-kai federation – Kodama's unfulfilled vision of a national alliance of rightists and gangsters; who had formed a historic truce with the Yamaguchi-gumi in 1972; and Inagawa again, the skilled fighter and gambler, who had built a postwar band of ragtag street toughs into Japan's fourth largest crime syndicate, stretching into twelve prefectures and across the Pacific. With Taoka's death, Kakuji Inagawa had become a senior statesman of the yakuza.

The Japanese were not the only ones taking note of Inagawa's accomplishments. U.S. Customs officials, in a 1981 intelligence report on Inagawa-kai members setting up shop in Hawaii, warned about the organization's abilities:

> *Although this 4,600 member gang with its 100 sub-groups is not the largest OCR [organized crime] entity in Japan, it is possibly the most efficiently organized and more than compensates for its relatively small numerical strength through a combination of "political" skills at the strategic level and the uninhibited employment of muscle at the tactical levels. . . . The power of the Inagawa-kai is also significantly enhanced by its close alliance with Japan's largest OCR organization, the Kansai-based Yamaguchi-gumi.*

Like the Yamaguchi-gumi, the Inagawa-kai is structured in traditional pyramid fashion, and lays great stress on the familial ties among its members. Smaller than the mammoth Yamaguchi-gumi, the syndicate enjoys greater discipline and tighter organization, while at the same time remaining more flexible. The Inagawa-kai, though, is by no means a small organization. Its more than 4000 members put it at just about the size of the Italian-American Mafia in the United States.

Another factor strengthening the Inagawa-kai is the composition of its membership. Inagawa gangsters traditionally come from bakuto, or gambler, stock. The Yamaguchi-gumi, by contrast, throws together all three of Japan's traditional gangster classes – gamblers, street stall operators, and hoodlums. The Sumiyoshi-rengo can also claim bakuto roots, but because of its structure as a federation of gangs, it lacks what one NPA official called "the strong binding power" of the Inagawa pyramid.

A main source of income for the Inagawa-kai continues to be gambling: bookmaking, running high-stakes casinos, and organizing offshore gambling tours. The syndicate long ago expanded into other typical mob businesses as well, including loan sharking, drug dealing, and various forms of racketeering. According to a 1979 police estimate, the Inagawa gangs run 879 legitimate businesses, including construction and entertainment companies, bars, cabarets, and restaurants. Officials believe the syndicate's combined annual income is nearly $200 million, and that is very likely a conservative estimate.

Like other syndicates, the Inagawa-kai runs on tribute extracted from its member gangs. "Compulsory" donations from within the syndicate totaled at least 580 million yen (about $2 million) from just one bank account monitored by the Tokyo Metropolitan Police in 1974. Top bosses must pay 250,000 yen a month (about $1300); less is demanded from the lower ranks.

The syndicate is composed of 119 gangs, from which 12 bosses are selected to act as a board of directors. Among those who sit at the top is Inagawa's own son, a possible candidate for succession – unusual in modern yakuza gangs. Godfather Inagawa may be on the verge of creating a personal dynasty that will ensure a new generation of internationally minded Japanese gangsters. His old teacher Kodama would have been proud.

Getting in to see the man whom many consider Japan's most powerful godfather is a difficult, at times precarious, task. Introductions from proper go-betweens are required, and one must pass muster in a tense preliminary interview by the boss's top lieutenants. In addition, "face" must be saved by all parties involved, a complicated task because not all middlemen can be present at the final meeting. Compounding the problem is that such values as saving face, already treated quite seriously in Japan, assume new heights within the yakuza world. So arcane are some of the yakuza customs that even well-educated Japanese often do not understand the ways of this subculture. Attempting such an interview plunges one into a world of invisible strings and obligations that a foreign visitor can only stumble through noisily.

Inagawa does, however, meet the press on occasion, and apparently the interest of American journalists aroused his own curiosity. The final, deciding factor, according to one go-between, was Inagawa's personal fortune-teller, a seventy-eight-year-old sage who advised the powerful boss that such a meeting would be an auspicious one.

The gathering took place on the thirty-ninth floor of the posh, forty-floor Akasaka Prince Hotel in Tokyo. Inagawa-san held court that day in the hotel's executive suite, an elegant room bound by large windows and a fine view of the central city. Inagawa's top three lieutenants, who had conducted the pre-interview, were there again, stern-faced and businesslike.

Inagawa, though, was friendly, and offered a warm welcome. At seventy years of age, he looked remarkably well kept, perhaps ten years younger. A short, stout man, he wears a bit of a belly (but carries it well) and radiates confidence, success, and leadership. His balding, muscular head sits fastened onto a two-inch-high neck built like an anvil. Like his lieutenants, he was dressed in a dark blue three-piece suit.

The group was seated around a large, fragile glass table. Young, crew-cut servants from the gang rushed in and out with a procession of refreshments: green tea, delicate sweets, and, finally, coffee. These lay untouched.

"I like casual conversations," Inagawa began, "but it's difficult to do interviews. I don't want to become a showpiece. We're part of society's hidden world and not meant to be more."

There was nothing casual about this conversation, however. Inagawa-san spoke in the traditional Confucian manner, dictating philosophy to his students, throwing in his own anecdotes and little jokes. Still, the godfather tried hard to put his guests at ease, showing off his many scars from over the years. Part of an ear was cut off; there is a chest wound; and, most important, he pointed to the back of his head.

"Part of my brains were blown off, and I died, but somehow the doctors revived me. After that there was a new life for me and a change in my heart. Until then I was strong in physical strength – too strong in my younger days – and then my life changed, I went through a conversion."

Since that time, Inagawa-san has earned the reputation of a peace-maker among the yakuza gangs. His underworld diplomacy has helped make him a very wealthy man. But the seasoned godfather has not forgotten his origins.

"I grew up in a poor home, with no heating and few conveniences. Our meals were meager, just pickles and rice. . . ." His father, a graduate of prestigious Meiji University, lost everything to gambling. Said Inagawa, who never completed elementary school: "Now I've reversed that."

His father also was involved in a left-leaning farmers' group, although that had little appeal to the boy. As a teenager, the young Inagawa studied martial arts at a local judo school, until one day his teacher recommended him to a local yakuza boss in need of strong-arms. "Fighting was my business then. I was very simpleminded – I wanted to be strong."

The yakuza life surprised him, though. "I was just cleaning the floors. I didn't know yakuza did that sort of thing. I was up at five A.M. every day, washing the sliding doors with my hands and cold water during the winter. Before, yakuza training was severe. Our business changed drastically after the war."

Inagawa traces back the Inagawa-kai's all-important family tree to the Hansho-kane, a gang he calls the University of Tokyo of the Yakuza, roughly akin to a Harvard for the Mafia. But it was only in 1945, after his service in the war, that he founded the Kakusei-kai, predecessor to the modern-day Inagawa-kai.

As a sign of Inagawa's new status, he proudly related an anecdote about the Tokyo Metropolitan Police. "Each year we personally travel to police headquarters to give our traditional New Year's greetings. And each year the police ask, 'When are you going to disband your group?' But in 1983, for the first time I was encouraged to live a long life and play lots of golf [a favorite pastime]. It's interesting to hear the police celebrate my longevity now. They said I'm the only one now to chair the yakuza system and keep the peace. They want me to live a long life because they depend on me and I feel thankful and would like to help them. . . ." (Tokyo police deny any such statements were made.)

Inagawa loves golf. Every third and fourth Monday, he sponsors a golf competition at the Lakewood course in Kanagawa Prefecture, inviting professional golfers and well-known entertainers. He also enjoys taking his game on the road, traveling from one end of Japan to the other, at times followed by as many as seventy subordinates. The golf tours do more than improve his game: they are an opportunity to demonstrate his power to local gang bosses. At each stop, Inagawa gives banquets, inviting the region's reigning yakuza powers to dine with him. His travels aren't limited to the golf circuit, though. He often shows up at the VIP rooms of horse racing tracks as well. According to the *Weekly Mainichi,* wherever he goes, the yakuza boss is always followed by a guardsman who holds a large cash-filled paper bag.

Inagawa has a reputation for generosity – he collects hats and white shirts, and then gives them out to his younger members. Sometimes he will give $40 to a follower for a pack of cigarettes. He offers his visitors some sage advice: "Beware of the weak, for the strong will take care of themselves. And don't take any percentage from your direct subordinates; don't be greedy."

He is reflective about his old teacher, Yoshio Kodama. "It was unfortunate that Kodama-sensei was implicated in Lockheed, because we lost a great kuromaku. Yoshio Kodama was a great man and the world will never see the likes of him again." Indeed, Inagawa sees the end of the kuromaku era. "There will be no more kuromaku. This is the age of democracy. We needed kuromaku in an age of transition. . . ."

Inagawa-san complained that the Western press has never written anything favorable about the yakuza; he hopes this will change. "I like books that have a favorable aspect to the yakuza," he said pointedly, and suggested that the authors might want to submit their manuscript to him so it can be checked for wrong "assumptions." He proposed as a model an apparently endless series about him in the sensational weekly *Asahi Geino,* in which the author kindly submits his articles prior to publication. In one story, explained Inagawa, the author's assumptions were so wrong he had to edit out half the piece. The *Asahi Geino* series is a tribute to Inagawa's greatly increased stature in the yakuza world, but according to journalists familiar with the situation, the magazine cannot stop publishing the serial even if it wants to. Inagawa-san displayed the thirtieth installment; his aides would later assure him that many more are on the way.

More than two hours had passed, and the boss indicated that the audience was nearly over. "I'm sure there are things that will give you a bad impression, but we're trying. Our problem today is how to be more liked by the community, or at least not hated. . . ."

One of his top lieutenants, Keizo Tanaka, stressed a second point: "We'd like you very much to grasp the fact that our leader is a gentleman." Indeed he is. One is struck by the fine dress, polite manners, and hospitality shown by these top yakuza.

Before the meeting ended, however, Inagawa spent considerable time railing over a familiar theme among yakuza bosses: the young gangsters – less loyal, harder to control. "I can foster and educate the young people, and they hopefully will do so with the next generation, but beyond that it's difficult to grasp."

Inagawa is a traditionalist, a firm believer in the values of giri-ninjo and gangster chivalry. But he also sees room for change in many of the old customs, and has become something of a reformer among yakuza godfathers. He has, for example, shortened the once lengthy initiation rites entailing sakazuki, the formal exchange of sake. There are some rituals, though, such as the funeral ceremony, that he won't touch. Others, like finger-cutting, he has been less successful at changing. As noted earlier, if the Inagawa-kai is typical, 39 percent of its members are missing at least one finger joint. Because of the high turnover within yakuza gangs, a lot of former gangsters are walking around with nine fingers. This concerns the yakuza boss, who is fond of telling the story of how he tried to stop the practice within his own gangs.

A lowly soldier in the Inagawa army had committed some grievous error, so his immediate boss demanded he slice off a fingertip as punishment. When Inagawa learned of this, he was enraged, and berated the boss for ordering such an act. The boss, humiliated and ashamed, responded in the only way he knew how: he cut off his finger and presented it to Inagawa.

The godfather has been more successful at changing other long-held yakuza traditions. One reform that gained Inagawa wide attention in Japan was his abolition of the infamous *demukai,* the prison-release ceremony. When one of Inagawa's four arrests for gambling finally landed him in jail, his liberation, like most yakuza jail releases, was an occasion of great pomp. Hundreds of gang members arrived in dozens of expensive foreign cars. Once at the prison, the syndicate members carefully lined up according to gang, subgang, and personal rank. In Inagawa's case, as with other high-ranking yakuza, representatives of affiliated gangs were also present to pay their respects.

Demukai is an important rite of passage to the yakuza, a symbol that the state's rehabilitation effort has failed. Typically, the released gangster is given a significant promotion for doing his time for the gang. The gang publicly displays its commitment to its members and also engages in some recruitment, offering an opportunity for marginal members and potential recruits to interact with the organization.

Perhaps most important, the ceremony allows the gang to show off its power with a convoy of foreign luxury cars. There is something about large, black Cadillacs and Continentals that has great appeal to the yakuza. Indeed, in Japan, where after tax and refitting the price of a U.S. car doubles, the gangsters are Detroit's best customers. So closely identified are American cars with the yakuza that many parking lots ban the vehicles, and police reportedly advise the public to steer clear of anyone driving them.

Clad in their flashy outfits, with their close-cropped hair and aggressive driving style, the yakuza in their foreign cars are readily identifiable on the highways of Japan. In a land where the biggest vehicle usually determines right-of-way, the yakuza driver commands the road, sweeping past normally combative truck drivers and anyone else who dares get in the way. Like a renegade funeral procession, these criminal convoys converge on unsuspecting rest stops and neighborhoods, tying up traffic and scaring local residents out of their wits. As one might imagine, such blatant displays of gang power have dismayed both the police and the general public. It was in response to this, says Inagawa, that he decided to do away with the ceremony.

Befitting Inagawa's role in the yakuza, a movie based on the godfather's life was released in 1984 entitled *Shura no Mure* (A Band of Daredevils). As with many movies made about the yakuza, the Inagawa-kai has helped with production of this feature film. Inagawa must feel that his turn has arrived; a decade earlier, the Yamaguchi-gumi had seen to it that a trilogy on Kazuo Taoka's life was produced.

Inagawa's life story joins a central, firmly established cinematic tradition in Japan: the yakuza film. These films, descendants of the old samurai epics, bear little resemblance to American or European gangster movies; they are closer to the Western, in which cowboy and outlaw clearly define a code of morality. From the samurai, the yakuza has inherited the role of the last defender against the decadence and corruption ushered in by modernization and contact with the West.

Unlike the Western, though, yakuza films are as highly stylized as the Kabuki theater of a century earlier. The movies are "probably the most restricted genre yet devised," according to director Paul Schrader, writing in *Film Comment* magazine. "The characters, conflicts, resolutions, and themes are preset. . . . Yakuza films are litanies of private argot, subtle body language, obscure codes, elaborate rites, iconographic costumes and tattoos."

So similar are many of the films, with the same actors and the same stories, that often it is difficult to tell them apart. Japan's leading actor, Ken Takakura, who won his fame starring in gangster roles, has made one yakuza classic – *Abashiri Bangaichi* (Abashiri Prison) – more than a dozen times, according to Schrader.

Typically, a yakuza film opens with the outlaw's release from prison, the noble gangster having served years behind bars to spare his gang a police investigation. Other requisite scenes follow: the gambling den, the baring of the tattoo, the blood brother ritual, the evil oyabun, plenty of finger-cutting, and a final battle bloodying the screen with dazzling swordplay. Throughout, the film stresses the twin themes of giri-ninjo, as the yakuza hero struggles between his deeply felt virtues of absolute duty to his crooked gang and compassion for the oppressed. In the end, he dies a violent, but honorable, death. There is in these sagas an almost unrelenting obsession with death, a fatalism that runs through nearly every film. As one gangster on the big screen declared, "There are only two roads for a yakuza, prison and death."

If the human conflicts sound elaborate, the films themselves are not. Yakuza movies are mostly low-budget endeavors that Japan's big studios throw together within a matter of weeks. Schrader traces back the first authentic yakuza film to 1964, a movie titled, appropriately enough, *Bakuto* (Gambler). The genre quickly came into its own, and by the mid-1970s, 100 yakuza films a year were being churned out. And the Japanese loved them. Yakuza-film addicts range across the political spectrum, from leftist student activists to the ultranationalists of author Yukio Mishima's private army.

Toei Studios is the Warner Brothers of the yakuza movie industry, having made well over 300 of the films, most with the same plot structure. The studio owes much of its success to its general producer, Kouji Shundo, who pioneered the genre. Shundo learned about his subjects firsthand; he is a former yakuza. Present-day yakuza are employed in the industry as well. Most Japanese actors labor under contract to one of the country's four big studios, a system not unlike the worst days of old Hollywood. To enforce their will, some studios have reportedly hired gangsters over the years, resulting in a number of highly publicized assaults on Japan's leading stars.

Not surprisingly, the yakuza are among the yakuza films' biggest fans. On the big screen, they can see themselves portrayed as the noble gangsters they so rarely are. But these are mostly the older works, from the heyday of the genre in the 1960s and early 1970s. A newer subgenre has emerged, which strikes somewhat closer to reality. This is the *Jitsuroku Eiga* (True Document Films), in contrast to the more orthodox *Ninkyo Eiga* (Chivalry Films). In this later group, there is less honor and more treachery, less swordplay and more gunfire. The modern yakuza cinema has expanded along with the gangs as well; recent films have been set in Hong Kong and the Philippines. Complains godfather Inagawa, "In the movies nowadays, the yakuza is depicted as interesting, but he always loses to the authorities in the end. It's impossible to make a movie that's one-hundred-percent pro-yakuza."

Inagawa, though, has more to complain about than the role of yakuza in the movies. Like their fading heroic images on the screen, Japan's real-life outlaws are rapidly losing their honorable image. This is due in large measure to the changing times, as new opportunities for the syndicates appear with the growth of the nation's economy. The ruthless expansion pioneered by Taoka and his Yamaguchi-gumi, and matched by Inagawa and the others, had by the 1980s made the public weary of the everpresent gangs. The widespread drug dealing, extortion, racketeering, and violence were affecting more people than ever before. But just as the Japanese thought they had seen it all, the corruption fostered by the yakuza spread to places even they didn't expect.

Chapter 6
Corruption, Japanese-style

Like many good crime stories, this one began by accident. In March of 1982, a middle-aged woman strode into the Osaka District Prosecutor's office and lodged a complaint against her boyfriend for physically assaulting her. The alleged offender was a retired sergeant of the local police.

Japanese officials did not look kindly upon one of their own involved in domestic violence, or, for that matter, in other crime. Since the war, law enforcement in Japan has won the admiration and respect of not only the Japanese people, but of police forces around the world. The accomplishments of Japan's police seem to go hand in hand with those of the nation's "economic miracle." Women can safely walk the streets of Tokyo alone at midnight; rates of violent crime are among the lowest in the industrialized world; and the police have become a highly disciplined, dependable force of professional lawmen.

It was this image that was marred when the retired sergeant went about beating his girlfriend. Upon further investigation, officials learned that the former cop also worked for a gambling machine leasing company, the kind that rents out computer-operated poker games. There was nothing illegal in it per se, but, as with similar games in the United States, regulation has proved difficult for Japanese authorities. Under certain owners, and with a small adjustment, the machines can transform an amusement arcade into a gambling hall.

Still, there was no reason to suspect foul play beyond the morally reprehensible actions of an old policeman. Before long, however, the case would utterly transform the image of the Osaka police and raise for the first time in recent memory the specter of widespread systemic corruption within Japanese law enforcement, a corruption influenced, and at times inspired, by the yakuza.

It was while local investigators checked into the ex-sergeant's background that they first smelled something rotten within the ranks. Their suspect, apparently, was using his old police cronies to tip off contacts in the gambling business about upcoming police raids.

As Osaka police probed further, the broad outlines of a major scandal came into view. The tip-offs were being made not only by the former sergeant, but by a growing number of police on active duty. And they were receiving payoffs not only from gambling bosses, but from the operators of striptease theaters as well. The respected officers of Osaka's Finest – the prefectural police – appeared to be working hand in hand with the local mob, a shocking development for the Japanese.

Osaka is a town that, like Chicago, has always played second city to Japan's New York – Tokyo. Osaka's 3 million people live within a sprawling metropolis of 19 million, in one of Asia's leading centers of commerce. For 300 years, while the country's political and cultural life centered in Tokyo, Osaka concentrated on business and industry.

Also, like Chicago, Osaka became a mob town. Particularly hard hit was the adjacent port city of Kobe, home base of the legendary Yamaguchi-gumi, largest crime syndicate in the country. The Yamaguchi-gumi had cash and political clout, and its 13,000 members had made organized crime a fact of life throughout the region. So it was, perhaps, only a matter of time before such power corrupted the local police.

Investigators took eight months to build their case, but by November of 1982 they were ready. On the first of the month, the initial collars were made: a senior policeman and the manager of a game center were arrested on bribery charges.

The next day, a veteran police sergeant, apparently unconnected to the inquiry, committed suicide, claiming his innocence in a final, handwritten note. More arrests followed over the next week, including that of the retired sergeant whose domestic assaults first sparked the investigation.

Later the same week, on the morning of November 12, 1982, Tadashi Sugihara, former chief of the Osaka police, tied a sash to the central beam running along the ceiling of his storehouse. Around the sash's other end he snugly wrapped his neck and proceeded to commit suicide in its most commonly practiced form in Japan. Unlike the sergeant earlier that week, Sugihara left no note. Those closest to him knew only that he had recently made a volley of phone calls to Osaka and had grown increasingly concerned about the police scandal.

Sugihara's reign over Osaka headquarters lasted two years, until his promotion three months before his death to president of the National Police Academy. When he died, he was one of the highest-ranking policemen in all Japan. An elite bureaucrat with a bright political future, Sugihara was being groomed for the position of deputy minister of justice in the Nakasone cabinet.

Veteran Japanese cops were killing themselves because it was the only "honorable" way out of an unbearable situation. They had brought immeasurable shame to Japanese law enforcement, and their continued existence – not to mention their testimony – would only further bring humiliation upon those they had served so long. Sugihara, furthermore, was clearly under suspicion. He had been seen with another high-ranking police official frequenting almost nightly the expensive bars in a renowned Osaka entertainment district, according to an article in *Bungei Shunju,* a leading monthly. A typical night of such festivities – including a couple of restaurants and a nightclub – could easily have cost them $2000. A convicted police investigator would later testify he had given some $16,000 to Sugihara to bribe his way out of a transfer. Other evidence would also implicate Sugihara in bribes from local mob-controlled Turkish bath houses. These *turukos,* as they are called, are nothing more than houses of prostitution.

Although Sugihara's death firmly tied the scandal to the department's highest-ranking officers, it still wasn't clear how far the case would spread. Many citizens had long suspected that large-scale official corruption existed – even in the police departments. But the Japanese had felt that such problems were best swept under the tatami mat. Perhaps that was finally changing, for the Lockheed revelations were still fresh in the country's memory. Speculation on the police scandal was running rampant in the press, and seasoned reporters were betting that, with Sugihara's suicide, much more would be revealed. They were right.

By the beginning of 1983, the bribery scandal had snowballed. Investigators implicated scores of men from throughout the Osaka police force, and disclosed payoffs to individual cops as large as $20,000. When the dust finally settled, a record 124 lawmen had been fired or otherwise disciplined, enough officers to police a Japanese city of nearly 70,000. And still there was more.

In December, the national daily *Mainichi Shimbun* reported that two LDP politicians – including Akira Hatano, the justice minister in the newly appointed Nakasone cabinet – had acted as consultants to game machine associations whose members were linked to the Osaka bribery case. Hatano protested his innocence, explaining that he had never received any money for his services, and that he had assumed the organization was engaged in "wholesome forms of amusement." But despite

Hatano's claims, suspicion lingered around the justice minister, whose campaign for the Diet in 1980 had attracted donations from a Tokyo yakuza-rightist political party. A former Tokyo police superintendent, Hatano would later comment that seeking morality from a politician is like "asking for fish at a vegetable shop."

By February of 1983, the Osaka bribery scandal had spread to neighboring Hyogo Prefecture, home to the national headquarters of the Yamaguchi-gumi in Kobe. Authorities arrested a fifty-six-year-old vice squad chief and launched probes into the affairs of more than ten other officers. In what had become a familiar pattern to investigators, the vice chief, in return for bribes of about $1000 to $2000, leaked information on police raids to gambling machine operators. He would pass on payments of $50 to $100 to his subordinates to dissuade them from investigating the gambling shops, and invited officers of neighboring police stations to dinners and drinking parties with the machine agents and operators. Also part of his routine were visits to police stations, at times in the company of gamblers, who would arrive laden with gifts for the precinct's ranking officers.

The operations were as massive as they were corrupt. One gambling chain ran more than 10 shops with some 800 machines; the company employed more than 300 people and grossed above $350,000 daily. The shops, furthermore, stayed open 24 hours and most were located prominently along the region's major highways. Neon signs even advertised the machines to passing motorists. Yet despite this openness, only two of the company's shops were ever raided during its three-year existence. One day before an intensive, long-overdue police crackdown in November 1982, the operator abruptly closed all his shops, removed the machines, and disappeared.

One final, ominous blow would strike before the Osaka scandal faded from Japan's newspapers. In March, *Mainichi* reporters revealed the existence of a nationwide tip-off syndicate, run by retired police officers and businessmen and linked to the yakuza. The operation provided information on police raids to gambling clubs in twelve prefectures, including Tokyo, Osaka, and Hyogo. The syndicate, at least six years old, had gained a reputation for accuracy and timeliness, being able to warn its customers three to ten days before a raid. One contract with the Tokyo-based organization reportedly cost some $12,000, plus a monthly fee of between $500 and $2000. Among the organizers was a prominent gangster who ran numerous "Turkish baths" in the Tokyo area, a man whom reporters identified only by the nickname "Emperor of the Night."

The World's Best Cops

The Osaka bribery scandal was not the first problem to surface within the Japanese police ranks. While most other Japanese police forces continue to maintain records to be envied by any large U.S. city, a number of cases have surfaced that suggest, if nothing else, widening cracks within the system. The year 1984 seems to have been a particularly bad one: a former sergeant in Kyoto shot and killed a policeman and a bank employee before making off with about $2300; months later, officials arrested a former Tokyo police captain for double murder and possession of nearly $80,000 worth of precious stones. Also that year, a number of cases arose involving past and present lawmen in fraud, forgery, and kidnapping. Similar to the Osaka scandal, earlier cases had been revealed in which police around the country informed local gangs of impending raids.

Aside from a handful of reports on the yakuza, American accounts about crime in Japan are generally awash with praise for the police. Such points are usually made for good reason. The Japanese police do have a high standard of discipline, and violent crime is far lower than in the United States. A country with half the population of the U.S., Japan had only 922 homicides in 1981. (There were 1832 in New York City alone.) According to official statistics, Americans are 12 times more likely to be raped, and 20 times more likely to be victimized by property crime. Perhaps most striking of all is the fact that, since 1955, official crime totals in Japan have actually followed a downward curve. In other words, during a period of unprecedented economic and urban growth, while crime rates in America shot upwards, those in Japan actually went down.

The Japanese police have appropriately taken their share of credit for this admirable accomplishment, and pride themselves on being the world's best cops. Yet, so notable are their many achievements that it becomes difficult to understand the most persistent, overwhelming problem confronting law enforcement in Japan: how can a hundred thousand gangsters thrive on the islands?

The answer, in part, rests on the unique relationship that exists between Japan's cops and robbers. It is, in a Western sense, a much more far-reaching, more institutionalized form of corruption than anything suggested by the police scandals previously discussed. Over the years, for example, there have been massive police crackdowns on the yakuza. At regular intervals, police have staged these huge offensives, arresting more than a thousand gangsters in a single day. From reading newspaper accounts, one might easily surmise that officials have waged an unrelenting war on the underworld. But while they make for impressive reading, the raids are mostly a form of harassment and, in particular, of publicity, reminiscent of the police chief's order in the movie classic *Casablanca* to "round up the usual suspects." Questions about the effectiveness of the raids have been raised by anthropologist Walter Ames, who spent eighteen months in Japan doing fieldwork on the police. In his 1981 book, *Police and Community in Japan,* Ames wrote that ". . . these raids assume an almost ritual air because most of the gangsters are released in a few days through lack of evidence of criminal acts or because their offenses were minor." Ames further points out that the gangs usually receive warning before the huge raids, and that well before authorities arrive on the scene, virtually all contraband is concealed and the highest bosses have gone into hiding. The raids end with a uniquely Japanese twist: so the police can save face, the gangsters generally leave behind a few guns for the officers to confiscate.

In keeping with the unusual openness of the gangs, there is a great deal of personal rapport between the yakuza and the police; local cops know local gangsters by name, and there is an easy familiarity between them. Such amicable relationships help form the bridge to police corruption. Departing precinct captains, for example, traditionally collect cash gifts from local merchants, much as retiring bureaucrats and company officials do with their own contacts. For the police chief, however, this can mean substantial gifts from local operators of massage parlors, gambling halls, and other gang businesses – but not if he has made life too uncomfortable for the community's wealthier "businessmen."

Police, though, are drawn to the yakuza for reasons other than bribery. Most Japanese lawmen are quite sympathetic to the highly conservative views held by the yakuza. Indeed, part of the rigorous routine investigation into the background of police recruits is to screen out anyone with possible left-wing leanings. Japanese leftists, unsurprisingly, have long accused police of going easy on the yakuza's often suspect political activity on the right.

There are other similarities as well. Like their criminal counterparts, most police have high school educations at best, and come largely from families of modest means. Also, many Japanese police admire and identify with the gangs' professed ideals of giri and ninjo, and similarly fashion themselves as a kind of latter-day samurai. These traditional values are expressed in a genre of moving ballads that frequently have yakuza or oyabun-kobun themes, and are quite popular among the police.

For their part, the gangs respect the police and understand their duty to enforce the law. After a gangland murder, for example, the guilty yakuza will typically turn himself in to the nearest police station and make a full confession. The deed having been done, he is fully prepared to suffer the consequences. As syndicate boss Kakuji Inagawa commented when asked about his gang's relationship with the police, "We believe in the Japanese police. If they say that the Inagawa gang is bad, then it is so. I don't want to say this, but they are a very capable lot. It is their duty to watch me. I respect them. Please convey my best regards to them."

This attitude of complicity is reinforced by the enduring links between high-ranking government officials and gang leaders, which have served to legitimize the position of the yakuza in Japanese society. What are police to think when a former prime minister and education minister guarantee the bail of a convicted murderer from the Yamaguchi-gumi? Police actions thus often seem tailored toward dealing not with a menacing underworld, but more with a somewhat misguided loyal opposition.

Perhaps the most remarkable aspect of police-gangster relations is the yakuza's function as a kind of alternative police force. Says criminologist Eric Von Hurst, a fifteen-year resident of Japan, "The one thing that terrifies Japanese police is unorganized crime. That's why there's so little street crime here. Gangsters control the turf, and they provide the security. If some hoods come around the neighborhood and start making trouble, chances are the yakuza will reach them first. Japanese police prefer the existence of organized crime to its absence."

The Underground Economy

The unique symbiosis between Japan's police and gangsters is indicative of a much larger problem of structural corruption in the country. Some of it bears a strong resemblance to the grand old traditions of corruption in America's large eastern cities, where the politician, labor boss, and gangster get rolled into one well-greased machine. Other elements of graft and corruption in Japan, however, remain markedly different from those of the West, floating somewhere on the same cultural plane as the Japanese fusion between gangster and rightist.

To the distant observer, Japan's low crime rates can be misleading, depicting a society of completely law-abiding automatons. Even allowing for the highly defined role of the yakuza, a look at Japan's police statistics seems to reveal a people who simply don't break the law very much. The Japanese, however, can be just as devious and corruptible as the Americans, even more so. They do not, for one glaring example, cooperate very much with the National Tax Agency, Japan's version of the IRS.

Like Americans, the Japanese support a massive underground economy. Estimates of the size of Japan's so-called black money sector range from $50 billion to $150 billion, although officials concede these are only guesses. (A 1981 estimate by the IRS put America's underground economy at nearly $250 billion.) What Japanese officials do know is that the country's tax collectors face continued, widespread underreporting of incomes by both individuals and companies. Tax collectors unearthed a record 529.3 billion yen (about $2.3 billion) in undeclared earnings in 1982. Topping the list were owners of private hospitals, followed by operators of *pachinko* parlors and loan companies, two occupations often linked to the yakuza. (Pachinko, a pinball-like game, is perhaps Japan's most popular pastime.) Not far behind were Buddhist monks.

So widespread is the cheating that, for 1983, tax officials accused the Japanese of underreporting more than 40 percent of all service companies, ranging from computer software firms and baseball clubs to tourist agencies and massage parlors. Also that year, authorities uncovered hidden capital gains (from the sale of land and buildings) totaling 300 billion yen, or about $1.3 billion. In a pattern familiar to IRS officials, Japanese taxpayers widely practiced such techniques as lying about the actual sale price of property and claiming false exemptions. Particularly delinquent in their returns have been various professional groups. Audits of Tokyo entertainers and physicians revealed average unreported incomes of more than $20,000 per person.

At the urging of police in the early 1970s, the government finally began to tax the earnings of Japan's gangster class. It was hardly a novel idea. U.S. officials have used tax laws as a weapon against the mob since they put Al Capone away on income tax evasion in 1931. But Japanese tax officials, in their zeal to treat everyone equally under the law, announced in 1975 that gangsters were allowed to deduct "business expenses" from their income. "Included in the deductible expenses," read an Associated Press dispatch out of Tokyo, "were rental for gambling places, per diem allowances to gangsters sent out for intimidation, payment to lookouts during gambling sessions and expenses of pimps."

Despite the liberal interpretations of tax law toward the gangs, the vast percentage of yakuza income remains uncounted and untaxed by Japan's official auditors. As in the United States, the gangsters are only following the rest of the population in hiding their billions of dollars from the tax people. But if the Japanese penchant for tax-dodging strikes a familiar chord with Americans, certain crimes in Japan take on a decidedly different flavor. Particularly distinctive are white-collar crime and related endeavors such as bribery and extortion.

When it comes to payoffs, Japan at times seems like a refined version of Mexico or the Philippines. If Japan does indeed have a serious problem of structural corruption, then it reaches its highest point here, in what appears to be a formalized system of endless payoffs. The demand for such payola ranges from multimillion-dollar corporate deals to apartment rentals and college entrance exams.

The concept of bribery in Japan is a muddy one, largely because the custom of gift-giving is so widespread and thoroughly institutionalized, to a far greater level than in the West. Gift-giving in Japan is a traditional, subtle art closely tied up with the obligations involved in giri, and pushing heavily against a thin line that separates it (usually) from outright bribery. Gifts are given when visiting someone's home; twice a year – during July and December – to associates and to those for whom one feels giri; to employees who move or transfer jobs; when one returns home from a trip; and in a myriad of social situations that are often confusing and frustrating for the Japanese themselves. Gifts can range from inexpensive souvenirs to luxury items, or be crisp, clean bills sealed in special money envelopes. So deep-rooted is the practice that many households keep record books of gifts given and received with the prices listed. The Japanese recognize the importance of this custom with the saying that gifts are *junkatsuyu* – "the oil that lubricates society."

How does a Japanese recognize when a gift is in effect a bribe? Not easily. Police and others claim they can identify a bribe if the gift's value is excessive for the particular situation. But such judgments become easily confused; vice cops routinely accept free tickets from local porno show operators. Cash gifts – sometimes of $1000 or more – are given to teachers by parents of students around final exams and admissions time; presents are offered each day by patients to doctors at elite university hospitals to obtain preferred treatment in Japan's socialized medical system. Writes anthropologist Harumi Befu of Stanford University, "It may be difficult for a Western observer to believe that one would not know when he is committing bribery, but . . . because gift-giving is so pervasive in Japan, and the obligations to give, to receive, and to reciprocate are so strongly entrenched . . . it is extremely difficult, if not impossible, to discern whether a gift is legitimate."

Often the bribery is so embedded in ritual that no questions can be asked. Japanese culture simply does not provide any appropriate way to refuse a gift once offered. A good example is the mah-jongg game. During contract negotiations between firms, the representative of one company is frequently invited by his counterparts in the other company to play the popular gambling game. Despite the skill of all the players, the hosts begin to lose huge bets in game after game to their client. Everyone knows what is going on, but the matter is never voiced. When the game ends, it is understood that the winner will do his best to get a contract with that firm.

According to Japanese law, it is a crime for public officials to accept any compensation, outside the legally specified salary, in connection with their recognized duties. The law relating to private citizens is much less clear. There is, in fact, no stated rule; judgment is based on what is socially acceptable. For example, company officials might entertain their business associates at $300 per night. The law allows for this. But if they spend such money on government officials, it can be considered a bribe. Practically, though, the law is seldom applied.

While prime minister, Kakuei Tanaka used the cover of traditional gift-giving to disburse his political funds. The politician's generosity was legendary: summer gifts, year-end gifts, bon voyage gifts, and various campaign contributions all came out of the prime minister's office. There are indeed times when the courts recognize that disbursement of funds has clearly gone beyond the realm of custom. But even then, it takes an event the stature of the Lockheed scandal to draw concerted public attention to the issue.

Many of Japan's more astute political observers readily concluded that the only unique element in the Lockheed case was that the officials were caught and prosecuted, and this only because the case involved a foreign company and such vast amounts of cash. The relative absence of major scandals, say critics, reflects more than anything else the system's ability to cover them up.

How corrupt, then, is Japan? Anthropologist Befu jokes that to really enforce the law, the Japanese government would have to create a huge Department of Bribery Investigations. So pervasive is its use that virtually every major contemporary Japanese politician has had some brush with the nation's postwar bribery law at one point in his career. Some scholars suggest, however, that this may be changing. For many years, they argue, the Japanese public tolerated the sale of access by their politicians, but the Lockheed scandal seems to have signaled a new era, in which the old ways of doing business may have to meet new standards.

If indeed the old ways are dying out, it will be a long process, for such cultural traits seldom change quickly in Japan. Those who have made a clever use of bribery in the past – be it Yoshio Kodama with Lockheed or the Yamaguchi-gumi with the Osaka police – will have equally skilled successors. Furthermore, it is not only bribery that will have to meet new standards. Hand in hand with bribery and kickbacks go blackmail, extortion, and intimidation, crimes that seem to grow exceptionally well in the refined culture of Japan.

Sarakin and Saving Face

At least twice a week, a small news story appears in the Japanese press that reads something like this: Mitsuru Takahashi, heavily in debt to creditors, can no longer bear the shame of being unable to pay off his loans. Rather than have his two children grow up penniless, he kills them and then tries unsuccessfully to take his own life.

The story appears with a number of variations throughout Japan. There was the insurance saleswoman from the west coast who drove her car into the sea, drowning herself and her family because she could not repay $40,000. Or the family of three in Nagano, in central Japan, who shot themselves to death over a $4000 debt. And the story in Tokyo of the confessed killer of a prostitute who committed murder to escape his creditors by going to prison.

These are the victims of Japan's notorious *sarakin,* a word that literally means "salary man financiers" but that translates more directly as "loan sharks." Through widespread use of public humiliation and strong-arm intimidation, police believe the yakuza-dominated sarakin drove nearly 2400 people to suicide in 1982, or about 11 percent of the nation's total suicide cases. The National Police Agency estimates that 7300 others that year fled the sarakin by abandoning their families and their work, an almost unforgivable act in modern Japan. Those who vanish are called *johatsu* – "the disappeared people," or, literally, "evaporated."

Some 42,000 sarakin firms are believed to operate in Japan, although some estimates put the number as high as 220,000, many of them "ghost" companies whose whereabouts are unknown. These loan sharks have become as successful as they are notorious, largely because the country's mainstream financial institutions have until recently shied away from granting consumer credit. Government policy and social custom have long encouraged the Japanese to "save now, buy later." Personal savings thus average about 20 percent of one's total income, nearly four times the U.S. rate. That, however, is changing, as a younger generation grows increasingly consumer-oriented and moves closer to the American habit of buying on credit. As a result, the consumer loan market in Japan has grown at a remarkable 33 percent annual rate, ballooning from $1.03 billion in 1973 to $9.58 billion in 1981. But in a land where few Japanese own checking accounts (banks often pay customers' bills directly), the granting of consumer credit is still a new phenomenon, and the primary beneficiaries have so far been the sarakin, many of whom are now trying to transform their operations into respectable businesses.

Four sarakin firms are so large that they gave out more consumer loans in 1982 than all of Japan's banks combined. The larger sarakin companies were helped by $1 billion in loans from Japan's leading insurance companies until mounting criticism stopped the practice. U.S. and Canadian banks, however, have helped fill the financial void by lending capital to the fast-growing sarakin industry. One leading sarakin operation has counted among its creditors American Express International Bank (6 billion yen in loans), Bank of Montreal (4 billion yen in loans), and Bankers Trust Bank, Bank of America, and Chase Manhattan Bank.

So lucrative is Japan's burgeoning consumer loan market that it also has attracted American finance companies like AVCO, Beneficial, and Citibank to set up competitive operations. U.S. firms have been helped to a degree by the Japanese government, which in 1983 passed long-overdue legislation aimed at cleaning up the industry. Legal interest rates, once as high as 110 percent annually, are now limited to a still-hefty 73 percent until 1987, and to 40 percent thereafter.

Yet, despite the offering of far cheaper credit by U.S. firms (18 percent to 29 percent), most Japanese borrowers still seem to prefer the no-questions-asked approach of the sarakin. Almost any adult Japanese can walk into the local sarakin office and – with nothing more than simple identification – walk out twenty minutes later with $2000 in cash and a 60 percent annual interest rate. Roger Broms, an officer with Beneficial in Tokyo, complained in 1983: "We can consolidate a guy's loans, but then he can go around the corner and borrow himself into a hole again."

Perhaps the biggest problem for U.S. firms is surviving in a business that has "heavy gangster overtones," according to Richard Huber, vice president of Citibank's Tokyo operations. In a *Business Week* story entitled "U.S. Bankers Take On the Japanese Mafia," Huber stressed that the major task for American lenders lies in persuading the Japanese that they don't run their businesses like the yakuza. "We're trying to convince consumers that we're different," he said, "that we won't break your kneecaps if you don't pay."

The power of the sarakin, though, is based on far more than the threat of violence. Harassing phone calls and nasty letters are a secondary concern to the Japanese. They fear the sarakin's power to repeatedly punch a sensitive nerve on which so much depends in Japan – saving face.

In its broadest sense, the ability to save face – or to "clear one's name," as some put it – remains a central fact of daily life in Japan. Businessmen devote enormous amounts of time to saving face, prompting more than a few Western salesmen to wonder how their Japanese customers ever earned their reputation for efficiency. It is of paramount importance, however, for such relations to be kept in balance.

The loss of face displayed before the public – by noisy sarakin visits to one's home or office – pushes the Japanese to abandon their work and family, to commit suicide and even murder. Sarakin tactics are in fact typically designed to maximize loss of face. There was, for instance, the case in 1983 when three sarakin charged into a wake and demanded that the bereaved widower pay up or they would disrupt the funeral. Or the case, also that year, of sarakin express-mailing "reminders" of money due to debtors' children – care of their elementary schools.

Ironically, the sarakin themselves are also sensitive to loss of face. When *Gendai* magazine published an exposé of Yasuo Takei, the leading sarakin boss, in July 1983, all 300,000 copies of the issue disappeared within three days of release. *Gendai* editors accused the racketeers of buying up virtually the entire print run to keep the story from the public. The article, entitled "King of the Sarakin Business," details Takei's career as a juvenile delinquent, black marketeer, and finally, sarakin boss.

The need of the Japanese to save face creates a unique climate in which a whole range of extortionist crimes can thrive. Much as gift-giving and giri contribute to the practice of bribery, so do these values make the Japanese particularly vulnerable to blackmail, intimidation, and a host of related acts.

Because of the emphasis on saving face, many crimes take on a different form than they would in the West, although the end is often the same. In 1984, for example, police in Tokyo accused four men of black-mailing a private dental college into handing over $85,000 by threatening to expose "back door" admissions of students with poor grades. The blackmailers, members of an obscure rightist "political party," vowed that unless payment was made, they would send a car equipped with a loud-speaker to the college campus to publicly denounce school officials.

In certain lines of business, the practice of blackmail and extortion is particularly entrenched. One such area is what the Japanese call *mizu shobai* – literally, "water business" – bars, restaurants, and nightclubs. When police in 1980 questioned more than 12,000 businesses in the densely populated Yokohama area, they found that 70 percent of all the region's bars, cabarets, steambaths, game centers, and strip theaters paid protection money to the yakuza. Officials estimated that local gangs each year grossed well over $6.5 million from these shakedowns – and that was just one city.

Sokaiya: "The General Meeting Mongers"
Japan's underworld showcase of extortion, however, is not in the "water business," or even in the sarakin. It thrives among a remarkably brazen,

professional class of corporate racketeers whose activities have traditionally centered around the company shareholders' meeting: the *sokaiya*. The word translates directly as "shareholders' meeting men" or "specialists," but the sokaiya gangs have been variously described in English as "financial racketeers," "general meeting mongers," "black gentlemen in the shadow," and "rent-a-thugs."

For years, virtually every company listed on Japan's stock exchanges dealt with them. They could be seen forming long queues in front of the general affairs bureau of any bank or securities firm. Most wore light-colored business suits similar to those of ordinary employees; others sported loud jackets adorned with wide neckties. At the larger banks, they would check to ensure their names were still officially listed in a special registry, enabling them to receive payoffs at least twice annually. Some made daily rounds through Japan's business districts, visiting several hundred corporations each year. At one major shipping firm, as many as eighty sokaiya visited each morning. They would be serviced by a company official who had been paying off sokaiya for twenty-five years. At another firm, a leading bank, some 2,000 persons, including known gangsters and rightists, were registered to receive twice-annual payments of typically between $20 and $200; certain callers were quietly handed as much as $15,000.

Although not operating as overtly as it once did, Japan's sokaiya industry is alive and well. And if they are not queueing up for corporate payoffs each morning, these racketeers are still blackmailing the country's largest businesses out of millions of dollars.

Why are these extortionists paid off? Largely to leave the companies alone, to stop disrupting the staid world of Japanese business. Typically, the groups operate by buying several shares of a company's stock, digging up scandalous information, and then demanding hush money. They ferret out embarrassing facts about the company's top management: high-ranking officials who cheat on their income tax, ignore safety rules in their plants, or keep mistresses. If the corporation refuses to pay up, at its next general meeting the sokaiya will appear armed with these unpleasant revelations and loudly berate the company management. The executives, highly concerned over losing face before their employees and the public, have traditionally anted up. As one police official put it, "It's not threats of violence that scare corporate executives. They're more afraid of damage to the reputations of friends and family members. We live in a culture of shame."

The larger sokaiya groups play both sides of the game by also selling companies their services as strong-arm guards to ensure that shareholder meetings run without serious questions being asked. Dissident stock-

Occupational Background of Yakuza

Occupation	Full-status Members	Marginal-status Members	Total
Bakuto (gamblers)	26,960	5,148	32,108 (31%)
Tekiya (peddlers)	21,438	2,570	24,008 (23%)
Gurentai (hoodlums)	9,861	1,639	11,500 (11%)
Seaport racketeers	3,221	0	3,221 (3%)
Sokaiya (corporate racketeers)	47	2,417	2,464 (2%)
Scandal sheet extortionists	41	803	844 (1%)
Prostitution gangsters	495	74	569 (1%)
Others	39	29,202	29,241 (28%)
Totals	62,102	41,853	103,955 (100%)

Source: National Police Agency, 1980.
Note: These categories are fluid; there are frequent crossovers. For example, many bakuto and tekiya may act as sokaiya or as other racketeers. Also, many sokaiya and right-wing gangsters are not counted as yakuza in official statistics and do not appear here. The total number of yakuza in 1984 officially stood at 98,771.

holders who dare protest company policy usually find themselves shouted down – and often beaten up – by the boisterous troop of sokaiya on hand. Occasionally, the larger companies have played one sokaiya group against another, at times with violent consequences. But most frequently, the result is to render the Japanese shareholder meeting useless, a highly staged, sometimes farcical performance that usually lasts less than twenty minutes.

Some scholars suggest that the sokaiya tradition can be traced back to the ronin (unemployed samurai) of the Meiji era who went into the "protection business." The first actual sokaiya reportedly appeared after 1890, when the nation's original commercial code was enacted. Until the occupation, though, few companies were publicly owned, and it was only with the rapid economic growth of the 1960s that the sokaiya business took off.

Among the leading bosses of the sokaiya world was, until his death, Yoshio Kodama. He is said to have systematically advanced into sokaiya circles after 1965, starting his own racketeering groups and making alliances with others. Taking their lead from Kodama, the mainstream yakuza syndicates began moving heavily into the field around 1972, and the sokaiya business started to boom, increasing fourfold between 1972 and 1977. At their peak in 1981, a police survey revealed 6800 sokaiya in 500 separate groups extorting as much as $400 million annually.

Police today estimate that some 70 percent of the sokaiya's annual take ends up in the hands of yakuza syndicates. A survey by the NHK public broadcasting network (Japan's equivalent of Britain's BBC) reported that one out of every four sokaiya is in fact a yakuza gang member. Other reports put the number of yakuza far higher. At least one sokaiya, though, was careful to mark the distinction between the two crime groups. "I don't like people to use the terms 'sokaiya' and 'yakuza' interchangeably," said Jiro Morimoto, boss of a thirty-member sokaiya group. "Yakuza are inheritors of the old bushido, the samurai spirit, who stick to one principle. On the other hand, sokaiya could tell a story in ten different ways."

The scams devised by the sokaiya over the years are as ingenious as they are lucrative. Often they pose as legitimate consultants from "economic research institutes," gathering corporate intelligence and, with the help of private detectives, maintaining dossiers on leading executives – down to the names and addresses of their mistresses. Many pose as publishers of small magazines and newsletters who are only too happy to accept money for "subscriptions" and "advertising" in exchange for not printing scurrilous stories. Management views such scandalous press with the same horror as threats against its general meetings. The contents of such stories are typically leaked to the company before the issue is distributed, and the company buys up all the copies, often at premium rates.

Some sokaiya set up booster clubs that seek "donations" from the companies for a range of rather dubious causes. Another favorite tactic is to host "parties" at which businessmen are expected to bring cash gifts. One such party, in May of 1975, attracted 600 executives from 450 leading companies, each visitor bearing gifts of between $75 and $300. Police estimated that the thirty-two-year-old host, Ryuichi Koike, collected more than $100,000 that night. Koike was unable to attend his own party, however. He had been arrested earlier that day for threatening the president of a vinyl company.

Other bands of sokaiya have branched into more enterprising efforts. One group arranged a beauty contest that companies were persuaded to "sponsor." Another organized a golf tournament for Tokyo businessmen – with exorbitant entrance fees. A third group hosted an "irresistible" Kabuki play at which tickets cost five times their normal price.

The practitioners of these varied exploits fall into several classes. Those who run sophisticated organizations – working at times closely with company management – receive salaries comparable to the best-paid corporate executives. They are chauffeured around town in limousines and maintain powerful political connections. Most sokaiya, though, are petty thugs hoping for an easy payoff. Their members come from varied walks of life: taxi drivers, tradesmen. There are even the reputed "bartender sokaiya," former barmen who switched to extortion after listening to conversations between top executives over drinks. Also in the lower ranks of the business is the so-called banzai sokaiya, who walks around company offices shouting the exclamation "Banzai!" When questioned, he states that he has just become a shareholder and is merely expressing his joy and desire to encourage greater worker productivity. Several thousand yen is usually enough to convince him that his joy is better expressed elsewhere.

So lucrative is the field that many corporate officials who once dealt regularly with sokaiya have switched roles and turned up as sokaiya at company meetings – much to the surprise of management. The sokaiya's rationale, like that of the yakuza in general, is that they play a critical role in society. "The stockholders' meeting is a solemn function," one sokaiya told the newspaper *Yomiuri*. "We help it proceed smoothly and protect the interests of the innocent shareholders. We are the prop men of modern capitalism."

The sokaiya are effective largely because Japanese companies shy away from confrontation. Decisions are made through behind-the-scenes talks; management will go to great lengths to avoid head-on clashes. Therefore, the *sokai* – or general meeting – should be only a legal formality, a harmonious gathering to recognize what is a *fait accompli*.

At the heart of this love of order and calm lies the concept of *wa*. Although the accepted translation of wa is "harmony," the word is somewhat misleading, for it encompasses a far broader concept. Wa is emphasized not just in business but throughout Japanese life, and manifests itself in such ways as the Japanese reluctance to give negative answers. If dissident shareholders sharply question management, it is considered disharmonious – a serious violation of wa. But if the company hires yakuza to assault and silence the shareholders, the violation of wa would not be as great.

Unfortunately, such a mind-set allows for a rather remarkable array of extortionists and blackmailers. Although their stories don't appear in popular how-to books about Japanese management, their activities occupy a central place in the operation of Japan's largest corporations.

A good example of the sokaiya's influence can be found in Eiji Shimazaki, president of the Shimazaki Economic Research Institute, with offices in the Tokyo and Osaka areas. Claiming a staff of sixty and a $6 million annual budget, Shimazaki's sokaiya perform research, analyze corporate finances, and publish magazines. "It is well within my power to make or break corporate mergers," he once said, "let alone change board line-ups." Among the many achievements he cites is the merger of three large Mitsubishi firms into the present Mitsubishi Heavy Industries. A former teacher, Shimazaki's motto is "Be strong, just, and cheerful."

Police were not impressed, though, and in a 1973 raid confiscated fifteen cardboard boxes revealing three years' worth of unsecured loans totaling nearly $3 million *from sixty-three banks nationwide,* including many of Japan's largest. Shimazaki's leverage over the corporations: threatening to disrupt their shareholders' meetings.

Were the activities of the sokaiya limited to exposing the sexual affairs and tax scams of Japan's executives, the impact of men like Shimazaki might be more easily overlooked. But the reach of these full-time racketeers goes deep into the heart of corporate responsibility and social policy. Just as Japan's largest corporations have been used by racketeers, so have they employed sokaiya and yakuza strongmen in controlling the unwanted airing of the most heinous corporate crimes. Nowhere is this better seen than in the historic Minamata case.

The Case of Minamata
For over a generation, the Chisso Corporation dominated the political and economic life of Minamata, a country town of 36,000 on Japan's southern island of Kyushu. The long-established fertilizer company had grown since the war into a leading manufacturer of petrochemicals. From its Minamata plant – a huge, gray complex of pipes, towers, and tanks – the company had for years routinely dumped its lethal by-products into the heavily fished waters of Minamata Bay.

The Chisso Corporation had run into pollution problems before. Three times – in 1926, 1943, and 1954 – the company paid local fishermen for losses caused by its dumping practices. But by 1953, the early effects of a far more serious development could be seen – the outbreak of one of the world's largest environmental poisoning disasters.

In their book about environmental problems in Japan, *Island of Dreams,* authors Norrie Huddle and Michael Reich describe the chilling progression of what would come to be called "Minamata Disease":

*Birds seemed to be losing their sense of coordination, often falling
from their perches or flying into buildings and trees. Cats, too,
were acting oddly. They walked with a strange rolling gait, frequently stumbling over their own legs. Many suddenly went mad,
running in circles and foaming at the mouth until they fell – or
were thrown – into the sea and drowned. Local fishermen called
the derangement "the disease of the dancing cats," and watched
nervously as the animals' madness progressed.*

Soon the malady spread to the fishermen and their families. The
symptoms of the disease were horrible to watch. Although it was still
undiagnosed, physicians knew the disease attacked the central nervous
system and the brain, crippling its victims and eventually rendering them
bedridden and incoherent. Forty percent of those poisoned died. Autop-
sies showed that their brains had become spongelike as cells were eaten
away. Hundreds of families were affected, while medical authorities
warned that thousands more were in danger.

By 1958, the victims and their families, treated as pariahs by a
fearful public, demanded compensation and better pollution control at
the Chisso plant. The company, however, resolutely denied that its
operations were responsible, as it would for the next fifteen years. Yet,
as early as 1959, Chisso knew from its own secret tests that its massive discharges of organic mercury were the cause of Minamata disease.
A long-overdue official government report would much later reveal that
for thirty-three years – until 1965 – Chisso dumped 80 tons of mercury
into the shallow waters of Minamata Bay, mixed in with 600,000 tons
of sludge.

To local fishermen, who had watched the number of victims grow as
their catch steadily declined, Chisso's conduct was inexcusable. In a
series of protests, they stormed the factory, at one point holding the
executive director hostage overnight and causing extensive damage to
company buildings. After the Japanese press picked up the story, the
company eventually agreed to pay a small amount in compensation
money to those affected. The Chisso Corporation, however, never admitted any responsibility in the matter.

Despite misgivings among the victims, the issue remained dormant
until 1965, when another outbreak of mercury poisoning occurred far to
the north in Niigata Prefecture. This time the cause was a Showa Denko
Corporation factory, employing an industrial process identical to that of
Chisso's Minamata plant. Niigata victims organized and took the historic
step of filing the first large-scale suit against a polluter in postwar Japan.

In September 1968, fifteen years after the poisonings first appeared, the Japanese government officially recognized organic mercury as the cause of Minamata Disease. Before another year would pass, Minamata victims followed the lead of those from Niigata and filed suit against Chisso. Supporters of the Minamata group, however, went a full step farther. They took their cause directly to Chisso's corporate headquarters and stockholders' meetings in Tokyo and Osaka. This was as good as a declaration of war to Chisso, and the company promptly enlisted the help of two groups closely associated with the underworld – the sokaiya and the *hosho kaisha,* or "security companies."

Borrowing a tactic from the sokaiya, Minamata victims and supporters began purchasing single shares of the company's stock, entitling them to attend Chisso's general meetings and introduce motions. Although some 500 members of the Minamata delegation arrived at the company's meeting in November 1970, few got much farther than the front door. The activists were barred by a line of guards who looked as if they'd been recruited from the seediest realms of the Tokyo underworld. One protestor who did make it inside found his attempts at amending a management proposal futile. Waiting for the man were a host of sokaiya, who easily drowned him out with a chorus of jeers and promptly called the meeting to a close. Total time of Chisso's shareholder meeting: five minutes.

The company's next general meeting, in May 1971, took place in an atmosphere of increasing tension. Minamata victims and their supporters grew increasingly frustrated as their lawsuit dragged through the courts. Chisso, meanwhile, stood as resolute as ever, and came to its stockholders' meeting prepared to do battle.

In a replay of the November meeting, the protesters were met at the door by a menacing line of guards, sokaiya, and members of local ultranationalist gangs, and were again shouted down. The meeting lasted twelve minutes.

Outraged by the abrupt conclusion this time, the protesters remained at the site, arguing fiercely with company shareholders and sokaiya. Suddenly, about twenty guards stormed into the hall and attacked the Minamata contingent, smearing the green seats of the auditorium with blood. Within two minutes they were gone, leaving behind a shaken and battered group, and sending one badly injured youth to a hospital emergency room.

Police until now had stood by, letting Chisso and the protesters fight it out. But such a blatant attack – with wide press coverage and serious injuries – prompted a raid on the offices of Chisso's specially hired guard services. That Chisso's guardsmen had strong underworld ties should not have surprised the police. The yakuza-dominated security companies were a suspect lot, frequently called on by firms to harass striking workers during labor disputes.

Chisso's next shareholders' meeting took place in November 1971. This time, both sides came prepared. Nearly 300 protesters, each owning one share of Chisso stock, slept on the concrete outside the convention hall the night before. At about 8:15 A.M., company supporters, including a mass of sokaiya and what one newspaper described as "18 members of a local rightist group," were allowed into the hall through two back doors. The main entrance, where the protesters stood assembled, remained locked. As Chisso corporate officials arrived, skirmishes broke out between protesters and the company's hired musclemen barring the entrance. Some 200 riot police moved in and broke up the fighting, evicting protesters from the entrance and making a number of arrests.

Meanwhile, inside the building, the handful of protesters who had made it in were unable to introduce motions, or even be recognized by the chair. Frustrated, they threw their bodies together and stormed the stage, shouting "Murderer!" and "You swallow mercury!" The burly troops of sokaiya lining the front rows responded, and as in a lopsided football scrimmage, the activists were violently thrown back.

Shielded from the battle below him, the chairman called for a vote on the company's audit report, and a "unanimous" approval echoed through the hall. With no more items on the agenda, the proceedings were promptly adjourned. Total duration of Chisso's forty-fourth shareholders' meeting: nine minutes.

The scene was a bit too much for journalist Bo Gunnarsson of the large Swedish daily *Expressen*. At a Chisso press conference later that day, Gunnarsson, accompanied by his Japanese wife and small daughter, confronted the corporation's president, Kenichi Shimada. "I saw the stockholders' meeting for the first time, and it was terrible," insisted Gunnarsson. "Do you mean to say you have money to pay gangsters but not patients?"

Shimada, composed and polite, preserved his humble posture with a modest smile, although his eyes began to twitch. "I think it's a misunderstanding," he replied cautiously. "I believe we are taking full responsibility toward the patients."

If that responsibility entailed unleashing its hired thugs, Chisso clearly didn't mind. Indeed, it appears that the company made a careful decision to escalate this undeclared war. At its Minamata plant two months later, Chisso guards and company union thugs surrounded and viciously attacked a patients' negotiating group. Among the victims was W. Eugene Smith, the eminent fifty-three-year-old American photographer whose images had focused worldwide attention on the Minamata tragedy. In what Smith later described as "a deliberate company setup," Chisso toughs singled him out, destroyed his cameras, beat him, and smashed his body into the pavement, crushing several vertebrae and causing serious damage to his most valued photographic asset – his eyesight. Smith, the veteran photographer for *Life, Collier's,* and the *New York Times,* never fully recovered, although he and his wife remained in the city to finish their devastating photo essay, *Minamata.*

The assault on Smith was a serious mistake by Chisso, for it brought a barrage of criticism both in and out of Japan. Chisso, however, seemed undaunted. At its stately Tokyo headquarters, workmen installed iron bars at the front door and hired twenty-four-hour guards. Meanwhile, outside, a militant faction of the so-called victims' groups pitched a scraggly tent on pavement alongside the entrance. Despite constant threats by police and ultranationalist groups to tear it down, the tent stood for months as a haunting reminder to the company, the press, and the public.

In what was becoming an almost ritual confrontation, Chisso's forty-sixth general shareholders' meeting took place in December of 1972. The number of protesters had by now dwindled to fifty, although the company came well prepared with what the *Japan Times* called "a horde of pro-management shareholders." Once again, Chisso's critics were prevented from introducing a motion by the jeers and cheers of sokaiya on hand. With each item voiced from the president came a resounding "No objection" from the audience, despite attempts by protesters to scale the speaker's platform and demand an emergency motion. As the president declared the meeting closed, about twenty protesters rushed the stage, shouting "Down with Chisso!" and running straight into the lines of company guards and sokaiya; chairs flew, tables overturned, and police soon moved in. Total time of the meeting: four minutes, possibly a sokaiya record.

Justice finally prevailed on March 20, 1973, when a federal judge found Chisso guilty of gross negligence and ordered damages paid to the plaintiffs. Still unclear, though, was Chisso's attitude toward those not directly represented in the suit. Nearly 400 victims had so far been officially identified, although some medical authorities put the total number at more than 13,000.

With momentum now on the victims' side, a series of tense, emotional negotiations followed. Two days after the verdict, Chisso management relented by agreeing "to accept all responsibilities concerning

Minamata Disease. . . ." But those who for so long had fought Chisso's corporate irresponsibility, its delaying tactics, and its use of the underworld were still not satisfied. The company's offer was accepted only after Chisso president Shimada, in a classic act of Japanese contrition, lay on his hands and knees and formally apologized to the victims of Minamata. A day later, the iron bars blocking the company's main office were removed.

On July 9, 1973, twenty years after Minamata residents first noticed "the disease of the dancing cats," Chisso Corporation signed a final, public statement agreeing to pay compensation to all recognized victims. By early 1975, the company had paid out over $66 million to Minamata sufferers, and a new chapter in environmental protection had begun in Japan.

Extortion, Inc.

Ironically, the role of the sokaiya was virtually unaffected by the Minamata case. Companies continued to make extensive use of the racketeers – and vice versa – for another decade. It was only after some twenty years of pressure for reform, largely by scholars and influential journalists, that the Diet finally cracked down in 1982 by tightening up the nation's Commercial Code. The new regulations make it illegal for companies to pay off sokaiya where no tangible service is rendered, and limit participation in annual meetings to persons holding substantial amounts of stock. Company managements, furthermore, are required to stop evading questions from common stockholders at their general meetings.

At first the new laws seemed to work. Early police reports indicated that the number of sokaiya had dropped dramatically (scores of "retiring" sokaiya demanded and received "severance pay" from their corporate victims). Officials worried, though, that the crackdown was only forcing the highly adaptable sokaiya into new ventures. Many of the racketeers began to lean more heavily on publishing scandal sheets. Some have homed in on hospitals, threatening to expose details of faulty care unless they are bought off. Others have merely shifted gears and begun receiving their payoffs from the overseas offices of targeted firms, or are taking their gifts in company goods instead of cash. And still others, in a time-honored tradition, have founded right-wing political groups, disguising their payoffs as political contributions.

Japan's business community has apparently had trouble changing its old practices as well. In one example, after the boss of a major sokaiya gang was hospitalized for hepatitis in 1983, phone calls went out to Tokyo's largest corporations advising them of the hospital's location and a date for an appointment with the ailing boss. Police suspected some 100 companies of sending representatives to the gang leader's bedside, many of whom bore cash gifts of between $100 and $200.

The Commercial Code reform, however, did encourage some companies to break their ties to the traditional sokaiya – the "general meeting mongers." In a key confrontation in early 1984, Sony Corporation's annual meeting lasted for a record 13 1/2 hours, as officials were grilled by angry sokaiya and other shareholders until almost midnight. So embarrassing was the meeting to Sony officials that it scared off many companies from breaking free of the sokaiya. By the summer of 1984, the *Asian Wall Street Journal* was reporting that "the sokaiya are on the comeback trail," and that "a majority of companies listed on the Tokyo stock exchange had either resumed payoffs or begun to seriously consider doing so."

Given the culture in which the sokaiya operate, it will be extremely difficult to dislodge them. Like so much of organized crime, the sokaiya have survived because there is a demand for their services, a demand that most observers expect will continue in some form, whether legal or not. They occupy a secure niche as the hired muscle of corporate Japan, breaking strikes, fomenting scandals, contesting mergers, and continuing to ensure order and "harmony" at shareholders' meetings.

The new laws did successfully drive many sokaiya out of the general meeting business. As they have moved into other areas of extortion, however, a handful have gone to extremes that have shocked the Japanese public. Among the most notable was the 1984 assault on former foreign minister Kiichi Miyazawa, then a candidate for prime minister. Miyazawa's assailant was a fifty-four-year-old racketeer who had first tried blackmailing the politician by writing stories on his private life for sokaiya-style newspapers.

The day following the attack, one prominent newspaper in a scathing editorial branded Miyazawa's attacker one of the "Hyenas of Nagatocho" (Nagatocho being the home of Japan's parliament). The editors complained that "these political leeches can be found roaming inside the Diet," and that although politicians are quick to denounce them, "they quite contrarily use such leeches to supply bits of juicy gossip and scandals with which to attack their political enemies. . . . In short, the politicians themselves are fostering this hotbed of corruption."

One month after the Miyazawa incident, another sensational case began making headlines across Japan. To Americans, the episode bore a striking resemblance to the poisoning of Tylenol pain-relievers a year and a half earlier. The case involved a clever band of shakedown artists who, for more than a full year, became an obsession with the Japanese police and public. In letters mailed to the media, the blackmailers identified themselves as "The Man with 21 Faces," taken from the name of a popular series of children's mystery books and television shows in the 1950s. Demanding millions of dollars in ransom money, the group threatened to place cyanide in the products of six major food companies, causing bankruptcies and huge financial losses. At least eighteen boxes of cyanide-laced candies were in fact found on store shelves in various cities. Attached to each package was a typewritten note warning: "Danger. Contains poison. Eat this and die. – The Man with 21 Faces."

Through circumstantial evidence, including rumors in the sokaiya community, police became convinced that a sokaiya gang was behind the extortion attempts. But the sokaiya rackets had never escalated to this level before; these were renegades. One police expert called the case "a new type of crime for Japan."

Japan's police departments came under unprecedented criticism for their inability to apprehend the gang. Added to their frustration and loss of face was a constant stream of letters from the group itself, ridiculing police efforts before the nation. The gang addressed their notes to "Fools of the Police Force" and referred to officials as "poor, stupid cops." One letter sarcastically asked how many persons could be killed by a 30-gram lump of cyanide the gang had mailed to the NHK-TV network, and suggested that answers be mailed to the Osaka Metropolitan Police. Ten winners, said the note, would be selected by lots, and awarded prizes of Morinaga candy – one of the targets of their cyanide poisoning campaign. In another note, the extortionists apologized to the director of the National Police Agency, saying they were sorry to have caused the balding director to lose even more hair over their activities.

For at least five consecutive weeks in 1984, police mobilized more than 44,000 officers on the case. At one point in late October, nearly half the nation's police force – 130,000 officers – participated in a door-to-door search of 3.2 million homes and offices in the Osaka-Kyoto area. But Japan's finest were still unable to track down the extortionists, and officials admitted that their inability to solve the case imperiled police credibility as never before.

How Many Crimes, How Many Criminals?
Police credibility, already stretched by the Man with 21 Faces gang, is being further challenged on other fronts. Since the early 1970s, a growing number of journalists, lawyers, and social scientists have drawn attention to a nagging question posed by the existence of a 100,000-man underworld – is Japan really as crime-free as police say? Few could argue that the country's rates of violent crime are far lower than in the United States.

All an American need do is walk the streets of Japan's largest cities at midnight to notice the difference. But if violent crime is far lower in Japan than in the United States, how do white-collar and related crimes compare, particularly in such areas as bribery and extortion, where a vast number of acts go unreported?

The Japanese propensity for saving face influences not only the susceptibility to but the reporting of such crimes as well. To prove an extortion case in Japan is quite difficult without causing considerable embarrassment to the individual or company involved. Much as loan sharks employ public embarrassment as a means of intimidation, so do sokaiya and other extortionists depend on the risk of losing face to keep their victims silent. While the same might be said for similar crimes in America, it should be remembered that the importance of saving face in Japan far outweighs that of similar values in the United States.

Another overriding factor not reflected in Japan's crime rate is the society's emphasis on apologies and resolving disputes outside the police and the courts. One unhappy foreigner learned the hard way how the country's criminal justice system worked when he and two friends were attacked with fists and beer bottles by a pair of thugs in 1981. After summoning police and confronting their assailants, the foreigners were surprised to learn that the officers showed little interest in pursuing the case.

"You could choose to prosecute and that is your right," explained the police to the three victims. "However, you may not be able to prove your case . . . so we suggest you pursue a more Japanese approach and accept an apology. We realize how you feel and an apology may seem inadequate to compensate you for the harm you have been done, so you will, naturally, only accept a sincere apology."

The victims were a bit surprised, to say the least. "There was really no choice," one said. "We shook hands with our assailants and accepted their 'sincere' apology."

What, then, is the actual rate of crime in Japan? Like all statistics, figures on crime can be manipulated to say whatever those employing them would like to say. Authorities admit that, as in America, much crime in Japan goes unreported. They caution, furthermore, that their own data on underreporting – what they call "the dark figure of crime" – are dated and may be inaccurate due to problems in research methods. Nevertheless, the statistics are worth reporting. According to the National Police Agency, cases of extortion for all Japan in 1970 – the latest year available – were 238 percent higher than reported; fraud was 236 percent higher; and cases of vandalism and "destroying" were 2536 percent higher. Statistics on bribery, which may be the most unreported crime in Japan, are not available.

Kenji Ino, perhaps the leading journalistic authority on the Japanese underworld, believes that police statistics on the yakuza are also wildly inaccurate. Although 100,000 gangsters is a large number to Western ears, Ino believes that if one takes into account the rightist gangs, young thugs employed by the yakuza, and other related groups, the overall figure is actually several times that released by police. Ino blames the discrepancy on the tendency of police to release only the number of "registered members" of the yakuza – meaning those whom officials find on formal lists seized during raids, or those allowed to wear gang badges or pins.

Ino, author of twelve books on the yakuza and the right wing, also casts doubt on police figures for the overall income generated by the yakuza. He estimates yakuza income at well over $16 billion annually, more than three times the amount usually cited by police. Others estimate the amount to be as high as $22 billion. Even this, however, still is dwarfed by recent estimates for American organized crime, which have ranged anywhere from $50 billion to more than $120 billion.

Also under attack is another critical crime statistic: Japan's much-heralded conviction rate of suspects taken to trial, which hit a whopping 99.88 percent in 1981. There is no such directly comparable U.S. statistic; typical city-by-city figures for felony convictions range between 64 percent and 84 percent. Central to Japan's success has been the remarkable fact that nearly all of those brought to trial signed confessions during interrogations by police and prosecutors. In 1981, for example, the confession rate stood at 89 percent.

Although confessing one's errors occupies an important place in Japanese culture, some observers believe officials have gone much too far in trying to obtain them. Critics have accused police of using physical abuse against suspects during routine interrogations. According to a 1984 report by a group of Tokyo lawyers, marathon interrogation sessions lasting fourteen hours or more occur in many cases. After arrest, suspects are placed in tiny, brightly lit cells known as "birdcages" in which they are forced to sit cross-legged on the floor and forbidden to lean against the wall. Defense attorneys are not allowed in the interrogation rooms. Police, furthermore, can routinely detain suspects for twenty-three days without charging them, and sometimes re-arrest them on a series of separate charges, thus extending detention time as needed. (Some European countries, it should be noted, allow detention for as long as six

Illegal Yakuza Income, 1982

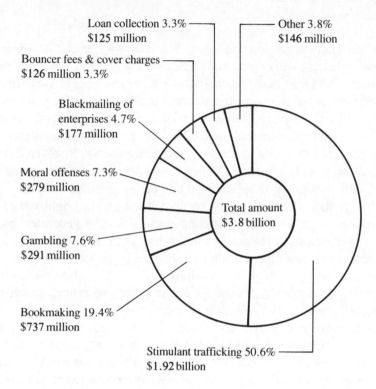

Loan collection 3.3% — $125 million

Bouncer fees & cover charges — $126 million 3.3%

Blackmailing of enterprises 4.7% $177 million

Moral offenses 7.3% $279 million

Gambling 7.6% $291 million

Bookmaking 19.4% $737 million

Other 3.8% $146 million

Total amount $3.8 billion

Stimulant trafficking 50.6% $1.92 billion

Source: National Police Agency, 1983.

Note: Some NPA analysts estimate total yakuza income may reach $8 billion. Independent figures range as high as $22 billion.

months for crimes deemed serious enough.) Some Japanese judges even refuse to grant bail until a suspect confesses.

These conditions, say critics, virtually ensure that those arrested will confess, and have led to many cases of false imprisonment. There have, in fact, been a string of widely publicized cases of false confessions that recently resulted in overturned verdicts after years of imprisonment. Police deny these charges and have claimed that such criticisms are motivated by "leftist ideology."

There is a final statistic on crime in Japan that merits serious questioning: the number of yakuza living abroad. Statements by the NPA put the answer simply: there are none. For years, in fact, NPA officials have refused to publicly acknowledge that the yakuza have gone international. While admitting that connections exist with foreign crime groups, they resolutely maintain that not a single yakuza has set up operations abroad. This position stands in sharp contrast to those adopted by police in the United States, Korea, and Southeast Asia, and conflicts as well with news accounts and interviews by reporters on both continents. Japanese officials rationalize their statements by simply declaring that all those who have left the country for extended periods are no longer "registered members" of their respective syndicates.

This is, after all, a face-saving gesture. After the hard knocks Japan's proud and skilled police force has taken, it must be hard to admit that the country's worst crime problem – the yakuza – is now being exported alongside television sets and automobiles. But eventually these attitudes must change, for even by the late 1960s police in Japan were aware that the yakuza was expanding abroad. Their delay in checking the international expansion of the syndicates helped ensure that underworld connections were made for much more than smuggling guns, drugs, and other contraband. By the early 1970s it was clear that the yakuza had made some very powerful friends outside Japan, both economically and politically.

Yakuza relaxing at a bath. Note the missing fingers on both hands of the man holding a newspaper. (Bernard Krisher)

Kazuo Taoka, Japan's "godfather of godfathers," here making one of his many court appearances. Until his death in 1981, Taoka headed the nation's largest syndicate, the Yamaguchi-gumi, and was widely regarded as the most powerful mobster in Japan. (Yomiuri Shimbun)

A rare shot of Taoka (right) with Kakuji Inagawa, head of the powerful Inagawa-kai. Once rivals, with Kodama's help the two bosses concluded a peace treaty that gave them influence over 43 of Japan's 47 prefectures. (Tokuma Shoten)

Masahisa Takenaka, Taoka's successor as Yamaguchi godfather, in 1984. Takenaka was gunned down later that year by assassins from a Yamaguchi splinter group. (Yomiuri Shimbun)

Members of Zen Ai Kaigi, the fiery ultranationalist alliance, clash with police at a 1974 convention of their favorite target, the leftist Japan Teachers' Union. Zen Ai Kaigi's membership, like that of many far-right groups, is heavily yakuza. (Yomiuri Shimbun)

Takeshi Takagi (far left), *one of the richest, most sophisticated yakuza to set up shop in the United States. Until his forced departure in 1978, Takagi was under investigation for gunrunning, prostitution, and heroin smuggling. He is shown here at a 1978 Honolulu court date.* (*Honolulu Advertiser* photograph by Ron Jett)

The 1985 funeral of slain Yamaguchi godfather Takenaka. Yakuza on right, riot police on left. (*Yomiuri Shimbun*)

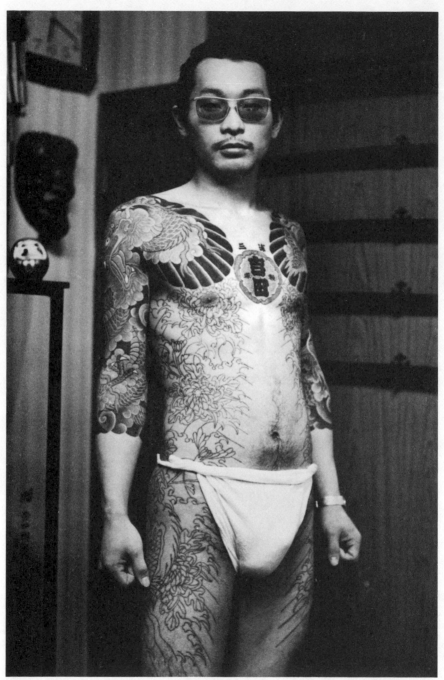

Yakuza with a partially completed tattoo. Many gang members still insist on traditional tattooing, done with a bamboo sliver in a long series of painful jabs. The full design can take months and, when completed, cost more than $5,000. (Photo by Michio Soejima)

A bosozoku (hot-rod) gang, a prime source of recruits for the yakuza. Police estimate more than 42,000 members in 700 gangs nationwide. (Seiji Kurata)

A scuffle involving sokaiya (financial racketeers) at a general meeting of Mitsubishi Shoji Corporation. In response to police crackdowns, the yakuza-dominated sokaiya have expanded into a wide range of extortion and racketeering crimes, and have begun exploring opportunities overseas. (Provided by Kyodo News Service)

A large haul of amphetamines, discovered hidden in surfboards. The East Asian trade in "speed," or "shabu," has become one of the world's greatest drug routes, supplying as many as 600,000 users in Japan and spilling into Europe and North America. (Provided by Kyodo News Service)

Hisayuki Machii, reputed godfather of the heavily Korean syndicate Towa Yuai Jigyo Kumiai (East Asia Friendship Enterprises Association). Machii and other yakuza allegedly helped arrange the 1973 kidnapping in Tokyo of political activist Kim Dae Jung by the Korean CIA. (Provided by Kyodo News Service)

Sasakawa jogging with former president Jimmy Carter in May 1984. Carter, who praised Sasakawa's "good work for peace," found the aging rightist a willing donor to his presidential library and center at Emory University in Atlanta. (AP/Wide World Photos)

Part IV
The Move Abroad

Chapter 7
East Asia:
The Yakuza Expand

A worried look seemed permanently drawn on the face of Kim Dae Jung, the leading opposition figure in the repressive world of South Korean politics. It was the summer of 1973, and Kim had just arrived in Tokyo from the United States. For a politician who had recently earned worldwide recognition, Kim acted like a fugitive. For the last three years, he'd been dodging the often violent attacks of the Korean government. It didn't matter where he traveled: Korea, Japan, the United States. At each stop, it seemed, there were government-hired goons following him, breaking up his political rallies, preventing him from reaching appointments with key foreign officials. In Tokyo, every public gathering seemed a target of these government squads – criminal gangs of ethnic Koreans who since the war had gained a permanent place among the Japanese yakuza.

Kim's major sin was to have challenged Korea's strongman, Park Chung Hee, in a 1971 presidential election, a contest that Park won, it is widely acknowledged, only through massive government fraud and manipulation. Even after the election, the immensely popular Kim remained a major headache for the Park regime, as he toured the United States and Japan speaking out for human rights and democracy in Korea. It was no accident that just after the election, a large truck smashed into Kim's car, killing three people and causing Kim serious hip injuries that left him with a severe and permanent limp. Korean officials later acknowledged that the attack was the work of the regime's notorious KCIA – the Korean Central Intelligence Agency.

The KCIA, established in the wake of Park's 1961 coup d'état, had become the most feared means of repression wielded against South Korea's 35 million people. The organization employed more than 100,000 agents, according to some estimates, and its influence extended to every walk of Korean life. Few doubted the allegations of torture, kidnapping, and murder made against the corrupt agency. The KCIA, bluntly put, was an instrument of terror unleashed against any Korean who dared to challenge the authoritarian rule of Park Chung Hee.

Following the 1971 election, as Kim predicted, Park issued an emergency decree, abandoned the constitution, and placed the nation under martial law. Kim, who was out of Korea at that time, decided that to return home at this point would be risking death. Instead, the forty-nine-year-old politician sought audiences with influential figures in the United States and Japan, and addressed overseas Korean groups regarding the dangers he saw awaiting his country. His demands for democracy and free elections only incensed the Park regime even further. By 1973, Kim was gaining more international attention and prestige than ever, and in July of that year he was invited to Tokyo to address a powerful group within the LDP.

"When I arrived in Tokyo," Kim recalled, "my friends warned that Korean yakuza members were seeking to hurt me, so they asked me to be careful. They said there was some kind of plot against my life, and that they had received the information from sources close to the yakuza. The Koreans in the yakuza had a strong connection with Mindan [the South Korean residents' association] and with the KCIA."

Kim took the advice to heart. Upon his arrival in Tokyo, he led the life of a fugitive. Every two to three days he changed hotels, using false Japanese names to avoid his enemies. But on August 8, 1973, the KCIA finally caught up with him.

At about 11 A.M. of that day, Kim knocked on room 2211 of Tokyo's Grand Palace Hotel. He was there to meet with a fellow opposition politician, Yang Il Tong, then in Japan for medical treatment. About two hours later, Kim left the room and headed into the hallway for the elevator. Suddenly, six or seven powerfully built young men appeared in the corridor, shoved Kim into an adjacent room, beat him, and pushed a cloth saturated with anesthetic onto his face. Four of the men then dragged him into an elevator and down to a waiting car in the hotel basement. For the next five to six hours, still conscious despite the drug, Kim was kicked in the stomach and forced to kneel down in the back of the car with his mouth stuffed and his face held against his assailants' laps. Evading police roadblocks, the kidnappers stopped near Osaka, where they bandaged with masking tape first Kim's hands and feet, then his face so thoroughly that only his nose showed through. Shoving their prize into a second car, they drove for at least an hour to the oceanside.

It was an elaborate, well-planned abduction. Kim was placed aboard a small motorboat, sped away from Japan, then transferred to a larger, more powerful vessel. As the ship moved farther out to sea, Kim – still bound, gagged, and blindfolded – had weights tied to his hands and feet and heard crewmen talking of how to ensure that his body would never rise to the surface. A devout Catholic, Kim began saying his final prayers.

Suddenly, a helicopter or plane appeared overhead, causing a great deal of commotion among the crew. After considerable debate, Kim's abductors unexpectedly removed the weights and loosened his bonds. Apparently, someone had changed the day's agenda. Most observers credit rapid actions by outraged U.S. and Japanese officials with saving Kim's life that evening.

The next day, the ship landed somewhere in South Korea, and after another journey by road, switching cars twice, they arrived in Seoul. There Kim was held for two days and, still blindfolded, finally released at night about 65 yards from his home. The Korean government welcomed Kim back by placing him under house arrest and subjecting him to years of persecution, including a jail term and a death sentence nearly carried out by President Park's successor, Chun Doo Hwan.

Shortly after the abduction, Tokyo police tied the kidnapping to the KCIA. At the kidnapping site, investigators found the fingerprints of Kim Dong Woon, first secretary of the Korean Embassy and believed to be the Tokyo-area KCIA director. They further identified one of the getaway cars, tracing it to the Korean vice-consul in Yokohama. Japanese officials believed that as many as four groups were involved, totaling twenty to twenty-six men. Reports from former government officials in both the United States and Korea would later confirm KCIA involvement at the highest levels, and implicate President Park himself. What never became clear, though, was the widely suspected role played by leading members of the yakuza. Japanese officials have not been anxious to shed light on the controversy. Despite repeated calls from opposition members of the Diet, after eleven years the Tokyo Metropolitan Police Department has still not made public the results of its investigation into the kidnapping.

At the center of suspicion stands Hisayuki Machii, said to be the most powerful Korean yakuza in Japan. Machii – blood brother to the late Yamaguchi boss Kazuo Taoka, oyabun of Tokyo's notorious Tosei-kai, and close ally of Yoshio Kodama – is the leader of a whole generation of Korean gangsters operating in Japan since the war. A report in the respected *Far Eastern Economic Review* cited "informed sources" who had "clearly identified a big Korean operator in Japan, Chong Gwon Yong, alias Hisayuki Machii, . . . as a leading participant in the abduction" of Kim. Machii's alleged role was to have "leased" virtually the entire hotel floor from which Kim was taken, and made the rooms available to the

KCIA. These allegations were never proven. The suspicions were enough, though, to have prompted *Newsweek* Tokyo bureau chief Bernard Krisher to wire his home office: "Machii . . . appears to have been behind the Kim Dae Jung kidnapping, having worked closely with the Korean CIA, but no Japanese newspaper has been willing to run this, for Machii's henchmen don't hesitate to torture or even kill their detractors."

Two other prominent ethnic Korean gangs in the yakuza have been implicated in connection with the kidnapping – both reportedly part of the Yamaguchi-gumi. One of them, the Yanagawa-gumi, headed by Jiro Yanagawa, is of particular interest, as the gang boss reportedly played a key role in leaking to the Japanese press a defamatory report on Kim from the Korean government. According to journalist Takao Goto, a Japanese expert on the Kim kidnapping, it is likely that Yanagawa – like other underworld characters in Japan – obtained contacts in Korea through one key man: Yoshio Kodama.

The close links between Korean intelligence and the mob were readily apparent to those who investigated at any length. In 1978, Pharis Harvey, then a Tokyo-based consultant to the Christian Conference of Asia, researched the KCIA's connections in Japan at the request of the U.S. House Subcommittee on International Organizations. This was the high tide of America's "Koreagate" scandal. Congressional hearings were focusing on influence-peddling and harassment in the United States by the KCIA and such friends as Tongsun Park and Sun Myung Moon. Harvey came away convinced that the ". . . KCIA and the Korean yakuza were certainly intermingled, so it was never certain what was an official KCIA initiative and what was from a mobster organization."

If the yakuza were making deals with the KCIA, it was not wholly surprising to seasoned observers in Japan. Those who had watched the increasing sophistication brought to the syndicates by Kodama and other fixers had seen the early connections being made, until, by the late 1960s and early 1970s, the yakuza had set their sights far beyond the home islands. By the time of Kim Dae Jung's kidnapping, the yakuza were already exploring opportunities around the Pacific Rim, homing in on the guns, drugs, and sleazy sex trade of Southeast Asia.

In the 1920s and 1930s, during the heyday of ultranationalism, yakuza joined with rightist groups like the Black Dragon Society in raising havoc across mainland Asia. And, during the war, they had gone to China and helped pillage the continent, paying special attention to the opium trade.

But this was a new era, and the new generation of yakuza had little experience in international matters. Through much of the 1960s, while their legitimate counterparts swept across the world cutting billion-dollar deals in everything from cars to curios, the yakuza had kept to the homeland, feuding over territory and sharing in the riches of an increasingly affluent Japan. That outlook would change by the end of the decade, and its impact would be felt first and foremost in the nearby nation that had already borne the brunt of so much of Japan's dark side: the Republic of Korea.

The Korean Connection

The relationship between Japan and Korea is a complex and often tragic one. Geography alone ensured that the history of these two peoples would be intertwined. Separated by as little as 120 miles across the Korean Strait and Sea of Japan, these two economic powers of Asia have come to a mutually beneficial, if at times uneasy, truce. Great animosity remains between Koreans and Japanese, dating back at least to the 1895 assassination of the Korean queen by members of the Dark Ocean Society. That murder helped create the pretext for Tokyo to order an invasion of Korea; the Japanese would not leave until their defeat by the Allied powers in 1945. During their 40 years of occupation, the Japanese ruled ruthlessly over Korea. By 1945, hundreds of thousands of Koreans had been shipped to Japan for forced labor.

Many Koreans who stayed in Japan after the war turned to the black markets and organized crime, forming gangs that were eventually absorbed into the larger Japanese syndicates. The yakuza, strangely, have been among the few institutions to open their doors to the Koreans in Japan. Even second- and third-generation Korean-Japanese, most of whom speak Japanese far better than they speak Korean, suffer severe discrimination in employment, housing, and education. Despite the fact that the majority of Japan's 676,000 ethnic Koreans were born in Japan, they are legally still considered aliens.

Such conditions have driven large numbers of Koreans in Japan into the yakuza, with some surprising effects. As Japan and South Korea finally strove toward normalized diplomatic relations in the mid-1960s, among those ready to act as intermediaries were top Korean yakuza bosses in Japan. Perhaps the most successful of those Korean bosses was the man thought by many to be involved in Kim Dae Jung's kidnapping, Hisayuki Machii.

Machii was born in Japanese-occupied Korea in 1923 and lived in Japan a number of times before settling there permanently after the war. The son of a small-time steel merchant, he was a college dropout who felt more at home on the streets than in the classrooms. During the occupation, he immediately moved into the lucrative black market activity and just as quickly ran afoul of the law. He was charged with one murder, and was believed to have committed at least one other, but managed to avoid any time in prison for the alleged crimes.

Machii formed Tosei-kai ("Voice of the East Gang") in 1948, a largely Korean band of yakuza. It was during these tumultuous postwar years that he and his men seized control of Tokyo's famed Ginza entertainment district. So thoroughly did Tosei-kai run the area that they were known as the Ginza Police, and undoubtedly they outnumbered the district's civil police in manpower and strength. Machii himself became known as the Ginza Tiger and the Ox, among other titles. He and his gang supplied concessions to the burgeoning, pinball-like pachinko industry, and soon moved on to control of restaurants and bars. Police also suspect that the Tosei-kai moved into the booming amphetamine trade in the early years and never let go.

Machii also capitalized on his status as a non-Japanese to make connections under the occupation. He served American authorities as a strikebreaker and an anticommunist thug. Through the U.S. Army's Counter Intelligence Corps, Machii was reportedly introduced to Yoshio Kodama, and the two men began a long and mutually profitable relationship. Machii, in fact, became close to a number of prominent rightists. A common enemy, communism, plus the chance to make money, did much to smooth over race relations.

Later, Machii would claim that Tosei-kai had never been more than a political strong-arm group. "As some of our members broke the law, the police referred to us as gangsters," he told the newsweekly *Shukan Shincho*. Machii was not arguing a point; he was lying. Between 1946 and 1958 Machii would be arrested ten times, for crimes ranging from extortion and fraud to robbery and assault; he received three prison sentences, but served very little time. Some Japanese journalists believe Machii's early luck with the law was due to his work with G-2 in strikebreaking and attacking leftists. As for his Korean gangsters, they were hardly angelic either: in 1964 Tokyo police raided the Ginza headquarters of the Tosei-kai and found a sizable cache of firearms and explosives. The newspaper *Mainichi* called the gang "one of the most feared and strongest underworld organizations."

Machii paid special attention to the problems of Koreans in Japan. Placing his gang at the disposal of key leaders, he quickly became a major power within Japan's Korean community. Machii's role became even more pronounced during the Korean War, as Koreans in Japan fought violently over which Korea to support. Two groups grew out of the turmoil in Japan: Chongnyon, supporting Communist North Korea; and Mindan, supporting South Korea. Machii, of course, threw in his lot with the staunchly anticommunist Mindan, and through his work of providing bodyguards began to meet agents of the KCIA.

By 1960, Machii had built up his Tosei-kai to some 1500 members. Although it never rivaled the other major syndicates in sheer numbers, it achieved prominence through ferocity, position, and connections. Among Machii's connections was Yoshio Kodama, who recruited his Korean friend for the yakuza army being massed to protect Ike during the 1960 security treaty disturbances. Later, under Kodama's auspices, Machii would befriend former prime minister Kishi, and forge an alliance with Kazuo Taoka that allowed the Yamaguchi-gumi to move into Tokyo. It was Machii, again, who served as "auditor" of the yakuza-ridden Japan Pro-Wrestling Entertainment Company, with Taoka as vice-chairman and Kodama as chairman. Kodama was good for other matters, too. By investing with Kodama in a series of highly questionable real estate deals, Machii became an extremely wealthy man.

In 1965, stung by police crackdowns, Machii formally disbanded his infamous Tosei-kai, but he immediately founded a "legitimate" successor organization, the Towa Yuai Jigyo Kumiai (East Asia Friendship Enterprises Association). Two years earlier, he had formed Towa Sogo Kigyo (East Asia Enterprises Company), with Kodama as chairman of the board, and out of these two organizations Machii would build a financial empire.

It was at about this time that Machii's foreign diplomacy ventures blossomed, with help again from Kodama. The ever-present kuromaku and Machii reportedly played an active role in promoting approval of the Republic of Korea–Japan Normalization Treaty, which mandated Japanese reparations to Korea and restored full diplomatic relations. Thanks to this new alliance, Machii and Kodama were soon meeting with leading Korean politicians, and finally with President Park himself, who apparently liked what he saw. With the blessings of Park, and the help of such friends as Kishi and Kodama, in 1970 Machii won control of the major ferry line between Pusan, South Korea, and Shimanoseki, Japan – the heavily traveled shortest route between the two countries.

By now Machii had become what one Japanese weekly called "a political merchant," a kuromaku of Japanese-Korean relations. Since the treaty normalizing relations between the two countries, Japanese businessmen were swarming into Korea, and vast amounts of graft, political contributions, and questionable payments of all sorts flowed both ways across the Sea of Japan. Machii set up new clubs and cabarets in Seoul and refurbished old ones in Tokyo; they would serve as meeting places for top Korean and Japanese officials, providing all the comforts available in an exotic "hostess" bar. While Machii was hobnobbing with the powerful, though, his gang members were still plying their traditional trades, now in both countries, enough so that Japanese officials considered the Towa Yuai Jigyo Kumiai one of the nation's top ten yakuza syndicates.

On a summer evening in 1973, Machii staged the gala opening of his new TSK-CCC (Celebrities' Choice Clubs), a multimillion-dollar reception at his new seven-story entertainment complex in Tokyo's fashionable Roppongi district. More than twenty-five star entertainers and sports figures celebrated his lavish new facility along with 7000 other people, among them corporation presidents, the head of the Tokyo Bar Association, and a leading editor of the huge *Yomiuri* newspaper. Machii had made it big. TSK-CCC featured high-class restaurants, cabarets, discos, saunas imported from Finland, a Beverly Hills beauty salon, and much more. Machii, it was reported, had personally overseen the design of each room. Membership in TSK-CCC featured access to sixteen "deluxe private clubs" in Tokyo's Ginza. In addition, a giant recreation center for members was in the works, including a ski area, a thirty-six-hole golf course, an amusement park, and a housing development. The cost to get in on the ground floor of Machii's venture was a mere $700 per person, $1900 per company. The genial Korean host called his creation "an oasis in the desert of dry, contemporary human relationships."

Machii, by now fifty, had become the archetypal refined syndicate boss. A multimillionaire with a taste for Picasso and fine antique porcelain, he had taken TSK into entertainment, restaurants, real estate, tourism, even oil. Some 1500 employees worked under him, from the operators of the Pusan ferry to the Korean "hostesses" in his bars. But there were storm clouds gathering.

On the same day in 1976 that Yoshio Kodama hobbled into his first and only Lockheed court appearance, TSK-CCC went bankrupt. In fact, Machii's dream collapsed in the wake of revelations spilling over from investigations of the Lockheed scandal and of Kodama. Saddled with a $72 million debt, TSK could no longer meet the payroll; the press, meanwhile, began asking pointed questions about the company's odd financial transactions. Of particular interest was the 1969 sale of vast tracts of land from Machii's planned giant recreation center. TSK's own directors admitted that Kodama had forced the company to sell the land at far below market cost to a favored company, then apparently embezzled more than $3.3 million of the money in a subsequent deal.

Despite his losses, by the mid-1980s the Ginza Tiger still wielded considerable power in both Japan and South Korea. Although he would "retire" from his Towa Yuai organization, he was still honorary director of the syndicate, a fact not lost on authorities when Machii's investments expanded beyond East Asia.

Thanks to Machii's diplomacy, the Republic of Korea became a yakuza playground, refuge, and investment center. Fugitives from Japanese justice would steal across the Sea of Japan, hiding out in the coastal cities of Korea until the heat passed. Syndicates like the Inagawakai set up casinos and arranged high-stakes gambling tours of the coun-try, shaking down corporate executives in cooperation with their new Korean friends. In major cities like Seoul and Pusan, money was laundered in the traditional yakuza "water trades" of bars, cabarets, and restaurants. By autumn of 1974, the Inagawa-kai were busily gaining a foothold in construction by setting up a gravel business on the large southern island of Cheji, a Korean province long popular as a resort. And all the major syndicates appeared to have their fingers in two key areas: prostitution and drugs.

Despite the presence of so many Koreans within the yakuza, establishing the Korean connection has not always been easy, due largely to the vastly different form of organized crime in Korea. There is no counterpart to the Mafia or the yakuza in that country. An unwritten rule appears to prevail in highly authoritarian societies like South Korea: organized crime is successful only when the government allows it to be. As one knowledgeable U.S. official in Seoul put it, "Between the KCIA, the civil police, and military intelligence, you've got such a powerful security state here that it's impossible for organized crime to operate without official sanction. If it exists, it's state-sponsored or state-sanctioned."

Instead of large syndicates, small crime rings have arisen, and these form the hard core of the yakuza's Korean connection. These enterprising bands, comprising from five to twenty-five people, take their chances in smuggling, the black market, pickpocketing. Their gang names come from hometown cities, smuggling boats, or whatever strikes their fancy: names like Seoulpa, Pusanpa, and Insonghopa. The black market is an especially lucrative niche, fueled by the presence of 40,000 American GIs. One PX on a U.S. base, according to embassy officials, actually sells more merchandise than the combined salaries of all its customers. Korean officials are too often on the receiving end of these deals to seriously consider cracking down.

U.S. officials worry about the long-term implications of Korean organized crime, for in tandem with the yakuza, it could become a formidable new force in the Pacific underworld. Like Japan, South Korea has become an economic giant of the region; the United States is the largest market for Korean goods, and Korea the ninth largest trading partner of the United States. Expansion of the seamy underside of Korean trade, warned one U.S. Customs official, "could transform exports here into a morass of influence-peddling, bribery, and commercial crime."

The market in Korea ranks among the best in Asia for smugglers. The nation's rapidly growing middle class has developed a great appetite for such foreign goods as Japanese electronic items, imports heavily restricted by the Korean government. The stocks of American PX stores can be depleted only so often, so for a wider range of contraband the Koreans turn to the yakuza and Chinese crime gangs operating out of Taiwan and Hong Kong. One estimate put the worth of Hong Kong goods seized at Seoul's Kimpo Airport at more than $20 million; similar figures are believed to exist regarding Japan.

The smuggled contraband ranges from cameras and watches to counterfeit dollars, gold bars, and precious stones. Mink stoles, jewelry, and textiles are also popular items, secreted into the country by sea and air. Chinese medicines, too, are in demand – traditional concoctions whose distribution is for some reason strictly controlled by the Korean government; deer antlers are a favorite item in this category. In January 1980, authorities seized three boats and arrested twenty-three Chinese and fifty-seven Koreans for smuggling in 137,000 pills of *uhwangchongsimhwan*, a Chinese herb the Koreans swear by to counter hypertension and paralysis. Authorities estimated the shipment of uhwangchongsimhwan (a Korean word) to be worth more than $6.5 million. But far more lucrative goods lure the yakuza across the Sea of Japan.

The Meth Capital of the World
For the yakuza, Korea's greatest attractions lie not in smuggling exotic Chinese remedies or consumer goods into the country, but in smuggling drugs out of it. Korea is the center of drug traffic for the yakuza, and the drug is methamphetamine, known on the streets of America as speed, crank, and meth, and on the streets of Japan as shabu and white diamonds. It is quite possibly the world's most massive unpublicized drug route, a dope connection of little interest in the West because so far it has affected only East Asia. But that will likely change as crime syndicates from both countries expand their activities across the Pacific.

Through the 1970s and early 1980s, at least 70 percent of the yakuza drugs peddled across Japan originated in South Korea. So great is the demand for the drug, and so lucrative are its sales, that Japanese police believe the meth trade accounts for fully half the yakuza's income – an amount measured in the billions of dollars. Markups of the drug, according to the police, increase 40 to 50 times from the factory to the street. A single gram of the drug sells for as much as $1300, and one "fix" – .01 to .03 gram – goes for more than $40. The preferred method of getting high is by injection.

To foreigners accustomed to the image of Japan as crime-free, the number of amphetamine abusers may come as a shock. Estimates typically put the number in Japan at between 300,000 and 600,000, roughly the number of known heroin users in the United States. As one Tokyo drug abuse expert put it, "Japan is the meth capital of the world." After halting a boom in stimulant use during the early 1950s, police in the 1980s have again rushed to combat what one newspaper called a "Blizzard of White Powder" pouring into the country from abroad. From 1975 to 1983, drug-related arrests tripled. Among the leading offenders: housewives, students, taxi drivers, firemen, and soldiers.

"Japan is the type of society that needs methamphetamine," remarked one longtime resident of Tokyo. "The treadmill is very fast and people use it to stay on." Indeed, at least one psychological study indicates that the pace of life in Japan is measurably faster than in such countries as England, Taiwan, and the United States – a fact to which resident foreigners in the country will readily attest.

Stung by concerted crackdowns at home, the yakuza have found Korea an inviting place to set up shop. In clandestine laboratories scattered throughout Korea, local crime gangs – typically with yakuza financing – manufacture vast stores of the drug. Conservative estimates put the international stimulant trade into Japan at two to three tons per year, but recent arrests suggest that these figures are low. Newspaper accounts indicate that one relatively obscure gang in southern Japan, the Sadaoka-gumi, alone were moving from Korea an estimated 600 kilograms annually (about two-thirds of a ton).

The prime smuggling route lies between Pusan – South Korea's second-largest city – and the nearby Japanese port of Shimanoseki. Pusan, a bustling seaport and trading center, is a favorite city of the yakuza. It is a smuggler's paradise, teeming with thousands of seamen, small boats, and Japanese tourists. Hidden among the city's industrial sections and offshore on nearby islands lie perhaps dozens of drug factories. An entire community of fugitive yakuza reportedly are holed up in Pusan apartments with their Korean girlfriends, waiting out the heat from their latest crimes in Japan.

Responding to two years of requests by Japanese police, in 1983 Korean officials finally staged a crackdown, raiding fifteen secret drug labs. Traditionally, though, Korean authorities have winked at the enormous traffic, influenced by well-placed bribes as well as by anti-Japanese feelings within the government. This laissez-faire attitude is slowly changing as speed use has spread to U.S. soldiers and, most recently, to the Koreans themselves. But cooperation between Korean and Japanese police remains at best lukewarm. No systematic relationship exists between law enforcement in the two neighboring countries; leftist legislators in Japan have vociferously opposed closer cooperation out of fear that the KCIA's successor, the National Planning and Security Agency, will make use of intelligence gleaned from Japanese police files. The tendency on the part of both countries has been to blame the other. In an unusually frank article on the traffic, Korea's leading monthly, *Wolgan Chosen,* nicely summed up the Korean position: "The Japanese say that Japan is the victim of amphetamines made in Korea. But we insist that behind the manufacture of amphetamines in Korea are Japan's terrorist crime gangs."

The Yakuza and Sexual Slavery

By the late 1960s, various forces were tugging at the Japanese syndicates to move abroad. Their early experience with Korea helped convince many yakuza that their criminal talents were best plied on an international scale. Some had become managers of multimillion-dollar companies, who watched with fascination as their legitimate counterparts circled the globe making trade deals and investing capital. The gangs' younger members were better educated and more internationally minded; some had even picked up the mandatory English taught in Japanese schools. The greatest incentive, though, was the explosion of the nation's tourist industry in the late 1960s and 1970s. With a strong yen, the easing of currency export controls, and increasing amounts of disposable cash in their pockets, the Japanese traveled abroad as never before. But few travelers saw tourism as a means of building up cross-cultural understanding. Instead, men from around the country lined up for prostitution junkets across much of East Asia. As many as 200 Japanese men at one time would descend from their jumbo jets into these cities, on prearranged three-day junkets whose sole purpose was an orgy of drinking and whoring. The "sex tour" was born.

The Japanese sex tours encouraged the yakuza to follow the excesses of their countrymen across East Asia. But more than widen their horizons, the tours introduced the gangs to the international trade in sexual slavery, a merciless enterprise that they would soon help expand around the Pacific. It is a trade that affects hundreds of thousands of mostly poor Third World women and children, forcing them into prostitution at home and abroad. Feminist Kathleen Barry, author of *Female Sexual Slavery*, defines the international trade in women widely to include sex tourism, prostitution around military bases, traffic in women and children, "mail-order" marriages, and pornography. The yakuza have had a hand in nearly all of these, helped out by conniving local crime syndicates in the poorer countries of East Asia.

The sex industry in the West simply does not compare to the massive scale of prostitution now practiced in many of these developing countries, a condition closely related to the rise in tourism from the world's wealthier modernized countries. Until the mid-1970s, Western Europe had served as the slave traders' main market, with the countries of the Middle East not far behind; by the 1980s the international focus had shifted to East Asia, with Japan and the yakuza playing a key role.

The early signs could be seen in Taiwan by the end of the 1960s, as planeloads of Japanese men arrived in special tours to take advantage of the nation's cheap brothels. Geopolitics interrupted that trade in 1972, as Japan resumed diplomatic relations with mainland China. With flights into Taiwan curtailed, the Japanese tour companies quickly shifted their operations to the increasingly popular nocturnal attractions of Korea.

Tourism had mushroomed in Korea after the nation normalized relations with Japan in 1965, with more than 650,000 Japanese visitors annually by the late 1970s. Few of the tourists were visiting temples, however. In a survey by the Korean Ministry of Tourism, no less than 80 percent of the men cited "Kisaeng parties" as "what was most impressive about Korea." The word *Kisaeng* historically applied to professional female entertainers, quite similar to Japan's highly refined tradition of geisha. But today the term is synonymous with prostitute.

In every major Korean city, large, government-registered "Kisaeng houses" sprang up. One pair of houses sat in a wealthy area of Seoul, on either side of the Japanese ambassador's official residence. Each could accommodate 800 men at one time. The owner was reportedly a top politician with past service in the KCIA. Along with the official Kisaeng houses arose hundreds of brothels, and tens of thousand of prostitutes.

The sex tours became big business, prompting large hotels, tourist agencies, and airlines to jump into the trade. Japan Air Lines, which was flying about one-third of all Japanese international travelers by the end of the 1970s, coaxed its passengers rather directly. Read one JAL guidebook: "In order to embellish and relish the nights of Korea, you must start, above all else, with a Kisaeng party. . . . There is no doubt whatsoever about the well-established reputation that a night spent with a consummate Korean girl dressed in a gorgeous Korean blouse and skirt is just perfect. . . . Every travel agent organizing trips to Korea makes it a must to include a Kisaeng party in his client's itinerary."

The realities of the Kisaeng houses are somewhat less pleasant. Generally, the women are impoverished migrants from the countryside, sold as minors on the black market for as little as $200 and forced into a life of prostitution. In the highly structured society of Korea, they are forever marked as "unpersons," a status comparable to that of India's untouchables. Managers rake off most of their pay, acts of violence against them are frequent, amphetamine use is widespread, and the living conditions are inhumane. There is a slave market atmosphere in some Kisaeng houses, where the women stand half naked in large rooms by their lockers as the Japanese men parade by and pick out their lady of the night.

The sex tours became so popular during the 1970s that, despite a resurgence of tourism to Taiwan and the booming trade with Korea, the Japanese began exploring other lands. They set their sights on the countries of Southeast Asia, an easy hop from their old forays in Taiwan. It was here that the sex trade – and the yakuza – would reach new heights.

It is hard at first to imagine how this corner of the world, so full of devout Buddhists, Christians, and Moslems, could develop such huge, industrial-scale centers of prostitution. But much of the market lies only a four- to five-hour plane ride from Tokyo, and the ravages of Third World poverty, combined with the power of the Japanese yen, fostered the massive sex trade, possibly involving as many as 80 percent of the one million Japanese men traveling abroad each year during the late 1970s. Thailand and the Philippines would bear the brunt of the assault, with considerable help from the British colony of Hong Kong.

As the richest country in Asia, Japan's role as lead buyer in the sexual slave market of the Orient could have been predicted. The aggressiveness of Japanese businessmen had already prompted taunts of "economic animal" throughout the region. Now to that was added a host of new names, including "sex animal" and "sex imperialist." Drunk, rowdy Japanese stumbling through the streets with their "girls" on arm renewed old hatreds in places like the Philippines, where Japanese atrocities during the war are not forgotten. In much of Asia, the Ugly American had found his match. Farmers, doctors, dentists, realtors, gangsters, and others line up at Tokyo's Narita Airport for jets bound not only for Seoul and Taipei, but now for Bangkok and Manila as well.

Japanese Overseas Travel — 1979

Country	Visitors	Men	Women
Republic of Korea	525,326	93.7%	6.3%
Taiwan	618,538	91.4%	8.6%
Philippines	190,637	83.7%	16.3%
Thailand	80,140	78.9%	21.2%
USA	1,410,320	59.4%	40.6%
France	166,622	50.5%	49.5%

Source: Immigration Bureau, Ministry of Justice, Tokyo.

Here again, the women involved may be sold directly into prostitution by their families in the countryside; in Thailand, daughters are sold for as little as $50. Some women go off willingly, seeking work in the big cities but finding no doors open but those of the local sex clubs. They tell their faraway parents they are working as "receptionists," a long-standing joke among prostitutes in Manila. Typically, they will support their entire family, sending home from one-third to one-half of their earnings. Their fees usually run from $50 to well below $10. Most of the money they make, however, ends up in the hands of tourist agencies, hotels, club owners, pimps, and organized crime syndicates. It is not a good life for the women. As in Korea, drug use is high, venereal disease rampant, and violence commonplace.

Many of the brothels do, in fact, resemble slave auctions. In the largest of these flesh markets, as many as several hundred women sit in huge warehouselike buildings, with numbers pinned to their dresses. Some clubs have one-way glass show windows so customers can "shop" more at ease, "rather as you would select a fish from the tank in a seafood restaurant," explained one guidebook to Thailand.

Critics point to the establishment of U.S. military bases and the Vietnam War as the first great catalysts for prostitution in the region. It was the tourist industry, though, that brought the Asian sex trade to the fore in the 1970s. Thailand in particular has earned a reputation among travelers as the brothel of Asia, although the Philippines has begun to vie for that dubious honor. In 1982, Thai police estimated that there were 700,000 prostitutes in the country, nearly 10 percent of all Thai women between the ages of fifteen and thirty. In the Philippines, estimates run over the 300,000 mark, with 100,000 women working as "hospitality girls," or prostitutes serving the tourist industry. In South Korea, independent estimates put the total number as high as 200,000, vast numbers of them under the control of local Korean racketeers who work closely with their yakuza kin in arranging the tours.

The yakuza did not originally create these conditions, nor do they now control most of the local action, which is handled by various bands of local gangsters, pimps, and businessmen. But the yakuza do play a key role in the trade in several ways. They have accompanied the tours, setting up contacts with local pimps and guiding their fellow Japanese toward women, drugs, or whatever else they desire. And, in many cases, they have financed the clubs.

Among the biggest boosters of the sex trade was none other than Ryoichi Sasakawa, the yakuza-connected Sugamo cellmate of Kodama who built up a fortune in motorboat racing. Sasakawa, a personal friend of then Philippines President Marcos, founded in 1979 the World Safari Club, a private, Japanese-only tour operation with exclusive rights to develop the unspoiled island of Lubang into a "tourist paradise." Sasakawa's advance advertisements in Japan touted unlimited fishing, hunting, diving, and "nudist areas" that of course included "private companions." But his plans for the island were soon discovered by women's and church groups, which claimed the resort amounted to a giant outdoor brothel. Bowing to the unfavorable publicity, Sasakawa and company canceled the project in 1981 "to avoid misunderstanding."

Employers, too, arranged for their workers to go on the sex tours. In one celebrated incident, the Casio Company in 1979 held a banquet in a Manila hotel for its 200 leading salesmen of the year. After wining and dining them, and inviting the elderly among them to call it a day, a huge folding screen parted to reveal 200 "hostesses" for the night, each one bearing a number on her corsage.

The Japanese, however, have not been wholly responsible for the Asian flesh trade. Sex tours from Western Europe, notably from West Germany and the Netherlands, have been visible as well, if not as numerous; and, worst of all, the women's own governments are complicit.

With tourism as the third or fourth largest earner of foreign exchange in these countries, and most of the visitors men, local government officials have condoned and even boosted the sex trade as a means of gaining hard currency. A 1984 report by the respected Korea Church Women United condemned the nation's Kisaeng houses as "an auction block where girls are bartered in exchange for foreign money." Indeed, these critics charge that the sex trade has become so pervasive that without it Korea's all-important tourist trade would collapse – and with it a startling percentage of the cash needed to pay off the nation's huge foreign debt. Despite a

1947 ban on prostitution, claim the church women, Korean tourism officials even sponsor ideological lectures for the prostitutes about patriotism and the importance of the foreign exchange they earn. At best, the governments in the region have followed a tragic policy of benign neglect.

Despite the apparent government sanction of the sex trade, there has been increasing opposition to the Japanese tours. In 1973, Korea's highly politicized student groups began protests at Kimpo Airport outside Seoul. They were joined by Christian women's organizations, which soon linked up with their Japanese counterparts.

Opposition within Japan was spearheaded by the 4000-member Women's Christian Temperance Union, a seasoned band of activists who had played a key role in the passage of Japan's antiprostitution laws in the 1950s. In the Philippines, a coalition of women's and church groups began organizing as well, and in 1980 filed its first formal protest with the Japanese embassy in Manila. This was at the height of the sex junkets, as the tourist industry pushed more than 1.8 million Japanese into the region.

Then, in June of 1981, a chain of carefully planned demonstrations followed Prime Minister Zenko Suzuki around his heavily publicized tour of Southeast Asia. By the time the prime minister reached Jakarta, he was willing to admit something was seriously wrong with Japanese tourism in the area. So effective were these protests that Thailand and the Philippines reportedly experienced a 25 percent drop in Japanese male tourists over the next few months.

The demonstrations and continued protests forced a number of overdue changes. Travel associations in Japan and the Philippines jointly condemned the sex tour business. Japan's Ministry of Transportation, after ignoring the trade for a decade, threatened to publicly name and chide the tour operators. In 1981, Japan's four major labor organizations finally joined in to stop the national embarrassment, appealing to the prime minister's office to halt the sex tours. And advertisements in the Japanese media, once filled with blatant references to the beautiful ladies of Manila and Bangkok, now stress the countries' natural beauty.

It was no coincidence that in the early 1980s, as the protests turned back the worst of the sex tours, the yakuza moved in force to another, equally exploitive aspect of the sex trade – the international traffic in women. The Japanese gangs simply began turning the trade around, luring to Japan tens of thousands of women throughout Asia with the promise of legitimate jobs and good money. But instead of a new start, their victims have been plunged into a world of forged passports and faked visas, and ultimately into sexual slavery, forced to work as poorly paid prostitutes in the brothels of Japan.

The "import" of foreign women into Japan is not new to the yakuza. Police records show "white slavery," as the Japanese also call it, dating back to the early 1970s. But the practice has now become big business, and it has enraged its Japanese critics even more than the sex tours. The reason lies in a sensitive bit of Japanese history: around the turn of the century, Japan itself was a victim of the very same trade.

By the late 1800s, impoverished Japanese families in large numbers were selling their daughters to international slave traders, who shipped the young women throughout East Asia and even to Hawaii and California. Other women, like the yakuza's modern-day victims, were tricked into the trade by being promised well-paid, legitimate jobs, only to be forced into prostitution upon leaving Japan. The government even supported the trade, encouraging the slavers to follow the conquest of the Japanese Imperial Army and Navy across Asia, and "drafting" as many as 70,000 Korean women to "entertain" imperial troops at the front.

These unfortunate women were called the *karayuki-san*; the Japanese today have modified the term to describe the foreign women now ensconced in yakuza bars and brothels in Japan. They are called the *Japayuki-san*, the Japan-bound prostitutes. Japanese police have been slow to act on this more recent manifestation of the sex trade. Even when they do act, their efforts have not been very successful, due in good part to the attitudes of the principal supplier nations: Korea, Taiwan, Thailand, and the Philippines. As a result, according to one senior police official in Japan, the trade has reached "critical proportions."

The horror stories are legion. Impoverished women, lured to Japan on various pretexts, find themselves at the mercy of gangsters who confiscate their passports and force them to work as prostitutes, dancers, and hostesses. Without friends and unable to speak Japanese, they are packed into tiny rooms and find themselves trapped in a life of virtual slavery.

The demand for foreign prostitutes in Japan is tremendous. A series of arrests over the years provides an idea as to the scope of the trade:

• In 1973, police in Hong Kong uncovered a ring operating out of a tailor shop and tour agency, coaxing about fifty women per month to Tokyo from Hong Kong and various other Southeast Asian countries. Once the women arrived in Japan, they were forced into work as strippers and prostitutes; their promised wages never appeared and they were unable to leave Japan.

• Japanese police in 1974 cracked a sexual slavery ring, allegedly run by two Korean men out of Hong Kong and Bangkok. Officials claimed the pair regularly visited Japan carrying catalogues of Thai girls, and took orders from brothel and bar operators.
• Police in Thailand in 1984 arrested a Japanese man and his Thai wife for having sent some 200 Thai women to Hong Kong and Japan via the Portuguese enclave of Macao. Over the previous two years, the couple had moved as many as two groups of eight women each month. Police also seized videotape equipment used to send "samples" of the women to interested parties.

The traffic in women is attractive to the yakuza gangs. A well-run brothel brings in good money, and the penalties are far less severe than those for moving guns or drugs. The women, furthermore, are inexpensive: young Filipinas can be bought for as little as $1000, and then "leased" to Japanese clubs for the same amount each month. One Japanese hotel operator bragged that he controlled more than seventy Southeast Asian prostitutes earning up to $100,000 per month: "Men who recruit prostitutes come to me regularly and ask if I need new women to run my establishments. . . . It is as simple as . . . delivering a bowl of noodles." A publication of the Asian Women's Association in Japan asserted that actual slave auctions occur along a row of cheap hotels lining Showa Avenue in Tokyo's Ueno district. During one auction, dealers allegedly came from around the country to make their bids, which ranged from $3000 for six months' service to $800 for "one little black girl."

Figures on the numbers of women involved are at best rough estimates, but it is clear that the trade has reached massive proportions. In the red-light district of Osaka alone, some 10,000 women, mostly Southeast Asians, reportedly work "selling spring," the Japanese slang for prostitution.

Servicing such a massive trade requires hundreds of recruiters, pimps, and assorted middlemen. The Korea Church Women United has accused fifty "talent" agencies in Osaka of engaging in the trade. By the early 1980s, about half the women were coming from the Philippines, where yakuza worked with local recruiters, called *bugaws,* who scoured the poorer provinces in search of prey. These rings of slave traders are as crude as they are criminal. One group based in Manila specialized in the export of young girls – ten to seventeen years old – to Singapore, Kuala Lumpur, and Tokyo. All were branded with an identical tattoo on their right thigh.

Certainly some of the women – those who have plied the trade in their native lands – know that they are being recruited as prostitutes. "The slave trade stories are about 30 percent true," says Tatsuo Saito, a Manila correspondent for Japan's Kyodo News Service. "I've interviewed almost 500 women here over a three-year stay. More than 90 percent who were in Japan want to return. The money is excellent for them and they got along with the yakuza just fine." Indeed, some are lucky enough to have jobs as hostesses, in which their principal duties consist of conversing with customers and getting them to buy drinks. Those with a good boss make as much as ten times what they could in their impoverished native countries, and much of that money goes back home to their families. Yet, despite the demand for these women, they usually receive half of what their Japanese counterparts make, and few are prepared for the often brutal treatment meted out by their yakuza caretakers.

The situation has become grave enough that Japanese police in 1984 created a special office to deal with illegal women workers in the country. In Tokyo, the Women's Christian Temperance Union announced plans to build a shelter for those who escaped their captors. Protests by women's and church groups have also continued, including a February 1985 march by 10,000 through Manila's tourist district. As the protesters burned pornographic books, a sound truck blared the activists' message to the predominantly Roman Catholic nation: "Our land, once the only Christian nation in the Orient, is now known as a country of murderers, adulterers, and fornicators."

The Philippines: A Second Home
Despite the protests of Manila's citizenry, the yakuza appear to have found a permanent home in the Philippines. As it has through much of East Asia, the sex trade introduced the Japanese gangs to the area, and since then the islands have become a center of the yakuza's international operations second only to South Korea. It is an exciting place for the younger, more aggressive yakuza. The Philippines, a former American colony, is a hazy, humid, sweat-soaked archipelago of 7000 islands centered around the 8 million residents of Metro-Manila. English is widely spoken, and, with an economy constantly teetering on the brink of disaster, it is a land where the dollar and the yen will go very far indeed.

Employing some well-honed techniques from Japan, the yakuza have made important political connections among those who rule over the Philippines' 48 million people. Capitalizing on the country's rampant corruption, the gangs have bribed their way into a lucrative, long-term relationship with both local businessmen and bureaucrats. Through well-placed "gifts," the more enterprising yakuza have avoided jail as well as extradition, maintained dubious business ventures, and repeatedly cleared Customs with no questions asked.

Senior members of the Yamaguchi-gumi, Inagawa-kai, and Sumi-yoshi-rengo have opened luxurious offices in Makati, the so-called Wall Street of Manila, according to a confidential U.S. Drug Enforcement Administration report. Makati's complex of skyscrapers, malls, and international hotels, set up alongside some of the city's worst slums, makes an ideal home to the import-export firms and travel agencies the yakuza prefer using as fronts. Other yakuza gangs have taken root as well. The Korean syndicate of Hisayuki Machii, according to press reports, has acquired "coral reef exploration rights" in the country. But the biggest investments have been made in the city's Ermita district, the sleazy center of the Philippine sex trade. In 1982 the *Times-Journal,* a leading Manila daily, cited police officials as saying that at least thirty clubs and restaurants in the area were yakuza-owned. The businesses, with Filipino "dummy" owners, were said to serve as fronts for gunrunning, drug smuggling, and trafficking in women.

By the early 1980s, Manila newspapers were abuzz with sensational reports of yakuza activity. One daily even ran a huge box on "Spotting a Yakuza," complete with photos of a tattooed back and a hand sans pinkie. Another paper ran banner headlines, YAKUZA SLAVE TRADERS HUNTED. Manila police, meanwhile, drew a confession out of one resident yakuza who claimed that up to several hundred of his ilk were active in the Philippines at any given time.

Working with the increasingly sophisticated Filipino gangs, the yakuza expanded into gambling, fraud, and money laundering. But next to the sex trade, the Japanese gangs have prized the Philippines most as a base for smuggling operations. With 7000 islands, most of them undeveloped, the Philippines offer ideal locations for the yakuza's foul-smelling amphetamine factories. Of even greater interest are handguns, which are illegal in Japan – but abundant in the Philippines – and are an increasingly necessary item among the gangs. Military men and police are suspected of selling their weapons to the gangs. When Manila police raided the headquarters of one gunrunning ring, dubbed the "Manila Connection," they reportedly discovered machine guns, automatic rifles, fifty pistols, enough ammunition for a small siege, and various drugs. The mastermind of the gang, one Hiroaki Kumitomo, a thirty-one-year-old yakuza, had earlier been found dead in a parked car in suburban Manila. Police believed the murder was linked to an abortive drug deal. Several other yakuza have been found floating in the murky rivers of Manila following disputes with their own groups or Filipino partners. But sometimes the victims are unfortunate Japanese who wandered into the jaws of these renegade mobsters.

Between 1978 and 1981, police tied at least four homicides to murder-for-insurance schemes in the Philippines. First, the gangs would intimidate businessmen in Japan into taking out huge insurance policies, listing the gang members as beneficiaries. Then, after somehow luring their victims to Manila, the yakuza hired Filipino assassins for as little as $2500. After the fourth homicide of a visiting Japanese, authorities finally got wind of the scam, and in 1981 police and soldiers raided a training camp for the assassins in a town south of Manila. Officials seized eight suspects, targets, shells, and a small arsenal of handguns.

Not all Philippine officials condone the presence of the yakuza. Indeed, many Filipinos on both sides of the law deeply resent the entry of Japanese gangsters into their homeland. Philippine authorities have in fact launched a series of crackdowns on the yakuza. Smuggling boats have been seized, fugitives tracked down, contraband seized, and mobsters deported. Between 1975 and 1983, according to press reports, police arrested and deported eighty-three yakuza suspects, and were seeking twenty-one others. Unfortunately, at this point it will take more than periodic crackdowns to drive the yakuza out of the country. The tattooed men from Japan have set up shop in the Philippines, and will not easily be dislodged.

Southeast Asia and the Chinese Triads
In the mid-1970s, reports began filtering in to Japanese police of gang activity throughout Southeast Asia. Yakuza members were sighted in Indonesia, Malaysia, Thailand, Singapore, Hong Kong, and Taiwan. In most places, they have practiced a familiar pattern: the procurement of guns, drugs, and women. As they have expanded, though, the yakuza have also had to learn a kind of underworld diplomacy, for their travels have introduced them to another, equally powerful set of crime syndicates whose size and sophistication rival their own – the Chinese Triads.

The linkup of the Japanese gangs with the leading syndicates of Chinese organized crime is the most ominous result of the yakuza's move into East Asia. Bound by ethnicity and codes of silence, the Triads exist in various forms in Hong Kong and Thailand – where they finance much of the world's heroin trade – and wherever most of the world's 20 million overseas Chinese have settled. The Chinese are, in fact, the main multinational link in organized crime today, with connections ranging from

Sydney, Singapore, and San Francisco to Amsterdam, Yokohama, and New York. As such, it is of no small importance that alliances have been struck, and business begun, between the yakuza and the Triads – the largest crime syndicates of the world's largest continent.

The danger here is not of a monolithic Asian Mafia invading the West. Such ideas are at best misinformed. Differences in language, custom, and history ensure that no great mergers will occur within the Asian underworld; indeed, the varied gangs are as likely to be fighting amongst themselves as cooperating. Nevertheless, alliances do occur between the world's powerful crime syndicates, like the narcotics trade between the U.S. Mafia and the Chiu Chao Triad, and they pose a powerful challenge to both law enforcement and the general public. To understand the significance of the Triads and their relationship to the yakuza, some history is in order.

Like the yakuza, the Triads represent a set of diverse, often feuding crime syndicates. The Chinese gangs exhibit many of the same traits as their Japanese counterparts: ancient rituals, strict discipline, and a history dating back some 300 years. The Triads similarly have carried a Robin Hood image through the years and are romanticized in movies and television series. And, like the yakuza, the Triads also have a history of heavy political involvement.

Some Chinese scholars trace the Chinese secret societies, from which the Triads arose, to as far back as A.D. 21. Most accounts, though, cite the year 1674 as the legendary beginning of the first Triad society, when a group of Buddhist monks at a monastery in Fukien became a rallying point against that nation's oppressive Manchu rulers. The monks refined a highly effective form of self-defense that came to be called kung fu, and though their cause was a lost one, they founded a set of secret societies that would endure for generations.

Years later, when Sun Yat-sen established the Chinese Republic in 1911, the Triads were there to help him. In his bid to control China, Sun's successor, Chiang Kai-shek, repeatedly turned to the Triads, which by then had become largely a criminal force with a heavy involvement in the opium trade. Chiang, in fact, was himself a Triad member, and relied so heavily on his underworld allies that they served as generals, soldiers, spies, businessmen, and hired thugs in his Kuomintang (KMT), the Chinese Nationalist Army.

Mao's 1949 victory spelled death for the Triads in mainland China. Smugglers, dealers, and hardened crooks of all sorts were summarily rounded up and imprisoned; many were simply shot. The Communist takeover of China, it is generally agreed, ended the nation's long ordeal with opium addiction. It did not, however, end the Triads. Wherever Chiang's Nationalist Army fled, the Triads went along – to Hong Kong, Taiwan, and from the south of China into Burma.

Hong Kong already had a serious problem with Triad gangs, thanks in part to the Japanese. After falling to Japan during the war, the colony's new masters organized cooperative Triads into the Hing Ah Kee Kwa, the "Aid Asia Flourishing Association," and used them to help keep order. The Japanese shared with their collaborators the profits from prostitution and gambling, and allowed the gangs to control the opium trade in the colony. The occupying Japanese, like the British before them, relied heavily on opium addiction to keep the population docile.

After the war, the Triads sank their roots deeper into Hong Kong (again in British hands), aided by the mass exodus of fellow members from the mainland. The British then made the grave mistake of banning opium in the colony, which immediately gave rise to a thriving black market and a steady source of income for the postwar gangs. Soon the local Triads were playing a central role in the world's narcotics trade, and were expanding like a young typhoon. By the 1980s, despite three decades of police crackdowns, Hong Kong's syndicates stood at 80,000 strong, with a solid core of professional criminals estimated at 12,000. Considering Hong Kong covers only 403 square miles, and has a population of 5.5 million, the colony must have among the highest per capita number of gangsters on the face of the earth. Police have identified 200 gangs grouped under at least 33 separate syndicates.

Of even greater importance to the future of organized crime was the fate of those Nationalist Army units that fled south across the Chinese border into Burma. It was there in the early 1950s that the U.S. Central Intelligence Agency, anxious to set up a second front along with Taiwan against Mao, helped form the remnants of Chiang's army into a guerrilla force of some 10,000 men. It was a critical mistake. As they had in China, the Nationalists turned to opium as a way to finance their activities. Without much hope of defeating the Communists, they soon degenerated into a private drug militia, which today, in concert with Thai and Hong Kong Triads, controls a considerable amount of the world's heroin traffic.

The region settled by Chiang's renegade KMT soldiers is Southeast Asia's notorious Golden Triangle, a remote, mountainous area where the ill-defined borders of Thailand, Burma, and Laos meet. Fiercely independent hill tribes, who have made the cultivation of opium poppies a way of life, sell the illicit crops to the Kuomintang remnants and to a bizarre array of warlords and drug merchants. From there the raw opium is moved in heavily armed mule caravans to remote refineries, where it is processed into heroin.

It is at the point of refining that the 16,000-member Chiu Chao Triad comes into play. Generally acknowledged as the most tightly organized of the numerous Triad societies, the Chiu Chao took over control of heroin distribution in Thailand in the 1950s and never let go. Today, they continue to wield a near-monopoly over international narcotics shipments out of Southeast Asia. Together with their brother Chiu Chaos in Hong Kong, these ethnic Chinese finance billions of dollars in heroin shipments worldwide. Highly skilled chemists, imported from Hong Kong or nearby Macao, oversee production of the narcotic. During the 1960s, much of the opium was refined in Hong Kong itself; now the colony serves largely as an entrepôt and financial center for the region's narcotics traffic. It is the Chiu Chao syndicates, operating out of Bangkok and Hong Kong, that over the years have made deals with the U.S. Mafia, with the Corsican mob, with other Chinese gangs, and, most recently, with the yakuza.

The Chinese are not solely responsible for the boom in Southeast Asian heroin, however. In his groundbreaking 1972 book, *The Politics of Heroin in Southeast Asia,* journalist Alfred McCoy meticulously described how the CIA, and the French intelligence service before that, played key roles in the development of the region's narcotics trade. It is a complex story, involving U.S. dealings with Corsican, Sicilian, and Chinese gangsters, the Vietnam War, corrupt governments, and mercenary armies that ultimately caused a heroin epidemic among America's youth. America's obsession of allying itself with any group willing to stem the flow of "Communist aggression," argued McCoy, blinded it into supporting many of the key figures in the postwar heroin trade. "The CIA's role," concluded McCoy, "was simply an inadvertent but inevitable consequence of cold war tactics."

Little has changed since McCoy's book. Despite concerted international efforts and more than $30 million of foreign assistance since 1970, the Golden Triangle still provides between 20 and 40 percent of the heroin entering the United States. Although vast quantities of the drug are now produced in Mexico and Southwest Asia's "Golden Crescent" – Iran, Afghanistan, and Pakistan – America's narcotics dealers continue to prefer the generally higher quality of Golden Triangle heroin. And though the U.S. heroin epidemic no longer gets the press it once did, the country's 500,000 heroin users still account for a huge percentage of the street crime nationwide.

It is difficult to gauge the full extent of yakuza involvement in the international narcotics trade. Law enforcement officials familiar with the

Chinese Organized Crime Syndicates

Name/Home Base	Members	Gangs	Area of Operations
14K/Hong Kong	24,000	23	Southeast Asia, North America, Western Europe
Wo Group/ Hong Kong	29,000	10	Southeast Asia and overseas
Chiu Chao (Chao Zhou)/ Hong Kong	16,000	6	Southeast Asia and overseas
United Bamboo Gang (Chu Lien Pang)/Taiwan	10,000– 15,000	NA*	East Asia, North America, Saudi Arabia
Luen Group/ Hong Kong	5,000	4	Southeast Asia and overseas
Tung Group/ Hong Kong	3,000	2	Southeast Asia and overseas
Others/ Hong Kong	4,000	9	Southeast Asia and overseas
Four Seas (Shih Hai)/Taiwan	thousands	NA	East Asia and overseas
Niu-Pu Gang/ Taiwan	1,000	NA	Taiwan

Sources: Law enforcement reports, 1980; miscellaneous press reports, 1984–1985.
*NA = Not Available.

situation worry that if the Japanese gangs continue to enter the Southeast Asian heroin market, they will be almost impossible to stop. With the yakuza's manpower, money, and organization, and the massive trade between Japan and the rest of the world, huge quantities of the drug could be moved to the United States, Australia, Europe, and Japan itself.

Since the yakuza first began setting up base in Southeast Asia, gang members have increasingly experimented with heroin, making purchases in Thailand and Hong Kong and smuggling it into Japan and elsewhere. By the mid-1970s, the Inagawa-kai, Sumiyoshi-rengo, and other syndicates had allegedly set up nightclubs and travel services in Hong Kong to facilitate their varied smuggling operations. At about the same time, the 2500-member Matsuba-kai began promoting kick-boxing and female professional wrestling shows in Thailand and Singapore. Perhaps, then, it was no coincidence that in 1971 Japanese police arrested ten members of the Matsuba-kai for selling some $45,000 worth of heroin to bar hostesses in Tokyo. According to police, it was the first time in several years that yakuza had been arrested for selling heroin.

A series of gang-related heroin crackdowns have since occurred that, though some of the quantities are small by U.S. standards, reveal interest on the part of the yakuza in entering the narcotics trade. Authorities seized an annual average of only 2.8 pounds of heroin from 1977 to 1982. But more recent raids have alarmed both Japanese and foreign police. In November 1984, police grabbed their largest single haul in years: 7.3 pounds, worth some $4.5 million, carried by a middle-aged Thai man. Only two months later, they seized 9.5 pounds of Golden Triangle heroin in the bags of a Thai Airlines stewardess.

The big shock, though, came in September 1985, when U.S. and Hong Kong police arrested 10 people in connection with smuggling 52 pounds of speed and 12 pounds of heroin into the United States. The case, the result of a yearlong investigation by DEA and Customs undercover agents, allegedly involved a series of high-stakes drug, firearms, and murder-for-hire deals. U.S. officials in Honolulu arrested two of the Yamaguchi-gumi's highest-ranking bosses, who they charged had flown to Hawaii to personally oversee the deals. It is unclear how unusual this particular transaction was. The case convinced many U.S. narcotics intelligence agents, who had previously looked at yakuza heroin only as a worrisome possibility, that the gangs are already funding, or stand on the brink of funding, large-scale shipments of the drug into the West.

Despite the image of Japan as heroin-free, traffic in the drug is not entirely new to the Japanese. Yakuza attached to the imperial forces during the country's expansion through Asia gained firsthand experience in the opium trade. And from the late 1950s to the mid-1960s, as demand for stimulants fell, the gangs helped smuggle substantial amounts of narcotics into the country, peaking at 121 pounds of opium, morphine, and heroin in 1966. The Triads are familiar with Japan as well, for over the years they have regularly used that country as a transfer point. Because Japan is not commonly thought of as a source of drugs, goods shipped from there are less suspect than those from Hong Kong or Singapore. What agreements, if any, have been made with the yakuza are unknown, but the Japanese syndicates are sophisticated enough, and have enough ethnic Chinese within their ranks, to ensure that such connections can be made quickly.

Before his downfall, the notorious Hong Kong Chiu Chao godfather, Limpy Ho, flew to Japan on several occasions in 1970 and 1971 to meet buyers from the United States. Limpy arranged a maritime smuggling route via Japan, and moved large quantities of high-quality heroin into the U.S. market. English author Sean O'Callaghan, in his book *The Triads,* asserted that this route still existed by the late 1970s, and that considerable quantities of heroin reach Amsterdam – the center of the European narcotics trade – from Japan hidden in refrigerators, fans, and other electrical appliances.

Japanese police dismiss the possibility that the yakuza will ever enter the heroin trade in force, and cite the minuscule number of arrests for opiates in the country (only twenty-two in 1983). Other factors contribute to keeping the Japanese out of the heroin trade. Not the least of these is the impropriety of smuggling heroin into the United States or Europe; impropriety still counts for something in Japan. Yakuza leaders would take a good deal of heat if the United States and other nations were to blame Japan for their heroin problems; Japanese still care deeply what the rest of the world thinks of their country. This concern with social probity may change, however, if the new guard of yakuza leaders is as indifferent to tradition as some observers now believe. (Japanese officials are concerned, however, that the yakuza may turn to large-scale marijuana smuggling as that drug becomes popular among young Japanese. With Japan's close proximity to growing areas in Thailand and the Philippines, pot shipments could become a major source of income for the yakuza.)

Another factor that must be considered is the status of Hong Kong. With the crown colony reverting to China's control in 1999, Hong Kong's role as a center for the region's heroin trade may well change. The Triads have already begun looking for new bases of operation, transferring enormous sums of money abroad. If they fail to retain control of the Hong Kong pipeline, it would become easier for the yakuza, with their center intact, to step in and take over large portions of the trade. The Chinese syndicates might, in fact, welcome an alternative source of distribution that is both well financed and trustworthy.

Historically, elements of the American Mafia hedged for years before deciding to go into heroin in a big way, and the yakuza may simply be waiting until someone decisive and ruthless enough takes the initiative. According to John Y. Y. Lee, former chief of the U.S. Drug Enforcement Administration in Honolulu, the major obstacle to the yakuza in the heroin business is the lack of an adequate distribution system outside of Japan. "Not many of them speak English well enough to negotiate a major deal," says Lee. And, it might be added, not many American mobsters speak Japanese.

But the yakuza, like other Japanese businessmen, have proved themselves highly adaptable. The gangs' wide experience in dealing in guns, stimulants, and women shows that they can and will make deals with foreign crime syndicates. And if a foreign distribution system does not yet fully exist, a sophisticated supply network certainly does. Since the mid-1970s, the yakuza have been moving large quantities of their prized methamphetamine along the same routes as the region's heroin traffic. Their new suppliers: the Triads in both Thailand and Hong Kong.

The heart of the Southeast Asian narcotics belt holds many attractions for the yakuza. Hong Kong in particular, with its heavy Japanese presence, is a natural for the gangs. The tiny colony is at the same time one of the world's busiest ports, a leading financial center, and a magnet for tourists. Twenty percent of the colony's 2.6 million visitors in 1982 were Japanese. Some 10,000 of the yakuza's countrymen reside in Hong Kong, and more than 800 Japanese firms are active there. While the tourists are, as always, a favorite target for vice, the companies have become a target for the sokaiya, who, unsatisfied with their returns at home, have moved their unique brand of extortion abroad.

A 1980 confidential report by the Interpol bureau of the Royal Hong Kong Police concluded that the Sumiyoshi-rengo was most active in the colony, but warned of a serious lack of knowledge of yakuza activity. Citing the flood of Japanese visitors and money pouring into the colony, officials wrote: "It would be naive and shortsighted to assume that they are not active here. . . . We have seen the ubiquitous line of Japanese tourists being led dutifully to a particular shop. One wonders – just who is doing the leading?"

At least a partial answer to that question was provided in 1978, when Japanese police netted 16 Yamaguchi-gumi members who were believed to have moved as much as 100 kilograms of amphetamines out of the British colony. Suspicions were confirmed in 1979, when local police in Japan tied another 100 kilograms to the 24,000-member 14K Triad. The reach of the Hong Kong–based 14K stretches around the world, from Chinese street gangs in San Francisco to drug kingpins in Amsterdam, where they control much of the heroin entering Western Europe. In 1985, the syndicate's name surfaced again as the apparent source of 64 pounds of heroin and speed seized from Yamaguchi couriers by police in Hong Kong and Honolulu.

From Hong Kong it is only a short plane ride to Bangkok, the teeming capital city and marketplace of Thailand. Like elsewhere in Southeast Asia, the yakuza were originally attracted to Bangkok by the sex trade. But Thailand is a bit like the Wild West set in the tropics, and has a strong pull for the more adventurous Japanese gangsters. Three wars are being fought on Thai soil at any one time: with opium barons to the north, the Vietnamese Army to the east, and Moslem secessionists to the south. Such conditions create a massive flow in illicit arms; in 1977 police investigated the "disappearance" of 700,000 rounds of ammunition from a Bangkok gun shop. Four years later, they raided a house in that sprawling city and seized 100,000 cartridges for military rifles, 71 hand grenades, booby traps, and fuses. Add to this atmosphere a corrupt police force, and the yakuza have an ideal base for gunrunning operations.

In keeping with the nature of Thailand, smuggling by the yakuza at times takes on an exotic flavor. One operator concealed a sizable shipment of handguns in seven boxes of 70 poisonous snakes, including 15 cobras and 30 chain vipers. Somehow the shipment cleared Japanese Customs, but police soon panicked the entire city of Hakone when they disclosed that the gangsters had dumped the snakes into a local river.

Operating out of first-class hotels in Bangkok, the yakuza have made deals for women, guns, and drugs. The local Chiu Chao Triads have apparently become involved in channeling European-made stimulants as well as Thai heroin to the gangs. One smuggling ring dissolved in Tokyo claimed its main contact in Bangkok was a captain in the Thai state police. Another operation involved an enterprising gang boss in Saitama Prefecture who ran a construction business and exported tractors to his Chinese customers in Thailand. The yakuza businessmen received his payment in guns, gold bars, jewels, and wristwatches.

After the Communist victory in China, the Triads fled not only to Hong Kong and the Golden Triangle but also to Taiwan, where they set up equally impressive criminal cartels. Taiwan, like Korea a Japanese colony for 40 years, lies only 700 miles from the southern tip of Japan and holds a great attraction for the yakuza. This rapidly industrializing island of 18 million people served as the original sex tour destination for Japan's male travelers, and continues to supply women for the yakuza's booming trade in sexual slavery. The gangs have invested heavily in real estate and run a number of import-export companies, moving everything from carrots and bananas to folk art.

Unlike their counterparts in Thailand and Hong Kong, the Taiwanese syndicates handle only small amounts of heroin, but have moved heavily into meth production. Police believe the "Taiwan Connection" first began in 1975, when – borrowing a tactic from the Hong Kong Triads – the yakuza sent Japanese chemists to train their Chinese allies in amphetamine production. Police got an idea of the vast scope of the operation when in 1984 they uncovered a ring of smugglers that in a five-month period moved an estimated 163 kilograms from Taiwan into Japan, an amount worth $135 million. The gang's leading courier was alleged to be one Tancredo Duluc, the ambassador to Taiwan from the Dominican Republic. The diplomat, according to Taiwanese officials, had made more than forty-eight trips out of Taiwan in the past year.

To engage in such large-scale smuggling, strong crime syndicates are needed, and these Taiwan has in abundance – more than 700 different gangs, most of them grouped under a half dozen major syndicates. The nation's leading Triad is the powerful United Bamboo Gang, whose membership has been estimated at 40,000, although most figures range from 10,000 to 15,000. Along with the next largest group, the Four Seas Gang, they reportedly control more than 60 percent of the nation's prostitution, gambling, and protection rackets. As they had in China, the Nationalist Chinese ruling Taiwan have continued to use the gangs for political purposes. Through much of the 1970s, the gangs were used to spy upon and disrupt political opponents of Chiang Kai-shek. Then, in 1984, the Taiwanese Defense Ministry Intelligence Bureau recruited leading Bamboo Gang members to silence Chinese-American journalist Henry Liu, whom they murdered in his suburban garage outside San Francisco.

So close are relations between crime syndicates in Taiwan and Japan that the yakuza have entered into an unprecedented formal alliance with their Chinese counterparts. United Bamboo members admit to having formed an important pact with Japan's leading gang, the Yamaguchi-gumi. Similar alliances are believed to exist between other syndicates from the two countries.

The Bamboo Gang is something of a pioneer in setting up overseas ventures. It has long had affiliated members in Los Angeles and other U.S. cities, and in the early 1980s the syndicate hosted a lavish reception in Hong Kong to clinch a peace pact with the local Triads. Using as a front its Churan United Sports Association, the Bamboo hierarchy sent out engraved dinner invitations proclaiming "We are all members of a big family." Details are sketchy about this meeting of the mobs, but varied reports assert that in attendance were some 350 well-heeled Triad leaders representing virtually every major Hong Kong group.

Such alliances worry law enforcement officials, who see in them the possibility for endless sources of trouble. Growing international activity on the part of both Chinese and Japanese crime syndicates, coupled with the increasing sophistication of the gangs, means that new avenues of cooperation will emerge – new types of crimes, new investment scams, new smuggling routes. Some experienced lawmen, however, are cautious about how far-reaching the changes might be. "The alliances are mostly personal relationships," says a ranking Hong Kong police inspector with long years in combating the Triads. "The links between organized crime groups in Asia depend on initiative – by the criminals, and by the police to stop them. It's not a static situation." Whatever the situation, it's a safe bet that the world will be seeing more of Asia's great crime syndicates working together.

Western Europe, South America, and the Mid-Pacific

Once the yakuza tasted the excitement and profit of doing business abroad, the more enterprising gangsters began seeking out opportunities around the globe. Their travels have taken them far beyond East Asia – to South America, Western Europe, and the countries of the Pacific Basin. Little is known about the yakuza's activities in many of these places. Few of the crimes get reported, and local police seldom know what to look for. Missing fingers and body tattoos are not regularly on the minds of Customs inspectors in Sydney and São Paulo.

Regardless of face-saving denials by the Japanese police about yakuza expansion abroad, since the mid-1970s the gangs have shown an eagerness to make connections in virtually every non-Communist nation where an opportunity has presented itself. Like the Chinese, though, they have tended to go mostly where large ethnic Japanese communities reside. Nowhere is this truer than in the surprising case of Brazil.

Japanese have been migrating in large numbers to Brazil since the 1930s, when many came to work as agricultural laborers. After the end of World War II, a huge wave of immigrants arrived, many of them former soldiers who, once repatriated to Japan, left their war-torn homeland to seek a new life abroad. As a result, today there are an estimated one million ethnic Japanese living in South America. More than three-quarters of them live in Brazil, making it the largest Japanese settlement outside of Japan. Another 80,000 reside in Peru, 30,000 in Argentina, and 10,000 in Bolivia. The huge number living in Brazil has helped make that country one of Japan's top three centers of foreign investment. It has also helped nurture a Japanese underworld, both imported and homegrown.

Brazil has its share of organized crime problems without the yakuza, with a rising cocaine trade spilling over from nearby Bolivia and Peru, active associates of the Italian Mafiosi, and down-and-out members of the country's varied ethnic groups. The yakuza have found their niche in the heart of Brazil's Japanese community, the Liberdade (Liberty) district of the huge city of São Paulo. Some 250,000 Japanese live there, squashed into twenty square blocks of that city of more than 10 million.

The yakuza apparently first caught the attention of the Brazilian media in the late 1970s, when violence erupted between Japanese and Korean gangs in Liberdade. Those involved have rightly been called gurentai, or hoodlums, by the Japanese community there. These young gangsters don't cut off their fingers or go in for tattooing. But many have kept up ties with yakuza in Japan, and much of their criminal activity sounds surprisingly familiar. In tandem with yakuza from abroad, they have set up commercial businesses as fronts, with a preference for restaurants, bars, import-export companies, and floral shops. They are heavily into smuggling – Brazilian goods out of the country, and Japanese goods (mostly electronic items on which Brazil has strict quotas) into the country. Within the Liberdade area they control gambling, drugs, prostitution, and protection rackets, and have helped their associates from Japan procure Brazilian women for the sex trade. Other reports suggest that the Brazilian yakuza have moved into vending and slot machines and construction.

The yakuza made another media splash in Brazil in 1979, when police cornered two gangsters involved in a murder-for-insurance scheme strikingly similar to those occurring in the Philippines at about the same time. After insurance companies alerted police, the yakuza, apparently then in Japan, fled to Taiwan, where they met Chen Quan, a fifty-three-year-old naturalized Paraguayan and alleged Triad member. Quan arranged passage for them to Paraguay, and eventually the yakuza made their way to the Japanese community in São Paulo. As Brazilian police, alerted by Interpol, closed in on the fugitives, the gangsters fled northward to the town of Araguaia outside Brasilia, where they died in a shootout with federal agents. As for Chen Quan, the yakuza's Chinese connection was arrested in 1985 for smuggling into the country nearly a pound of heroin, reported at the time as the largest single quantity of the drug ever seized in Brazil.

The yakuza have caused other troubles in South America. Recruiters for the sex trade have conned women from Colombia as well as Brazil, and probably other countries, into trips to Japan. At least two gun smuggling operations have been tied to Argentina, and considerable money is suspected of being laundered on the continent. Also, according to reliable sources, the yakuza have established a Peruvian connection for moving cocaine into Japan. Considering the wild popularity of stimulants in Japan, cocaine might someday rival methamphetamine as the country's drug of choice.

*   *   *

It is not surprising, perhaps, that if the yakuza had made their way to Colombia and Paraguay, they would turn up in Western Europe. Still, it was a shock to the Japanese police commissioner visiting Paris for a seminar when he bumped into several leading members of the Yama-guchi-gumi. Among other crimes, a series of gunrunning cases has been traced to Europe. As early as 1965, an Air France pilot was caught smuggling guns to the yakuza. More recently, an Italian connection has surfaced. In 1982, Japanese police stopped a twenty-eight-year-old member of the Kyosei-kai, and charged him with smuggling 300 .25-caliber Garesi handguns and 20,000 bullets he had picked up in Milan. A year later a second smuggler was nabbed with 37 of the guns, leading police to comment on how popular the Italian models had become among the yakuza rank and file.

Europe's huge pornography industry also holds an attraction for the Japanese gangs. Sumiyoshi-rengo associates smuggled both guns and hard-core porno films out of Northern Europe in 1980. The gangs have turned to Europe for drugs as well. Methamphetamine has been bought up in West Germany and, with the help of the Triads, shipped to Japan. Germany has also attracted yakuza-owned trading companies specializing in the export of expensive cars to Japan. Cases of slave trading are suspected as well, based upon the yakuza's central role as brokers for the Southeast Asian women so popular among Dutch and German men.

The yakuza have found Europe attractive for at least one other scam: fleecing Japanese corporations. Pushed by the crackdown on sokaiya in Japan, a handful of these professional extortionists have explored Europe as a new hunting ground. Japanese companies, always conscious about their public image, are easy targets for sokaiya clever enough to learn how to operate abroad. Seiji Hamamoto, a notorious practitioner of the trade, opened a "foreign correspondent office" in London in the fall of 1981. Police in Tokyo lost little time in labeling it a front for blackmailing subsidiaries of Japanese companies. Another leading sokaiya group, Ron-dan Doyukai, invested thousands of dollars during the early 1980s in the stock of at least three large European firms: Rotterdamsch Beleggings Consortium, Compagnie Francaise des Petroles, and Compagnie Financiere de Paris et des Pays Bas (PARIBAS). The group followed up its investments in 1984 when, fresh from shaking down the Isetan department store in Japan, it sent eleven of its members on a whirlwind tour of Europe in 1984, taking in the sights of London, Paris, Geneva, and Rome.

Despite their attractions, South America and Europe are somewhat far afield for the yakuza. If they're doing business abroad, most of the gangsters prefer to keep matters confined to the Pacific Rim. This area –

with its Asian drug markets, cheap prostitutes, and fast-growing economies – is the land of yakuza opportunity. With the Japanese tour industry as a base, the gangs can invest, smuggle, and steal while blending into the huge numbers of Japanese travelers and businesses. Such conditions have encouraged the gangs to expand on their operations throughout the region. They have arrived in Australia, where, amid large-scale legitimate Japanese investments, they are suspected of laundering drug money and running ranches, casinos, and construction companies. And they have sought out a number of small Pacific islands to use for a variety of scams.

Those few U.S. officials concerned with the yakuza, though, have had scant time to worry about what might happen in other lands – they've been too busy coping with what's happening on our own soil. For by the early 1970s, the yakuza were already setting up base in the United States, embarking on a sometimes sloppy campaign of crime that would take them first to Honolulu, and then to Los Angeles, San Francisco, New York, and around the country.

Chapter 8
Hawaii:
The Forty-eighth
Prefecture

From 6 A.M. to 10:30 A.M., Al Gano and Bill Sweet study the crowds of Asian visitors as they queue up behind the Customs inspection line at Honolulu's sprawling airport. During these hours, 747s arriving from Taipei, Manila, Osaka, and Tokyo disgorge their passengers into the controlled bedlam of the international arrival area. The passengers are tourists, immigrants, businesspeople, and yakuza.

It is January of 1982. Gano and Sweet are plainclothes Customs Patrol Officers (CPOs), and they watch for smugglers and undesirables, which include the yakuza. In fact, lately the two seasoned Customs men have had their hands full, as a seemingly endless supply of Japanese mobsters head to Honolulu, then to the mainland. For by now it has become painfully clear to Sweet, Gano, and all concerned lawmen that the yakuza have made a dramatic impact on Hawaii, investing over $100 million, according to official estimates, and linking up with the islands' most powerful crime figures.

It is the U.S. Customs Service, a usually underrated branch of American law enforcement, that has put up the first line of defense against incoming yakuza. And it is at Honolulu International Airport that they have developed the crucial, if not always successful, techniques of tracking down the tattooed men.

"There's a couple of ways you can spot a yakuza," Al Gano says. He's a trim, alert man with a thin mustache, sharp eyes, and a New Jersey accent. "For one thing, your average Japanese tourist . . . well, walks humbly. Yakuza, they strut. Another easy sign is when they arrive in a group. The boss – the oyabun – is usually surrounded by his boys – the kobun – and they're carrying his bags, lighting his cigarette, and saying, '*hai! hai!* (yes, yes)."

Bill Sweet offers an observation: "Of course, you might get lucky and spot a missing pinkie."

Missing pinkies, though, are awfully hard to spot at 10 or 20 yards. Dress styles are a better clue. On the departure deck, Gano points out a knot of yakuza waiting for a JAL flight home. There was no legal reason for Customs to detain the gangsters, but neither could the yakuza stop anyone from looking them over carefully.

"They used to all wear crewcuts," Gano says. "But now a lot of them wear punch perms. Of course, so do a lot of people who aren't yakuza."

This was a low-class bunch. A few were sporting punch perms – short, frizzy hair – but the overriding similarities were tough, expressionless faces and a lot of tasteless polyester clothing. If they had been Americans, they could have been a couple of small-town nightclub owners with their hired help.

Back on the line, an inspector moves across the vast waiting area and murmurs to the CPOs, "We've got a hit."

Another CPO escorts a stocky, smiling Japanese male into one of the back rooms. His wife, looking worried, is asked to wait outside. There's nothing sinister about the room – a lot of desks, charts, and file cabinets. The suspect is led into the Yakuza Documentation Center (YDC, or less formally, Yak Doc). The YDC is by far the best single source of information on the yakuza in the United States, a testament to years of hard work by Honolulu Customs and to general apathy elsewhere. Sweet and Gano are two of a mere handful of U.S. lawmen with any degree of sophistication in understanding the nature of Japanese organized crime.

Sweet begins interrogating the man in fluent Japanese. Except for his punch perm and black slacks, though, the man doesn't look very criminal, and he is far from sullen. He cheerfully answers questions and unhesitatingly allows a reporter to be present. "That doesn't mean anything," says Gano. "Even the oyabun are ridiculously polite."

Customs keeps a "J/OCR Debriefing Outline" (Japanese Organized CRime) for use with yakuza suspects. In addition to such expected data as name, address, occupation, and purpose of trip, there are more specialized blanks to be filled in:

> How subject recognized as possible yakuza: profile, informant, associates.
> Identifying characteristics: fingers, toes, tattoos, hairstyle, scars.
> Excessive jewelry that could be converted to cash.

Also included on the form is a list of crimes in Japanese, with English translations, for the criminal record. These include *kyohaku* (extortion), *tobaku* (gambling), *satsujin* (homicide), and *baishun torimochi* (pimping).

Sweet doesn't get very far in filling out the form when he realizes that this is a mistake. The man owns a small construction firm in Hokkaido – a fact occasionally consonant with yakuza ties or even membership – but the subject is not their man. He just happens to have the same name as a known yakuza. It is a common error.

Despite the problems, the unassuming, raspy-voiced Sweet has managed to build data on the yakuza from virtually nothing into a sophisticated criminal intelligence system. The fourteen-year veteran of the Customs Service spends many twelve-hour days expanding YDC files and fielding requests from curious lawmen in Hawaii and on the mainland. He is, at any given time, the only bilingual law enforcement official in the United States assigned to the yakuza.

Sweet first encountered the Japanese mob as an undercover agent with the Army's Criminal Investigation Division during the occupation. Since then, he has spent some twelve years on and off working in Japan and building up connections with police there. Aided by his Japanese wife, he translates volumes of reports and articles on the yakuza, paying special attention to a favorite source of intelligence, *Shukan Jitsuwa,* which translates as "Weekly Truth," but which might better be dubbed "Gangster Times" for its constant flow of bloody yakuza stories. The magazine was of particular help to Sweet when it published an article on the hundred biggest up-and-coming oyabun.

Sweet and others at YDC face more problems than the lack of funding, manpower, and recognition common to offices far from Washington. The most immediate problems stem from bureaucratic and linguistic roadblocks, which often stymie the YDC's efforts at basic identification of visiting mobsters.

In its present form, though, the YDC goes a long way toward solving the problem: cross-indexed in three cabinets – the "brain" of the YDC – are 7000 names and records of the 100,000 or so known yakuza in Japan and abroad. That Sweet and Gano have compiled data on even 7 percent of known yakuza is remarkable, for Japanese officials have proved to be highly reluctant to turn over their own intelligence on the subject. As a result of the poor flow of information between the two countries, U.S. officials must proceed on a case-by-case basis with their Japanese counterparts, a frustrating process that leads to frequent misunderstandings, both legal and linguistic.

Nowhere are the problems more serious than in the most fundamental area of all – names. The man from Hokkaido was just one of an almost constant stream of incorrectly identified suspects. The problem is built into the language. It's not unusual even for well-educated native speakers of Japanese to fail to properly read a given name from the written characters, or to correctly "spell" a name after hearing it. The *kanji,* Chinese-based ideograms that form the basis of written Japanese, are not phonetic; they can typically be read several different ways. Korean names in Japanese can be even more difficult to interpret properly. (According to Bill Sweet, there are thirty-five different kanji just for the Korean name Lee.) Ethnic Koreans, who make up a sizable portion of incoming yakuza, usually use a Korean name, such as Lee, Kim, or Park, plus an adopted Japanese name. To make matters worse, the YDC must also contend with Chinese gangsters passing through Honolulu, who may have the same written name, but often with very different pronunciations from either Japanese or Korean.

If Sweet is attempting to obtain the records of a suspected yakuza, he faces a complex problem. To ensure accuracy, he must first translate the American approximation of the name, in Roman letters, into kanji. For this he employs an array of Asian dictionaries, including an overweight index of 36,000 Japanese names and a Korean-Japanese guidebook. For verification he turns to a near-antique set of U.S. Army codebooks used for changing the kanji into telegraphic signals.

Thus translated, the name and request for information are sent by phone or wire to Tokyo – but not directly to Japanese authorities. Due to diplomatic considerations, the request must go first to the Customs attaché at the U.S. Embassy in Tokyo, who then hand-delivers it to bureaucrats at the National Police Agency. If all goes well, Sweet receives a return answer within thirty-six hours, but many requests take considerably longer. Information compiled by Sweet will also go into the Treasury Enforcement Communication System (TECS) computer, which is in turn linked to the FBI's massive National Crime Information Center database.

Often, the YDC is overwhelmed by incoming yakuza. For example, Customs each year contends with "Holy Week," a Japanese holiday period that coincides with Christmas and New Year's. Thousands of Japanese tourists – and hundreds of yakuza – stream into Honolulu during that period.

"Most of the yakuza arriving here are just tourists," explained Al Gano. "They need vacations like anyone else, I suppose. They come and spend money, lie on the beach flashing their tattoos, and go home. Except that some of them don't go home. They check out the action and stay."

In early 1982, American policy toward the yakuza was still relatively laissez-faire. Minor visa and currency violations did not usually keep yakuza out of the United States. For the most part, these were tourists; since that time, those who stayed and ran rackets have increasingly come under official scrutiny. For the people of Hawaii, though, the yakuza was simply one more gang to contend with, and not necessarily the worst.

Gangsters in Paradise

Like their fellow Japanese, the yakuza have found Hawaii a very congenial spot. Prior to World War II, the Japanese came to Hawaii for vacations, and following the war, as soon as prosperity settled upon Japan, waves of tourists returned, this time in much larger numbers. In 1984, 814,000 Japanese went to the islands, spending a hefty $1 billion. So popular is Hawaii as a destination for Japanese that some people in that country have taken to calling it the forty-eighth prefecture, as an American might dub Canada the fifty-first state. And, like tourists everywhere, many Japanese leave not only their cares at home, but also their inhibitions. Although Hawaii has never equaled the fleshpots of Southeast Asia, it has similar attractions for Japanese men.

Police estimate there are at least 500 prostitutes working in Honolulu at any one time, with much of the action well in the open. Massage parlors advertise in the newspapers. "Beach boys" pass out cards with telephone numbers advising of the location of American women. Apartments, hotels, and condominiums serve as floating whorehouses. And given that prostitution is part of the tourism industry, law enforcement isn't generally too severe on violators of the law. Some judges won't touch a prostitution case unless drugs are involved as well.

For those tourists who want drugs, though, there is a ready supply. Hawaiian marijuana – Maui Wowie, Puna Purple, Kona Gold – is renowned throughout the United States for its potency. The production of marijuana is a massive cottage industry, generating more than $600 million a year and supporting a host of well-financed, well-armed criminal gangs. Other drugs, including the amphetamines so prized in Japan, are as available here as they are in most mainland cities.

If Hawaii is not the most crime-ridden state in the country, it's certainly in contention. The state's major industry, tourism, provides both cash and victims for criminal organizations. It also provides the troops, underpaid locals working legitimate jobs in the tourist industry.

Apart from their colorful pidgin slang, the local soldiers of organized crime tend to be pretty ordinary, elementary thugs. According to a 1978 report of the Hawaii Commission on Organized Crime, Hawaiian criminals have a lot to learn:

> . . . the visible street-level criminal organizations in Hawaii are crude. The core of the group may consist of no more than three to twelve individuals who self-consciously feel themselves as part of an ongoing conspiracy. Compared to mainland models, there is a notable lack of sophistication and complexity in their structures.
> . . . The different groups base their operations on geographic areas, like Maui, or on enterprises like prostitution or gambling. The gangs also cluster themselves in rough groupings based on ethnic ties or extortionate relationships.

The largest of the Hawaiian gangs comprise, appropriately enough, native Hawaiians. Although they represent only 12 percent of the population, Hawaiians and part-Hawaiians are very well represented in organized crime. Like Native Americans on the mainland, they also tend to be among the poorest residents of their own state. But there are many other groups in the picture as well. In a celebrated 1984 trial, mob boss Henry Huihui was portrayed as overseer of a vast and varied collection of gangs whose members included Asians, Polynesians, and Caucasians. The Hawaiians tend to ally themselves with Samoans, who have proved to be as tough as they are big. Koreans, Filipinos, Chinese, Japanese, haoles (whites), and blacks provide the rest of Hawaii's criminal membership. Despite this apparent glut of gangs, the yakuza have had little difficulty joining the ranks of Hawaiian mobsters. Evidence isn't hard to find.

Just take a stroll any warm evening on Kalakaua Avenue in Waikiki. Along with the Pizza Huts, Woolco, seven-story Japanese shopping plazas, and other mundane emporia, you'll see as fine a collection of massage parlors, bottomless clubs, porno movie houses, and adult bookstores as exists between San Francisco's Tenderloin district and Subic Bay in the Philippines. The signs on these shops tend to be bilingual, often with Japanese in larger characters. Red Japanese script reads "Poruno," and the massage parlors are labeled "turuko," or Turkish bath. A number of turuko have mama-san sitting lazily on beach chairs on the sidewalk in front of the store, waiting to explain the setup and prices to interested men.

Nearly all have some relationship to the yakuza. A sweeping investigation of massage parlors conducted by the Honolulu Police Department in January of 1981 revealed that half of the fourteen parlors raided had Japanese-surnamed operators, and of those seven, two were definitely linked to the yakuza. One, a diminutive porn shop operator named Tsuyoshi

"Bambi" Bamba, was tied to the Inagawa-kai and was subsequently deported. Another was linked to a major yakuza operator, and owned a sushi bar and a gun shop as well as a porno shop with a live sex show. The remaining non-yakuza sex merchants are usually forced to buy protection from yakuza and yakuza associates. But the yakuza today have ventured far beyond pimping and dealing drugs. They are into gunrunning, gambling, and perhaps most important, money laundering.

The yakuza are faced with the problem that plagues all highly successful criminals – what to do with all that money. The huge profits that the yakuza wring out of the shabu (amphetamine) trade pose to them the same problem that cocaine profits do to Colombians and Americans. One solution that occurred to the yakuza was simple: invest it in Hawaii. Japanese police and tax officials would make life uncomfortable for known yakuza investing billions of yen in Japan, but no such problem faces yakuza and their front men in Hawaii. There are plenty of Hawaiians who will sell to Japanese with cash, no questions asked. How much yakuza money is invested in the Pearl of the Pacific? One Honolulu official responded to a guess of $100 million by scoffing at the figure. "It's many times that," he said cheerfully.

For the yakuza, as for other crime syndicates, the investment doesn't necessarily have to turn a profit to be successful. "If the yakuza get $1 back for every $2 invested," said former Honolulu detective Bernie Ching, "they're happy." The reason, of course, is that now the $1 is clean, and can be used or returned to Japan. The money is simply declared as a profit or sale of a legitimate business, or just moved to Japan by wire transfer with no explanation. Japanese bankers, as a rule, are not particularly curious as to the source of funds.

But the yakuza did not arrive as high-level money launderers, or even as criminals – at first. The yakuza first entered Hawaii sometime in the 1960s, arriving as restaurateurs, cooks, dishwashers. They often took any kind of menial job that would enable them to look around unobtrusively. Later, in the early 1970s, yakuza began meeting people from the local crime syndicates and worked out alliances, or at least nonaggression pacts. The first yakuza did not seem to pose a threat to Hawaiian criminals. They were, in fact, a generally graceless and inept lot, certainly not the finest of Japan's 250-year gangland tradition. But they did, if nothing else, pave the way for others.

The First Wave
By 1973, the police were keeping a handful of yakuza under surveillance, and were beginning to conclude that their presence was no fleeting phe-

nomenon. If they needed further proof, it came in the form of Wataru "Jackson" Inada, an all-around criminal who rather flamboyantly, and not too effectively, set up headquarters in Honolulu and proceeded to run a series of scams that ultimately led to his premature death in 1976.

Inada was a member of the Tokyo-based Takahashi-gumi, a Sumiyoshi affiliate, who wandered into Hawaii in 1972. Shortly after his arrival, he teamed up with a local gangster of Korean descent named John Chang Ho Lee, and together they went into a variety of legal and illegal businesses, backed by Inada's yakuza funds. Lee hadn't been a notably careful criminal, and since 1961, when he had been caught removing a safe from a Honolulu theater, he had been arrested and sentenced to prison a number of times. But Inada found Lee a kindred soul and a man with valuable connections, for Lee knew just about everyone in the Honolulu underworld.

Together the two hoods formed Mitsui Tours, which catered exclusively to Japanese visitors, and which probably originated the now common feature of furnishing tourists with trips to gun ranges. There, Japanese could indulge in the forbidden pleasure of shooting handguns. The idea was a worthwhile one, but something of Lee's poor luck infected the enterprise. In July 1974, at the Koko Head range, one of the gun-happy shooters attempted to clear his jammed .45 automatic with the muzzle pointed toward himself, and put a bullet through his heart. Koko Head then denied Inada and Lee further use of the facilities, but Inada had already seen the need to diversify their operations and was not caught without employment.

Over the next two years, Inada would begin a prostitution racket, a gambling casino, and a shakedown of local porno shops. Back in 1973, though, Inada had seen that there was really big money to be made in the heroin business. With his cash reserves, his Asian connections, and Lee's distribution network, he could make a fortune. Unfortunately for both Inada and Lee, it didn't work out that way.

Inada had no trouble finding the heroin in East Asia, but it was in the United States that his lack of experience was evident. Inada and Lee had enlisted the help of reputed Los Angeles Mafia boss Peter John Milano, who, for $100,000, would help run a kilo of heroin through L.A. and on to a buyer in the Midwest. It was to be the beginning of a regular operation. But by late 1973, Lee was arrested for selling heroin to an undercover agent and, in return for a reduced sentence, agreed to testify against his former partners in future trials. As a result of the Lee case, Milano and six other mainlanders were arrested and tried.

Inada never took the hint that perhaps the heroin business was not for him. In July of 1975, he was arrested for the sale of $165,000 worth of the drug to yet a different undercover agent. The next year, Inada was preparing to go to court, aware that Lee would be testifying against him. It promised to be a dramatic, highly publicized trial. However, Lee, for his part, had no intention of testifying publicly and being branded a snitch for the rest of his criminal career.

Five days before the scheduled beginning of the trial, Inada, forty-three, and his Korean girlfriend, Ju Nam Song, twenty-six, were found murdered. They were shot in the head and arranged to look like a double suicide. Inada had been trouble for a lot of people on both sides of the law, and it is doubtful that he was missed. The case is officially unsolved, although police have long suspected it was Lee who arranged the hit. Because Lee never testified in court, the government was not bound to its pledge, and Lee earned himself fifteen years in prison and a ten-year parole.

If Jackson Inada was a bungler, he was also a pioneer. In barely over three years, he had put together virtually every tourist scam that the yakuza would later use, and some that went beyond the tourist game. Like many pioneers, though, Inada will be best remembered for his efforts rather than for the results.

The one operation that Inada apparently chose to ignore, or simply didn't get around to, was gun smuggling. It was left to another Takahashi-gumi thug, a small ex-boxer named Takatsugu Yonekura, to begin regular gun smuggling. Yonekura was not a typical yakuza. He had attended college and had been on the Japanese Olympic boxing team. In Japan, he met and married an American woman; they emigrated to the United States, where he obtained legal residency and a green card from Immigration.

It was in 1975 or so that Yonekura went into the gun business, but he didn't last very long. In May of 1976, U.S. Customs arrested Yonekura in Hawaii with a cache of fifty Raven .25-caliber automatics and 900 rounds of ammunition. In December of that year, Yonekura was convicted and sentenced to a term in Halawa Correctional Facility in Hawaii. (At his sentencing hearing, Yonekura's attorney insisted that the tattoos covering his client's body were merely the result of a "deep depression," and had no connection with the yakuza.)

While on parole, Yonekura displayed the same brazen lack of judgment that his friend Inada had shown. According to a federal undercover officer, the yakuza began operating a profitable mah-jongg game for Japanese tourists. In addition, he began a technically legal but highly suspect partnership with boxing promoter Kuwashi Shimizu and former chef Yoji Kawakami. The Takara Sogyo Company, ostensibly an investment firm, was partly devoted to the export of bulletproof vests to Japan, where guns are illegal. The customers for the vests were likely the same people who failed to receive their Raven .25s when Yonekura was arrested. In addition to this quixotic scheme, Yonekura joined with Inada's old partner John Chang Ho Lee in shaking down Waikiki businesses.

As if that weren't perilous enough, Yonekura flagrantly violated his parole by visiting Japan without notifying American authorities. He returned with more than $10,000 in cash, but missing the top knuckle of his right pinkie. Yonekura evidently apologized in the time-tested way for his bungling in America, and was rewarded with a new allowance from his Takahashi boss.

On his return to Hawaii, Yonekura fell into still more trouble. Not only was his parole revoked, but he was charged with importing $10,000 and not declaring it, a currency violation. At his trial, the U.S. attorney decided to make an example of Yonekura for other yakuza eager to try their luck in America. The hapless kobun was given five years in federal prison and fined $10,000, the amount found on him at the airport. Federal prosecutors argued that Yonekura's fine was justified as "a 'tax' on those who willfully engage in criminal activity as representatives of an organized crime group." The judge agreed.

Yakuza are known for stoically doing their time in prison, but this was America, and Yonekura apparently didn't feel bound by giri-ninjo here. In 1981, he left his confining accommodations at the federal prison at Lompoc, California, and expertly disappeared. For all his ineptitude as a thug, Yonekura showed great ingenuity as an escapee, and U.S. marshals searched Los Angeles in vain for him. Six months later, he showed up in Mexico City, where he complained bitterly to a Japanese reporter before disappearing again. Five years, said Yonekura, was a wholly unjust sentence for currency violations, as was undoubtedly true. The sentence also failed to deter any incoming yakuza.

By the late 1970s, the yakuza tried with varying results to gain a foothold in the American heroin market – the world's largest. Their own ineptness at first served to alert both local and federal officials. But more than any single event, it was the Case of the Three Mules that tipped off American lawmen that the yakuza were serious about heroin.

On May 9, 1979, Customs Line Inspector Yenlyn Shadowens was checking out an incoming Japanese air passenger at Honolulu International Airport. She looked over Satoshi Meguro and asked him for his passport. It showed, according to Customs, extensive travel to and from Bangkok, Honolulu, and Guam, pivoting around Tokyo. Meguro had been in Bangkok only a week before his arrival in Honolulu. Shadowens summoned a Customs inspector and voiced her suspicions.

Meguro was hustled into the interrogation area and, through an interpreter, told Customs that he worked at a bar in Japan. He had with him only a small valise and a duty-free bag containing a bottle of Rémy Martin and a carton of Dunhill cigarettes. When inspectors opened the Dunhill carton, they found packets of white powder. Two other companions of Meguro's, Tamotsu Omori and Yasuhiro Ono, were located in different parts of the air terminal – after they had passed inspection. A second search yielded duty-free bags containing Dunhills and a white powder.

The powder turned out to be #4 heroin – a high-quality Southeast Asian brand – a pound to each carton. The DEA was called in and found a fourth man, Kiyoshi Yoshioka, in a Waikiki hotel. This man was believed to be the team leader, but no evidence could be turned up to hold him.

Tokyo Metropolitan Police revealed that Yoshioka was a member of another Sumiyoshi affiliate, the Seishi-kai. The Japanese police searched the residences of the three drug runners, or "mules." Among the seized papers were detailed schematic drawings of customs facilities at Bangkok, Hong Kong, and Tokyo airports, and instructions on how to most easily clear those facilities.

But most fascinating among the seized papers was a meticulous set of instructions on required behavior for mules. Naturally, unquestioning obedience was demanded, but in return the compensation and expenses were precisely laid out. Said the code of practice:

You should obey whatever you are told to do by your group leader. You have no choice, you cannot refuse or complain of the leader's instructions. The above instructions are given at the request of the financier in order to protect ourselves and to accomplish our work. Therefore, if you want to work and get paid for it, you should follow instructions.

[The pay schedule is] five thousand dollars for the trip plus $500 more or less for your pocket money. Your group leader will determine the amount. You must pay for your souvenirs yourself.

*Your leader will pay for your hotel and three meals. He will also
pay for your drinks, up to $75.*

Although the flat payment was the same whether the couriers had to
go to America or Southeast Asia, trips to the United States placed a
curious restriction on the mules. Said the instructions, "Your group leader
will pay for your tickets, hotel and meals. You will have to pay for your
other expenses, like drinks or snacks."

And, concluded the missive, "If you have any objections, it means
you will be out. You are again advised that you will not get a penny if you
fail to obey instructions given by the financier or the middlemen." Many
U.S. or South American drug dealers must have often wished for that kind
of deference on the part of the runners.

On August 28, 1979, the trio of hapless mules were sentenced to
terms ranging from ten to twelve years in federal prison for their part in
the heroin scheme. Their fellow gang members and associates back home,
who had undoubtedly cashed in on the previous trips, weren't touched.
Whatever the final outcome for the runners, it is clear that Americans have
not seen the last of yakuza heroin smugglers. Police have since monitored
a host of Japanese drug couriers working their wares through such ports
of entry as Los Angeles, San Francisco, and Vancouver. If officials
needed any further proof, it came in the 1985 seizure of 12 pounds of
heroin and 52 pounds of methamphetamine in Honolulu and Hong Kong.
Police in the two cities arrested seven Japanese and three Chinese in
connection with the case – including two of the highest-ranking bosses of
the Yamaguchi-gumi, as well as associates of the notorious Hong Kong
14K Triad.

The Big-Time and the Mongoose

To some influential Hawaiians, a yakuza contact brings with it a certain
cachet. For one thing, there is the tangible benefit of links to muscle and
money as well as yakuza connections in Japan that can often result in
lucrative contracts – legal and illegal. For another, hanging out with the
yakuza is in some ways exotic, and Japanese mobsters are known for
lavish entertaining. For the Japanese, the benefits of knowing powerful
Hawaiians are obvious: access to business connections, legitimizing their
presence, and more ways to make money.

Among the Hawaiians who sought out the yakuza was Charles Higa,
one of the wealthiest men in the islands. Actually, Higa had been extremely wealthy until, by his own doing, he dissipated a multimillion-
dollar shipping fortune built up by his father and grandfather. Higa

Enterprises was into trucking and storage, with branches on the mainland, and government contracts in Japan.

Charlie Higa began to keep poor company – among them Samoan thugs and Japanese gangsters. When his trucking enterprise began to show obvious signs of decline, Higa tried the same hustle that Inada, Yonekura, and a host of anonymous hoods have tried – shaking down marginal businesses to get some extra cash. On September 22, 1983, Higa and two others were arrested and charged with extortion and conspiracy, specifically for attempting to pry $300 a month from the manager of the Tsukoba Book and Video Store in Waikiki, a porno operation.

In the court proceedings following his indictment, Higa admitted to links with organized crime. According to reporter Jim Dooley, writing in the *Honolulu Advertiser,* Higa was quite candid about those ties:

> *[Higa] said he first met the yakuza in Japan in the late 1950s. He said his family trucking business in Japan depended on a labor force controlled by the yakuza and he complied with local custom by making a gift – money or sake – to yakuza representatives. Since that time, he said, he has met with other yakuza leaders. He acknowledged a personal acquaintance with the top three leaders of the Sumiyoshi-rengo, a large Tokyo-based yakuza group which has been active in Hawaii in recent years. And he said he had met twice in Hawaii with Kazuo Taoka, the now-deceased boss of Yamaguchi, the single largest yakuza organization. Higa also said he was acquainted with Kaoru Ogawa, identified by Tokyo police as Japan's "most influential racketeer."*

Higa received a five-year sentence for extortion, and what favors he did for the various yakuza oyabun were never made public in his trial. At the time Higa admitted to knowing Kaoru Ogawa, the Japanese racketeer had already left the islands, apparently for good. But in 1978, Ogawa actually moved his family from Japan to Hawaii, indulging in a variety of investments and generally avoiding the glare of unfavorable publicity in Japan.

Ogawa was, in fact, Japan's most famous sokaiya at that time, and the National Police Agency estimated that he and his cohorts had shaken down over 100 Japanese businesses in a two-year stretch. In 1982, Ogawa was subpoenaed to Hawaii to testify in a rather acrimonious and complex court battle over control of stock in the City Bank of Honolulu. Ogawa himself was charged with secretly attempting to gain control of the bank. In the short time he was in Honolulu for the trial, Ogawa was accused of intimidating employees of the bank in an apparent attempt to squelch their testimony. Whether any of Ogawa's real estate investments remain is uncertain, but Ogawa was certainly close to a number of well-heeled Hawaiians, including Higa.

Ogawa was not, in fact, a full-fledged member of the yakuza, but one other visitor to the island can claim no such exemption. Hisayuki Machii, the "retired" boss of Towa Yuai Jigyo Kumiai, is occasionally seen in Hawaii. On one trip, in 1982, he claimed that he had simply come for the purpose of having oral surgery, but just managed to find the time to visit alleged Towa associate Ken Mizuno, investor and Las Vegas restaurateur. Police think that Machii has kept company in Hawaii with far more disreputable characters than Mizuno, and believe that Machii has invested some of his millions in the islands.

Perhaps the major figure of interest in Hawaii has been famed kuro-maku Kenji Osano. Osano is often spoken of in the same breath as Kodama and Sasakawa, but excepting his major role in the Lockheed scandal, he has maintained a cleaner public image. Still, many associate Osano with the dark world of politics and business in Japan.

By 1973, Osano's wealth was estimated at over $1 billion, and he used that money to become the largest individual Japanese investor in the United States. His investment company, Kokusai Kogyo Co., Ltd., established a Honolulu branch back in 1961, but it wasn't until 1976 that Osano began buying property as if he were playing Monopoly. When he finished his mainland and Hawaiian buying spree, he owned a lot of hotel rooms – 6000 in all. Five Waikiki hotels fell to Osano: the Sheraton Waikiki, Royal Hawaiian, Surfrider, Moana, Princess Kaiulani, plus the Sheraton Maui on that island.

Although known as a real estate investor, Osano revealed another side to his operations. Honolulu police have kept a regular watch over the prosperous kuromaku from the time of his early purchases. One of the things they noticed was the identity of his companion, Susumu Ishii, the number-two man in the Inagawa-kai. On other trips to Hawaii, according to press accounts, Osano was again seen in the company of top officers of the same syndicate. Osano's company had sponsored a number of gambling junkets for high rollers, including, allegedly, top yakuza. A Honolulu detective further claimed that Osano's hotels serve as landing spots for yakuza, although he didn't say that Osano personally intervened for the gangs. "They'll get a job there, work for a while, and then go into their own hustles."

*　　*　　*

By the mid-1980s, it was clear that the yakuza had firmly established themselves in the islands. According to some police sources, the Japanese gangs have become the second most powerful criminal syndicate in the state, right behind the native Hawaiians. There is no doubt that the yakuza are thoroughly insinuated into the billion-dollar Japanese tourist trade, and that they are using the island for smuggling guns, pornography, and increasing amounts of drugs.

It is also likely, given the dollar value of yakuza-related enterprises, that Hawaii is becoming dependent on yakuza investment. How dependent is difficult to say. One hundred million dollars is an impressive sum, but Honolulu is not yet in Miami's league. At the present time, however, volumes of yakuza cash ensure that the Japanese gangs, or at least their oyabun, will be sought after by some Hawaiians. The money is now part of the economic structure of the islands. As Honolulu policeman Bernie Ching said glumly, "The yakuza are here to stay."

Hawaiians may find that the yakuza are similar to another visitor from Asia, the mongoose. Years ago, Hawaiian sugar growers brought the mongoose to the island from Asia to rid the canefields of a previous import, the rat. The weasel-like mongoose, however, failed to make a dent in the rat population, but did take a liking to Hawaiian chickens and other livestock. Today it has become an ineradicable pest. The yakuza, welcomed by some for the money they bring in, may prove to be as larcenous and parasitic in the long run as the mongoose, and just as hard to dislodge.

Chapter 9
North America: Foothold on the Mainland

In 1975, an unusual gangster film starring Robert Mitchum and Japanese actor Ken Takakura opened in the United States to generally indifferent audiences. The unconvincing plot, the strange and highly stylized Japanese acting, and the exotic setting didn't send Americans flocking to the box office. But viewers were probably amused by the outlandish and anachronistic swordplay, and found the finger-cutting sequences both compelling and gruesome. In any case, the movie, entitled simply *The Yakuza*, enjoyed a short run to nearly empty houses. It deserved better. It still plays occasionally on late-night television, but in 1975 Americans neither knew nor cared about the subject matter – Japanese organized crime.

By the early 1980s, that began to change. Americans other than Hawaiians slowly became aware of the yakuza through the news media, and indirectly because of the new posture of U.S. law enforcement. Press reports of official statements about the yakuza conveyed a note of panic, with headlines like "Japanese Organized Criminals Invading West," and "FBI Chief Warns of Japanese Crime Ring."

A number of top Washington law enforcement officials, including Attorney General William French Smith and FBI chief William Webster, warned on several occasions that the yakuza presented a threat to the nation that warranted swift action. Partly as a response to this clamor, members of the Reagan administration decided to include the yakuza in the agenda of the President's Commission on Organized Crime, formally created in July 1983. Some previous legislative panels, like the Kefauver and McLellan Senate committees, had a discernible impact on organized crime by putting pressure on law enforcement and increasing citizen awareness. But the Reagan commission was the first to acknowledge the fact that organized crime is changing, and that it is no longer the exclusive domain of the Mafia, if ever it was.

California authorities recognized this change rather early, owing perhaps to the weak position of traditional Italian syndicates in that state. In the 1980s, state authorities paid less attention to the Italian groups and more to the "nontraditional" gangs, which include everyone else. In its 1981 report to the legislature, the California Bureau of Organized Crime and Criminal Intelligence (BOCCI) devoted as much space to Israeli, Vietnamese, and Japanese groups as to the Mafia. Three years later, it was clear that this broader version of organized crime was firmly entrenched on the national level, and that it included the yakuza.

In its initial public hearing, held in November 1983, the President's commission devoted its agenda to the direction and scope of American organized crime, and Smith, Webster, and Drug Enforcement Administration chief Francis Mullen urged new strategies for dealing with its changing structure.

The second public hearing, in New York in March 1984, focused on money laundering, a requisite task of all organized crime groups in and out of the United States, including the yakuza. Cash, according to commission director James Harmon, is "the life-support system without which organized crime cannot exist." The commission discovered that the money to be laundered for the $80 billion annual U.S. drug trade, for example, comes from all points of the compass – East Asia as well as Latin America – and many U.S. bankers have been only too willing to oblige organized crime.

Finally, in its third hearing, held on October 25, 1984, the commission gathered in New York to address the issue of Asian organized crime, and the yakuza was to occupy one-third of the agenda. Certainly, the attention was justified. Verifiable police reports placed yakuza from Roanoke, Virginia, to Arizona to Seattle. The yakuza were highly involved in the Japanese tourist industry, were smuggling guns and pornography out of the country, allying themselves with American gangsters and gamblers, and laundering funds. They were, in short, getting well entrenched in America, and it was time to place them under closer scrutiny.

The first witness called before the President's commission appeared shrouded in a black robe and hood, looking somewhat like a *ninja*. He was led across the floor of the high-ceilinged, columned hall to a seat behind a screen that shielded him from the press and audience. Chief Counsel Harmon then revealed to the commission and audience that the man was an oyabun, or leader, in a major Japanese organized crime gang.

The twelve commission members present listened carefully as the witness described tattooing and yubitsume, or ritual finger-cutting, and provided a graphic recounting of how that painful act is accomplished.

"The actual procedure is to take . . . what they in Japanese yakuza call a little silver knife – on a table – and you pull it towards you and bend over and your body weight will snap your finger off. . . . The finger that is severed is put in a small bottle with alcohol and your name is written on it and it is sent to whoever you're repenting to as a sign that you are sorry."

The nameless oyabun also elaborated on the organizational charts of the Yamaguchi-gumi and Sumiyoshi-rengo that the commission had provided, and explained how the yakuza are active in his own specialty, economic crime. Gangsters in Japan, he told the panel, try to find companies in financial trouble, and engage in a number of schemes to take them over. Through bogus notes and threats to company officials and creditors, they would assume control of the ailing business, sell off the assets, and profit from the failure.

This yakuza had personally run high-stakes card games two or three times a month in Japan. Because of his status, he retained 40 percent of the profits, which amounted to from $40,000 to $60,000. After expenses, he realized about $16,000 per game. Money, though, had to be passed up to the very highest echelons; yakuza leaders maintained control through money, and lower members rose by passing it on. Nonetheless, said the witness, "I would say that I lived a very good life, probably equivalent to the presidency of a company employing three hundred to five hundred people."

Later in the day, another hooded witness made an appearance. Also a Japanese national, this anonymous informant had been a U.S. resident for ten years, and he described yakuza activity in New York. Card games, with stakes in the many thousands of dollars, were being run by a combination of yakuza, yakuza associates, and Italian-American hoodlums. The customers were both Japanese nationals and Japanese-Americans. He believed that the Italians, who wore guns and sold stolen goods at the games, were actually in charge of the action.

Less dramatic than the hooded witnesses, perhaps, but equally revealing was the testimony of three American policemen, all knowledgeable in the workings of the yakuza in the United States: Inspector John McKenna of the San Francisco Police Department; Detective George Min of the Los Angeles Police Department; and Bernard Ching of the Honolulu Police Department. The three intelligence cops described in brief how the yakuza were gaining crucial footholds in their respective communities.

Bernard Ching described the Hawaiian yakuza scene in much the same terms he had used to reporters nearly three years earlier: gun smuggling, prostitution, pornography, extortion, and drugs. What was new to some observers, however, was the admission that yakuza activity was not confined to the islands. Detective Min of Los Angeles presented an impressive list of yakuza activities in the large Japanese communities of southern California. "I have seen many crimes instituted by the yakuza," he told the panel. "We have cases of homicide, prison escape, gun smuggling, money laundering. . . ." Inspector McKenna, for his part, added that the SFPD had identified members of the Sumiyoshi-rengo in the San Francisco area. He believed that a pattern of intimidation and extortion existed within the Japanese business community.

None of the testimony by police, and little by the witnesses – except the finger-cutting and other exotic Japanese customs – was particularly startling crime news. Activities from money laundering to murder are, of course, the basic stuff of organized crime. No, the news was that it was Japanese, and it was occurring both in Japan and in the United States, and it contradicted popularly held beliefs. The public, to the extent that they thought about it at all, believed that the Japanese had virtually no crime problem, and that Japanese-Americans were the most law-abiding of citizens. Now, the issue of yakuza coming to America would stir up some ugly ghosts from the past.

Ron Wakabayashi, the national director of the Japanese-American Citizens League, told the *New York Times* that yakuza-hunting could "fan anti-Asian sentiment," and given the American predilection for periodic attacks on Asians, it was a well-founded warning. Because of economic competition from Japan, many Americans have begun to blame Asians – any Asians – for their problems. In 1982, for instance, two disgruntled and intoxicated auto workers in the Detroit area attacked a bachelor party of Chinese-Americans, killing the prospective bridegroom. The assailants' defense was that they thought the victims were Japanese, and the court handed down extremely lenient sentences.

At the same time, Americans are openly fascinated with things Asian in general and things Japanese in particular. This motive, as much as that of racism, could also result in misapprehending the nature of Japanese organized crime. Americans will probably be very disappointed to discover that Japan has no magic solution for the problem of crime in its own country, much less one that translates to the problems of the United States.

Given the love/hate attitude the Americans have toward the Japanese, it isn't surprising that the yakuza are either under- or overestimated. What is somewhat surprising, though, is the total lack of historical perspective that law enforcement, the press, and the public have brought to the whole issue of Japanese organized crime in America. When the attorney general, for instance, raised the specter of large-scale Japanese drug dealing in the U.S., he was missing something. Not only *might* the Japanese be able to deal heroin here, they already have.

The Cotton Connection

Early in the 1930s, some Japanese in America were drawn to the narcotics trade for the simple reason that the Japanese Empire, in its conquest of East Asia, had acquired much of the opium, morphine, and heroin business there. Connections between the drug distributors in Asia and America were logical and fairly easily made.

Harry J. Anslinger, the crusading chief of the U.S. Bureau of Narcotics for much of its existence, commented that in the prewar years, "We should not be far short of the mark if we said that ninety percent of all the illicit 'white drugs' of the world are of Japanese origin, manufactured in the Japanese Concession of Tientsin, around Tientsin, in and around Dairen, or in other cities of Manchuria, Jehol, and occupied China, and this always . . . under Japanese supervision." Unfortunately, a good deal of prewar propaganda colored evaluations of Japanese criminal activity, but even if Anslinger exaggerated by two or three times the percentage of Japanese-manufactured narcotics, that still left a lot of white drugs. And some of them found their way into the United States.

The Bureau of Narcotics began to notice Japanese morphine, called "cotton morphine" because of its appearance, as early as 1932, just one year after the Japanese takeover of Manchuria. The following year, the grave concern voiced by the bureau began to show signs of justification, although the quantities seized were still rather small. Japanese were arrested with cotton morphine in Tacoma, Washington; Portland, Oregon; and Hawaii. All the arrests involved Japanese residents of America. In Portland, four tins seized in a February 24, 1933, raid bore the label "Japan Pharmaceutical Establishment" and contained morphine hydrochloride. The other arrests involved a similar type of morphine.

For the next five or six years, there were numerous arrests of Japanese passengers and crew members of steamships, most sailing under Japanese flags. They brought in morphine, heroin, and sometimes even cocaine, a drug obviously made not in Tientsin, but in South America. There were also functioning American distribution networks, headed by Japanese.

In April of 1935, California authorities arrested Fujiyuki Motomura, a major San Pedro drug trafficker, with over $5000 worth of cocaine and morphine, about 10 pounds in those days. Police believed that Motomura was tied to an additional 50 pounds of drugs found elsewhere in southern California. The following year, California authorities again made a major arrest when state narcotics police in Los Angeles arrested Toshiyoshi

Nagai for attempting to sell 5 pounds of morphine to undercover officers. Nagai told the prospective buyers that his brother owned a morphine factory in Japan and that he, Toshiyoshi, could supply any amount the buyers wanted. The smugglers were apparently using a number of routes, most of them successful; in 1938, the American representative at the Geneva drug conference told the assembled officials that 650 kilos of heroin from Japan had been captured by American agents on the West Coast. Using the usual law enforcement formula of ten to one – for every pound or kilo seized, police assume that ten get through – the Japanese may have accounted for some 6500 kilos of heroin in the period described.

In addition to their own operations, the Japanese were responsible for supplying huge amounts of heroin to the biggest drug rings in the United States. These gangs at the time were under the control of Jewish and Italian gangsters, operating all over the country. In San Francisco, for instance, mobster Mario Balestreri, successor to the mob run by "Black Tony" Parmagini, decided to increase his take and buy directly from the producers. He sent his men to purchase from Japanese dealers in Kobe, Japan, and Shanghai, China, then in Japanese hands. In 1939, police discovered that two of Louis "Lepke" Buchalter's lieutenants, Yanis Tsounias and George Mexis, had fled to the Japanese Concession at Tientsin and set up a heroin operation. The two were shipping enough to the United States to supply 10,000 addicts for a year, according to the Bureau of Narcotics.

The Japanese connection, of course, ceased to operate in the United States after December 7, 1941. Japanese and Korean drug dealers continued to work in the occupied territories of Asia, and a substantial body of evidence indicates that the Japanese were responsible for spreading, or at least maintaining, a very high level of narcotic addiction, particularly among the Chinese.

The Japanese also had their hand in gambling in the United States, although here it was controlled by resident Japanese for the most part. By 1910 there were over 70,000 people of Japanese descent in the United States, with at least a third of those living in and around Los Angeles. The center of Japanese activity in the United States was in the downtown L.A. community of Little Tokyo. And controlling all the gambling, as well as other aspects of the community, was the Tokyo Club, situated atop a three-story building at Jackson Street and Central Avenue.

Although it was based in Los Angeles, the Tokyo Club had branches – or more correctly, franchises – all over the West, from Seattle to the

Mexican border. The bulk of the operation was in California, with eight Tokyo Clubs in the Central Valley alone. It was a very successful operation. In the 1920s, it counted a profit of more than $1 million a year, a considerable sum in those days. Because it held the biggest accumulation of capital in the Japanese community, the Tokyo Club functioned as a bank as well. It also supported sports teams and lined the pockets of police and city officials.

The men who ran the Tokyo Club were businessmen-gangsters. Recalls Howard M. Imazeki, the retired editor of the San Francisco Japanese-American daily *Hokubei Mainichi,* "We didn't call them yakuza then, but now I think that's probably what they were." Power struggles frequently occurred within the club, sometimes erupting into gunfire. Wrote criminologist Isami Waugh, "In the cases of insubordination and disobedience Club President Itatani was severe in meting out the penalty; he sent his gang of powerful burly men to take care of these rebels in the Chicago gangland manner. . . . In two or three extreme cases, so the grapevine reported, men were actually murdered and their bodies were disposed of so well that even the police detection failed."

The gangsters who ran the Tokyo Club and the drug smuggling rings were interned along with the rest of the Japanese population early in 1942. Like the yakuza in Japan, many of them appeared to harbor ultranationalist sentiments. Openly rightist Japanese in the camps were sent to a special section at the camp in Tule Lake, California, and many of these were repatriated to Japan after the war. There have been no follow-up studies on the Tokyo Club leaders, but it's more than possible that many of them returned to their ancestral land. In any case, after the Tokyo Club closed its doors in 1941, it never reopened.

With the criminal leadership gone, and the post-internment community far too traumatized to engage in open lawlessness, organized crime in the postwar Japanese community was at a virtual standstill. Study after study reported a phenomenally low arrest rate among Americans of Japanese ancestry through the 1950s and 1960s. Gambling did not disappear, of course, and the Japanese were part of the poker clubs that made their appearance in the Los Angeles suburb of Gardena, but these were legalized operations. It was, according to Los Angeles police, not until the late 1960s that Japanese-Hawaiian gamblers drifted over from the islands and began to set up illegal bookmaking operations.

Southern California Yakuza

Los Angeles today has a lot to attract the yakuza. Besides the climate, the money, and the glamour, Los Angeles has the largest Japanese community on the mainland. All told, over 200,000 people of Japanese descent reside in the L.A. area. More than 99 percent of these have no connection with the underworld, but a growing number of yakuza have slipped into the Japanese community here, and some are doing quite well.

One of them, Tetsuo "Leo" Orii, runs the Club Niji, a modern-day successor to the Tokyo Club. A hostess bar that offers an assortment of barely dressed Asian and white women as companions, Niji caters mostly to businessmen from Japan. Orii has been involved in various business ventures in and around Los Angeles, and at least one police intelligence report called him "the most influential figure of the Japanese organized crime faction" in the city.

Orii is quite open and respectful of his links with the yakuza. "I've entertained the oyabun of Sumiyoshi when they come here," he boasts. "We are brothers of the same family. When the chief of Sumiyoshi came to the U.S., he stayed at my house. They come to my bar."

Orii says he joined the yakuza at age sixteen, and spent the next ten years fighting his way through prison and the tough Sumiyoshi-rengo gangs that dominate much of Tokyo. He made a name for himself by extorting money out of college kids in Tokyo's busy Ginza district. But, he says, after a decade with the yakuza, he'd had enough. "The only way out was to leave Japan, but I'm still in. They won't let you out."

So, young Tetsuo arrived in America, went into legitimate business, and claims he kept up his unbreakable link with the yakuza only by putting up oyabun at his Pacific Palisades home. Even if he wanted to, he says, he could not be a real yakuza in America. He admits there is some yakuza activity in Hawaii, but not on the mainland. "Yakuza are not into California because it's not profitable," he argues. "They can make twice as much money in Japan. They can't speak English very well, so they go where the Japanese are."

The problem, maintains Orii, is the police. The LAPD's Asian Task Force, he says, picks him on because "they need to show a reason for their existence." Most gangsters, of course, like to claim that they are simply honest citizens who just happen to have a few shady associates. Orii, however, got caught. In 1975 he and his partner, Tomonao Miyashiro, a.k.a. Tony Kawada, were arrested and convicted of shaking down a Japanese businessman. LAPD brought charges of conspiracy, extortion, kidnapping, and assault with a deadly weapon against Miyashiro, who tried to shoot the victim. Orii, apparently not present at the shooting, was charged only with attempted extortion.

Orii is only one individual in a rather large, fluid group of yakuza-connected Japanese in the Los Angeles area. Members of this group allegedly engage in racketeering and investment scams. Names appear and reappear on various watch lines, but there have been few arrests.

It has remained for police intelligence to piece together what the yakuza are up to. The most definitive statement comes from BOCCI, an arm of the California Department of Justice. In its 1981 annual report, BOCCI assessed the yakuza:

> *Law enforcement authorities have noted during the past several years that a number of Japanese organized crime members have immigrated from Japan and are now residing in the San Francisco and Los Angeles areas. There are approximately 50 gang members and associates now living in California.*
>
> *Law enforcement sources indicate that Japanese organized crime groups are operating tour agencies, Japanese gift shops and night clubs. Their criminal activities include extortion of Japanese businesses, harassment of Japanese tourists, prostitution, gun and pornography smuggling, narcotics distribution and laundering money.*

For deeply held cultural reasons, and because they are strangers in the United States, Japanese nationals here are extremely reluctant to talk with American police about their troubles with the gangsters. Victims of yakuza shakedowns will most likely just suffer the loss and try to forget it. One group in Los Angeles that has tried hard to break through this barrier is the LAPD's Asian Task Force. Criticized by some as a public relations outfit, the Task Force has indeed put a lot of effort into simply maintaining a presence in the various Asian communities in Los Angeles, including the Japanese. One problem in dealing with the yakuza is that they have yet to cause as much trouble as America's Chinese or Vietnamese gangs, and therefore do not lead police to spend the time or money to pursue them.

Nonetheless, as the exploits of Orii's partner, Miyashiro, demonstrated, the yakuza in California are not necessarily delicate in their tactics. A pair of unsolved crimes, reminiscent of the Tokyo Club killings of fifty years earlier, is evidence that the yakuza have to be taken seriously. Two Asian male bodies found in remote parts of southern California, one in a shallow grave near Oxnard on the coast north of L.A., and a second found near Castaic Lake in the Angeles National Forest, pointed strongly to yakuza skulduggery. "We never could identify the bodies," said LAPD Detective George Min, "but one was heavily tattooed, and the other was also believed to be yakuza."

In February of 1984, a Japanese murder victim was positively identified by police and was also believed to be the victim of yakuza violence. Hiroshi Eto, reportedly running from massive gambling debts in Japan, had been found strangled in his room at the Los Angeles Hilton. A Japanese newspaper reported that Eto, a "dating club" operator, had heavily insured his life with an American carrier prior to his leaving Tokyo. Upon Eto's death, a Taiwanese male stood to collect about $315,000 in yen in what is by now a standard, and gruesome, yakuza method of collecting back debts. Some yakuza in L.A. apparently make their living as hit men for this and similar tasks.

Beyond the shakedowns and outright murders, the yakuza's principal activity in southern California is money laundering, a very difficult operation for police to detect. Here, as in Hawaii and elsewhere, the easiest, most efficient money laundry is a high-volume cash business, such as a bar, restaurant, or gift shop. But the yakuza are also investing in noncash businesses in the Los Angeles area, according to Detective George Min. As in Japan, construction companies are a favorite of the gangs, and the LAPD has kept watch over a number of Japanese-owned firms. As officials in Hawaii noted, though, law enforcement can trace money back to Japan and run into a stone wall. "Japanese bankers," said one Honolulu official, "are like Swiss bankers. They reveal nothing."

The largest U.S. firm with known ties to a yakuza or former yakuza is headquartered in the Los Angeles area. This is Machii-Ross Petroleum, an investment of one of Japan's best-known yakuza leaders, the ubiquitous Hisayuki Machii. Apparently, when the Korean head of the Towa Yuai Jigyo Kumiai decided to invest in an American enterprise, he chose a prestigious type of business, and one that is decidedly non-yakuza: oil. Machii-Ross was incorporated in 1970 as an oil exploration company, but today owns over 100 wells, principally in the Wattenburg field in central Colorado. From its Santa Monica offices, Machii-Ross has also explored in Texas and, through a subsidiary operation, built and runs a natural gas processing plant. Machii has invested over $1 million in the business, which today has a future net income, based on oil reserves, of $100 million.

The American partner of the company is Kenneth Ross, a genial former lobbyist and California state assemblyman. Ross claims that he was a little surprised when informed of his partner's colorful background. "When we began the company," said Ross, "all I knew was that he was a wealthy Korean living in Japan. I had never heard of the yakuza."

Over the past fifteen years, Ross says that he has gotten to know Machii quite well, despite the fact that they need a translator to communicate. Machii's criminal activities, says Ross, are in the past, and his partner now regrets the reputation he must carry. Nonetheless, Machii told Ross, "I'm proud of what I did. Proud of my activities fighting communism."

Machii, of course, fought communism so successfully that he was able to amass considerable wealth. "Machii," says Ross, "lives almost like Howard Hughes, in a huge five-story home that he rarely leaves. I suspect that he's worth well over a billion dollars . . . maybe twice that."

Machii's American investments do not represent, then, a significant part of his overall fortune. They have, however, attracted the attention of U.S. officials. Ross, who is regarded by American police as clean, has been visited a number of times by both local and federal authorities and questioned about Machii. No specific charges or even allegations came out of these visits.

In a police intelligence report, however, an unnamed but remarkably similar company was accused of using suspect funds. The report referred to a "Japanese-based oil leasing and exploration company with offices in California and Colorado." The suspicions were anything but vague: "It is suspected that money made from illicit drug trafficking is being funneled through this company." Other police intelligence places Machii-Ross in a network of yakuza-related enterprises, without leveling specific charges.

Ross, who runs the American end of the business without much help or interference from Machii, denies any possibility of wrong-doing. He points to the reputably obtained audits of the firm, and the records of funds transferred from Japan to the United States by way of Mitsui and Manufacturers Hanover banks. He did not know the exact source of the funds invested, though, but added, "As far as I know, the [gang] disbanded in 1967."

The West Coast Sex Trade
Although Japanese newsweeklies frequently feature nude photos of young women, hard-core pornography is outlawed in Japan. The demand is filled, then, from overseas countries, including the United States. Similarly, live women are imported from the United States to Japan, either with their consent or, as often, through subterfuge and trickery. The so-called white slave trade from the United States isn't comparable to the trade in women that exists between Thailand or the Philippines and Japan, but it exists and shows no sign of abating. The reason is simple: novelty.

Tokyo-based journalist Jean Sather, in her investigation of the problem, found that American women hold a special attraction for Japanese men. Sather, now with the Asahi newspapers, wrote:

Many expensive clubs, and their customers, prefer the "exoticism" of Western women. This is part of a general tendency in modern Japan to see caucasian women as more beautiful and much sexier than Japanese women. Caucasian models are used heavily in advertising, porno films that feature white women are popular, and many Japanese women still visit plastic surgeons to have their eyes made rounder and their noses more prominent.

Gyo Hani, executive editor of the *Japan Times,* told Sather:

Attitudes are not really changing towards caucasians. They're not creatures from outer space, but close to it. Asian aliens look like us, but if you have a woman who's fair-skinned, blue-eyed, with blond hair, then you have a treasure.

Japanese technology is still incapable of filling this particular domestic need, and Japan, in this case, requires imports. The yakuza, naturally, are only too willing to attempt to cash in on the market, but they have a problem: few yakuza speak English well enough to entice women to come to Japan. They have, therefore, tended to operate through fronts or paid agents on the West Coast. According to various police reports, these agents usually obtain women by placing ads for singers and dancers in the entertainment press, publications such as L.A.'s *Drama-logue* and *Music Connection*. These have listings for "cattle-call" drama auditions, as well as for seamier performances, such as nude modeling and porno pictures. The ads by talent agents are designed to appeal to the starving actress or singer.

What happens to the women in Japan varies, but not much. Instead of straight jobs as singers or dancers, the women are expected to add tasks ranging from "hostessing" in bars to outright prostitution. As *Playgirl* magazine reported, "One American woman told of a club where she was forced to dance nude with half a dozen other women until a mob of audience members swarmed onto the stage and molested the performers. Another described a club where dildos were thrown out randomly to the audience for use on the performers."

Often, no matter what the duties of the woman, she will either not be paid, or be paid far less than she was promised, so that escape from Japan

– and even escape from the employer – becomes nearly impossible. One American woman recruited from Los Angeles told her story to the *Japan Times* just hours before she fled Japan. Her stay included two attempted rapes and violations of her contract. Her employer, one Kanji Chiba, "insisted that she relinquish her [return air] ticket for 'safekeeping,' which she did." Even when exploited, the women sometimes cooperate with their exploiters to an unnecessary degree. Said one: "A lot of the mistakes have been mine. You're naive, vulnerable, ambitious – you dream. That's what these people capitalize on – your dreams."

Women who return from what is often a hellish experience in the yakuza clubs often seek revenge, but usually get little satisfaction. Few of the agents can be located, and the victims have little in the way of legal recourse against those few who can be found. American law holds that the agents must have knowingly sent the women to houses of prostitution, and this is difficult, if not impossible, to prove.

There have been a number of civil suits launched by women against the talent agents. Lisa Petrides of Berkeley, California, answered an ad in the *San Francisco Chronicle* for entertainers. Petrides, who aspired to be a singer, went to an agency in San Francisco for "a very professional audition," and wound up at the Little Club in Tokyo, where her yakuza bosses insisted that she forget about singing and concentrate on hostessing. She called the agency from Japan, but her old agent refused to help her. When Petrides returned to California, she sued the agency and got a small out-of-court settlement. This agency is still in business.

Another victim of the talent ruse, Kristina Kirstin of Los Angeles, filed a $3.5 million lawsuit in May 1982. She named three defendants: her American agent, its counterpart in Japan, and Alexander Haig, then secretary of state. Haig was charged because Kirstin alleged that the U.S. Embassy in Japan refused to help her when she wished to flee Japan. The embassy, maintained Kirstin, was indifferent to her plight at the Mil Members Club in Kyoto, despite the fact that it was a known yakuza operation. U.S. officials at the State Department had told her that, by law, she was on her own and they could do nothing.

Even if the State Department were to get actively involved, it is unlikely it could stop the racket. There is simply too much money at stake. Japanese men pay an enormous amount for the thrill of having sex with a Western woman, and the profits to be made are immense. Even in the somewhat tamer area of hostessing, the bars make out handsomely from the presence of white women.

Trying to stem the trade at the American end appears likewise impossible. For one thing, although some victims have stepped forward, most do not. LAPD Detective Fred Clapp, a national expert on the vice trade, estimated that by 1982 the number of victims in the Los Angeles area alone had run into the hundreds. Clapp had, in fact, received over fifty reports from women who had been recruited and deceived through American talent scams, but expressed hopelessness over any attempt to end the trade. "The demand for Caucasian prostitutes," said Clapp, "is so great over there it can't be filled."

The Arming of Japan

When one thinks of the trade in precision machinery between the United States and Japan, the flow seems to be entirely toward the States. But there is one instrument that is entirely an export item from the United States to Japan. Thanks to a combination of high quality, great availability, and minimal legal encumbrances, American firearms are sought and acquired by the Japanese. The distributors, and in this case the customers, of the product are primarily the yakuza. Americans have competition from various foreign producers, but the yakuza's second most popular source – the Philippines – also sells a great many American-made weapons. The United States is, in effect, arming the Japanese underworld.

Eddie Kurimata (not his real name) is typical of the yakuza's mainland connections. A Japanese-American, naturalized here, he was no stranger to the world of crime before he met any yakuza. After he did time for drugs, he met a few Japanese gangsters in San Francisco and took them up on what he thought was an excellent offer. He became a gun scout for them. "I'm straight now," he insists. "But I've made money off the yakuza here. They need us. There's no way they can get all the guns they need in Japan."

For three years, Eddie traveled to scores of gun shops throughout the Bay Area. He'd purchase three pistols in Daly City, four in Oakland, two in San Rafael. A good sale to his yakuza customers could be as few as twelve guns, but it paid off. "I worked for them," he said, "but just for the money. It was too good to pass up." Kurimata could realize a profit of $1000 per handgun.

The possibility of such profits exists largely because of the discrepancy between Japanese and American gun laws. For all practical purposes, guns aren't allowed in Japan, and they are freely permitted in the United States. This, in turn, creates a huge price differential. A pistol that sells legally for $250, a Smith & Wesson Chief's Special, for instance, will command up to ten times that amount in Japan. Ammunition frequently sells for $5 to $12 a bullet there.

For gun buyers, America is a wide-open gun supermarket with only slightly restrictive rules. As one West Coast official of the U.S. Bureau of Alcohol, Tobacco, and Firearms put it, "Most foreign police regard American gun laws as a joke." Japanese laws, however, are anything but a joke.

The idea of a civilian population with easy access to firearms flies in the face of a Japanese tradition that stretches back nearly four centuries. For 200 years, the Japanese conducted a remarkable social experiment by banning all firearms on the islands. It began in the early seventeenth century, largely as a reaction to the cold-bloodedness of combat with firearms, and as a gesture of commitment to the sword, an enduring symbol of honor and stature in Japan. It was also an expeditious way to maintain power in the central government.

As Noel Perrin details in his fascinating book *Giving Up the Gun,* Japan's gunsmiths were summoned to a single city in 1642, forced to work for a government monopoly, and slowly starved out of business. Japan's feudal rulers impounded massive numbers of firearms, and for the next 200 years the development of modern weaponry virtually stopped. When Commodore Perry arrived in 1853, his sailors wryly noted that the Japanese shore batteries defending Tokyo harbor could fit inside and be fired out of their ships' cannons.

A tradition of gun control survived the Industrial Revolution and even World War II. In 1958, the Diet enacted the Firearms and Swords Control Act, which had the effect of making Japan relatively free of handgun murders. In 1980, for instance, 48 people died from handgun wounds in Japan, compared to more than 10,000 in the United States. There are guns in private hands in Japan – 881,204 as of 1981 – but this official figure is misleading. It includes antiques and construction guns (devices for punching holes in concrete) as well as hunting rifles and shotguns. There are virtually no legal handguns at all, except those used by military and police.

To help Japan with its "gun gap," enterprising Japanese have been moving thousands of handguns illegally into Japan in ever-increasing numbers. Guns smuggled into Japan do not go to collectors or to citizens interested in protecting their homes; they go to the gangs. A 1981 National Police Agency report noted that 89.5 percent of all handguns seized came from "criminal syndicates." For gun couriers, the varied syndicates have employed Japanese-Americans, Guamanian-Americans, U.S. military, tourists, students, and anyone else who might slip through Customs with a small arsenal.

Americans have been involved in gun smuggling ever since the first days of the postwar firearms ban, and many of these Americans have been military personnel. This is hardly surprising, considering the approximately 48,000 personnel stationed at 118 facilities in Japan. Many of them are bored, lonely, and low on cash, and many have access to stores of American weapons.

The yakuza have found it convenient to exploit the American military gun pipeline, while also cultivating members of the U.S. merchant marine for the same purposes. The point of contact, suggested a 1980 internal DEA report, is the off-base bars where GIs and others go for drugs, women, and drink.

Just how this connection can work for the yakuza was revealed to law enforcement officials by Air Force veteran James Anthony Bridgeport. In early 1983, a joint BATF-Customs-Air Force operation broke up a twelve-man smuggling ring headed by Bridgeport. Based in Tucson, Arizona, the ring had been sending guns to Japan via military air transport.

Bridgeport began his association with the yakuza while stationed in Japan. "It basically started with little favors, money loans . . .," Bridgeport later testified. "I just got in over my head, began to meet people, and borrow. And it ended up where I was a little bit deeper than I should have been. And then when I tried to get out, it was impossible."

Bridgeport claimed that he had been pressured by the yakuza into smuggling – first amphetamines, then guns. When he failed to recover a package of amphetamines – his first assignment – Bridgeport was beaten by yakuza members and threatened by having a gun placed in his mouth. He later succeeded in smuggling a shipment of speed from Korea to Japan. When he returned to the United States, the yakuza tracked him down and forced him to move guns. All told, over a two-year period, Bridgeport netted a total of $250,000 for gunrunning. Although the money was sweet, he ran in fear for his life, until one of his cohorts was seized in San Francisco with thirty-eight handguns and revealed the operation.

More recently, the majority of gun shipments to Japan have been handled by civilians rather than military people. Some of the smuggling methods show a great deal of ingenuity. Guns are taken from the United States into Japan in false-bottom bags, inside folk craft articles, in cassette players and travel irons, television cameras, and even inside pineapples, an item commonly carried by Japanese returning from Hawaii. Larger quantities require roomier conveyances, and in 1980 Japanese police discovered five pistols in the gas tank of a British Jensen arriving from the United States. American-built cars are used as well, and it is perhaps no coincidence that yakuza oyabun are the principal purchasers of imported American cars.

The trans-Pacific gun route was, by 1985, sufficiently well developed that smugglers could respond to particular crises in Japan with special orders for guns. For instance, when Masahisa Takenaka, newly crowned oyabun of the Yamaguchi-gumi, was assassinated in January 1985 by a hit team from the recently splintered Ichiwa-kai, U.S. police knew that shipments of guns would soon be leaving for Japan. DEA agents were able to turn early leads into a yearlong investigation of gunrunning, drug dealing, and murder conspiracy that ended with the arrest of two of the Yamaguchi-gumi's highest-ranking bosses in Honolulu. But even this, police agree, made only a small dent in the yakuza's activity abroad.

It is a dismal way to alleviate the foreign trade crisis: Japanese gangsters buying American handguns and hiring American entertainers and prostitutes. But the yakuza, as recent events have shown, are not content simply to buy American. Like good businessmen everywhere, they are investors, and they have expanded activities here mainly because of a strong foothold in their favorite base of operations abroad – the tourist trade.

The Tourist: An Easy Mark

Along with oranges and sinsemilla, Japanese tourists ought to be considered lucrative cash crops for the state of California. Some 463,000 Japanese visited the state in 1983, leaving behind hundreds of millions of dollars. Yet most of this booming Japanese tourist industry is a closed system. Tourists typically fly in aboard Japan Air Lines, stay at Japanese-owned hotels, eat in Japanese restaurants, shop at Japanese-owned boutiques, ride about in Japanese tour buses, and patronize Japanese purveyors of drink, guns, and vice. Police suspect yakuza involvement in a good deal of the racket. In a 1981 report, state investigators noted that the gangs had apparently launched a drive "to dominate the Japanese tourism industry in San Francisco and Los Angeles." The report described a common pattern of accosting cash-laden Japanese tourists and, through deception or intimidation, forcing them to participate in selected tours.

Inspector John McKenna, veteran chief of San Francisco's Gang Task Force, is one of the nation's experts on Asian organized crime. But McKenna's men, though aware of racketeering by yakuza and associates in the city for years, have been unable to make many cases, due in part to the reluctance of witnesses to come forward. Another problem is figuring out exactly what is going on in the often sleazy tourist districts.

North America: Foothold on the Mainland | 257

The Gang Task Force is not the only enemy of the yakuza in San Francisco. There is, for example, Stuart Eugene "Steve" Conn. The fifty-year-old businessman is as unlikely an opponent as the yakuza are apt to find, but Conn has taken on the entire Japanese tour industry. In July 1984, the pugnacious Conn was found by police near the city's Japan Town with bullet holes in his leg and shoulder. From his bed in San Francisco General Hospital, Conn claimed to any who would listen that his assailants were yakuza. Police were not entirely convinced, however; given the victim's checkered career – he is suspected of ties to the Bonnano mob – some thought Conn was attacked by someone with a debt to pay or a grudge to settle. Regardless, the roots of his troubles come from the fact that he decided to compete with the Japanese for some of the tourist yen. Declared Conn angrily, "I'm just trying to make a buck the way our Constitution says I can."

So, Conn opened a gift shop in San Francisco near the downtown area and began selling boutique items. The store – sometimes known as Nikkaido (Upstairs) and sometimes as Sakura (Cherry Blossom) – offered designer clothing and accessories, real and counterfeit. A specialty was Western wear, which for a time the Japanese loved. And, in a separate room in the back, there was a huge selection of pornographic magazines, films, videotapes, and plastic paraphernalia. The operation was typical of Japanese tourist traps up and down the West Coast.

According to one police report, Conn put on a very hard sell: "Japanese are lured into the shop by Japanese-speaking 'hustlers.' Once inside the shop, they are intimidated into buying gifts at very high prices. Victims rarely complain to police for fear of retaliation and losing face among their people." This report, if accurate, is consistent with the normal victimization of Japanese tourists. It ranges from browbeating gift shop customers to robbing prostitutes' clients. Not only is the element of losing face present, according to police, but few tourists – Japanese or otherwise – are able to remain in a foreign country in order to testify against the accused.

With the apparent enmity of the Japanese tour operators working against him, Conn began to lose money on the store. Suddenly, a savior appeared. Through intermediaries, Conn was introduced to a wealthy and influential Japanese who, he was told, would back the store and put in a word with Japan Air Lines and other tour operators. Conn had never heard the name of his backer before, but was advised it was well known in Japan: Sasakawa. The same Sasakawa with the billions of dollars, the speedboat racing monopoly, the rightist organizations, and the yakuza ties.

Sasakawa, acting through his son, Takashi, did put some money into the store, but just enough, apparently, to fulfill the terms of his agreement. Conn continued to lose business; he had trouble replenishing his stock and the tour operators failed to come through. Eventually Steve Conn went out of business, complaining to an uncomprehending press that he was the victim of a conspiracy.

Who was responsible for Steve Conn's near-murder? The case was never solved. But clearly, there is a very large amount of money involved in Japanese tourist scams in the West, and no individual or group making that kind of money is about to give it away. If Steve Conn wasn't put out of commission by the yakuza, his case is a good lesson for anyone with aspirations to muscle in on such a lucrative racket.

The Wrong Side of Japanese Business

While there is no record of eminent rightist Ryoichi Sasakawa ever wanting to own another overpriced, failing gift store, he did lose an immense amount of money in another tourist-related scheme 3000 miles from San Francisco. It was a business deal that called attention to Sasakawa's yakuza ties in Japan, and that made American law enforcement sit up and take notice.

In 1978, Takashi Sasakawa, Ryoichi's second son, publicly joined with well-known Japanese restaurateur, speedboat racer, and balloonist Hiroaki "Rocky" Aoki to announce plans to lease the aging Shelburne Hotel in Atlantic City and turn it into a casino. The gambling boom was hitting the East Coast, and Sasakawa, for one, wanted to be in on it. Aoki, owner of the famed Benihana chain, felt that a touch of Japan would add some exoticism to the Jersey Shore.

The actual deal was a hopelessly complicated affair involving several paper corporations in both America and Japan, and several hundred million dollars. Of this, Takashi openly owned 47 percent of the enterprise, although no knowledgeable observer believed Takashi was the real investor. His New York attorney asserted to the press that Takashi's father was "far removed from the deal," but few were convinced.

Within months, the U.S. Securities and Exchange Commission charged Takashi Sasakawa and Aoki with insider stock trading. The two men had purchased 60,000 shares of the Hardwicke Company, knowing that they would later engage that company to manage the planned Shelburne Benihana. This move inflated the value of the stock, a patently illegal move. Sasakawa was forced to make restitution to the sellers of the original Hardwicke stock.

The Sasakawas were reportedly quite taken aback with this wrinkle; Ryoichi was used to manipulating stock values for his own profiteering without a peep from the Japanese government. Following that unpleasantness, Sasakawa continued to pump money into the Shelburne project, but without his previous enthusiasm. There were indications that the casino would not fly, and not only because the Securities and Exchange Commission was on his tail. Sasakawa's seedy background had caught up with him. Because of Sasakawa's dossier, American banks refused to "anchor" the project with domestic loans, and New Jersey law enforcement let it be known that any project with the Sasakawa name on it would have a hard time getting a casino license. If New Jersey wanted to keep mob-connected Americans out of Atlantic City, it could hardly open the door to yakuza-connected Japanese.

Sasakawa's interest in Atlantic City made a good deal of sense, and he brought to it plenty of expertise. The boat-racing czar already knew the gambling business from the ground – or the water – up, and could run large-scale betting operations as well as anyone. Some law enforcement people worried that, had it succeeded, it could have served as the biggest Japanese-owned laundry in the United States, which is why they helped scuttle the deal. When the Sasakawas, Aoki, and the silent partners bailed out – selling their interest to a Philadelphia real estate developer in 1981 – they had lost an estimated $27 million. The aging rightist had become quite used to leaving large bundles in the United States, but it must have galled him to involuntarily drop a sum of this magnitude.

Undaunted, in February of 1983, Ryoichi arrived in San Francisco to receive the Linus Pauling Medal for Humanitarianism for his generous donation of $770,000 to the Linus Pauling Institute of Science and Medicine. The man who once called himself "the world's wealthiest fascist" was now out to become the world's greatest philanthropist.

Sasakawa's efforts at self-aggrandizement are boggling. Prior to the black-tie dinner given by the Pauling Institute, he held a luncheon at San Francisco's posh Bohemian Club – which is anything but – and spent the morning giving interviews to the local media. At the luncheon, Sasakawa received the guests bobbing like a buoy in a rough sea and smiling continuously. His publicist, flown out from the giant New York firm of Doremus, told the assembled that Sasakawa was, among other things, a patriot, a man unashamed to love his country and his mother. In fact, Sasakawa erected a statue in Japan of himself carrying his aged mother on his back, but the object of his veneration was less the mother than the bearer.

He also denounces, as he did in San Francisco, accusations of his ultranationalist past and war profiteering as Communist inspired, secure in the knowledge that he has outlived most eyewitnesses. When the authors pointed out to him that U.S. Army documents were quite explicit about his plundering in China, he proclaimed, "I have not exploited one yen or one penny. What I did was to donate several million tuberculosis injections to China." He was equally imaginative in denying any relations with the yakuza, conveniently forgetting that he had publicly boasted of including the late Yamaguchi boss Kazuo Taoka among his drinking companions.

In spite of Sasakawa's indifferent results in cleaning up Japanese history and his place in it, the grand old kuromaku continues to make a name for himself as a philanthropist and promoter. He has funneled millions through his Japan Shipbuilding Industry Foundation to charities throughout the world. He is the largest private donor to the United Nations and has funded international health centers, Ivy League universities, and even the presidential library of Jimmy Carter, who praised his "good work for peace." As an industrial promoter he has had less success, spending millions in a vain attempt to introduce the Shinkansen, the Bullet Train, to southern California.

Sasakawa's most ambitious giveaway in America is the U.S.-Japan Foundation, headquartered in New York and begun in 1980 with a generous $48 million endowment from Sasakawa. To orchestrate its efforts, the foundation chose as its staff president Richard W. Petree, former political section chief at the U.S. Embassy in Tokyo, and a man accused in the Diet of being an active CIA official (an accusation Petree will neither confirm nor deny). The foundation's original "American Working Group" included such luminaries as Henry Kissinger; Chairman Angier Biddle Duke, former ambassador to four countries and heir to a tobacco fortune; James A. Linen, former president of Time, Inc.; former RCA chairman Robert Sarnoff; and former New York mayor John Lindsay.

The expressed goal of the U.S.-Japan Foundation is to enhance, through grants and education, cooperation between the two countries, primarily of an economic nature. But there is another, more covert goal, and that is to raise the value of Sasakawa's personal stock among the movers and shakers. According to Rocky Aoki, Sasakawa's former business partner, the old ultranationalist is angling for the Nobel Peace Prize, and it appears he is willing to spend almost any amount of money to get it. He has even set up an office in Oslo, Norway, in order to better lobby the Nobel Committee, and in 1985 he was actually nominated for a prize.

Despite all his do-gooding and donating, Sasakawa remains a gambling czar with strong ties to the extreme right in Japan, and with less overt but definite ties to the yakuza. If, as Dr. Linus Pauling said of Sasakawa's philanthropy, "Perhaps he's just trying to make up for past misdeeds," he still has a long way to go – and time is running out.

Sasakawa is not the only questionable financial figure in the United States to arrive from Japan. An equally worrisome development has evolved in the form of major sokaiya groups arriving at America's doorstep. Sasakawa's clumsy casino attempts and showy humanitarian gestures are easy to see through; the tactics of the sokaiya are considerably more opaque.

On April 21, 1982, the manager of the powerful sokaiya group Rondan Doyukai, a gentleman named Shigeru Kobayashi, attended a stockholders' meeting at the Chase Manhattan bank in New York. Kobayashi sat through Chairman David Rockefeller's opening remarks, and forty minutes of questioning from the floor – undoubtedly fighting the urge to silence the dissenters – and then turned and addressed the crowd. Said Kobayashi: "We represent your stockholders from Japan. I am happy to be here at your general meeting. Now I have the honor of seeing Chairman Rockefeller. . . . He is a great man because he met with His Majesty the Emperor when he visited Japan a couple of years ago, and very few people in Japan can shake hands with the Emperor. I would also like to express my sincere appreciation for your high dividends."

Kobayashi's statement probably amused those stockholders present, but some were also puzzled. Why should Rondan Doyukai send one of its top people to New York merely to flatter the company? Kobayashi later told a Japanese newspaper: "We rode into New York to show them what Japanese sokaiya are. But, just before the meeting, the *Wall Street Journal* carried a sensational article with banner headline saying, 'The Sokaiya are coming, the Sokaiya are coming,' as if the Japanese gangsters were invading the U.S. This raised a stink. We know that the public peace is bad in New York, so we thought we might be eliminated by the Mafia."

Kobayashi somehow avoided a trip to the bottom of the East River, but he needn't have worried in the first place. Nearly six years earlier, in equally violent Los Angeles, another sokaiya group made its appearance. In 1976, according to police sources, fifty Japanese executives filed into one of the ballrooms of the Biltmore Hotel in downtown L.A. They were the top-ranking officers of the largest Japanese corporations operating on the West Coast, and they had come to pay their respects to a group of visiting sokaiya (who had neglected to announce their presence to the press). Police at the same time observed sokaiya Masato Yoshioka making a tour of Los Angeles to present himself at Japanese-owned banks, conglomerates, and securities investment firms, possibly to hit any companies missed at the Biltmore meeting. Although the businesses were reluctant to talk about the incident, informants revealed to law enforcement agents that, as in Japan, it was cheaper to pay up than to risk the consequences.

Rondan Doyukai also had made earlier trips to America. They had sent representatives to the 1981 annual meeting of the Bank of America in San Francisco. They were, in the words of corporate secretary John Fauvre, "polite but insistent." The group approached the microphone, said Fauvre, with their own photographer and translator, and introduced themselves with lengthy formality. The sokaiya then did little more than wish the bank good luck, much as Kobayashi would do to Chase Manhattan a year later.

Rondan Doyukai, Japan's largest sokaiya group, has faced the 1982 Japanese crackdown by diversifying. This group, most of whose members all attended one high school in Hiroshima, has invested $232,000 to gain shareholder status in a strategic handful of American and European companies, according to the *Wall Street Journal* report that so terrified Kobayashi. Among those targeted besides Chase and Bank of America were General Motors, IBM, and Dow Chemical.

Other sokaiya operations are underway. Los Angeles and New York City police have discovered that sokaiya-type scandal sheets are being used to extort money from Japanese corporations, and it appears that the sokaiya remain a threat to American branches of Japanese companies, particularly the smaller ones. But it also looms that as Japanese investment capital pours into the United States, and American firms do more and more business with Japanese corporations, American-owned companies, too, may have to deal with the extortion that accompanies so much of Japanese capitalism. It may be subtle at first, but the remarkably versatile and wily sokaiya will surely find a growing international niche within the $85 billion worth of business done annually between the two nations.

Meeting of the Mobs

The New York Police Department has a hard time keeping track of yakuza activity in that city. Said one Chinese-American officer in a heavy New York accent, "There's only one Japanese-American on the whole force, and he doesn't speak Japanese."

Nonetheless, Asian cops in the intelligence division have noted reports of yakuza shakedowns of Japanese businesses and individuals. The NYPD was dubious of any large-scale ongoing criminal operations in the area, though. Said one officer: "If there were any rackets, like prostitution, the Five Families would be interested. You can't do anything for very long in New York without the traditional mob becoming aware of it. In the bar business, you have to deal with them. They're in restaurant supply, in liquor, and related activities. I think New York is just geographically inconvenient for the yakuza to get anything going in. That's one reason they have done so much better in L.A. – less structured organized crime."

Less than a year after this pronouncement, the President's Commission on Organized Crime revealed that the New York mob was perfectly willing to play ball with Japanese gangsters in organizing gambling setups. The NYPD was correct up to a point: the mob doesn't want competitors in its territory, but it loves to have more customers. The yakuza don't pose a threat to American organized crime anywhere on the mainland, but they certainly can form alliances with gangsters in the United States, alliances that will benefit both parties.

It is, in fact, precisely this nascent alliance that gives American law enforcement the jitters. Ties between American and other mobs have always increased the strength of domestic gangsters. In some ways, American organized crime went international at the turn of the century, when arriving Sicilian gangsters kept in touch with their cousins in the old country, and Jewish and Greek drug smugglers maintained ties to relatives in strategic locations. Over the years, American organized crime became more involved in the international drug trade and, during Prohibition, in bootlegging. After World War II, big-time American gangsters took gambling operations to Havana, the Bahamas, and Europe.

Although there were links between American and Asian mobsters in the narcotics trade beginning in the 1920s and 1930s, the growing criminal ties between the U.S. and Japanese mobsters could eventually dwarf those links. They would bring together two of the world's most powerful mobs, rivaled perhaps only by the great Chinese syndicates. Furthermore, both the Japanese and American Mafias engage in similar activities – from white-collar crime to control over sidewalk food stands. And both have troops, political power, and money.

One possible consequence of a working alliance between the mobs would be an increase in international theft. Presently, one of the Mafia's biggest money earners is organized theft from Kennedy International Airport and from the New York docks. The huge volume of commerce between the United States and Japan now exceeds that of the Atlantic trade, and any mob-controlled theft from those cargoes could bring in billions.

The amount of power such an alliance would create truly worries American lawmen. Warned former U.S. attorney Michael Sterrett, one of the country's most astute yakuza-watchers: "There are now shadow governments in the U.S. and Japan that collect their own taxes, make their own rules, and enforce their own laws. An alliance between the yakuza and U.S. organized crime means that drugs and guns and huge amounts of money will be moving across the world accountable to no one but the mobs themselves. It means an international shadow government."

Perhaps the major difficulty the mobs face in cementing such a union is a large cultural and linguistic barrier, and lack of any existing ties. Few mafiosi have cousins in the yakuza, and not many speak even pidgin Japanese. Consequently, the element of trust is lacking, and it is impossible to set up a cross-Pacific theft or smuggling scheme without that trust. In organized crime, several million dollars does not change hands on the basis of a written contract.

What the two mobs need, then, is a place to meet and get to know one another – maybe a place to relax, to eat, to drink, maybe to whore and gamble; to exchange, even through an interpreter, the amenities that bring about an aura of trust required before business can be planned. This place ought to be open enough to ensure that these meetings don't raise too much suspicion. Fortunately for the mobs, there is such a place: Las Vegas.

Japanese mobsters and high rollers have been coming to Las Vegas for over a decade as operators and participants of gambling junkets. Pleasure has clearly led to business. As long ago as 1975, American and Japanese investigators believe they uncovered a link between Caesar's Palace in Las Vegas and organized crime in Japan. Caesar's, long suspected of being under the direct control of mob families, in 1973 appointed an allegedly yakuza-connected movie producer, Kikumaru Okuda, to help find customers and to collect debts owed to the casino. Two years later, according to Japanese press reports, Okuda associates threatened a number of debtors who together owed more than $200,000. The collectors would, they said, have the yakuza kill them if they didn't pay up. Caesar's Palace officials denied that Okuda had any mob connections on either continent, but the case in Japan was strong enough to send Okuda and two others to jail for extortion.

The Japanese have found that they could profit from a permanent base of some sort in Las Vegas, and have made several attempts to secure one. As early as 1971, billionaire kuromaku Kenji Osano began negotiations to purchase the Sands Hotel and Casino. Like Sasakawa seven years later, Osano knew that a giant casino operation, with its enormous flow of cash, its facilities, and its location in a gambling capital, could only help him and his friends in the gambling business. Osano, however, was forced to withdraw from the deal when his troubles with Lockheed began.

In 1982, a former professional baseball player and golfer, Ken Mizuno, attempted to secure a liquor license for a Japanese restaurant in the Tropicana Hotel and Casino. According to the *Las Vegas Valley Times,* he entered the United States with $3 million in traveler's checks – an unusual way to transfer money. Police, however, claimed that Mizuno had not $3 million, but $100 million at his disposal, and charged furthermore that it was yakuza money. When Mizuno actually applied for his license, Las Vegas police charged him with close association with members of the yakuza. Mizuno nonetheless received his license while at the same time enduring continuous surveillance and protest from a variety of police agencies.

The fact is, Las Vegas has laundered cash since Bugsy Siegel built the Flamingo in 1946, and continues to do so. That the Japanese would take advantage of this service is not surprising, and that they would enter into agreements with American gangsters is even less so. Many U.S. law enforcement reports have commented upon meetings between Japanese and American mobsters in Las Vegas, and it is only a matter of time before they strike major deals – if they haven't already done so.

Secret meetings have been taking place every two or three years, between Japanese and Americans. The first meeting was in 1980 on the island of Kauai in Hawaii. Another occurred in December 1983 in Honolulu. The subject was the yakuza, and the participants were cops. The meetings are called the U.S./Japan Organized Crime Conferences, but they are really one-sided: American organized crime, according to an NPA participant at the 1983 meeting, is not active in Japan.

The meetings are a counterpoint to the generally poor communication between American and Japanese police officials regarding the yakuza. Representatives of most federal law enforcement bodies – from the FBI to the IRS – and of Hawaiian and West Coast local police departments attend on the American side. Japanese police from the NPA and the Tokyo Metropolitan Police have attended all three.

Although some Japanese police belittle, or even deny altogether, the problem of yakuza in the United States, there have been exceptions. By 1982, a twenty-year veteran of the Tokyo Metropolitan Police, Masanori Kita, had been assigned to the Japanese Consulate in Honolulu to serve, in part, as liaison to local and federal police. It was not wholly an act of generosity. Kita observed that the yakuza in Hawaii appeared to be more of a problem for the Japanese than for the Americans, since much of their activity was smuggling guns and pornography back to Japan.

Despite the otherwise low level of cooperation from the Japanese, American police have decided on a novel approach to an organized crime problem: stop it before it gets entrenched.

Although there is some skepticism about the effectiveness of the new aggressive approach, there is no doubt that, at the federal level at least, law enforcement has taken the offensive, with or without the cooperation of the Japanese. The laissez-faire attitude that Honolulu Customs officers Bill Sweet and Al Gano had described in 1982 had hardened considerably within two years, and yakuza were being caught and dispatched in record numbers. Late in 1983, Customs joined the Immigration and Naturalization Service (INS) and the FBI in the semi-secret Operation 893, "whereby Yakuza are identified, prosecuted, or deported for violation of visa or other entry requirements." The tool is identification, and it has been employed rather unfairly, but apparently with considerable effect. Incoming yakuza are caught in a bind: if they account for their past police record, they may be denied entry on grounds of undesirability; if they fail to declare the arrests and they're caught, they may suffer more than deportation for the crime of making false statements on a visa application. A surprising number of Japanese gangsters confess when confronted with mere suspicions.

Throughout 1983, Customs turned suspected yakuza over to the INS. Those admitting to having omitted criminal records were allowed to take the next plane back to Japan. But by 1984, the United States got tougher still, and took arrested yakuza suspects to court. By May of that year, thirteen yakuza had been convicted, fined a total of $100,000, sentenced to probation, and deported.

The yakuza, however, didn't take the hint. In early 1985, eight were caught in one stretch, and one of them was found to be wearing a false fingertip, a device that apparently didn't fool Customs. It remains to be seen what "counter-countermeasures" the yakuza devise next, but they undoubtedly will attempt to elude the crackdown. The opportunities for money laundering, gambling, and other scams make the United States well worth the risk. Many yakuza, according to police, simply bypass the efficient Customs points in Honolulu and Los Angeles, flying instead to a different gateway where inspectors don't yet know a yakuza from an Eskimo. Yakuza can then easily fly to Hawaii or California on a domestic carrier, bearing a valid entry visa.

Nonetheless, the crackdown, particularly in Hawaii, has put a crimp in some yakuza plans. One Sumiyoshi boss claimed in 1984 that he had been unfairly treated in the United States, a victim of yakuza scare stories. He had, he said, been pulled from his tour group – a tour organized by a bank

– and interrogated for two hours, then followed for the remainder of his trip. Complained yakuza godfather Inagawa, "Please tell the American people we wish them no harm. All we want to do is go to Hawaii and play golf."

The question is, however, does the border crackdown have an effect on the serious moneymaking yakuza ventures? Honolulu's Bernie Ching, for one, doubts that any really important deals were sidetracked. "The guys they're getting," he confided, "are just the ones over here on vacation. The ones who are coming over now are slicker, harder to keep track of. Previously, we had no trouble knowing which yakuza were arriving. They'd show up with an entourage at the airport to greet new ones. Now, the good ones sneak in and that's that."

By spring of 1985, it appeared that the crackdown might be petering out. In spite of the publicity generated by the President's commission, enthusiasm for anti-yakuza programs runs hot and cold in Washington, and funding is constantly in jeopardy. The Yakuza Documentation Center at Honolulu International Airport may well become a victim of budget cutbacks, a paradox in the Reagan administration's commitment to the fight against organized crime.

At the same time funds were being withdrawn from the fight against the yakuza, one committee on Capitol Hill sounded perhaps the strongest alarm over yakuza drug smuggling. On February 22, 1985, the House Committee on Foreign Affairs released a staff study entitled *U.S. Narcotics Control Programs Overseas: An Assessment*. The section on Japan was both succinct and accusatory:

> 1. Japan is a likely transshipment point for narcotics: It is one of the commercial hubs of the region, has a huge organized crime network (the Yakuza), and such a clean international image that U.S. Customs does no incoming cargo checks on shipments coming from Japan.
> 2. It is impossible to know Japan's significance as a transit point for narcotics, due to lack of cooperation from the Japanese. The Japanese share very little narcotics intelligence with the United States, refuse to permit "controlled deliveries" through their territory, will not provide conviction records or their list of names of 100,000 known Yakuza members, or other important information.

The yakuza threat to the United States, then, is both present and potential. The yakuza continue to work the tourist racket; shake down Japanese businessmen and personnel; smuggle guns, pornography, and women to Japan; launder and invest funds; and now have a hand in importing Asian heroin to the United States. But how active and autonomous yakuza groups become, and how firmly entrenched in the various Japanese communities, is a big question. With little or no active opposition, they will continue to expand as have other organized crime groups. It is possible that shortsighted American officials, hampered by unhelpful Japanese authorities, are missing a chance to severely curtail one of the world's largest and best-organized criminal syndicates.

If there were one overriding element to the success of modern organized crime, it would be complicity. In the case of the yakuza, complicity of both officials and local crime groups is needed. And because the yakuza are in no way able to confront either group, they must win them over. It will be, if successful, a painstaking process.

By virtue of their immense cash resources, yakuza members can always buy some officials. Certain subtle rulings and policies can, for instance, make it easier for "investors." Police officials might receive quiet advice that there are other priorities than yakuza. Friends in and around government will help yakuza frontmen obtain necessary licenses and permissions to do business. Very little will be overt, and if the yakuza are lucky, nothing will come to the attention of the press or public.

On the other side of the fence, American mobsters will find that those who play ball with the yakuza stand to make a lot of money in one way or another – at first in gambling, perhaps later in drugs – and there is no need to view the Japanese with suspicion. Those Americans who can broker deals for the yakuza and their friends will also find that they can make small fortunes.

The yakuza, then, do not have to take over America in order to succeed here. Indeed, they cannot. But if they proceed with caution and ally themselves with the right people, they can do extremely well. And by the time they succeed, the gangs will come to be regarded as part of the cost of doing business here, as they are in Japan.

Epilogue
A New Yakuza

"Ultimately, the yakuza will become like the U.S. Mafia," explains Kakuji Inagawa, Japan's most esteemed godfather. "In the future," he says, "there'll be one national mob. Like my organization, the bigger firms will take over. You can see the move towards a more corporate structure."

Inagawa, though, is clearly not happy about this turn of events. "The Mafia will kill for profit," he warns. "The yakuza must respect morals and regulations and obey them – but that tradition is fading. . . . It would be easy if we could turn back the pages of time. It is because of the generation gap that I worry."

Inagawa is not alone. The most common complaint among Japan's underworld chieftains today is that the new yakuza are more violent, less obedient, and interested most in honoring fat profits, not feudal traditions. Perhaps worst for Inagawa and his aging peers, there is little they can do about it. They are no longer in full command of a generation raised with jet travel, biker gangs, television, leisure time, and growing consumer credit.

The yakuza are in the midst of a transformation. Their structured, insular world of giri-ninjo, tattoos, finger-cutting, total obedience, and all the other trappings of gangster chivalry is in danger of obsolescence. In a way, this change is long overdue. Few other Japanese run their lives by these hoary tenets of feudalism, although bits and pieces of the oyabun-kobun system persist in postwar Japan. As the samurai did a hundred years ago, when they dropped their swords and picked up profit-and-loss statements, the yakuza are finally shedding their medieval past, and the changes may be equally far-reaching. Japan's gangsters have recently discovered that the criminal world of the late twentieth century does not require ideology, chivalry, or absolute loyalty. Instead, the times seem to call for sophisticated crooks and cunning, adventurous schemers. As a result, for the first time the yakuza are beginning to act as much for themselves as for the gang as a whole, and it is changing the face of organized crime in Japan.

These are not changes that are occurring wholesale, as they did, for instance, in the early 1930s in New York. It was then that Charles "Lucky" Luciano engineered the elimination of the leading old-line bosses, and with them went all the "Moustache Petes," the Sicilian-born gangsters with their old-world ways. The modernization of the Japanese underworld began in the broken rubble of 1945, and has been going on ever since.

As early as 1954, an anonymous oyabun warned of the dangers befalling the underworld:

> *What is happening today has never happened before. The traditional yakuza used to fight among themselves and sometimes steal, but it was only a matter of living in underworld society. If a yakuza caused injury to ordinary people, we used to punish him immediately. It was not permitted by our rules to hurt the weak; however, today, force is used against the weak people indiscriminately, and there is no longer a sense of order in the yakuza world.*

Skeptics might ask if the yakuza were ever truly chivalrous. Throughout their long history, Japan's gangster class has acted foremost as an undeniably criminal force, extorting, bullying, and robbing those with the bad luck to fall in their path. But even the members of Japan's famous police force will admit in confidence that their nemesis has a noble side. Like so much of the Japanese culture, the nation's organized crime syndicates exist in a maze of contradiction. The yakuza have played the role of that society's honorable opposition, integrated yet rejected, legal yet criminal. The answer is a qualified yes – the yakuza do have a chivalrous side, and that is indeed part of what has changed so dramatically. As the gangs arm themselves with America's handguns, and are increasingly unaccountable to both their bosses and the general public, the substance and the image of the noble outlaw are finally disappearing.

The breakdown in traditional lines of authority has much to do with the changing structure in many of the syndicates. No one really knows for sure if, as Inagawa believes, there will be one great national mob in the future. But like the Mafia, Japanese crime groups are becoming integrated into huge centralized syndicates. And of those syndicates, the model is not the top-down, tightly knit Yamaguchi-gumi; it is, instead, the looser, more Mafialike federation, on the lines of the Sumiyoshi-rengo. The narrow, pyramid-shaped Yamaguchi syndicate has been dependent on an all-powerful oyabun-kobun tie running throughout the organization, with little or no room for dissension. The death of its leader, Taoka, and the subsequent bloody infighting, is perhaps the most dramatic evidence of the weakening of these feudal ties. An entire generation of Japanese mobsters is passing, and the police are as worried as the godfathers.

The Tokyo Metropolitan Police, who rank among the most astute yakuza-watchers in Japan, publicly aired in 1984 what the gangs had long since realized. "There is a clear trend of declining solidarity and obedience" among the yakuza members, officials reported. "This stems from the retirement of aging gang bosses who maintained strict discipline as well as changes in the temperament of rank-and-file gangsters." No longer, it seems, will kobun say that the passing crow is white just because the oyabun so observes.

The issue of retirement is crucial, according to Kanehiro Hoshino, one of Japan's leading yakuza experts. Hoshino, a senior researcher at the National Research Institute of Police Science, believes that the most profound changes in the major syndicates will come when the last of the great bosses, those who came to power during the occupation, passes on. Despite the turmoil in the Yamaguchi-gumi, Inagawa and the other traditionalists are still largely in control – for now. It is their death or retirement, argues Hoshino, that may prompt younger elements to dramatically alter the structure and tone of the gangs.

Directly related to the breakdown in traditional authority is the move abroad by the yakuza. Once again, the comments of godfather Inagawa are revealing. "The yakuza in Hawaii are outsiders and misfits," he says. "They cannot adapt themselves to Japan." These very misfits, however, have spearheaded the yakuza's move abroad. Most are the members of a new, more adaptable generation of Japanese criminal, far too busy making money in Honolulu or Hong Kong to worry about severed fingers and *sake* ceremonies. Regardless of whether they are full members or just knowledgeable associates, they continue to work in concert with the yakuza back home.

Not every restless yakuza is a misfit, however. Most are simply of another generation. The younger yakuza, those who came to crime not through the waterfront, the labor gang, or the black market, but through gangs of street punks and hot-rodders, are simply not very enamored of gangland tradition. They are less willing to obey their bosses at every step; few are ready to give their lives for some abstract devotion to duty. Even the most common traditions are changing: the younger yakuza are forsaking the full-body pictorial tattoos. They opt instead for a simple line drawing or phrase on their upper arm, more similar to the tattoos of Western youths. The reason, says researcher Hoshino, is not a change in aesthetics: the old-style tattoos cost a fortune, and are simply no longer worth either the physical or financial stress.

Nor is it worthwhile for the more aggressive yakuza to pay heed to the old tradition of never harming *katagi no shu,* "the citizens under the sun." This is the creed, as old as the yakuza itself, of never hurting the common people. The anonymous oyabun who railed about the underworld's lost sense of order in 1954 might keel over in disbelief at the state of affairs today. Fast profits and plentiful handguns have become the standards of power throughout the Japanese underworld, and the two have combined to cause an explosion of violence by the gangs. Gangland shootouts doubled in 1983 alone, reaching a postwar high in Tokyo. Officials now complain that shootouts in broad daylight have victimized innocent bystanders. But the violence is not confined to gang wars. Gunplay is being used to back up everything from corporate shakedowns to loan-sharking, a radical change for both the police and the yakuza.

In his 1976 study of Japanese police, American scholar David Bayley could write that "Japan . . . is a totally disarmed society; criminals hardly ever carry firearms." So great are the changes that just eight years later they would lead one police official to say, "We are convinced that literally every yakuza owns or carries a handgun even on the streets, an entirely different situation from the past." Even allowing for overstatement, the National Police Agency knows now that the yakuza – thanks to the huge traffic in gun smuggling – is heavily armed in a society that forbids the ownership of handguns. Yakuza are carrying more guns in part because there are more guns to be had in Japan. The vaunted ban on handguns is becoming less effective, at least within the underworld. For this the U.S. bears some responsibility; America, with its 200 million firearms, is the primary source for smuggled guns among the yakuza.

Japan's prestigious newspaper, the *Asahi Shimbun,* devoted an editorial in 1983 to denouncing the wave of mob violence. Focusing on a rash of shootings in smaller cities, the paper noted that the underlying causes of violence are no longer confined to the old territorial wars. A gunfight will erupt as easily over the profits from a racetrack as over who will sing along with recorded music in a pub.

For once, the cops, too, are ducking bullets. In August 1983, two leaders of the Kawai-gumi tried to raid the office of the rival Kyokuto-Sekiguchi gang in Tokyo's Ikeburo district. When the gangsters were stopped by four policemen, the yakuza pulled guns and began firing. One officer was seriously injured. In the past, an attack on police – particularly for something as minor as an ID check and a possible weapons charge – was about as likely as a yakuza attack on the emperor.

Beyond the changes in structure, authority, and violence, the yakuza have come to resemble the American mob in at least one other way: more and more gangsters are opting for crimes of greater sophistication. There still is the bottom layer of simpleminded thugs, of course. But now there are the *interi yakuza,* the so-called intellectual gangsters: white-collar crooks, financial racketeers, and the overlapping groups of sokaiya. The economic crimes of these modern gangsters, as American police know all too well, are hard to detect and even harder to prosecute. These changes go hand in hand with other developments bearing on the future of the gangs: the newer yakuza are better educated and more traveled, and an increasing number can speak English, still the language of commerce in much of the world.

The shifts within the yakuza, however, are part of a broader set of changes occurring within Japan. It is not only organized crime that is undergoing a major transition; it is crime itself. In 1979, for example, police reports indicated that drug arrests were up 20 percent per year, women were committing more and more crimes, and juvenile delinquents were getting younger and younger. Moreover, crime in general has become more violent, with bank robberies increasingly common, leading the Japanese press to conclude that "Western-style" crime has finally arrived. Although most of these figures are still quite small by U.S. standards, many are comparable to those in Western Europe. They certainly represent a significant rise for the Japanese, and pose unwelcome questions about the future of public safety in that country.

The changes sweeping through the yakuza world, and through Japan as a whole, have also affected the underworld's place in Japanese politics. Few organized criminal groups in the world are so closely linked to one political force as are the yakuza to the Japanese far right. Certainly in the United States, the idea of a politically extreme group interchangeable with a Mafialike organization is all but unknown. But Japan of the 1980s is not the world of the occupation, nor even the world that spawned the huge rightist/gangster coalitions of the 1960s. The far right itself has changed, if not in purpose, then in impact and acceptability to the public at large.

To a degree, the Lockheed scandal made the rightists, particularly underworld rightists like the heirs of Kodama, a little less savory, and a little more outside the ruling structure. And, for the time being, Japan's unprecedented economic success has meant that fewer Japanese than ever have heeded the call of the far right. Most people's expectations are being met, and any appeal that the ultranationalists might have to the masses has been blunted by paychecks and consumer goods.

Another milestone is that, much as the traditional yakuza godfathers are fading, the great rightist kuromaku – the power brokers of twentieth-century Japan – are dying out. Of that strategic trio of Sugamo Prison war criminals released in 1948, Kodama is dead, and Sasakawa and Kishi are both in their late eighties. The new kuromaku of Japan are by trade businessmen, not ultranationalists. And while they may have underworld ties, the times have changed since the heady days of the Drawn Sword Regiment and Ampo. There are no longer American occupation officials in need of yakuza spies and strikebreakers; no longer justice ministers who make it their business to unite the underworld into an anticommunist militia; and no longer a Yoshio Kodama to organize a yakuza army to protect the visit of an American president.

Nevertheless, it would be a mistake to dismiss the far right in Japan. The underworld continues to be closely tied with the ultranationalist movement, and organizationally the far right is still alive and active. Some groups, such as Seiran-kai, the Diet members' faction, have disbanded, but others, such as the twenty-six-year-old Zen Ai Kaigi, continue to prosper.

Although its charismatic leader, Keizo Takei, has retired, Zen Ai Kaigi still claims thousands of followers and 400 offices stretching the length of Japan, from northern Hokkaido to the southern island of Okinawa. A 1984 visit to the group's main headquarters in Tokyo's Ueno district – long a center of ultranationalist activity – revealed that the yakuza-ridden organization still sponsors paramilitary exercises and demonstrations around the country.

Using a tactic dating back to the Dark Ocean Society – the nation's first modern ultranationalist group – Zen Ai Kaigi exacts ad money from many leading corporations in Japan. Like the sokaiya and other financial racketeers, the group is accused of threatening to disrupt major corporations in order to extort contributions. In 1983, two issues of the Zen Ai Kaigi tabloid *Kaibyaku* (meaning "foundation" or "beginning") revealed impressive advertising. There were many of Japan's largest banks: Fuji, Mitsubishi, Mitsui, Sanwa, Sumitomo, and others. Leading financial brokers such as Daiwa, Nikko, Nomura, and Yamaichi Securities were also represented. Kawasaki Heavy Industries, Kawasaki Steel, Iwatate Road Co., and many more also added to the group's coffers. Clearly, the far right still possesses sufficient clout to lean on major institutions and get away with it.

The danger from the ultranationalist camp is for now a potential one. But even a quiescent far right is not to be ignored. According to many scholars, Japan needs only a generally perceived threat from the left – such as prolonged demonstrations or a Socialist move toward power – for the far right to again become a major force in the country. The rapid rearming of Japan's long-dormant military makes this prospect more worrisome than ever before in the postwar era. In 1960, Columbia University professor Ivan Morris, one of the foremost chroniclers of Japanese culture and of the right wing in that country, speculated on what the reaction might be to a leftist threat. His words are as appropriate today as they were a quarter-century ago. Wrote Morris:

The fact that on the whole rightists have become far less radical and anti-capitalist in their stand would probably make it easier for them to cooperate with the conservatives than it was in the prewar days. A number of the post-war nationalist organizations have combined politicians, business men, and professional rightists in their leadership and such groups would probably become more numerous and important. . . . The less respectable strong-arm groups could usefully cooperate with the police in breaking strikes and in obtaining information about leftists and trade unionists. In case a full-fledged police state should come into being many of them could profitably be mobilized as anti-Communist shock troops. As the government steadily came to adopt extreme undemocratic policies, prominent rightist personalities would be likely to gain positions of influence in the state, and many middle-of-the-road conservative leaders would probably become increasingly right wing in their orientation . . . virulent xenophobia and the various other irrational factors associated with extreme nationalism would come into play, and would tend to make the country's foreign policy unstable and unpredictable.

The deaths of Kodama and lesser kuromaku have helped make this a less likely scenario. Their passing, combined with the impact of the Lockheed scandal, has at least partly diminished yakuza power at the governmental level. A surprising number of politicians still use the gangs to raise money and do dirty work, but political figures increasingly avoid any connection with gangsters, ultranationalists, and anything that smacks of the nation's corrupt "Black Mist."

A key element in this change is that the press and the public have become more aware of yakuza involvement in the seamier aspects of politics, and less forgiving to those involved as a result. The yakuza's widely acknowledged role in events ranging from the Minamata mercury poisoning case to the kidnapping of Kim Dae Jung have angered broad cross sections of the public. Since the Lockheed scandal, the press has grown bolder in exposing these types of incidents, and in looking for ties between the establishment and the underworld. This, combined with the continuing shakedowns of the country's biggest corporations, the mushrooming drug traffic, and the increasing violence, has finally begun to erode the longtime social acceptance of the gangs.

The police have responded to an increase in public pressure, and to a decrease in political protection for the gangs, by more freely attacking their most serious crime problem. But while officials claim that their crackdowns have nearly halved the underworld's total membership since 1963, the population of the gangs has now largely stabilized, and those remaining yakuza tend to be the shrewdest, richest, and most ruthless. In addition, police inadvertently have strengthened the bigger syndicates, as smaller gangs have adapted by either joining larger groups or disbanding altogether. Still another unforeseen consequence is that the continued pressure has helped drive growing numbers of yakuza overseas, where they can evade the reach of Japanese authorities.

In the postwar world, the yakuza were quite late in moving overseas. They lagged behind other crime syndicates – Corsican, Italian, American, and Chinese – in part because the occupation kept the gangs at home until 1952. But it was inevitable that the yakuza would eventually follow the striking successes of Japan's businessmen around the world. And follow they have. If the events since 1970 prove anything, it is that the yakuza have shown a willingness to expand wherever opportunities have presented themselves. They have gained footholds in Japanese communities from Honolulu to São Paulo, invested huge sums through much of the Pacific Rim, and formed working alliances with Chinese and American crime syndicates.

Beyond the yakuza's murder-for-insurance schemes, overseas shakedowns, and varied smuggling operations, it is the question of alliances that remains most troubling. The yakuza's appearance on the international scene coincides with the shift of the world's central market activity from the North Atlantic to the Pacific Rim. This idea of the Age of the Pacific, an increasingly popular concept among businessmen, will soon gain many adherents among law enforcement agencies, as the yakuza combine with other underworld organizations to cash in.

The modern roots of crime in the Pacific are sunk in the heroin trade carried on by the Chinese Triads and the American Mafia. But now the criminal trade is moving far beyond drug smuggling to a wide range of international scams. The danger here is not from an international turf war disrupting the civil peace, but from alliances that pit several highly mobile, sophisticated groups against law enforcement. These criminal coalitions, furthermore, are by no means limited to the region's big three syndicate groupings: American, Chinese, and Japanese. Officials in South Korea now foresee the emergence of highly capable crime syndicates from that rapidly emerging industrial power. In the Philippines, seasoned crime rings have sprung up with links to immigrants in the U.S. In fact, through much of Southeast Asia, and in Latin America as well, a trans-Pacific trade controlled by organized crime is slowly coming of age. It is in Hawaii, perhaps, that the future can best be seen, where a panoply of Eastern and Western gangsters cooperate, shifting their language in a single drug deal from Chinese, Japanese, and Filipino to the local pidgin English.

The biggest moneymaker is the narcotics trade, and it will probably stay that way. Although the field seems adequately serviced by Chinese and Western gangsters, there is still room for more, particularly any gang that is richer, stronger, or tougher. The yakuza's massive trade in amphetamines, still virtually unnoticed outside East Asia, has created and supplied up to 600,000 drug users in Japan. The gangs' long experience in the drug market proves that they have the manpower, the money, and the expertise to work the international narcotics trade. The connections, furthermore, already exist: Japanese gangs now move significant quantities of speed through the Chinese Triads, the same gangs that control most Southeast Asian heroin – the source of between 20 and 40 percent of the American domestic market. For the yakuza, it may simply be a business decision to move bulk lots of heroin through Japan and Southeast Asia to the West. Japanese syndicates already wield considerable influence over the huge docks of Kobe and Yokohama, and one Toyota full of heroin could make a lot of yakuza very rich.

It is the potential of massive Japanese heroin imports, with its historical precedent in the U.S., that has caused some American authorities to eye the yakuza with perhaps greater fear and suspicion than the present danger calls for. Clearly, the yakuza do not yet maintain a huge presence in this country, as they do in South Korea and the Philippines. But they are most certainly active and visible in Hawaii, and present though less visible on the mainland.

Japan's National Police Agency officially maintains otherwise. In numerous interviews, government spokesmen have repeatedly discounted the presence of yakuza in America. Some officials have gone so far as to deny altogether that the yakuza operate outside Japan, although informed Japanese lawmen will privately admit otherwise. This contradictory stance, due in part to the need for saving face, is typical of the cultural differences that American police must understand if they are to foster a strong working relationship with Japanese agencies. American traditions and values play an equally complicating role.

American observers attempting to assess the impact of the yakuza in the U.S. risk either over- or underestimating the Japanese gangs. It is very easy for Americans, when viewing a foreign "menace," to be misled by the outer trappings rather than the reality of the threat. Certainly the frightening images of tattoos, missing fingers, and suicidal loyalty all contribute to misunderstandings. It has happened before.

Perceptions of the Mafia have long been colored by ignorance and racism, both of which interfere with a sober assessment of the phenomenon. The tragedy of such a view is that other people of the same ethnicity are likely to be tarred with the same brush. On the other hand, it is likely that when the "threat" fails to live up to early expectations, it is then downplayed, and potential problems are ignored. The early Mafia grew exponentially during Prohibition, but some law enforcement people refused to take it seriously. The FBI's J. Edgar Hoover, throughout most of his forty-eight-year tenure, stoutly maintained that the Mafia, in fact, did not exist.

Things have come a long way since 1976, when U.S. Strike Force attorney Michael Sterrett was told to delete observations about yakuza tattoos and finger-cutting, for fear his reports would not be believed. Many American law enforcement groups have today a passing knowledge of the yakuza, if not necessarily a clear plan of action. For some yakuza activities, though, such as large-scale money laundering, it may already be too late to stop operations even with a clear plan. For others, such as drug dealing and sexual slavery, well-informed and aggressive police action could prevent untold misery and save lives in a host of countries. Most important for Americans, decisive moves taken today by law enforcement on both sides of the Pacific can stop the yakuza from becoming a permanent fixture of criminal life in the West.

The 1980s are a critical time for the yakuza as well as the police in the United States. The fifty-year dominance of the Mafia over organized crime is eroding, and other groups have the opportunity to step in. Black and Hispanic criminals stand to take over the lion's share, but on the West Coast and in New York, Asian gangs also have a chance to carve out a growing piece of the action, and among these the yakuza is certainly well organized, well financed, and ready to expand. It remains to be seen whether they can capitalize on this opportunity, and whether U.S. law enforcement can stop them in time.

Like the blind men examining the elephant, observers of organized crime "see" only a small part of the whole beast. It is inevitable; what comes to light at any one time may be important or may be trivial. Furthermore, the line between some kinds of criminal and legitimate commerce is often blurred, changing with the laws and the times. Racism, self-righteousness, political opportunism, and fear color perceptions of organized crime and render many appraisals suspect and indistinct.

But beyond the indistinction, opportunism, and bigotry, there is the raison d'être of organized crime. It lies under the patina of colorful characters, exotic rituals, nicknames, and legends. At the core lies one undying principle – theft. Gangsters may provide goods and services, but usually at a vastly inflated cost. In its most basic form, organized crime is simply institutionalized robbery.

For the average citizen, the presence of gangsters – be they Japanese or American – adds an invisible tax to every dollar or yen. Gambling, bribery, extortion, prostitution, and drugs all demand a human and economic toll of society. In those areas in which organized crime holds a substantial interest – bars, restaurants, construction, entertainment, trash collection, longshore work – a direct cost is passed along to the public. Gangsters, unlike most business people, are not content with reasonable profits, and they rarely put money back into the community in any constructive way. They want an exorbitant return, and they want it for nothing. They are, as Jonathan Kwitny of the *Wall Street Journal* wrote, "a class of persons who live like kings but whose only contribution is to innovate new ways to steal the wealth produced by hard-working citizens."

Despite the greatest efforts of police and the public, this robbery of the commons continues unabated, and increasingly reaches into every corner of society. By serving as muscle for the worst elements in business and politics, organized criminals have impeded progress in everything from representative government to a clean environment. They have prevented new unions from protecting workers and have seriously compromised many existing unions. They have protected corporations from those seeking redress for dangerous and insensitive policies. They have worked as hitmen and hired muscle for repressive governments and corrupt politicians. They have served in Japan, among other places, as the most virulent exponents of male dominance, buying, selling, and enslaving women for the sex trade. And they have robbed entire communities not only of their money but of their youth as well, spreading a deadly trail of narcotics addiction that stretches around the world. There is, quite literally, nothing that organized crime won't do for money.

The yakuza are an exceptional organized crime group. In the twentieth century, they have often been a major key to political power in Japan. They have carved out a secure niche for themselves and have arrogated more open wealth than gangsters anywhere else in the world. In the West, one can look only to Sicily, perhaps, to find such overtly powerful gangland figures. Through the years, the Japanese have learned to live with the yakuza and to render unto them as much as necessary to keep the peace. This method has in the past provided a certain public harmony, but that social contract is finally breaking down.

Whether the Japanese can use this period of flux in the underworld to dramatically alter some of the ancient relationships between the public and the yakuza, and to build a higher wall around the gangs, is impossible to foretell. Organized crime in Japan has grown remarkably powerful since World War II, and like organized crime everywhere, once entrenched it is nearly impossible to eradicate. It can, however, be contained, and it remains to be seen if the yakuza will be prevented from further applying their proven techniques to the rest of the world. What is clear is that over the past 300 years, the yakuza have become one of the world's most successful criminal organizations, and that whatever the public does, these once honorable outlaws of Japan are apt to be around another 300 years.

A Note on Research

Research for this book began with work undertaken by the authors for the Center for Investigative Reporting in early 1981. The results of that initial investigation appeared one year later in a segment of ABC's *20/20* newsmagazine. The authors subsequently wrote a series of articles on the subject for a variety of magazines and newspapers, and eventually devoted full time to researching this book.

The work ultimately involved no fewer than 400 interviews in the U.S. and abroad over a four-year period. The authors met with diplomats, scholars, policemen, former intelligence agents, businessmen, political activists, journalists, and organized crime figures. Our reports and conclusions are based on these interviews and on extensive use of material from public and private libraries, government archives, and law enforcement files.

Japan is a highly literate society with thousands of publications – daily newspapers, weekly magazines, journals, and newsletters – ranging the political spectrum from right to left. Whenever possible, we relied on direct translations from these publications, as well as from books, academic papers, and government reports. There is, unfortunately, no grand tradition of investigative reporting in Japan, as there is in the United States; critical, in-depth coverage of important issues occasionally finds its way into the big dailies, but more often ends up in the usually sensational weekly press. Where we have used weekly press accounts, they are typically backed up by other, more reliable sources.

Of great help was the remarkably vital English press in Japan. Tokyo today can boast five English daily newspapers, more than most American cities; all but one are based on Japanese editions, and generally these papers cover the yakuza with interest. For copies of these stories and other relevant documents, the authors made use of the extensive clipping files at the Foreign Correspondents' Club in Tokyo, the back files of major publications, and the National Diet Library for hard-to-get documents.

Most important, perhaps, was access to the private library of John Roberts in Tokyo. This remarkable collection of indexed clippings, studies, and reports from throughout Japan deals not only with the yakuza and the right wing, but also with Japanese business and politics dating back to the 1950s. It is a unique resource, one that richly deserves funding to preserve its contents and make them available to other researchers.

During a six-month tour of East Asia to research this book, the authors also gained access to reports of yakuza activity in South Korea, the Philippines, Hong Kong, and Thailand. Again, the English press in the capital cities of these countries proved most helpful, as did local journalists, government officials, and businessmen. Through a network of sources around the globe, we were able to garner reports of yakuza activity from other regions as well, including South America, Western Europe, Australia, and the mid-Pacific.

Written materials on the yakuza are rather scarce in the United States, but they do exist. A number of journalistic reports have appeared over the years, but these are nearly all based on Japanese press accounts. One helpful source was the small but lively Japanese-American press, usually, alas, unindexed. Previously, only one general book has appeared on the subject, *The Tattooed Men,* written by Florence Rome and published in 1975. Sections of other books pertain: "Underground Empire" in Harry Emerson Wildes' memoir of the occupation, *Typhoon in Tokyo;* also parts of Mark Gayn's recollections of that same period, *Japan Diary.* A handful of key academic reports are available in English as well. Particularly noteworthy are the field studies of anthropologists Walter Ames and David Stark, both sponsored by the University of Michigan at Ann Arbor; the research of George De Vos at the University of California at Berkeley; and in Tokyo, the works of Glenn Davis while at Sophia University and of Kanehiro Hoshino at the National Research Institute of Police Science.

We made use of a number of American libraries. Of particular help was the University of California at Berkeley, including the Bancroft Library and the various departmental libraries, and the Government Documents Section of Doe Library. The East Asia Section at the University of Maryland's McKeldin Library had the most extensive occupation materials outside the government. The Gordon Prange and Justin Williams collections rest there, each containing bits of history ranging from critical documents to the flotsam of bureacracy.

The most boggling trove of materials resides at the National Records Center in Suitland, Maryland. The NRC contains twenty acre-sized rooms, each filled with towering shelves of the most important and obscure records of the country. It is here that the bulk of American papers on the occupation of Japan are stored. The records of the Supreme Commander of the Allied Powers, or SCAP, are still stored in the boxes in which they were packed in Tokyo in 1952. Indexing is crude at best, but these are the primary documents of a unique period in American and Japanese history – one for which there is still no definitive history written in English. There are, in addition, other materials available, particularly the Embassy Post Files at the National Archives in Washington, D.C.

Other primary documents proved equally challenging to obtain. The authors filed numerous Freedom of Information Act requests to nearly a dozen federal agencies, some of which responded, and some of which were less than helpful. Court records, as well as FOIA materials, were useful for yakuza-related figures who had dealings in the U.S., and those we found in California and Hawaii. Finally, confidential law enforcement reports were made available to us; these often supplied key documentation of yakuza movements in Japan and abroad.

Notes

Chapter 1

Pp. 14–16: Historical material for this section is drawn from George Sansom, *A History of Japan* (1963), pp. 32–36, 57–60; George A. De Vos, *Socialization for Achievement* (1973), pp. 286–287; and *The East* magazine, vol. XVII, October 1981, pp. 46–48.

Pp. 16–18: Chobei Banzuiin background is from *The East* magazine, vol. XVII, October 1981, pp. 47–48; Sansom, *A History . . .*, p. 60; and *Asahi Evening News,* January 31, 1979.

Pp. 18–20: Oyabun-kobun description is based on Kanehiro Hoshino, "The Recent Trend of Underworld and Organized Crime in Japan," research paper of the National Research Institute of Police Science, Tokyo (1979), p. 16; Iwao Ishino, "The Oyabun-Kobun: A Japanese Ritual Kinship Institution," *American Anthropologist,* December 1955, pp. 696–698; Hiroaki Iwai, "Delinquent Groups and Organized Crime," *Japanese Culture and Behavior* (1974), p. 390; Chie Nakane, *Japanese Society* (1970), p. 42.

P. 19: Mafia and Triad initiation rites are described in Sean O'Callaghan, *The Triads* (1978), pp. 37–42; Ed Reid, *The Grim Reapers* (1969), p. 26; Eric Hobsbaum, *Bandits* (1969), p. 34.

Pp. 19–20: Yakuza initiation rites are from Iwai, "Delinquent Groups . . .," p. 388; Walter L. Ames, *Police and Community in Japan* (1981), p. 108.

Pp. 20–22: Tekiya background is based on De Vos, *Socialization . . .*, pp. 284–285; Hoshino, "Organized Criminal Gangs in Japan," research paper for the National Research Institute of Police Science (June 1971), pp. 5–6, 11–12.

Pp. 22–23: Information on burakumin is from Mikiso Hane, *Peasants, Rebels, and Outcasts* (1982), pp. 139–143; Hoshino, "Organized Criminal Gangs . . .," p. 13.

P. 24: Origin of the word *yakuza* comes from Ames, *Police and Community . . .*, p. 108; George De Vos, *Socialization for Achievement*, pp. 282–283; David Harold Stark, *The Yakuza: Japanese Crime Incorporated*, doctoral thesis (1981), pp. 27–28.

P. 24: Expulsion practices are described by Stark, *The Yakuza*, pp. 105–108.

P. 25: For a fuller description of finger-cutting customs and history see Hoshino, "Organized Criminal Gangs . . .," p. 8; Stark, *The Yakuza*, p. 111.

Pp. 25–26: Tattooing information comes from *Asahi Evening News*, March 29, 1984; Hoshino, "Organized Criminal Gangs . . .," p. 10, and "The Recent Trend . . .," p. 22; Florence Rome, *The Tattooed Men* (1975), p. 54; Stark, *The Yakuza*, p. 117.

P. 27: The description of the "travelers" can be found in *The East* magazine, October 1981.

Pp. 29–31: Shimizu no Jirocho story is drawn from *Asahi Evening News*, January 6, 1975, and February 7, 1979; George De Vos, "Organization and Social Function of Japanese Gangs," in *Aspects of Social Change in Modern Japan* (1967), pp. 290–291; Oliver Statler, *Japanese Inn* (1961), pp. 233–250, 271.

P. 33: Information on early Toyama years is from Glenn Davis, *The Right Wing of Japan*, Master's thesis (1976), pp. 6–8.

P. 34: Genyosha espionage activities are detailed in Richard Deacon, *Kempei Tai: A History of the Japanese Secret Service* (1983), pp. 40–41.

Pp. 34–35: Genyosha's role in the 1892 election is from E. H. Norman, "The Genyosha: A Study in the Origins of Japanese Imperialism," *Pacific Affairs*, September 1944.

Pp. 33–36: Other background on the Dark Ocean and Black Dragon societies can be found in Glenn Davis, *The Right Wing of Japan*, pp. 5–15; I. I. Morris, *Nationalism and the Right Wing in Japan* (1960), especially p. 88; John Roberts, *Mitsui: Three Generations of Japanese Business* (1973), p 134; and in an unusual two-part series by Andy Adams, "Behind the Mask of Japan's Black Dragon Society," *Black Belt* magazine, August and September 1969, pp. 44–47.

Pp. 36–37: Background on Takejiro Tokunami and the Great Japan National Essence Society is based on an interview with noted yakuza authority Kenji Ino on March 2, 1984, and on the following sources: *Uyoku Jiten* (The Right-Wing Dictionary) (1970), p. 45; Morris, *Nationalism and the Right Wing . . .*, pp. 314, 338–339; Roberts, *Mitsui*, pp. 209–210.

P. 38: Reports on the yakuza in Manchuria are from Tetsuro Morikawa, *Chi no Senkoku* (Bloody Verdict) (1979), p. 209; De Vos, *Socialization . . .*, p. 299.

Background on the Japanese wartime heroin trade can be found in Roberts, *Mitsui,* pp. 312–313; and Jonathan Marshall's superb article "Opium and the Politics of Gangsterism in Nationalist China, 1927–1945," *Bulletin of Concerned Asian Scholars,* vol. 8, no. 3, 1976, pp. 22, 29, 39–42.

Chapter 2

Pp. 43–44: Kades's press conference is from SCAP files, "Press Conference, Civil Information and Education Section," September 19, 1947, and from interviews with Mr. Kades, late 1984–early 1985.

Pp. 47–48: Sangokujin background is based on Florence Rome, *The Tattooed Men* (1975); Kazuo Taoka, *Yamaguchi Gumi Sandaime: Taoka Kazuo Jiten* (Yamaguchi-gumi Third Generation: The Autobiography of Kazuo Taoka) (1973); and interviews with Kenji Ino and Goro Fujita, February–March 1984.

Pp. 48–49: Shupak investigation comes from SCAP, "Public Safety Department Oyabun-Kobun System Report," 1948.

Pp. 49–50: Ando story is from Mark Gayn, *Japan Diary* (1948); and Justin Williams, *Japan's Political Revolution under MacArthur* (1979), p. 14.

Pp. 52–53: The record of SCAP's probe into the gangs is in Government Section's "Report of the Oyabun-Kobun Subcommittee," September 25, 1947; G-2's "Oyabun-Kobun Systems," October 1, 1947; and "Public Safety Division History," vol. I, pp. 165–183. Also useful are Harry Wildes' *Typhoon in Tokyo* (1954) and his "Underground Politics in Postwar Japan," *The American Political Science Review,* vol. 42, 1948.

Pp. 54–55: Background on occupation reforms is from Jon Livingston et al., *Postwar Japan* (1973), pp. 10, 116, 142.

P. 55: The gyakkosu debate is familiar to virtually all students of the occupation. See, for example, Williams, *Japan's Political Revolution . . .,* pp. 51, 71, 208.

P. 56: Status of the JCP comes from I. I. Morris, *Nationalism and the Right Wing in Japan* (1960), p. 60; and Livingston et al., *Postwar Japan,* p. 75.

P. 57: For a description of the CIA's secret war against the French left, see Alfred McCoy's excellent *The Politics of Heroin in Southeast Asia* (1972), pp. 43–47.

Pp. 57–58: The postwar involvement of U.S. intelligence in recruiting Japanese gangsters and ultranationalists is based on confidential interviews with former G-2 officials and, in part, on the following documents: John Dower, "The Eye of the Beholder," *The Bulletin of Concerned Asian Scholars,* October 1969, pp. 16–25; Ann Crittenden, "CIA Said to Have Known in 50's of Lockheed Bribes," *New York Times,* April 2, 1976; Tad Szulc, "The CIA's Activities in Postwar Japan," *Asahi Evening News,* April 23, 1976; Omori Minoru, *Sengo Hisshi* (Postwar Secret History), vol. 7 (1981).

P. 58: Willoughby background is from Frank Kluckhorn, "Heidelberg to Madrid – The Story of General Willoughby," *The Reporter*, August 19, 1952.

Pp. 59–60: Information related to Matsukawa and the other incidents comes from Chalmers Johnson, *Conspiracy at Matsukawa* (1972), especially pp. 4–5 and 377–381; Seicho Matsumoto, *Nihon no Kuroikiri* (Black Mist over Japan), vols. I and II (1974), especially pp. 224–225; Minoru, *Sengo Hisshi*, vol. 7, pp. 195–199.

P. 60: For details of the Kaji case see Morris, *Nationalism . . .*, p. 220; and Johnson, *Conspiracy . . .*, pp. 367–373.

Pp. 60–61: Details on the various secret organs can be found in SCAP files, Record Group 331, National Records Center; Morris, *Nationalism . . .*, p. 221; *Shukan Bunshun*, April 15, 1976; Ei Mori, *Kuroikikan* (Black Chamber) (1977), pp. 26–35; Minoru, *Sengo Hisshi*, vol. 7.

P. 61: Machii incident is from Hisatomo Takemori, *Miezaru Seifu* (Invisible Government) (1976), p. 72.

P. 62: G-2 use of ultranationalist groups is based on confidential interviews with former U.S intelligence officers; Delmer M. Brown, *Nationalism in Japan* (1955), p. 248; Morris, *Nationalism . . .*, p. 13, 68–69; Minoru, *Sengo Hisshi*, vol. 4, pp. 144–146.

Pp. 63–65: Early Kodama background is primarily from Yoshio Kodama, *I Was Defeated* (1951), and *Bungei Shunju*, January 1961. See also *Japan Times*, June 12, 1977; and Morris, *Nationalism . . .*, p. 443.

Pp. 65–66: Kodama's wartime exploits are from *Yomiuri Shimbun*, April 26, 1976; David Boulton, *The Grease Machine* (1978), pp. 47–49; Jim Hougan, *Spooks* (1978), p. 415; and *Uyoku Jiten*.

P. 66: The quotation on Kodama is from a G-2 report, May 24, 1947, marked to the attention of Col. R. E. Rudisill.

P. 66: For Kodama's apparent deal with G-2 see *New York Times*, April 2, 1976; *The New Republic*, April 10, 1976; and *Asahi Evening News*, April 23, 1976.

P. 67: Tsuji's background is from *Japan Times*, July 26, 1976; and SCAP, Government Section, "Memorandum for the Record," by Harry Emerson Wildes, August 16, 1946.

Pp. 67–68: Kodama's varied exploits here are described in *Japan Times*, April 28, 1976; *New York Times*, April 2, 1976; and Takemori, *Miezaru Seifu*, p. 130.

Chapter 3

Pp. 71–72: These scenes are from a privately translated copy of rightist historian Bokusui Arahara's *Dai Uyoku Shi* (The Great History of the Right Wing) (1966), pp. 483–485. The book is considered a classic among Japan's modern ultranationalists.

Pp. 72–74: Information on Tokutaro Kimura and his Drawn Sword Regiment comes from Kenji Ino in the respected monthly *Ekonomisto,* February 26, 1976; Tetsuro Morikawa, *Chi no Senkoku* (Bloody Verdict) (1979), p. 217; J. W. Dower's biography of Prime Minister Shigeru Yoshida, *Empire and Aftermath* (1979); *Japan Times,* October 26, 1961; and U.S. Archives at the National Records Center in Suitland, Maryland, Group 331, Box 2275G.

Pp. 77–78: The similarity between yakuza and rightists in the 1950s is from Marius Jansen's "Ultranationalism in Post-War Japan," *Political Quarterly,* April–June 1956, pp. 141–151. The *Daily Yomiuri* article cited is from October 20, 1959.

Pp. 78–79: For Kodama in this period, see Morris, *Nationalism . . .,* p. 444; *Asahi Evening News,* February 16, 1960; and *Japan Times,* June 12, 1977.

Pp. 79–81: Various occupation-era documents on Sasakawa were obtained from the U.S. National Records Center. The authors further received dozens of pages of later U.S. reports under the Freedom of Information Act. A key source of information on Sasakawa is also the superb work of Tokyo-based American journalist John Roberts. See his story in the Hong Kong monthly *Insight,* April 1978, under the title "Ryoichi Sasakawa: Nippon's Right Wing Muscleman," and related pieces in *Far Eastern Economic Review,* June 18, 1973, February 17, 1978, and June 23, 1978. Also useful is Hanji Kinoshita's "Rightists on the March," in *Oriental Economist,* November 1952; the authors' own "Soft Core Fascism" in the *Village Voice,* October 4, 1983; and numerous clips from the Japanese daily press. Sasakawa's boast of being "the world's wealthiest fascist" is noted in *Time* magazine, August 26, 1974. Finally, we have relied on an October 2, 1976, interview conducted with Mr. Sasakawa by Bernard Krisher while he was *Newsweek* bureau chief in Tokyo.

Pp. 81–82: Kishi's rather questionable background is covered in George R. Packard III's *Protest in Tokyo: The Security Treaty Crisis of 1960* (1966); and in John Roberts, *Mitsui.*

P. 82: Ohno's fondness for the yakuza is detailed in *Mainichi Daily News,* August 16, 1963, and July 18, 1964; and *Japan Times,* July 30, 1963.

P. 84: The quote on the Pine Needle Association appeared in the *Daily Yomiuri,* April 9, 1960. For an overview of the crisis, see Packard's *Protest in Tokyo.*

Pp. 84–86: The material on Kodama's organizing to protect Ike is from the late Koji Nakamura's "The Samurai Spirit," in *Far Eastern Economic Review,* October 16, 1971. Also see Kenji Ino, *Yakuza to Nihonjin* (Gangsters and the Japanese) (1974), pp. 254–258; and *Asahi Geino,* January 15, 1984. A decade after the Ampo battles, Nakamura and Ino were two of the few Japanese journalists willing to look critically at the collusion between the government and the rightist/yakuza groups.

P. 86: Ambassador MacArthur's remarkable notion about the Ampo demonstrators appeared in U.S. State Department telegram no. 4230, transmitted from Tokyo on June 15, 1960. Additional information on Ampo appears in Richard Storry's *A History of Modern Japan* (1960), pp. 274–276; and in Roberts, *Mitsui,* pp. 462–463.

Pp. 87–88: The only comprehensive look at Zen Ai Kaigi in English is in *The Right Wing of Japan* (1976), journalist Glenn Davis's prescient master's thesis at Tokyo's Sophia University. We have also relied on an April 2, 1976, unpublished interview by then Zen Ai Kaigi chief Takei to Mr. Davis and journalist Koji Nakamura, and on the following publications: *Kaibyaku* (the monthly newspaper of Zen Ai Kaigi), April 1983 and January 1984; Koji Nakamura's stories in *Far Eastern Economic Review,* October 16, 1971, and in *National Time* magazine (Australia), October 7, 1974; Donald Kirk's excellent look at the yakuza and the right in the *New York Times Magazine,* "Crime, Politics and Finger Cutting," December 12, 1976; and Kenji Ino's *Kodama Yoshio no Kyozo to Jitsuzo* (The Image and Reality of Yoshio Kodama) (1970).

Pp. 88–89: Even less exists on Seishi-kai than on Zen Ai Kaigi. See Ino, *Kodama Yoshio no . . .,* p. 35; *Sandei Mainichi,* November 2, 1969; *Daily Yomiuri,* March 17, 1969; and *New York Times,* January 7, 1970.

Pp. 91–92: The early life and rise of Kazuo Taoka is presented in the only other book in English on the yakuza, Florence Rome's lively account of her search for Japan's underworld, *The Tattooed Men* (1975). Much of her material evidently comes from Taoka's own three-volume autobiography, *Yamaguchi Gumi Sandaime* (Yamaguchi-gumi Third Generation) (1973). We have also relied upon a remarkable 1964 *Mainichi* newspaper series on the gangs (July 18–August 1, 1964) and on the *Mainichi Daily News,* May 24, 1982.

Pp. 92–93: Inagawa's early days are from a 1984 interview with him by the authors, and from numerous Japanese press clips. The U.S. cable on Inagawa's gang, dated August 9, 1950, is from the National Archives Embassy Post Files.

Pp. 93–96: All material and quotes on Kanto-kai are from a remarkable 14–part series on that coalition, the yakuza, and their links to Japanese politics that appeared in the newspaper *Mainichi* in 1964. The English version appeared in the *Mainichi Daily News* beginning July 18, 1964. It was a thorough and courageous look at the subject at a time when such investigative reporting was sorely lacking in the press.

Pp. 98–99: The alliance between the Yamaguchi-gumi and Inagawa-kai is described in the aforementioned *Mainichi* series and in Rome, *The Tattooed Men.*

The sakazuki ceremony was reported in *Mainichi Daily News,* December 6, 1972.

Chapter 4

Pp. 101–102: For Church's statement, and background on the Lockheed scandal, see "Hearings of the Subcommittee on Multinational Corporations of the Committee on Foreign Relations," U.S. Senate, February 4 and 6, 1976.

Pp. 102–103: Chalmers Johnson's quote is from his excellent three-part series on Kakuei Tanaka and the Lockheed scandal in the *Asian Wall Street Journal,* December 14, 15, and 16, 1983. The series is adapted from his paper, "The Rise and Decline of Tanaka Kakuei: The Problem of 'Structural Corruption' in the Japanese Political System." The events leading to Tanaka's resignation are detailed there and in Frank Gibney's *Japan: The Fragile Superpower* (1975), pp. 312–313.

Pp. 104–105: Kodama's dealings with Lockheed in the 1950s and 1960s are from the *New York Times,* March 1, 1976, and the *Sunday Times* (UK), March 7, 1976. His letter to Sato is cited in the *Asahi Evening News,* February 17, 1976.

P. 107: Kodama's ouster of ANA president Oba is described in the *Asian Wall Street Journal,* December 16, 1976, and *Asahi Evening News,* March 23, 1976.

P. 107: Sasakawa's role in the Lockheed scandal is reported in Robert Shaplen, "Annals of Crime: The Lockheed Incident," the *New Yorker,* January 23 and 30, 1978.

Pp. 108–109: The flow of Lockheed money into Japan, the role of Deak & Co., and the CIA's possible involvement are explored in the *New York Times,* March 1 and April 2, 1976, and in Tad Szulc's "The Money Changer," *The New Republic,* April 10, 1976.

P. 109: Osano's statement about his relations with Kodama is quoted in the *Japan Times,* July 22, 1976.

P. 110: Osano's Las Vegas tours and Hamada's huge losses are from varied press reports. See especially *Asahi Evening News,* March 14, 1980; *Daily Yomiuri,* March 7 and April 11, 1980; and *Japan Times,* June 24, 1974, and April 11, 1980.

P. 110: Mob connections to the Osano/Hamada tours are reported in *Asahi Evening News,* March 25, 1980; *Daily Yomiuri,* March 13, 1977; *Japan Times,* April 12, 1980; and *Mainichi Daily News,* April 12, 1980.

Pp. 110–111: Hamada's background is from "Hamada's Shady Past," a three-part series in *Mainichi Daily News,* April 12, 13, and 14, 1980; *Yomiuri Shimbun,* March 7, 1980; *Japan Times,* April 11, 1980; and *Mainichi Daily News,* February 25, 1978.

Pp. 112–113: Maeno's kamikaze attack on Kodama's home is from *Asahi Evening News,* March 24, 1976; *Far Eastern Economic Review,* April 2, 1976; *The Times* (UK), March 24, 1976; and David Boulton, *The Grease Machine* (1978), p. 270.

Pp. 115–116: Kodama's final days and funeral are described in *Japan Times,* January 24, 1984, and *Mainichi Daily News,* January 19, 1984.

P. 216: Kishi's dealings with the underworld are noted in *Shukan Asahi,* June 7, 1974; *Far Eastern Economic Review,* April 20, 1979; the *Los Angeles Times,* November 9, 1980; and *Mainichi Daily News,* October 9, 1971. A long list of prominent guests responding to the Taoka wedding invitation – including Kishi, Sasakawa, and Itoyama – is printed in the *Shukan Asahi* story.

P. 117: The younger Ohno's mob connections are detailed in various press clips. See, for example, *Daily Yomiuri,* December 12, 1982; *Japan Times,* October 27, 1980, and April 3, 1983; and *Mainichi Daily News,* November 28, 1982, and January 1 and April 3, 1983.

Pp. 117–118: Rokusuke Tanaka's use of yakuza in his campaigns is from *Japan Times,* December 23, 1983, and *Mainichi Daily News,* February 8, 1979.

P. 118: Dietman Tsukuda's affections for the mob are reported in *Asahi Evening News,* October 26, 1981; *Daily Yomiuri,* June 21, 1982; and *Mainichi Daily News,* October 26, 1981.

Pp. 118–119: Yakuza ties to local officials are detailed in numerous press reports. See, for example, *Asahi Evening News,* November 22, 1983; *Daily Yomiuri,* March 17, 1979, and February 7, 1981; and *Mainichi Daily News,* July 13, 1980.

Pp. 119–120: The expansion of yakuza political parties is reported in an *Asahi Shimbun* story, translated by the Asia Foundation and related to the U.S. press on September 21, 1981. Kamoda's brief political career is noted in *Japan Times,* January 27, 1980.

P. 120: The Eiji Sadaoka case comes from *Japan Times,* April 29, 1975.

P. 121: Statistics on the military are drawn from the Center for Defense Information's excellent summary of the debate over Japanese rearmament, "The Defense of Japan: Should the Rising Sun Rise Again?," *Defense Monitor,* vol. XIII, no.1.

P. 122: The shifting mood toward rearmament and glorifying imperial Japan is covered well in a series of Pacific News Service dispatches dated April 29 and December 1, 1982, and November 7, 1983.

P. 122: The sending of a gun to Prime Minister Sato by a yakuza was reported widely in Japan. See, for example, *Daily Yomiuri,* November 17, 1971, and *Japan Times,* September 30, 1971.

Chapter 5

Pp. 127–128: The Taoka shooting and its aftermath are described in numerous press clips. See, for example, *Asahi Evening News,* September 30, 1978; *Japan Times,* July 23, 1978; *Mainichi Daily News,* October 3, 1978; and *Shukan Jitsuwa,* August 13–20, 1978.

P. 129: The Yamaguchi-gumi press conference was covered widely. Clips were used from *Asahi Evening News,* December 16, 1978; *Daily Yomiuri,* October 12, 1978; and *Los Angeles Times,* November 9, 1978.

P. 130: Details of Taoka's death and funeral are from *Asahi Evening News,* July 25 and October 30, 1978; *Los Angeles Times,* November 9, 1978; *Mainichi Daily News,* October 21 and 27, 1981; and *Shukan Jitsuwa,* August 13–20, 1978.

Pp. 130–131: Fumiko Taoka's role is cited in *Mainichi Daily News,* June 16, 1982; and *Shukan Jitsuwa,* August 13–20, 1978.

Pp. 131–132: The Yamaguchi-gumi structure is described in *Mainichi Daily News,* June 3, 1981. Figures on the syndicate's income are from *Mainichi Shimbun,* February 13, 1984; *Mainichi Daily News,* April 16, 1977; and *Asahi Evening News,* March 29, 1979.

P. 133: Yakuza influence over the Japanese entertainment industry is from *Asahi Evening News,* June 9, 1976, and *Mainichi Daily News,* February 20, 1973.

Pp. 136–137: The Yamaguchi-gumi election and subsequent splitting are reported in numerous press clips. See, for example, *Asahi Evening News,* July 4, 1984, and *Mainichi Daily News,* June 20, 1984.

Pp. 137–138: The arrest of Takenaka's brother, Masashi, and Hideomi Oda quickly became one of Japan's biggest stories of 1985, and occurred just as this book was going into production. They are undoubtedly the most significant arrests yet of yakuza in the U.S. We've relied here on the criminal complaint filed in the case, no. 85–0207M in U.S. District Court, Honolulu, September 3, 1985; an attached affidavit by DEA Special Agent Robert A. Aiu; a related press release from the U.S. Department of Justice, also dated September 3; and interviews with law enforcement officials in Honolulu, September 4–13, 1985.

Pp. 138–139: Statistics on yakuza gangs and membership come from the National Police Agency's report, *Present State of Boryokudan (Organized Crime Groups) and Our Crackdown Operations* (1983), and miscellaneous press clips.

Pp. 139–140: Differences in syndicate structure were explained in an interview with Kanehiro Hoshino, Chief Researcher, National Research Institute of Police Science, Tokyo, March 7, 1984. The income of Sumiyoshi-rengo is cited in *Asahi Evening News,* March 29, 1979.

P. 141: Similarities between U.S. and Japanese organized crime groups are detailed in Chapter VI of anthropologist David Stark's *The Yakuza*, especially p. 241.

P. 141: Statistics on the number of U.S. Mafia members come from an interview with Lane Bonner of the FBI in Washington, D.C., August 1985; the President's Commission on Law Enforcement and Administration of Justice, *Task Force on Organized Crime Report* (1967); and Charles Grutzner, "How to Lock Out the Mafia," *Harvard Business Review*, March–April 1970, p. 47.

Pp. 144–145: Information on the bosozoku comes from Michael Uehara, "Japan's Nocturnal Nuisance," *PHP Magazine* (Tokyo), January 1984; *Japan Times*, May 4, 1982; and *Yomiuri Shimbun*, April 19, 1985.

Pp. 145–146: Stark's fascinating and gutsy field study was done as his doctoral thesis in anthropology at the University of Michigan, Ann Arbor, and is titled *The Yakuza: Japanese Crime Incorporated* (1981).

P. 146: The Yamaguchi-gumi's monthly magazine is described in Ames, *Police and Community . . .*, pp. 119–120; and in the *San Francisco Examiner*, July 25, 1981.

Pp. 147–148: The income and structure of Inagawa-kai is described in *Tokyo Shimbun*, February 5, 1975; *Shukan Sankei*, late August–early September 1981; *Asahi Evening News*, March 29, 1979; and *Daily Yomiuri*, November 27, 1974.

Pp. 152–153: The information on gang funerals and yakuza driving habits is from Stark, *The Yakuza*, pp. 136 and 139; *Hokubei Mainichi* (San Francisco), January 25, 1985; *Shukan Asahi*, October 26, 1984; and *Focus*, October 19, 1984.

Pp. 153–154: Paul Shrader's thorough analysis of the yakuza film genre is entitled "Yakuza Eiga: A Primer," and appears in *Film Comment* magazine, January 1974. Also used for this section are Ian Buruma's writings in the *Far Eastern Economic Review*, May 3, 1984, and in his book *Behind the Mask* (1984), especially pp. 189–190.

Chapter 6

Pp. 157–160: The story of the Osaka police scandal is based on numerous press clips and on a long article in the July 1983 issue of Japan's prestigious monthly *Bungei Shunju:* "Osaka Fukei Fushoku no Kozo" (The Corroded Structure of the Osaka Prefectural Police). Justice Minister Hatano's questionable actions, cited on pp. 159–160, are reported in the *Japan Times*, December 15, 1982; *Mainichi Daily News*, December 10, 1982; and the *Los Angeles Times*, November 5, 1983.

P. 161: The accounts of police corruption are described in various press reports. See, for example, *Japan Times*, September 9, 1969, and June 30, 1976; *Daily Yomiuri*, January 25, 1970, and July 6, 1976; and *Mainichi Daily News*, May 27, 1982, November 25, 1984, and January 15, 1985.

P. 161: Statistics on the crime rate in Japan come from the National Police Agency's *White Paper on Police 1983 (Excerpts),* p. 48; Ames, *Police and Community* . . ., p. 1; and "What Americans Can Learn from Japanese Prisons," *Parade,* January 15, 1984. No less than four books in English have appeared extolling the achievements of police in Japan. For a glowing account see David Bayley, *Forces of Order: Police Behavior in Japan and the United States* (1976). Bayley wrote of Japan as "Heaven for a Cop" and dismissed corruption as being "almost nonexistent." A more balanced account is Ames's *Police and Community in Japan* (1981); the remaining two are William Clifford, *Crime Control in Japan* (1976), and L. Craig Parker, Jr., *The Japanese Police System* (1984).

Pp. 161–162: The close relations between yakuza and police were detailed in confidential interviews with law enforcement officials in Tokyo; and in Ames, *Police and Community* . . ., especially pp. 107, 142, and 159.

Pp. 164–166: The section on bribery in Japan is based largely on the fascinating work of anthropologist Harumi Befu of Stanford University. See "Bribery in Japan: When Law Tangles with Culture," *The Self and the System;* and "An Ethnography of Dinner Entertainment in Japan," *Arctic Anthropology,* vol. XI–Suppl., 1974. Also useful is Gerald L. Curtis's *Election Campaigning Japanese Style* (1971), pp. 238–242. Tanaka's use of gift-giving to disburse political funds is from Chalmers Johnson's series on the prime minister in the *Asian Wall Street Journal,* December 15, 1983.

Pp. 167–168: Statistics on sarakin are based on reports in *Asahi Evening News,* April 12, 1984, and *Daily Yomiuri,* November 2 and 5, 1983. The investment of U.S. and Canadian firms in sarakin companies is cited in the *Asian Wall Street Journal,* October 30, 1984.

P. 169: The *Gendai* story comes from *Japan Times,* June 8, 1983, and *Mainichi Daily News,* July 9, 1983.

P. 169: The statistics on extortion in Yokohama are reported in the *Daily Yomiuri,* January 14, 1980.

Pp. 169–173: Background on the sokaiya comes from interviews with Japanese police and corporate executives, and from a wide range of newspaper and magazine articles. See especially *Nihon Keizai Shimbun,* January 10, 1978; *Daily Yomiuri,* August 30, 1978, and October 10, 1982; *International Management,* September 1983; the *Asian Wall Street Journal,* June 12, 1984, and July 4, 1985.

P. 172: Kodama's involvement in the sokaiya rackets is noted in *Asahi Evening News,* April 5 and June 7, 1976.

P. 172: Koike's antics are described in *Japan Times,* May 14, 1975.

P. 173: The importance of wa to the sokaiya is explained in an unpublished paper by Professor Eric M. von Hurst, "The Sokaiya Syndrome" (1973), pp. 2–3.

P. 174: Shimazaki's story is detailed in the *Daily Yomiuri,* February 20, 1973, and *Mainichi Daily News,* May 26, 1971.

Pp. 174–176: Background on the early history of Minamata Disease comes from Norrie Huddle and Michael Reich's important *Island of Dreams: Environmental Crisis in Japan* (1975), especially pp. 103, 107, 115, and 129.

Pp. 176–178: Chisso's repeated use of yakuza, sokaiya, and other thugs is described in countless stories from the Japanese press. See, for example, *Asahi Evening News,* June 4, 1971; *Japan Times,* June 2, June 4, and November 30, 1971; *Mainichi Daily News,* January 12, May 27, and November 30, 1971. The assault on W. Eugene Smith by Chisso's company goons was reported widely. See *Asahi Evening News,* April 10, 1974, and Eugene Smith and Aileen Smith, *Minamata* (1975), p. 86.

Pp. 178–179: The outcome of the Minamata tragedy is detailed in Huddle and Reich's *Island of Dreams,* pp. 129–131, and Smith and Smith's *Minamata,* p. 135.

Pp. 179–180: The sokaiya shift into new areas is from the National Police Agency report, *Present State of Boryokudan and Our Crackdown Operations* (1983); the *Asian Wall Street Journal,* June 12 and July 3, 1984; and *Daily Yomiuri,* October 10, 1982.

P. 182: The foreigners' description of their assault appeared in a letter in the *Japan Times Weekly,* December 19, 1981.

Pp. 182–183: Data on underreporting of crime in Japan comes from "The Police and the Situation of Public Safety in Japan," a speech given before the 1984 Interpol conference in Cairo by Masaharu Saitoh of the National Police Agency. See especially Table 3 of the appendix.

P. 183: Estimates of organized crime income in the United States are from *Newsweek,* January 5, 1981; and *Time,* May 16, 1977.

P. 183: Estimates of yakuza income are from an interview with Kenji Ino, March 1984; *Mainichi Shimbun,* January 4, 1984; *Mainichi Daily News,* November 3, 1984; National Police Agency, *Present State of Boryokudan . . .*; Ministry of Justice, *White Paper on Crime – 1978*; and press reports. Perhaps in response to criticism recent NPA estimates have been boosted from $4.5 billion to as high as $8 billion.

P. 183: Statistics on Japan's near-perfect conviction rate are cited in the *Christian Science Monitor,* March 11, 1981, and the *Los Angeles Times,* September 6, 1984. U.S. conviction rates are cited in the U.S. Department of Justice's *Report to the Nation on Crime and Justice* (1983), p. 65.

Pp. 183 and 185: The controversy over confessions in Japan is explored in the *Los Angeles Times,* September 6, 1984; *Daily Yomiuri,* March 4, 1984; Ames,

Police and Community . . ., p. 136; and Chalmers Johnson, *Conspiracy at Matsukawa*, Chapter 4.

P. 185: The attitudes of Japanese law enforcement toward yakuza operating abroad is based on numerous interviews with ranking officers of the Tokyo Metropolitan Police Department and the National Police Agency, January–March 1984, as well as with both local and federal U.S. law enforcement officials.

Chapter 7

Pp. 189–190: The events leading up to Kim's kidnapping are described in U.S. House of Representatives, *Hearings before the Subcommittee on International Organizations of the Committee on International Relations*, "Activities of the Korean Central Intelligence Agency in the United States," part I, March 17, 1976, pp. 12–13. See also *San Francisco Chronicle*, January 13, 1985; and *Mother Jones*, May 1985.

Pp. 189–190: Background on the KCIA is drawn from *Hearings* . . ., p. 12; Robert Boettcher, *Gifts of Deceit: Sun Myung Moon, Tongsun Park, and the Korean Scandal* (1980), pp. 23–30; and the *New York Times*, August 20, 1973.

Pp. 190–191: Kim's statements are from an interview with the authors in December 1984. His kidnapping is described in the *Asian Wall Street Journal*, August 17, 1978; *New York Times*, August 15, 1973; *San Francisco Chronicle*, January 13, 1985; and a U.S. Department of State cable, U.S. Embassy (Seoul) to Washington, D.C., "Account of Kim Tae Chung's Kidnapping," August 1973.

P. 191: The KCIA's involvement in Kim's kidnapping is from Ranard's testimony in *Hearings* . . ., March 17, 1976; *Japan Times*, February 8, 1984; *Mainichi Daily News*, September 25, 1973; and *Asahi Evening News*, September 26, 1973.

Pp. 191–192: Machii's alleged role in the kidnapping is discussed in *Shukan Gendai*, August 30, 1973; Takao Goto, *Koria Uochiya* (Korea Watcher) (1982), p. 94; and the *Far Eastern Economic Review*, November 12, 1973, and May 13, 1974. Other possible yakuza involvement is cited in *Koria Uochiya*, p. 93; and *Mainichi Daily News*, February 8, 1977.

Pp. 193–195: Machii's early background was pieced together from interviews with his American business partner, Ken Ross, and with Tokyo Metropolitan Police officials. Also consulted were the following articles: *Shukan Bunshun*, "Kankoku Kara Kita Otoko" ("The Man Came from Korea"), three-part series, June 23, June 30, and July 7, 1977; *Shukan Shincho*, July 26, 1973; and *Mainichi Daily News*, November 20, 1964.

P. 195: Machii's contacts with high-ranking Korean officials are detailed in *Ekonomisto*, March 16, 1976; *Shukan Shincho*, July 18, 1970; *Asahi Evening News*, March 20, 1976; and the leading Korean monthly, *Wolgan Chosen*, February 1984. His gang's continued criminal activities are noted, among other places, in *Yomiuri Shimbun*, June 8, 1975.

P. 197: The yakuza's big move into South Korea is reported in *Tokyo Shimbun,* February 12, 1975; and *Daily Yomiuri,* June 8 and October 20, 1975.

P. 198: Smuggling in Korea is detailed in numerous clips from the *Korea Herald,* an English daily in Seoul. The case of the smuggled uhwangchongsimhwan is from the *Herald,* January 30 and April 17, 1980.

P. 199: The markup on amphetamine sales is from the *Japan Times,* October 15, 1983; and the NPA's *Present State of Boryokudan.* . . .

P. 199: The striking number of speed users in Japan is cited in numerous press reports. See *Daily Yomiuri,* September 2, 1984; *Japan Times Weekly,* July 28, 1984; and *Japan Times,* March 14, 1982. Additional background comes from the NPA's "Drug Problem in Japan," 1979, and "Drug Problem in Japan," 1983.

Pp. 199–200: The Sadoaka-gumi report is featured in *Asahi Geino,* March 15, 1984. Also of note is a $200 million annual smuggling operation described in an *Asahi Shimbun* story translated by the Asia Foundation and released to the U.S. press on December 18, 1981. The quote from *Wolgan Chosen* is from its February 1984 issue.

Pp. 201–202: Information on Kisaeng tourism in this section is drawn from confidential interviews in Seoul and from Korea Church Women United, *Kisaeng Tourism* (1984), pp. 10–12, 19–20; the characterization of Korean prostitutes as "unpersons" is from Paul S. Crane, *Korea Patterns* (1967), pp. 29–30, 128.

Pp. 202–204: The state of prostitution in Southeast Asia is described in "Hospitality Girls in the Philippines," *Southeast Asia Chronicle,* January–February 1979; and in "Prostitution in Asia," a background paper prepared by Sister Mary Soledad Perpinan, Manila, for the General Assembly of the World Council of Churches, 1983.

Pp. 203–204: The number of prostitutes in East Asia is cited in *Kisaeng Tourism,* pp. 24–25; the *Progressive,* February 1985; *Far Eastern Economic Review,* January 9, 1976; *Action Bulletin,* a newsletter of the Third World Movement against the Exploitation of Women, March 1981; and Kathleen Barry et al., *International Feminism: Networking against Female Sexual Slavery* (1984), p. 39.

P. 204: Sasakawa's "tourist paradise" on Lubang is from *Action Bulletin,* March and July 1981; *Japan Times,* May 25, 1981; and *Mainichi Daily News,* April 15, 1981. The Casio story is from the *New York Times,* August 5, 1979.

Pp. 204–205: Government complicity in the sex trade was acknowledged by leading journalists in Seoul and Manila. See also *Kisaeng Tourism,* pp. 17 and 26; and the *Progressive,* February and March 1985.

P. 206: Background on the karayuki-san is from Mikiso Hane, *Peasants, Rebels, and Outcasts: The Underside of Modern Japan* (1982), pp. 207, 218–225.

Pp. 206–208: Background on the Japayuki-san is from "Women in Crisis in Japan," information sheet, Japan Women's Christian Temperance Union, Tokyo, undated (circa 1983); and *Daily Yomiuri,* August 5, 1984. For specific cases of the sex trade, see *Asahi Evening News,* September 7, 1974; *Daily Yomiuri,* April 25, 1984, and October 16, 1973; and *Bangkok Post,* February 17, 1984.

P. 207: The slave auction is reported in *Asian Women's Liberation,* no. 6, 1984, Asian Women's Association, Tokyo. Prices for buying and leasing Filipinas are from *Mainichi Daily News,* February 24, 1985.

Pp. 208–210: Yakuza investment in the Philippines is described in the *Times-Journal* (Manila), November 12 and December 8, 1982; and the U.S. Drug Enforcement Administration report, "A Brief History of Japanese Organized Crime" (1979). Machii's syndicate investments are cited in *Daily Yomiuri,* June 8, 1975, and *Mainichi Daily News,* February 16, 1975.

Pp. 210–211: Yakuza expansion across East Asia is reported in *Tokyo Shimbun,* February 5, 1975; *Yomiuri Shimbun,* June 8, 1975; and *Daily Yomiuri,* December 22, 1981.

Pp. 211–212: History of the Triads is taken from Fenton Bresler, *The Chinese Mafia* (1980), pp. 28–32, 39; and Sean O'Callaghan, *The Triads* (1978), pp. 11, 48–49. Chiang's Triad membership and close relationship with the gangs is covered at length in Sterling Seagrave's *The Soong Dynasty* (1985).

Pp. 212–213: The impact of the KMT Army remnants, Western intelligence agencies, and organized crime on the Golden Triangle heroin trade is detailed in Alfred W. McCoy's superb *The Politics of Heroin in Southeast Asia* (1972). See especially pp. 7–8, 92–95, 223, 232, and 315. See also the more recent work of John McBeth in the *Far Eastern Economic Review,* particularly December 27, 1984.

Pp. 214–215: Statistics on heroin and other opiate confiscations in Japan are from the NPA's "Drug Problem in Japan," 1983. Specific cases cited are from *Japan Times,* March 13, 1971; *Mainichi Daily News,* November 27, 1984, and January 23, 1985; and *Japan Times Weekly,* February 23, 1985.

Pp. 217: Yakuza activity in Hong Kong is described in a confidential report by D. M. Hodson, Interpol Bureau, Royal Hong Kong Police, "Organized Crime in Japan," December 19, 1980; *Daily Yomiuri,* March 4, 1978; *Far Eastern Economic Review,* December 27, 1984; and the NPA's "Drug Problem in Japan," 1983.

P. 218: The huge arms seizures are from the *Bangkok Post,* November 25, 1977, and October 26, 1981.

Pp. 218–219: Yakuza activity on Taiwan is reported in *Yomiuri Shimbun,* June 8, 1975, and *Mainichi Daily News,* February 16, 1975. The alleged involvement of the Dominican ambassador was reported widely. See, for example, Kyodo News Service dispatch, August 2, 1984, and *Mainichi Daily News,* July 30, 1984.

P. 219: Information on the alliance between Taiwanese and Japanese syndicates was obtained in an interview by our associate with Bamboo Gang members in Los Angeles, 1985. The alliances were also discussed in the *Far Eastern Economic Review*, December 27, 1984. The United Bamboo Gang's "meeting of the mobs" in Hong Kong was featured in *Newsweek,* April 1, 1985.

Pp. 220–221: Yakuza activity in Brazil is described in two of that nation's leading newspapers, *Folha de São Paulo,* September 18, 1983, and *Jornal do Brasil,* February 22, 1985; and in a series of 1984 interviews by our associate Michael Kepp with Antonio Carlos Fon of *Isto E,* Brazil's second-largest newsweekly; Ari de Moraes of *Diario Popular,* a São Paulo daily; and William Kimura, editor of *Diario Nipak,* a bilingual daily in São Paulo.

P. 222: Yakuza activity in Europe in described in an internal report by the U.S. Immigration and Naturalization Service, *Strategic Assessment: Asian Organized Crime,* March 1, 1985, and in various newsclips. See, for example, the *Guardian,* May 20, 1979; *Asahi Evening News,* May 22 and 23, 1979; *Japan Times,* March 1, 1983; and *Daily Yomiuri,* December 29, 1982. Sokaiya in Europe are noted in the *Wall Street Journal,* April 16, 1981; and *Daily Yomiuri,* October 10, 1982, and June 4, 1984.

P. 223: Yakuza activity in Australia is based on a 1985 radio report by the Australian Broadcasting Corporation, Sydney, "Background Briefing: The Yakuza," and is noted in *Newsweek,* February 11, 1985. Gang interest in the Pacific islands is from the Drug Enforcement Administration's "A Brief History of Japanese Organized Crime," 1979.

Chapter 8

P. 229: A good analysis of the Hawaiian tourist industry appears in Noel Kent's *Hawaii: Islands under the Influence* (1983). See especially p. 177.

Pp. 229–230: The 1978 report of the Hawaii Crime Commission, *Organized Crime in Hawaii,* was an excellent beginning for a state probe. This quotation comes from p. 9 of the report. It is unfortunate that the Crime Commission trod on too many sensitive and important toes; power was withdrawn from the commission, and its funding sharply curtailed, after this report intimated that the commission could name names among the powerful in Hawaii with links to organized crime. For background on the commission, see C. F. Wang, *Hawaii State and Local Politics,* pp. 523–528. The trial of Henry Huihui was covered by the Honolulu papers as well as the *New York Times* and Associated Press.

Pp. 230–231: Most day-to-day reporting on the yakuza in Hawaii appears in the *Honolulu Advertiser* under Jim Dooley's byline. Dooley, a transplanted Californian, has become the premier crime reporter on Hawaii, and has undoubtedly written more on the yakuza than any other American newspaper reporter.

Pp. 231–234: Much of the reporting on Inada, Yonekura, and other yakuza in Hawaii appears in various reports by Jim Dooley in the *Honolulu Advertiser*. See especially his four-part series on the gangs beginning March 19, 1978. We also relied on numerous interviews with Honolulu law enforcement sources, on a valuable internal 1979 U.S. Customs report, "Yakuza – Japanese Organized Crime," and on the following press clips: Inada – *Honolulu Advertiser*, March 20 and December 17, 1980; *Penthouse*, April 1983; Yonekura – *Honolulu Advertiser*, March 19, 1980, *Rafu Shimpo* (Los Angeles), March 31, 1982, and a federal sentencing memorandum on Yonekura, U.S. District Court (Hawaii), Cr. No. 79-00418.

Pp. 234–236: The Three Mules case is detailed in a U.S. Drug Enforcement Administration document obtained under the Freedom of Information Act, *Report of Investigation R4-76-0055,* May 11, 1979, Honolulu; U.S. Customs report, "Yakuza . . ."; and Jim Dooley's August 29, 1979, article in the *Advertiser.*

Pp. 236–237: Background on Charlie Higa is based on confidential interviews with Honolulu law enforcement officials; the *Honolulu Star-Bulletin*, January 25, 1984; and Jim Dooley's articles in the *Honolulu Advertiser*, September 22, 23, and 29, 1983.

Pp. 237–238: Background on Kaoru Ogawa is based on confidential interviews with police in Hawaii and Japan; *Mainichi Daily News*, January 19, 1980; *Shukan Yomiuri*, May 30, 1982; and the *Honolulu Advertiser*, August 15 and 18, 1982.

P. 238: Osano's activities in Las Vegas are covered in Chapter 4. For this section we've also drawn on confidential interviews with Hawaii law enforcement officials; *Asahi Evening News*, October 5, 1974; and *Japan Times*, June 24, 1974.

Chapter 9

P. 241: The headlines cited are from the *Los Angeles Times*, November 14, 1981, and *USA Today*, November 28, 1983, respectively. They are not the only inflammatory headlines to hit the stands.

P. 242 and 249: California's Organized Crime and Criminal Intelligence Bureau rearranged its name to Bureau of Organized Crime and Criminal Intelligence to take advantage of the acronym BOCCI. The agency issues a report yearly. The quote on p. 249 is taken from *Organized Crime in California: 1981.*

Pp. 242–244: Testimony at the President's Commission on Organized Crime was recorded in the commission's preliminary transcripts, dated October 23, 1984, and in numerous press clips.

P. 245: The quote on Japanese morphine in North America is from the U.S. government's *Annual Report of the Bureau of Narcotics*, 1932, p. 10.

Pp. 245–247: Information on prewar Japanese narcotics dealing in the U.S. appears, for the most part, in the Bureau of Narcotics annual reports, 1930–1942. These are not the most objective of reports, but they are based on arrest and court records. For a detailed and scholarly treatment of Chinese and Japanese involvement in the prewar heroin trade, see Jonathan Marshall's excellent study, "Opium and the Politics of Gangsterism in Nationalist China, 1927–1945," in the *Bulletin of Concerned Asian Scholars,* July–September 1977. For a propagandistic, but interesting, look at the Japanese narcotics trade, see Violet Sweet Haven's book *Gentlemen of Japan* (1944). Also see Harry J. Anslinger's *The Protectors* (1964), p. 31.

Pp. 246–247: Information on the Tokyo Club was gathered by Isami Arifuku Waugh, primarily from reports in the rich Bancroft Library collections at the University of California, Berkeley. Ms. Waugh's findings were published in her 1978 doctoral thesis for the University of California (Berkeley) School of Criminology, *Hidden Crime and Deviance in the Japanese-American Community, 1920–1946.* See also James Oda's controversial, self-published history, *Heroic Struggles of Japanese Americans* (1981); and *Rafu Shimpo* (Los Angeles), October 20, 1930, and other stories.

P. 247: The quote on the Tokyo Club appeared in the now defunct Japanese-American daily *Pacific Citizen* (Los Angeles), September 19, 1949. It ran under the "Nisei USA" column.

Pp. 248–249: The Leo Orii story is based on two interviews with Mr. Orii in 1982; on interviews with LAPD and other officials, 1982–1985; and on confidential law enforcement reports.

Pp. 250–251: Machii's activities in the U.S. are based on interviews with his American business partner, Kenneth Ross, in 1982 and 1985; on confidential law enforcement reports; and on a television segment from ABC's *20/20* newsmagazine, "Japan's Other Exports," May 27, 1982.

Pp. 251–254: Reporting on the "white slavery" trade is from interviews with hostesses and entertainers in the U.S. and Japan by the authors and our associates, and from numerous press clips. See, for example, *San Francisco Examiner,* May 6, 1982, and August 10, 1983; *Los Angeles Times,* April 13, 1982; *Japan Times,* April 17, 1981, and June 13, 1982; *Playgirl* magazine, "White Slaves," November 1982; and *Penthouse,* "Yakuza," April 1983. See also "Japan's Other Exports," from ABC's *20/20* newsmagazine, May 27, 1982.

P. 252: Sather's quotes on the image of Western women in Japan are from *Hostesses* (1984), her master's thesis in journalism for the University of California at Berkeley.

Pp. 254–255: For a historical look at guns and gun control in Japan, see Noel Perrin's fascinating *Giving Up the Gun* (1979). Information on gun smuggling comes from numerous interviews with U.S. and Japanese law enforcement officials and from varied press accounts. See especially *Japan Times,* July 15, 1966, December 20, 1980, April 17, 1981, and November 21, 1981; *Sankei Shimbun,* July 15, 1981; *Mainichi Daily News,* July 1, 1976; and *Asahi Evening News,* July 7, 1976. Information on the Guam case comes, in part, from a Bureau of Alcohol, Tobacco and Firearms investigative report, Honolulu, July 24, 1980; Indictment, U.S. District Court of Guam, Criminal Case CR82 00015; and the *Pacific Daily News* (Guam), March 5 and March 18, 1982.

Pp. 258–259: The Steve Conn case is drawn from interviews with law enforcement officials, Mr. Conn, and his publicist, Davy Rosenberg. See also *San Francisco Chronicle,* June 19, 1984.

Pp. 259–262: Sasakawa's activities in the U.S. are constant and fascinating. Our story is based on interviews with Mr. Sasakawa, Rocky Aoki, Richard Petree, and New Jersey law enforcement officials; various documents of the U.S.-Japan Foundation; and numerous press clips. See especially "Soft Core Fascism," by the authors, in the *Village Voice,* October 4, 1984; *New York Times,* July 11, 1978; and, for an in-depth look at Sasakawa and Atlantic City, John Mintz's excellent report in the *Trenton Times* (New Jersey), February 8, 1981.

Pp. 262–263: Sokaiya activities in the U.S. are from confidential police reports; *Wall Street Journal,* April 16, 1981; *Shukan Bunshun,* May 7, 1981; and "The Yakuza Are Coming," by the authors in *California Living,* the Sunday magazine of the *Los Angeles Herald Examiner,* February 6, 1983.

Pp. 265–266: Information on yakuza activity in Las Vegas comes from police sources and numerous press clips. See *Yomiuri Shimbun,* June 22, 1975; *Mainichi Daily News,* June 29, 1975; *Japan Times,* July 23, 1982, and October 19, 1975. The Mizuno case is based on various press reports. See, for example, Jim Dooley's piece in the *Honolulu Advertiser,* July 19, 1982.

Pp. 266–268: The crackdown on the yakuza is from police sources and, in part, the following documents: Memorandum, U.S. Department of Justice Organized Crime Strike Force, San Francisco Office, December 12, 1983; *Honolulu Advertiser,* April 23, 1983, and May 25, 1984; and *Honolulu Star-Bulletin,* December 1, 1983.

Epilogue

P. 271: Inagawa's comments are from his Tokyo interview with the authors, February 9, 1984.

Pp. 271–272: The changing nature of the yakuza was detailed in two interviews with Kanehiro Hoshino of the National Research Institute of Police Science, Tokyo, February 10 and March 7, 1984. Professor Hoshino's conclusions are backed up by the prolific work of the institute's researchers from 1968 to 1985, which includes many of the most comprehensive surveys and reports on the yakuza in Japan. See, for example, Hoshino with Fumio Mugishima and Kenji

Kiyonaga, "Boryokudan-in no Danshi to Shisei: Boryokudan no Dentoteki Fukuji Bunka no Kenkyu" (Tattooing and Finger Joint Cutting by Organized Crime Members) (1971); a series of subsequent studies by Fumio Mugishima, "Boryokudan-in to Dantai to no Kankei ni Kansuru Kenkyu" (Follow-up Survey of Organized Crime Members) (1974); and, in English, Hoshino's "The Recent Trend of Underworld and Organized Crime in Japan" (1979). A number of press clips also discuss the yakuza's transformation. See, for example, *Asahi Shimbun,* February 2, 1984; and *Mainichi Daily News,* October 24 and 25, 1984.

P. 272: The anonymous oyabun's quote is cited in George De Vos, *Socialization for Achievement,* pp. 294–295.

P. 273: The quote from Tokyo police is taken from *Mainichi Daily News,* February 9, 1984.

P. 274: The statistics on shooting incidents are from *Mainichi Daily News,* February 9, 1984; and *Japan Times Weekly,* August 11, 1984. The police quotes are from *Mainichi Daily News,* March 31, 1984. David Bayley's comment is from his *Forces of Order,* p. 6. The figure of 200 million firearms in the U.S. comes from a Bureau of Alcohol, Tobacco and Firearms internal report dated December 1, 1983, "Tracing of Recovered Firearms." The report further states that 55 million of these are handguns, and that an additional 5.5 million firearms are manufactured here annually, of which 2.4 million are handguns.

P. 275: The changing patterns of crime in Japan are reported in *Japan Times Weekly,* August 11, 1984; *Mainichi Daily News,* October 29, 1980, and October 31, 1979.

Pp. 276–277: The 1984 visit to Zen Ai Kaigi included an interview by the authors with Donshyo Kawasaki, office manager of the association's Tokyo headquarters, March 8, 1984. The copies of Zen Ai Kaigi's monthly tabloid, *Kaibyaku,* are dated April 1983 and January 1984.

P. 277: The Morris quote is from his landmark study *Nationalism and the Right Wing in Japan,* pp. 421–423.

P. 281: The characterization of organized crime as theft is explored at length in Jonathan Kwitny's fine book, *Vicious Circles: The Mafia in the Marketplace* (1979). Kwitny's quote is from p. 70.

Cast of Key Characters

Chobei Banzuiin – a famous seventeenth-acentury gangster with a reputation for protecting the common people. Chobei is seen by the yakuza as one of their earliest ancestors.

Kakuji Inagawa – the powerful godfather of the Inagawa-kai, and the senior statesman of the Japanese underworld today.

Tokutaru Kimura – known as "Japan's Joe McCarthy." As justice minister in 1952, Kimura organized yakuza into a nationwide anticommunist federation called the Patriotic Drawn Sword Regiment.

Nobusuke Kishi – prime minister from 1957 to 1960. Designated a Class A war criminal, but never tried. A close associate of Kodama's, Kishi returned to power a wide array of prewar rightists. His administration relied heavily on the underworld to counter leftist demonstrations.

Yoshio Kodama – one of Japan's most powerful men until his death in 1984. An extraordinary character: ultranationalist, multimillionaire, CIA agent, war criminal, yakuza godfather, LDP powerhouse. The one man most responsible for the postwar resurrection of the yakuza.

Hisayuki Machii – the immensly wealthy ethnic Korean godfather who became known as the Ginza Tiger for his gang's control of nightclubs in Tokyo. A close ally of Kodama and Taoka, Machii established ties with U.S. and Korean intelligence after the war.

Yasuhiro Nakasone – elected prime minister of Japan in 1982 and again in 1984. A former protégé of Kodama, Nakasone has long pushed for Japan's rearmament and revision of the antiwar constitution.

Kaoru Ogawa – Japan's most influential racketeer, according to police reports. One of the nation's leading sokaiya, who tried to export sokaiya techniques to Hawaii.

Kenji Osano – one of the richest men in Japan, with vast holdings in Hawaii. Found guilty of perjury in the Lockheed bribery case; widely associated with the "dark world" of Japanese politics.

Ryoichi Sasakawa – one of Japan's richest, most influential men. Controls the immensly lucrative monopoly over speedboat racing. Like Kodama, an ultra-nationalist, war criminal, multimillionaire, political powerhouse, and yakuza associate.

Shimizu no Jirocho – the most famous gangster in Japanese history. A nineteenth-century gambler, Jirocho's Robin Hood image is enshrined in dozens of songs, stories, and plays.

Kazuo Taoka – until his death in 1981, the unchallenged head of the Yamaguchi-gumi. Widely acknowledged as the Japanese "godfather of godfathers" during his reign.

Mitsuru Toyama – the grand old man of the Japanese ultranationalist movement. Instrumental in founding the Dark Ocean and Black Dragon societies, and in plunging Japan into World War II.

Charles Willoughby – the major general in charge of U.S. Army Intelligence under General MacArthur in the Pacific. His agents recruited yakuza to spy on and disrupt the left in U.S.-occupied Japan.

Glossary

Bakuto – gambler, used especially to refer to the roadside bands of gamblers in feudal Japan. One of the three historic types of Japanese gangster, along with tekiya and gurentai.

Boryokudan – literally, violence groups. Used by Japanese police to refer to yakuza.

Bosozoku – motorcycle and hot-rod gangs, a prime source of yakuza recruits.

Burakumin – the members of Japan's ancestral class of outcasts, perennial victims of discrimination. Another prime source of yakuza recruits.

G-2 – U.S. Army Intelligence under the occupation, headed by Major General Charles Willoughby. Used yakuza and rightists to spy on and disrupt the left.

Genyosha – the Dark Ocean Society, Japan's first modern ultranationalist group, founded in 1881. Pioneered the fusion between gangsters and rightists.

GHQ – General Headquarters of the Allied Powers during the occupation of Japan, led by General Douglas Mac-Arthur. The center of U.S. power in Japan from 1945 to 1952.

Giri – closest translation is debt or obligation, but the concept entails much

more. Often used with the word *ninjo* by yakuza to describe the basis for their "honorable" traditions.

Gumi – a suffix denoting association, company or gang, commonly used by both yakuza groups and construction firms.

Gurentai – ruffian or hoodlum, the ruthless gangsters who grew amid the black markets of postwar Japan. One of the three historic types of Japanese gangster, along with bakuto and tekiya.

Gyakkosu – or "reverse course." The abrupt political shift in U.S. occupation policy beginning in 1947 that turned against the left and labor movement.

Ichiwa-kai – the Osaka-based splinter group from the Yamaguchi-gumi. Japan's fifth-largest yakuza syndicate.

Inagawa-kai – Japan's fourth-largest syndicate, led by the powerful Kakuji Inagawa and based in the Tokyo-Yokohama region. Inagawa-kai was among the first syndicates to venture abroad.

Kai – a suffix denoting association or society, often used in gang names.

Kanto-kai – Yoshio Kodama's dream of a unified underworld fashioned into a national political force. A coalition of syndicates largely from Tokyo's Kanto plain, the Kanto-kai fell apart after 15 months, in 1965.

Kobun – "child role," used in conjunction with oyabun ("parent role") to connote the familial relationship within most yakuza gangs.

Kokuryu-kai – the Amur River Society, also known as the Black Dragon Society. A leading ultranationalist group founded in 1901 and a direct descendant of the Dark Ocean Society.

Kuromaku – literally, black curtain, a term from traditional Kabuki theater. Now used to connote a behind-the-scenes fixer, godfather, or power broker.

LDP – Liberal-Democratic Party, a coalition of largely conservative factions that have dominated Japanese politics since 1955.

Mizu shobai – "water business" or "water trades," meaning nightclubs, bars, restaurants, and related businesses.

Ninjo – compassion or empathy. Often used with "giri" obligation to describe the Japanese conflict between one's duty and one's feelings; a central theme in Japanese literature. Both are favorite terms of traditional yakuza.

NPA – the National Police Agency, the central agency for administration and control of Japanese police, including all prefectural and local forces.

Oyabun – "parent figure," used with kobun to describe the familial relationship within the gang. Somewhat similar to the use of "godfather" in the West.

Prefecture – the Japanese equivalent of a U.S. state, but geographically about the size of most U.S. counties.

Ronin – masterless samurai, the source of countless legends about good and evil in medieval Japan.

Sangokujin – "people of three countries." The name for the Taiwanese, Koreans, and Chinese who were brought to Japan as wartime labor. Yakuza fought pitched battles with them over control of black markets in the immediate postwar years.

Sarakin – "salary man financiers," or, more appropriately, loan sharks.

SCAP – Supreme Commander for the Allied Powers, the official title of General MacArthur's command during the U.S. occupation of Japan, 1945 to 1952.

Sokaiya – "general meeting specialists," Japan's unique breed of financial racketeer. Professional extortionists and strong-arm thugs who traditionally prey on shareholders' meetings, but are now diversified into wide areas of organized crime.

Sumiyoshi-rengo – the Tokyo-based federation of gangs with operations throughout much of Japan and abroad. The nation's second-largest yakuza group with an organization similar to that of the American Mafia.

Tekiya – street stall operators and peddlers. One of the three historic types of Japanese gangster, along with bakuto and gurentai.

Tokugawa era – Japan's final period of feudalism, ruled by a succession of shogun from 1603 to 1868. During most of this time, Japanese rulers deliberately isolated the nation from the rest of the world.

Towa Yuai Jigyo Kumiai – East Asia Friendship Enterprise Association, the heavily Korean yakuza syndicate founded by crime boss Hisayuki Machii. With fewer than 1000 members, the group is still one of the most active overseas.

Triads – Chinese organized crime syndicates. With strong bases in Hong Kong, Taiwan, and Thailand, the gangs

control the Southeast Asia heroin trade
and are perhaps the single biggest force in
international organized crime today.

Yamaguchi-gumi – Japan's largest crime
syndicate, with a membership of more
than 12,000 under the leadership of
Kazuo Taoka. After Taoka's death in
1981, the syndicate split into two
factions, but still boasts some 10,000
members. The syndicate is very active
overseas.

Yubitsume – the ritual act within the
yakuza of slicing the joint of the little
finger to atone for a mistake.

Zen Ai Kaigi – the fiery coalition of
ultranationalist groups in Japan. Jokingly
called Yakuza Kaigi because of its large
gang membership.

Bibliography

Books: English

Allen, Louis, *Japan: The Years of Triumph*. London: Purnell & Sons, 1971.

Ames, Walter L., *Police and Community in Japan*. Berkeley: University of California Press, 1981.

Anslinger, Harry J., *The Protectors*. New York: Farrar, Straus & Co., 1964.

Arifuku-Waugh, Isami, *Hidden Crime and Deviance in the Japanese-American Community, 1920–1946*. Ph.D thesis, University of California School of Criminology, 1978.

Barnett, Richard J., *The Alliance*. New York: Simon & Schuster, 1983.

Barry, Kathleen, et al., *International Feminism: Networking against Female Sexual Slavery*. New York: published by the authors, 1984.

Bayley, David H., *Forces of Order: Police Behavior in Japan and the United States*. Berkeley: University of California Press, 1976.

Beasley, W. G., *The Modern History of Japan*. New York: Praeger Publishers, 1963.

Benedict, Ruth, *The Chrysanthemum and the Sword: Patterns of Japanese Culture*. New York: World Publishing Company, 1946.

Boettcher, Robert, *Gifts of Deceit: Sun Myung Moon, Tongsun Park, and the Korea Scandal*. New York: Holt, Rinehart & Winston, 1980.

Boulton, David, *The Grease Machine*. New York: Harper & Row, 1978.

Bresler, Fenton, *The Chinese Mafia*. New York: Stein & Day, 1980.

Brown, Delmer M., *Nationalism in Japan*. New York: Russell & Russell, 1955.

Buruma, Ian, *Behind the Mask*. New York: Pantheon Books, 1984.

Craig, William, *The Fall of Japan*. New York: Dial Press, 1967.

Crane, Paul S., *Korea Patterns*. Seoul: Royal Asiatic Society, 1978.

Curtis, Gerald L., *Election Campaigning Japanese Style*. Tokyo: Kodansha, 1983.

Deacon, Richard, *Kempei Tai: A History of the Japanese Secret Service*. New York: Berkley Books, 1985.

De Vos, George A., *Socialization for Achievement*. Berkeley: University of California Press, 1973.

Dore, R. P., *Aspects of Social Change in Modern Japan*. Princeton: Princeton University Press, 1967.

Dower, J. W., *Empire and Aftermath: Yoshida Shigeru and the Japanese Experience*. Cambridge: Harvard University Press, 1979.

Duus, Peter, *The Rise of Modern Japan*. Boston: Houghton Mifflin Co., 1976.

Gayn, Mark, *Japan Diary*. Tokyo: Charles E. Tuttle, 1948.

Gibney, Frank, *Japan: The Fragile Superpower*. New York: W. W. Norton & Co., 1975.

Hane, Michiso, *Peasants, Rebels, and Outcasts: The Underside of Modern Japan*. New York: Random House, 1982.

Haven, Violet Sweet, *Gentlemen of Japan*. New York: Ziff-Davis, 1944.

Hobsbawm, Eric, *Bandits*. New York: Dell Publishing Co., 1969.

Hougan, James, *Spooks*. New York: William Morrow & Co., 1978.

Huddle, Norrie, and Michael Reich, *Island of Dreams: Environmental Crisis in Japan*. Tokyo: Autumn Press, 1975.

Johnson, Chalmers, *Conspiracy at Matsukawa*. Berkeley: University of California Press, 1972.

Kent, Noel, *Hawaii: Islands under the Influence*. New York: Monthly Review Press, 1983.

Kodama, Yoshio, *I Was Defeated*. Tokyo: Robert Booth and Taro Fukuda, 1951.

——, *Sugamo Diary*. Tokyo: Taro Fukuda, 1960.

Korea Church Women United, *Kisaeng Tourism*. Seoul: Catholic Publishing House, 1984.

Kwitny, Jonathan, *Vicious Circles: The Mafia in the Marketplace*. New York: W. W. Norton & Co., 1979.

Lebra, Takie Sugiyama, *Japanese Patterns of Behavior*. Honolulu: University of Hawaii Press, 1974.

Lebra, Takie Sugiyama, and William P. Lebra, *Japanese Culture and Behavior*. Honolulu: University of Hawaii Press, 1976.

Lee, Changsoo, and George De Vos, et al., *Koreans in Japan*. Berkeley: University of California Press, 1981.

Livingston, Jon, et al., *Imperial Japan: 1800–1945*. New York: Random House, 1973.

Livingston, Jon, et. al., *Postwar Japan: 1945 to the Present*. New York: Random House, 1973.

McCoy, Alfred W., *The Politics of Heroin in Southeast Asia*. New York: Harper & Row, 1972.

Morris, Dr. I. I., *Nationalism and the Right Wing in Japan*. London: Oxford University Press, 1960.

Nakane, Chie, *Japanese Society*. Berkeley: University of California Press, 1973.

Nelli, Humbert S., *The Business of Crime*. Chicago: University of Chicago Press, 1976.

Nishi, Toshio, *Unconditional Democracy*. Stanford: Hoover Institute Press, 1982.

O'Callaghan, Sean, *The Triads*. London: W. H. Allen & Co., 1978.

Oda, James, *Heroic Struggles of Japanese Americans*. Hollywood: James Oda, 1980.

Packard, George R., *Protest in Tokyo: The Security Treaty Crisis of 1960*. Princeton: Princeton University Press, 1966.

Parker, L. Craig, Jr., *The Japanese Police System Today*. New York: Kodansha International, 1984.

Perrin, Noel, *Giving Up the Gun*. Boston: Shambhala Publications, 1979.

Reid, Ed, *The Grim Reapers*. New York: Bantam Books, 1969.

Roberts, John, *Mitsui: Three Centuries of Japanese Business*. Tokyo: John Weatherhill, 1973.

Rome, Florence, *The Tattooed Men*. New York: Delacorte Press, 1975.

Sampson, Anthony, *The Arms Bazaar*. London: Coronet Books, 1977.

Sansom, George, *A History of Japan*. Tokyo: Charles E. Tuttle, 1953.

Seagrave, Sterling, *The Soong Dynasty*. New York: Harper & Row, 1985.

Smith, W. Eugene, and Aileen Smith, *Minamata*. New York: Holt, Rinehart & Winston, 1975.

Stark, David Harold, *The Yakuza: Japanese Crime Incorporated*. Ph.D. thesis, University of Michigan, 1981.

Statler, Oliver, *Japanese Inn*. New York: Harcourt Brace Jovanovich, 1961.

Storry, Richard, *A History of Modern Japan*. Middlesex, England: Penguin Books, 1960.

Toland, John, *The Rising Sun*. New York: Random House, 1970.

Wang, James C. F., *Hawai'i State and Local Politics*. Hilo, Hawaii: University of Hawaii Press, 1982.

Wildes, Harry Emerson, *Typhoon in Tokyo*. New York: Macmillan, 1954.

Williams, Justin, Sr., *Japan's Political Revolution under MacArthur*. Athens, Georgia: University of Georgia Press, 1979.

Books: Japanese

Aoyama, Koji, *Yakuza no Seikai: Kenka, Jingi, Tobaku, Sono Onna* (Yakuza Society : Fighting, Chivalry, Gambling, and Women). Tokyo: Kofusha, 1979.

Arahara, Bokusui, *Dai Uyoku Shi* (Great History of the Right Wing). Tokyo: Dai Nippon Kokumin To, 1966.

Berrigan, Darrel, *Yakuza no Sekai: Nihon no Uchimaku* (Yakuza Society: Behind the Japanese Curtain). Tokyo: Kindai Shisosha, 1948.

Fujita, Goro, *Koan Daiyoran* (Great Directory of Public Security). Tokyo: Kasakura Shuppan, 1983.

——, *Koan Hyakunenshi* (The 100 Year History of Public Security). Tokyo: Koan Mondai Kenkyu Kyokai, 1979.

——, *Ninkyo Hyakunenshi* (The 100 Year History of Chivalry). Tokyo: Kasakura Shuppan, 1980.

Goto, Takao, *Koria Uochiya* (Korea Watcher). Tokyo: Gendai no Rironsha, 1982.

Ide, Hideo, *Jissho: Nihon no Yakuza* (Documented Account: The Japanese Yakuza). Tokyo: Tatsukaze, 1972.

Iiboshi, Koichi, *Kaigenreiku no Yamaguchi Gumi* (Yamaguchi-gumi under Curfew). Tokyo: Gentaishi Shuppankai, 1983.

Ino, Kenji, *Kodama Yoshio no Kyozo to Jitsuzo* (The Image and Reality of Yoshio Kodama), Tokyo: Sokon Shuppan, 1970.

——, *Nihon no Uyoku* (Japan's Right Wing). Tokyo: Nisshin Godo Shuppan, 1973.

——, *Yakuza to Nihonjin* (Yakuza and the Japanese). Tokyo: Mikasa Shoto, 1974.

Kata, Koji, *Nihon no Yakuza* (Japan's Yakuza). Tokyo: Daiwa Shoten, 1973.

Makasa no Nihon (MacArthur's Japan), vols. 1 & 2. Tokyo: *Shunkan Shincho* editors, Shincho Bunko, 1983.

Matsumoto, Seicho, *Nihon no Kuroikiri* (Black Mist over Japan). vols. 1 & 2, Tokyo: Bungei Shunju, 1974.

Mizoguchi, Atsushi, *Chi to Koso* (Blood and Battle). Tokyo: Sanichi Shobo, 1970.

Mori, Ei, *Kuroikikan* (Black Chamber). Tokyo: Daiyamondo, 1977.

Morikawa, Tetsuro, *Chi no Senkoku: Don Taoka Sogeki Jiken* (Bloody Verdict: The Shooting Incident of Don Taoka). Tokyo: Sanichi Shubo, 1979.

Omori, Minoru, *Sengo Hisshi* (Postwar Secret History), vol. 4, *Akahata to GHQ* (Red Flag and GHQ); and vol. 7, *Boryaku to Reisen to Jujiro* (The Crossroads of Conspiracy and Cold War). Tokyo: Kodansha Bunko, 1981.

Takemori, Hisaakira, *Miezaru Seifu* (Invisible Government). Tokyo: Shiraishi Shoten, 1976.

Taoka, Kazuo, *Yamaguchi Gumi Sandaime: Taoka Kazuo Jiten* (Yamaguchi-gumi Third Generation: The Autobiography of Kazuo Taoka), vols. 1–3. Tokyo: Tokukan Shoten, 1973.

Uyoku Jiten (Right-Wing Dictionary). Tokyo: Shakai Mondai Kenkyu-kai, 1970.

Key Government Documents: U.S.

California Department of Justice, Bureau of Organized Crime and Criminal Intelligence, "Organized Crime in California: 1981."

——, miscellaneous reports.

Hawaii Crime Commission, "Organized Crime in Hawaii," vol. 1, August 1978.

President's Commission on Law Enforcement and Administration of Justice, "Task Force Report: Organized Crime," 1967.

President's Commission on Organized Crime, "The Cash Connection: Organized Crime, Financial Institutions, and Money Laundering," October 1984.

——, "Organized Crime of Asian Origin," Ocotber 1984.

——, "Open Hearing Transcripts," New York, October 25, 1984.

——, miscellaneous reports and memoranda, 1984–1985.

Supreme Command for the Allied Powers, "The Brocade Banner: The Story of Japanese Nationalism," September 23, 1946.

——, Civil Information and Education Section, press conference, September 19, 1947.

——, Civil Information and Education Section, press conference, November 7, 1947.

——, Government Section, "Political Reorientation of Japan," September 1945–September 1948.

——, Government Section, "Report of Oyabun-Kobun Sub-committee," September 25, 1947.

——, Military Intelligence Section, "Oyabun-Kobun Systems," October 1, 1947.

——, Military Intelligence Section, miscellaneous interrogations and reports of

Yoshio Kodama and Ryoichi Sasakawa, 1946–1948.

——, Public Safety Division, *Public Safety Division History*, vol. 1, 1948.

——, miscellaneous documents, especially Record Group 331, National Records Center, Maryland.

United States Bureau of Alcohol, Tobacco and Firearms, paper, "Tracing of Recovered Firearms," December 1, 1983.

United States Bureau of Narcotics, annual reports, 1932–1940.

United States Commission on Wartime Relocation and Internment of Civilians, "Personal Justice Denied: Report of the Commission," 1982.

United States Customs Service, "Yakuza – Japanese Organized Crime," 1979.

——, miscellaneous reports of Yakuza Documentation Center, Honolulu, Hawaii.

United States Department of Justice, "Criminal Complaint No. 85-0207M," U.S. District Court, Honolulu, September 3, 1985.

——, "Criminal Victimization in the United States," various years.

——, "Report to the Nation on Crime and Justice," October 1983.

United States Department of State, miscellaneous cables and memoranda between U.S. Embassy in Tokyo and Washington, D.C., 1946–1985.

United States Drug Enforcement Administration, "A Brief History of Japanese Organized Crime," 1979.

——, "Investigation Report R4-76-0055," Honolulu, January 31, 1978.

——, "Narcotics Intelligence Estimate," 1983.

United States Federal Bureau of Investigation, "Oriental Organized Crime," January 1985.

——, *Uniform Crime Report,* various years.

United States House of Representatives, Hearings before the Subcommittee of International Organizations of the Committee on International Relations, "Activities of the Korean Central Intelligence Agency in the United States," March 17 and 25, 1976.

——, Report to the Committee on Foreign Affairs, "U.S. Narcotics Control Program Overseas: An Assessment," February 22, 1985.

United States Immigration and Naturalization Service, "Strategic Assessment: Asian Organized Crime," March 1, 1985.

United States Senate, Hearings of the Subcommittee on Multinational Corporations of the Committee on Foreign Relations, February 4 and 6, 1976.

——. *Statement of the Senate Permanent Subcommittee on Investigations Minority Staff on International Narcotics Trafficking,* November 12, 1981.

Key Government Documents: Foreign

Royal Hong Kong Police Department, Interpol Bureau (D. M. Hodson), "Organized Crime in Japan," December 19, 1983.

Japan Foreign Press Center, miscellaneous handouts and reports.

Japan Ministry of Justice, "Summary of the White Paper on Crime," 1981.

——, "White Paper on Crime," 1978.

——, "White Paper on Crime," 1982 (Summary), October 1982.

Japan National Police Agency, "Drug Problem in Japan," 1979.

——, "Drug Problem in Japan," 1983.

——, (Masahiro Saitoh), "The Police and the Situation of Public Safety in Japan," 1984.

——, "The Police of Japan," 1982.

——, "Present State of Boryokudan (Organized Crime Groups) and Our Crackdown Activities," 1983.

——, "White Paper on Police," 1982 (excerpt).

——, "White Paper on Police," 1983 (excerpt).

——, "White Paper on Police," July 1984.

Japan National Research Institute of Police Science (Kanehiro Hoshino), "Organized Criminal Gangs in Japan: The Subcultures of Organized Crime Gangs," June 1971.

—— (Kanehiro Hoshino), "The Recent Trend of Underworld and Organized Crime in Japan," February 1979.

——, (Kanehiro Hoshino, Fumio Mugishima, and Kenji Kiyonaga), "Boryokudan-in no Danshi to Shisei: Boryokudan no Dentoteki Fukuji Bunka no Kenkyu" (Tattooing and Finger Joint Cutting by Organized Crime Members), 1971.

—— (Fumio Mugishima), "Boryokudan-in to Dantai to no Kankei ni Kansuru Kenkyu" (Follow-up Survey of Organized Crime Members), 1974.

Periodicals: United States

American Anthropologist

The American Political Science Review

Associated Press dispatches

The Bulletin of Concerned Asian Scholars

Business Week

Christian Science Monitor

The Defense Monitor

Film Comment

Hawaii Hochi (English-Japanese)

Hokubei Mainichi (English-Japanese)

Honolulu Advertiser

Honolulu Star-Bulletin

Long Beach Independent-Press Telegram (CA)

Los Angeles Herald Examiner

Los Angeles Times

Multinational Monitor

Newsweek

The New Republic

The New Yorker

New York Times

New York Times Magazine

Oriental Economist

Pacific Affairs

Pacific Citizen

Pacific Daily News (Guam)

Pacific News Service dispatches

Parade

Penthouse

Political Quarterly

The Progressive

Rafu Shimpo (English-Japanese)

Sacramento Bee

San Francisco Chronicle

San Francisco Examiner

San Jose Mercury

Saturday Evening Post

Southeast Asia Chronicle

Time

Trenton Times (NJ)

United Press International dispatches

The Village Voice

The Wall Street Journal

Washington Post

Periodicals: Japan

Asahi Evening News (English)

Asahi Geino

Asahi Jyanaru

Asahi News Service dispatches

Asahi Shimbun

Bungei Shunju

Daily Yomiuri (English)

The East (English)

Focus

Hoseki

Japan Economic Journal (English)

Japan Interpreter (English)

Japan Shipping and Trade News (English)

Japan Times (English)

Japan Times Weekly (English)

Kaibyaku

Kyodo News Service dispatches

Mainichi Daily News (English)

Mainichi Shimbun

Nihon Keizai Shimbun

PHP Magazine (English)

Sandei Mainichi

Sankei Shimbun

Shukan Asahi

Shukan Bunshun

Shukan Gendai

Shukan Jitsuwa

Shukan Sankei

Shukan Shincho

Shukan Yomiuri

Tokyo Mimpo

Tokyo Shimbun

Weekender (English)

Yomiuri Shimbun

Periodicals: Other Foreign

The Asian Wall Street Journal

Asiaweek

Bangkok Post

Bulletin Today (Philippines)

Chosen Ilbo (South Korea)

Daily Express (Philippines)

Der Spiegel (West Germany)

Deutsches Allgemeines Sonntagsblatt Hbg. (West Germany)

Far Eastern Economic Review

Folha do São Paulo (Brazil)

The Guardian (UK)

Insight (Hong Kong)

International Management (UK: Asia Edition)

Jornal do Brasil (Brazil)

Korea Herald

Korea Times

Maynila (Philippines)

National Time Magazine (Australia)

Oriental Economist

The Sunday Times (UK)

The Times (UK)

Times-Journal (Philippines)

Wolgan Chosen (South Korea)

Index

Chivalry, 14–16, 17, 82, 272
Chongnyon, 195
Christian Science Monitor, 44, 49
Chrysanthemum and the Sword, The
    (Benedict), 28
Chun-shu, Hsiao, 98
Churan United Sports Association, 219
Church, Frank, 101–102
Citibank, 168
City Bank of Honolulu, 237
Clapp, Fred, 254
Club Niji, 248
Cocaine trade, 220–22, 231, 245
Cold War, 55
Colombia, 221, 222
Colton, Kenneth, 58
Commerical Code, 179–180
Communism, 51, 55, 56, 57, 58, 60,
    61, 68, 71, 74, 83, 94. *See also*
    Japanese Communist Party (JCP)
Compagnie Financiere de Paris et des
    Pays Bas (PARIBAS), 222
Compagnie Francaise des Petroles, 222
Conn, Stuart Eugene "Steve," 258, 259
Consiglieri, 132
Construction companies, 49–50, 51,
    91
Consumer loan market, 168
Corruption. *See* Police; Political cor-
    ruption
Corsican mobs, 5, 57, 68, 213
"Cotton morphine," 245
Counter Intelligence Corps (CIC),
    49, 60–61, 194
Credit, 167–168
Crime, in Japan, 95, 157, 161–163,
    181–185, 275
Customs agents, 215, 225–228, 235,
    267

Dai-An Construction Company,
    49–50
Daikazoku principle, 145

Dai Nippon Butoku-kai (Great Japan
    Military Virtue Society), 73
Dai Nippon Kokusui-kai (Great Japan
    National Essence Society), 36
Dairen, 245
Dark Ocean Society (Genyosha), 33–
    36, 64, 78, 119, 193, 276
Deak, Nicholas, 108, 114
Deak & Company, 108, 109, 114
Demilitarization, 56
Democratic Party, 67, 75
Demukai (prison release ceremony),
    152
Diet, 37, 46, 93–94, 110–111,
    114–116, 118, 119–120,
    121–122, 179, 255
Dokuritsu Seinen Sha (Independence
    Youth Society), 64
Dooley, Jim, 237
Doshida-gumi, 141–142, 144
Drama-logue, 252
Drawn Sword Regiment (Aikoku
    Haukyo Battotai), 72, 73, 74
Dress, 27, 89, 98, 129 153
Drug abuse, 76, 199, 212
    fostering of, 38
Drug Enforcement Administration
    (DEA), 8, 215, 216, 233, 235,
    242, 257
Drug trade, 8, 57, 68, 133, 197–200,
    210–222, 229, 231–236,
    245–247, 256, 268, 279. *See
    also* Amphetamine trade;
    Cocaine trade; Heroin trade;
    Morphine trade; Opium trade
Duke, Angier Biddle, 261
Duluc, Tancredo, 219

East Asia, 189–223, 245
Eguchi, Toshio, 96
Ehime Prefecture, 119
Eisenhower, Dwight D., 84–86, 147,
    195